3/3

Institutions and the Role of the State

NEW HORIZONS IN INSTITUTIONAL AND EVOLUTIONARY
ECONOMICS

General Editor: Geoffrey M. Hodgson
Research Professor, University of Hertfordshire Business School, UK

Economics today is at a crossroads. New ideas and approaches are
challenging the largely static and equilibrium-oriented models that used to
dominate mainstream economics. The study of economic institutions – long
neglected in the economics textbooks – has returned to the forefront of
theoretical and empirical investigation.

This challenging and interdisciplinary series publishes leading works at
the forefront of institutional and evolutionary theory and focuses on cutting-
edge analyses of modern socio-economic systems. The aim is to understand
both the institutional structures of modern economies and the processes of
economic evolution and development. Contributions will be from all forms of
evolutionary and institutional economics, as well as from Post-Keynesian,
Austrian and other schools. The overriding aim is to understand the
processes of institutional transformation and economic change.

Titles in the series include:

Institutions and the Role of the State

Edited by

Leonardo Burlamaqui

Chair of Innovation and Competition and Director of Research, Faculty of Economics, University Cândido Mendes, Brazil and Adjunct Professor of Political Economy, Faculty of Economics, State University of Rio de Janeiro, Brazil

Ana Célia Castro

Chief, Graduate Program in Development, Agriculture and Society, Federal Rural University of Rio de Janeiro, Brazil

Ha-Joon Chang

Assistant Director of Development Studies, Faculty of Economics and Politics, University of Cambridge, UK

NEW HORIZONS IN INSTITUTIONAL AND EVOLUTIONARY ECONOMICS

Edward Elgar

Cheltenham, UK • Northampton, MA, USA

Published by
Edward Elgar Publishing Limited
Glensanda House
Montpellier Parade
Cheltenham
Glos GL50 1UA
UK

Edward Elgar Publishing, Inc.
136 West Street
Suite 202
Northampton
Massachusetts 01060
USA

A catalogue record for this book
is available from the British Library

Library of Congress Cataloguing in Publication Data

Institutions and the role of the state / edited by Leonardo Burlamaqui, Ana Celia
Castro, Ha-Joon Chang.
   — (New Horizons in institutional and evolutionary economics)
   Includes bibliographical references and index.
   1. Economic policy. 2. State, The. 3. Institutional economics. 4. Evolutionary
economics. I. Burlamaqui, Leonardo. II. Castro, Ana Célia. III. Chang, Ha-Joon.
IV. Series.

HD87 .I55 2000
338.9—dc21   00–034731

ISBN 1 84064 311 0

Printed and bound in Great Britain by MPG Books Ltd, Bodmin, Cornwall

Contents

Figures and tables

FIGURES

TABLES

Introduction

The last decade has witnessed the rediscovery, and rapid diffusion, of institutionalist and evolutionary approaches in economics and other social sciences (see for instance, amongst many others, Nelson and Winter, 1982, Dosi *et al.* (eds), 1988, Hodgson, 1988 and 1993, North, 1994, Maki, Gustafsson and Knuddsen (eds), 1993, Arthur, 1996, Shionoya, 1997). These two approaches, despite their remarkable potential for cross-fertilization have, until now, 'travelled alone'. Their common achievement has been the fact that their approaches and findings are increasingly posing serious intellectual challenges to the dominant neoclassical approach.

It is perhaps useful to observe that economic theory was, in its origins and for a long time thereafter, both evolutionary and institutionalist. Note, for instance, the discussion about the division of labour that opens Adam Smith's *Wealth of Nations*, or his statements on the theory of value and distribution. The analysis is deeply concerned with change and deals quite explicitly with historical time. To summarize, it is highly 'institution-dependent' and evolutionary. Excluding David Ricardo, whose approach lacked historical perspective and was aimed at drawing bold conclusions from simple hypotheses, inaugurating what Schumpeter would later call the 'Ricardian vice', the same can be said for all the other 'classical political economists' including Robert Malthus[1] and both James Mill and John Stuart Mill. The same approach is also present in Karl Marx's theory of industrialization and in Marshall's analysis of 'industry and trade'.

Obviously this is not to say that these were the exclusive, or even the main, features of the canonical works in classical and 'modern' political economy. What appears to have gone unnoticed in most studies of the development of economic analysis is the ambivalence and tension between the aforementioned concern with evolution and institutions – therefore, with history, path-dependence and the interplay between economic and other forces – and the focus on 'Newtonian' types of mechanisms and laws. That tension is still at the core of economic debate today, and it is probably not much of an exaggeration to say that the future course of economics depends on how the discipline will deal with Institutions and Evolution without ruining its reputation as 'the most rigorous' and 'the most prediction-oriented' social science.

Let us also acknowledge the fact that, although the word 'institutionalist' almost became a dirty word in Anglo-American academia after the fall of American Institutional Economics led by Thorstein Veblen, John Commons, and Wesley Mitchell in the early 20th century, by the early 1980s it was not difficult to find articles in 'respectable' journals that talked of a 'new' institutionalist approach (cf. Yonay, 1988).

The new institutionalist approach, inspired by the works of Ronald Coase, Douglas North, and Oliver Williamson, shares some basic attributes of the dominant neoclassical approach – for example, the emphasis on self-seeking and rational behaviour, and the neglect of the role of power in shaping the evolution of institutions. In fact, it sought to explain: (a) how economic institutions may arise due to transaction-cost-minimizing behaviour; and (b) how these institutions can affect subsequent economic behaviour – albeit, with more emphasis on the former.

In the 1980s and 1990s, the approach was applied to a wide range of issues, including property rights (e.g., Barzel, [1989] 1997), the firm (e.g., Williamson, 1985), rural land property and financial institutions (e.g., Bardhan, 1989) and international trading networks. The awarding of the Nobel Prize to Coase (1995) and North (1994) in the early 1990s symbolized the weight that this approach was gaining, even among mainstream economists. It must, however, be stressed that, important as it may have been, the New Institutional Economics was by no means the only institutionalist approach developed during the last two decades.

Another is the 'behaviouralist' school led by Herbert Simon, which emphasized the importance of the 'bounded' nature of our rationality and the consequent limitations of the maximizing approach – that the new institutionalists share with neoclassical economists. The behaviouralists argue that the world we live in is too complex and uncertain for human beings to operate without some kind of (often deliberately created) constraints on their choice. According to Simon (Simon, 1947 and the seminal work of 1983) organizations and institutions would accomplish these roles (for more recent examples, see Heiner, 1983 and Simon, 1991).

Quite independently from the behavouralists, the 'Austrian School', led by Friedrich Hayek, is also very much an institutionalist approach, emphasizing the role of what they call 'tradition' in determining human behaviour. Indeed, they share with the behaviouralists a view of the world as a complex and uncertain place and scepticism about both the perfect human rationality and the maximizing approach. The Austrians, however, parted company with the behaviouralist school when they claimed that the complex and uncertain nature of our world dooms attempts to control it by deliberately constructing new institutions – which they call 'rational constructivism'. This is exactly why we need institutions, according to the behaviouralists (classic statements of the Austrian view of institutions can be found in Hayek, 1949, 1978, 1994; Kirzner, 1992; and O'Driscoll and Rizzo, [1985] 1996 are some recent examples).

Finally, on the other side of the analytical spectrum, the works of Karl Marx and Karl Polanyi have emphasized the role of relationships of power in shaping the evolution of institutions. Polanyi's classic work shows how the birth and subsequent evolution of the actual foundational institutions of capitalism – property rights (especially of land and labour) and the market – have been shaped by relationships of power (Polanyi, [1944] 1980). This approach is shared today by authors such as Fred Block, Mark Granovetter, Peter Evans and many others (cf. Block and Sommers, 1985, Granovetter and Swedberg (eds), 1992, Smelster and Swedberg (eds), 1994, and Hollingsworth and Boyer (eds), 1997).

Marx's legacy gave birth to another new trend in economics (albeit in a fairly roundabout way) through his great admirer, and reluctant disciple, Joseph Schumpeter: the evolutionary approach. While Marx himself was influenced by the works of Charles Darwin, it was Schumpeter who first incorporated evolutionary biology into economics in an explicit and systematic way (Schumpeter, 1911, 1939, and 1942). Schumpeter argued that changes in technology and institutions should be understood as an evolutionary process, in which changes are made incrementally and with path dependency. Of course, Schumpeter did not argue that the mechanisms of biological evolution could be found in the economic sphere. He went to great pains to show that 'mutation' in the economic world (or what he calls innovation) is both conscious and purposeful – whereas in the biological world it is random.[2]

One of the fathers of the 'old' institutionalist school, namely Thorstein Veblen, was also very much committed to an evolutionary perspective, as the recent work of Geoff Hodgson and others have clearly shown (cf. Hodgson, 1988, 1993, 2000; Louçã, 2000; O'Hara, 2000).

In summary, although both the institutionalist and evolutionary approaches are increasingly posing serious intellectual challenges to the dominant neoclassical approach, as can be seen, for instance, in the flood of books and articles that fill the catalogues of Elgar, Routledge, Kluwer and several 'University Press' publishing houses, there is an element strikingly common to most of these works. Namely, despite their affinity, there has been relatively little interaction between these two potentially very complementary approaches.

It is our claim that both the institutionalist and the evolutionary perspectives in economics share the same core assumptions, way of theorizing, and key results. It is puzzling, therefore, that they have travelled along the same roads and fought the same enemies without ever borrowing from each other or, worse, without forging a 'strategic theoretical alliance'.

The present volume, resulting from a very successful conference held in Rio de Janeiro in November 1997,[3] is an attempt to begin to fill this theoretically challenging and policy relevant gap. It puts together eleven essays written by leading scholars in the field and has two chief objects: to contribute to the cross-fertilization of the aforementioned approaches and to apply them to one of the most controversial issues of our day, namely, the role of the state.

The choice of the role of the state as the common topic for this intellectual dialogue between the traditions was not a random choice. It was intended to fill a common and serious lacuna that can be easily noticed in these traditions. After all, despite the obvious relevance of their approaches for statecraft and policy issues, scholars writing in these traditions have been unusually silent on these topics (some obvious exceptions are the contributors to this volume such as Block and Chang).

The contributors to this volume have in common the understanding that the 'invisible hand' of the market is sustained by a complex and constantly evolving set of institutions, in whose design and enforcement both the state and other institutions play a critical role. Using the newly-developed theoretical frameworks of institutional and evolutionary economics, the essays in the volume emphasize (a) that the market and the state complement each other, (b) that the former would not be even able to exist (let alone 'work well') without the 'visible hands' of state bureaucracies and public policies and (c) that such interactions occur within a complex matrix of institutions.

More specifically, the book includes essays that provide an explicit theoretical discussion of the role of the state (Burlamaqui, Chang, Block), as well as essays which provide the theoretical foundations for this discussion (Storper on the social science of conventions and Hodgson on emergent properties). It also contains essays that focus on specific empirical cases (Wade and Dore on East-Asian developmental states, Bresser Pereira, Castro and Sola on Brazil and Drechsler on Estonia) and discuss policy issues.

Therefore, the volume offers a good methodological guide for researchers working in the two fast-evolving institutional and evolutionary traditions, for professionals unsatisfied with reductionist theoretical approaches and for people concerned with concrete policy discussions and proposals based on keen theoretical analyses as well as some careful studies of historical and contemporary cases.

The book is divided into two parts. The first part includes the more theoretically-oriented chapters on the role of the state, institutions and conventions.

The second part includes more empirically (and policy) oriented chapters, applying the institutionalist and evolutionary theoretical insights to the analysis of some important real-life cases.

NOTES

1. Whose *Essay on Population*, let us not forget, influenced Darwin's thought, which, in its turn, significantly influenced both Marx's vision of capital accumulation and evolutionary economics (Veblen and Schumpeter being clear examples).
2. Schumpeter's evolutionary approach was later expanded by Nelson & Winter (1982), who applied ideas from genetics, which had not really been developed in Schumpeter's own time, to the understanding of technological change.
3. 'Institutions and Economic Development: A State Reform Perspective', organized by Leonardo Burlamaqui, Ana Célia Castro and John Wilkinson – CPDA/UFRRJ (Graduate Course in Development, Agriculture and Society, Federal Rural University of Rio de Janeiro) and NUSEG/UERJ (Superior Nucleus of Governmental Studies, State University of Rio de Janeiro).

BIBLIOGRAPHY

Arthur, B. (1996), *The Economy as an Evolving Complex System*, Santa Fe: Santa Fe Institute of Studies in Sciences of Complexity, vol. 27.

Bardhan, P.K. (1989), *Land, Labour and Rural Poverty: Essay in Development Economics*, New York: Columbia University Press.

Barzel [1989] (1997), *Economic Analysis of Property Rights (Political Economy of Institutions and Decisions)*, Cambridge: Cambridge University Press.

Block, F. and M. Sommers (1985), 'Beyond the Economist Fallacy: The Holistic Social Science of Karl Polanyi', in T. Skocpol (ed.), *Vision and Method in Historical Sociology*, Cambridge: Cambridge University Press.

Coase, R.H. (1995), *Essays on Economics and Economists*, Chicago: University of Chicago Press.

Clemence, R. (ed) (1951), *Essays of J.A. Schumpeter*, New York: Addison Wesley.

Dosi, Giovanni, Freeman, Christopher, Nelson, Richard, Silverberg, Gerald and Luc L.G. Soete, (eds) (1988), *Technical Change and Economic Theory*, London: Pinter.

Evans, P. (1995), *Embedded Autonomy: States and Industrial Transformation*, Princeton, NJ: Princeton University Press.

Granovetter, M. (1985), 'Economic Action and Social Structure: The Problem of Embeddedness', *American Journal of Sociology*, **91** (3), pp. 481–510.

Granovetter, Mark and Swedberg, Richard (eds) (1992), *The Sociology of Economic Life*, Boulder: Westview Press.

Hayek, F.A. (1949), *Individualism and Economic Order*, London: Routledge & Kegan Paul.

———. (1978), *The Constitution of Liberty*, Chicago: University of Chicago Press.

———. (1994), *The Road to Serfdom*, Chicago: University of Chicago Press.

Hodgson, G.M. (1988), *Economics and Institutions*, Cambridge: Polity Press.

Hodgson, G.M. (1993), *Economics and Evolution*, Cambridge: Polity Press.

Hodgson, G.M. (1999b), *Evolution and Institutions: On Evolutionary Economics and the Evolution of Economics*, Cheltenham: Edward Elgar.

Hodgson, G.M.. (2000) *How Economics Forgot History: The Problem of Historical Specificity in Social Science* (forthcoming).

Hollingsworth, J. and Boyer, R. (eds) (1997), *Contemporary Capitalism – The Embeddedness of Institutions*, Cambridge: Cambridge University Press.

Kirzner, I. (1992), *The Meaning of the Market Process*, London: Routledge.

Louçã, F. (2000), *Is Economics an Evolutionary Science? – The Legacy of Thornstein Veblen*, Cheltenham: Edward Elgar.

Mäki, U., Gustafsson and Knuddson (eds) (1993), *Rationality, Institutions, and Economic Methodology*, London: Routledge.

Nelson, R. and S. Winter (1982), *An Evolutionary Theory of the Economic Change*, Boston: The Belknap Press of Harvard University Press.

North, D. (1994), 'Economic Performance Through Time', *American Economic Review*, **84** (3), pp. 359–68.

O'Driscoll, P. and J. Rizzo [1985] (1996), *The Economics of Time and Ignorance*, London: Routledge.

O'Hara, P. (2000), *Marx, Veblen and Modern Institutional Political Economy*, Cheltenham: Edward Elgar.

Polanyi, K [1944] (1980), *The Great Transformation*, New York: Rinehart.

Schumpeter, J. [1934, 1911] (1997), *The Theory of Economic Development*, Transaction Publishers.

———. (1939), *Business Cycles (2 vol.),* New York: McGraw Hill.

———. [1942] (1992), *Capitalism, Socialism and Democracy*, London: Routledge.

———. [1928] (1951), 'The Instability of Capitalism', in R. Clemence (ed.) *Essays of J.A. Schumpeter*, New York: Adison Wesley.

Shionoya, Y. (1997), *Schumpeter and the Idea of Social Science*, Cambridge: Cambridge University Press.

Simon, H. (1991), 'Organisations and Markets', *Journal of Economic Perspectives*, **5** (2), pp. 25–44.

Skocpol, T. (ed.) (1985), *Vision and Method in Historical Sociology*, Cambridge: Cambridge University Press.

Smelster, N. and R. Swedberg (eds) (1994), *The Handbook of Economic Sociology*, Princeton, NJ: Princeton University Press.

Williamson, O. (1985), *The Economic Institutions of Capitalism*, New York: Free Press.

Yonay, Yuval P. (1998), *The Struggle Over the Soul of Economics: Institutionalist and Neoclassical Economists in America Between the Wars*, Princeton, NJ: Princeton University Press.

Contributors

Antonio Barros de Castro is Professor of Economic Policy at the Federal University of Rio de Janeiro. He was a former President of Banco Nacional de Desenvolvimento Econômico e Social (BNDES). He has held visiting academic positions as Member of the Institute for Advanced Study (Princeton, USA) and at the Faculty of Economics, Cambridge University (England). He is the Editor of *Boletim de Conjuntura* and writes weekly for a column in *Folha de São Paulo*. His books include *Introdução à Economia: Uma Abordagem Estruturalista* (Rio de Janeiro: Forense, 1967) (in Portuguese and Spanish); *Sete Ensaios sobre a Economia Brasileira* (Rio de Janeiro: Forense, 1969); *A Economia Brasileira em Marcha Forçada* (Rio de Janeiro: Paz e Terra). Among his articles: 'Renegade Development', in William Smith, Carlos Acuña and Eduardo Gamarra (eds), *Democracy, Market and Structural Reform* (Transaction Publishers, 1993).

Fred Block is Professor of Sociology at the University of California at Davis. He has written on welfare policies, state theory, problems of economic measurement, the organization of the international financial system, and postindustrial change. His books include *The Vampire State* (New Press, 1996), *Postindustrial Possibilities* (California, 1990), and *The Origins of International Economic Disorder* (University of California Press, 1977).

Luiz Carlos Bresser Pereira has been Minister of Federal Administration and State Reform of Brazil in the Cardoso administration since January 1995, and is Professor of Economics of the Getúlio Vargas Foundation and editor of *Revista de Economia Política*. He was chief of staff of São Paulo (Montoro administration, 1985–86) and Finance Minister in the Sarney Administration (1987). Among other books he authored: *Development and Crisis in Brazil* (Boulder: Westview, 1984), *O Colapso de uma Aliança de Classes* (São Paulo: Editora Brasiliense, 1978), *The Theory of Inertial Inflation*, with Yoshiaki Nakano (Boulder: L. Rienner, 1987), *Lucro, Acumulação e Crise* (1986), *Economic Reforms in New Democracies*, with José Maria Maravall and Adam Przeworski (Cambridge: Cambridge University Press, 1993), and *Economic Crisis and State Reform in Brazil* (Boulder: L. Rienner, 1996).

Leonardo Burlamaqui teaches Innovation and Competition at University Cândido Mendes and Political Economy at the State University of Rio de Janeiro. He has written and published extensively on evolutionary economics, corporate strategy, economic sociology, and state-business relationships. He has also conducted research on the economic organization of East Asian capitalism, and on state reforms under an evolutionary and institutionalist perspective. Present position: Chair of Innovation and Competition and Director of Research at University Cândido Mendes and Adjunct Professor of Political Economy at the State University of Rio de Janeiro. Address: University Cândido Mendes, Joana Angélica Street, 63, Ipanema, Rio de Janeiro, Brazil, Zip code: 22411-003. Telephone: (55-21) 5234141; Fax: +55-21-2677495. E-mail: lburlamaqui@unikey.com.br

Ana Célia Castro teaches economics and agribusiness at the CPDA/UFRRJ, Federal Rural University of Rio de Janeiro. Her main publications are on Brazilian agribusiness competitiveness and her principal research interests are, presently, state reform in Brazil, and business enterprises. Present position: Chief of the Department of Development, Agriculture and Society, Federal Rural University of Rio de Janeiro. Address: Curso de Pós-graduação em Desenvolvimento, Agricultura e Sociedade, Universidade Federal Rural do Rio de Janeiro, Av. Presidente Vargas 417, 8th floor, Rio de Janeiro, Brazil, Zip code: 20071-003. Telephone/Fax: +55-21-2248577. E-mail: ancastro@gbl.com.br

Ha-Joon Chang teaches economics at the Faculty of Economics and Politics, University of Cambridge. He has written extensively on theories of the state, political economy, institutional economics, and development economics. Present position: Assistant Director of Development Studies, Faculty of Economics and Politics, University of Cambridge, UK. Address: Faculty of Economics and Politics, Sidgwick Avenue, Cambridge, CB3 9DD, UK. Telephone: +44-1223-335389; Fax: +44-1223-335475. E-Mail: hjc1001@econ.cam.ac.uk

Ronald Dore has spent most of his life studying Japanese society and the Japanese economy. He is a Senior Research Fellow at the Centre for Economic Performance at the London School of Economics and, with Wolfgang Streeck, is writing a book on the likelihood of Germany and Japan retaining their distinctive forms of capitalism.

Wolfgang Drechsler is Professor and Chair of Public Administration and Government at the University of Tartu. He has served as Advisor to the President to Estonia for Administrative Organization, as Executive Secretary in the German

Science Council during Reunification, and as Senior Legislative Analyst in the United States Congress. His independent publications include The Self-Governed Municipality (1999, ed., in German), On the Eminence of the Social Sciences at the University of Dorpat (1998), Foundations of Public Administration (1997, ed., in Estonian; some translations forthcoming), Johann Ulrich v. Cramer's Opuscula (5 vols., 1996, ed.), and Andrew D. White in Germany (1989, in German).

Geoffrey M. Hodgson is Research Professor in Economics at the University of Hertfordshire. He was formerly a Reader in Economics at the University of Cambridge. He has held visiting academic and research positions in Austria, Germany, Japan, Sweden and the United States. His publications include *Economics and Utopia* (1999), *Evolution and Institutions* (1999), *Economics and Evolution* (Polity Press, 1993), *Economics and Institutions* (Polity Press, 1988), *The Democratic Economy* (1984) and over 100 articles in academic books and journals.

Lourdes Sola is Professor of Political Science at the University of São Paulo. She is also President of the Brazilian Political Science Association and Researcher at the Instituto de Estudos Econômicos, Sociais de São Paulo (IDESP). She has conducted research on the politics of economic policy making and regime instability since 1945, in Brazil and Latin America. Presently she is engaged in a project on central banking, financial deregulation, and the ethos of responsibility. Her books in Portuguese are: (1) as editor: *O Estado da Transição. Política e Economia* (1987); *Estado, Mercado, Democracia, Política e Economia Comparadas* (1993); *Lições da Década de 1980* (São Paulo: EDUSP, 1995); (2) as author: *Idéias Econômicas, Decisões Políticas: Desenvolvimento, Estabilidade, Populismo* (São Paulo: EDUSP, 1998); in English: 'Heterodox Schock in Brazil. Tecnicos, Politicians and Democracy', *Journal of Latin American Studies*, **23** (1991); 'The State, Economic Transformation and Democratization', in William Smith, Carlos Acuña and Eduardo Gamarra (eds), *Democracy, Market and Structural Reform* (Transaction Publishers, 1993).

Michael Storper is Professor of Regional and International Development in the School of Public Policy and Social Research at UCLA. He is also Professor of Social and Human Sciences at the University of Marne-la-Vallée, in France, and researcher in the research center on societies, technologies and territories, at the École des Ponts et Chaussées. His research has concentrated on the processes of regional economic development. His most recent books include,

Worlds of Production: the Action Frameworks of the Economy, with Robert Salais (Cambridge, MA: Harvard University Press, 1997); *The Regional World: Territorial Development in a Global Economy* (New York: Guilford Press, 1997); and *Latecomers in the Global Economy* (Routledge, 1998).

Robert Wade is Visiting Scholar, Russell Sage Foundation, New York City, and Professor of Political Science and International Political Economy at Brown University. He has conducted research on the economic rise (and crisis) of East Asia, also on cooperation in India and Italy. He is the author of *Governing the Market: Economic Theory and the Role of Government in East Asian Industrialization* (NJ: Princeton University Press, 1990).

PART ONE

Theoretical Perspectives on the Role of the State, Institutions and Conventions

1. An institutionalist perspective on the role of the state: towards an institutionalist political economy

Ha-Joon Chang

1. INTRODUCTION

What is the appropriate role of the state? This has been one question that has constantly occupied economists for the last two or three centuries since the birth of the subject (for some excellent historical reviews, see Deane, 1989, and Shonfield, 1965). During this period, there have been a number of swings in the dominant opinion on the subject, but the two major swings that have occurred during the last half century after the Second World War are particularly remarkable in their scope and suddenness (Chang & Rowthorn, 1995a, Spanish translation appears in Chang, 1996).

The early postwar years witnessed the world-wide rejection of the *laissez faire* doctrine that failed so spectacularly during the interwar period, and the resulting emergence of a widespread consensus on state activism. By the 1960s, the end of *laissez faire* capitalism was announced in many quarters and there was a widespread consensus that we are now living in the 'mixed economy' (alternatively, 'modern capitalism' or 'organized capitalism'). However, this new consensus has been dramatically overturned since the mid-1970s, following the neo-liberal counter-offensive, which sought to end the mixed economy and reintroduce market principles to an extent that would have been unimaginable during the early postwar years.

The upsurge of neo-liberalism during the last two decades or so has fundamentally changed the terms of debate on the role of the state (Chang, 1994a, chapters 1–2). The state is no more assumed to be an impartial, omnipotent social guardian and is now analysed either as a 'predator' or as a vehicle for politically powerful groups (including the politicians and the bureaucrats themselves) to advance their sectional interests. No other motives than maximization of material self-interests are accorded to any agent even in the 'public' domains of life, denouncing the role of politics as a legitimate way to correct the market outcomes according to the 'collective will'. The resulting 'minimalist' bias in the terms of debate means that those who want to make a case for state intervention have to fight their adversaries at each and every step of their arguments, whatever the merits of their arguments may be, whereas those who want to discredit state activism can often do so with a very simplistic logic supported by often unrepresentative anecdotes.

Although the neo-liberal agenda itself has a lot of intellectual limitations and biases, as we will discuss in the rest of the paper, the legacy of the neo-liberal counter-offensive has not been entirely negative. For one thing, it exposed fundamental problems with the 'technocratic' view of the role of the state that prevailed in the heyday of welfare economics (1950s and 1960s) and brought politics back into economics (although it ultimately aimed to abolish politics; see section 3.4). And more importantly, its explicit engagement in 'political economy' discussions opened the door for the subsequent rise of 'institutionalist' criticisms (e.g., Evans, Rueschemeyer and Skocpol, 1985; Hall, 1989; Toye, 1991; Evans, 1995; Chang & Rowthorn, 1995b).[1] And following the institutionalist criticisms, even some proponents of neo-liberal doctrine have recently come to admit (but without necessarily recognizing the contributions of their critics) the importance of institutional factors in understanding the role of the state (North, 1994: World Bank, 1997).

However, having achieved that important, if unfairly unacknowledged victory over the neo-liberals, I think it is fair to say that the institutionalists still lack a full-blown political economy that can replace the neo-liberal political economy. In this paper, I will make some suggestions as to what I think should be the building blocks of what may be called an institutionalist political economy. For this purpose, I will dissect the neo-liberal research agenda on the role of the state from an explicitly institutionalist perspective and identify what I think are the fundamental flaws in it, and in that process suggest what should be the elements in the institutionalist theory of state intervention that can overcome these flaws.

2.   DISENTANGLING THE NEO-LIBERAL AGENDA

The Messianic convictions with which many proponents of neo-liberalism have delivered their messages have created the impression that it is a very coherent doctrine with clear conclusions. However, contrary to this popular belief, the neo-liberal doctrine is in fact a very heterogeneous and internally inconsistent intellectual edifice. So before going into the detailed criticisms of this doctrine, it will be useful to delineate the basic fault lines in the neo-liberal intellectual agenda and reveal some of its obvious weaknesses.

2.1 The Unholy Alliance: Neoclassicism and the Austrian-Libertarian Tradition

The biggest contradiction in the neo-liberal research programme comes from the fact that it was born out of a marriage of convenience between neoclassical economics as the source of intellectual legitimacy (given its dominance in academia) and what may be broadly called the Austrian-Libertarian tradition as the source of political rhetoric. The gap between these two intellectual traditions is not a minor one, as those who are familiar with, for example, Hayek's scathing criticism of neoclassical economics would know (e.g. Hayek, 1949). However, the marriage of convenience goes on, because the Austrian-Libertarian tradition supplies the popular appeal that neoclassical economics can never dream of supplying itself (who are going to risk their lives for 'Pareto optimality'? – but many have been willing to for 'liberty' and 'entrepreneurship'), while the Austrian-Libertarian tradition, given its lack of intellectual legitimacy in 'respectable' circles, needs the aura of 'science' that neoclassical economics carries around.[2]

But in return for the increased power of persuasion that they acquired by allying with the Austrian-Libertarian tradition, neoclassical economics had to pay a heavy price. In order to maintain the alliance, it has had to suppress its interventionist streak, given the strong anti-statism of the latter. So how is this done?

One such method of suppression is to accept the logic of 'market failure' behind welfare economics but then not to extend it beyond the set of 'politically acceptable' areas. So, for example, the externality argument is often applied to politically less controversial areas such as the environment or education, but is rarely applied to such politically more controversial areas as 'selective' industrial policy à la East Asia, which can be justified by the same logic equally well. Given that there is no theoretical way in neoclassical economics to determine what is the 'correct' boundary for state intervention, it becomes necessary to argue that market failures exist as logical possibilities, but rarely occur in reality – naturally without providing much evidence (Friedman, 1962, is a good example).[3]

The second method of suppressing the interventionist instinct of neoclassical economics is to separate, partly deliberately and partly subconsciously, the 'serious' academic discourse from the 'popular' policy discourse and compartmentalize them. So neoclassical economists in universities may be doing research justifying stringent anti-trust policy, but the 'lax' anti-trust policy of the government may be justified in terms of some other logic which has no place in neoclassical economics – say, by citing the need 'not to discourage entrepreneurship', etc. The recent 'reform' experiences in the former Communist countries mentioned above is a most poignant example of such practice.

The last method of suppression is to accept fully the logic of market failure and build models that may have strong interventionist conclusions, but later dismiss them on the ground that 'real life' states cannot possibly be entrusted with such policies that are technically difficult (due to informational asymmetry) and politically dangerous (due to the possibility of bureaucratic abuse and/ or interest group capture). Various writings by the American trade economist Krugman provide the best example, where frequently a few paragraphs of 'pop political economy' analysis dismissing the integrity of the state, at the end of an article, would be used to discredit his own elaborate 'strategic trade theory' model endorsing state intervention that went on in the rest of the article.[4] To put it bluntly, the name of the game is that a neoclassical economist may build a model that recommends state intervention as far as it is 'technically competent', but he/she has to prove his/her political credentials by rubbishing his/her own model on political grounds.

2.2 The Indeterminacy of the Neoclassical Position on State Intervention

Even when we ignore the above-mentioned tension between the neoclassical element and the Austrian-Libertarian element in the neo-liberal intellectual edifice, there are still disagreements amongst the neoclassical economists themselves on exactly what the role of the state should be, as we implicitly suggested above.

As I indicated above, neoclassical economics has a strong interventionist streak that is best manifested in welfare economics. Especially, as Baumol (1965) and others have pointed out, once we begin to follow the logic of externality faithfully, it seems doubtful whether we should have any market transaction at all. Most goods create some negative externalities in their production processes in the form of pollution, except in those few cases where proper compensation is actually made. When considering 'linkage effects' (Hirschman, 1958, chapter 6) or 'pecuniary externalities' (Scitovsky, 1954), many goods may additionally be classified as having positive externalities. Some economists even argue that some goods which have conventionally been treated as lacking externalities, say basic foodstuffs, can be seen as creating externalities when they are not consumed in the proper amount and therefore induce crime

(Schotter, 1985, pp. 68–80). Moreover, there exist interdependences between individual preferences. For example, people have what Elster (1983, chapter 2) calls counteradaptive preferences – 'the grass is always greener on the other side of the fence'. The psychology of luxury goods consumption – part of one's pleasure derives from the very fact that one consumes what others do not – is another example of interdependent consumer preference.

The list can go on, but the point here is that, even using a purely neoclassical logic, one can justify an enormous range of state intervention. Indeed, in the 1920s and 1930s people like Oskar Lange were trying to justify socialist planning on the basis of essentially neoclassical models (Lavoie, 1985; Pagano, 1985). Thus seen, whether a neoclassical economist is an interventionist or not depends more on his/her political preference rather than the 'hard' economics that he/she practises. Therefore, it is important to reject the myth propagated by neoclassical economists that the boundary between 'good' and 'bad' interventions can be drawn according to some 'scientific' rules.

2.3 Concluding Remarks

Neo-liberalism is based on an unholy alliance between neoclassical economics, which provides the intellectual legitimacy, and the Austrian-Libertarian tradition, which provides the political rhetoric. This, in turn, means that the interventionist streak of neoclassical economics has to be suppressed. Such suppression involves, we pointed out, intellectually and morally indefensible practices like drawing an 'arbitrary' boundary around the state without acknowledging its arbitrariness, using different discourses for 'serious' academic research and for 'popular' policy discussion (again without acknowledging such compartmentalization), and denouncing the interventionist conclusions of formal models with unsubstantiated 'pop' political economy. We then argued that even neoclassical economics itself does not provide us with any unambiguous 'scientific' criterion to draw the boundary between 'good' and 'bad' interventions. Thus seen, despite its pretence of intellectual coherence and clear-cut messages, neo-liberalism is an internally heterogeneous and inconsistent intellectual doctrine with confused and confusing messages.

3. SOME INSTITUTIONALIST CRITICISMS OF THE FOUNDATIONS OF THE NEO-LIBERAL ANALYSIS OF MARKET, STATE, AND POLITICS

Having pointed out the fundamental fractures in the very set-up of the neo-liberal doctrine, let us now make some detailed criticisms of it from an institutionalist perspective, questioning the very way they envisage the market, the state, and other institutions, as well as the relations between them.

3.1 What is a Free Market? Defining and Measuring State Intervention

3.1.1 Defining state intervention

The neo-liberal discourse on the state is basically about whether 'free' markets produce socially optimal results, which it thinks is the case most of the time, and whether therefore state intervention may be able to improve the free market outcomes, which it thinks is rarely the case. Whether or not we agree with the conclusion, the discourse seems straightforward enough, but is it?

This question may look stupid. Surely we know that a 'free' market is a market without state intervention? Of course, the argument may go, we may have disagreements on which is a 'good' state intervention and which is a 'bad' one, but surely we all know what state intervention means? I am not actually sure that we do. The trouble is that the same state action can be, and has been, considered an 'intervention' in one society but not in another (which could be the same society at a different point of time). Why is this? Let me answer this question with a few examples.

First, let us take the case of child labour. Few people in the OECD countries at present would consider the ban on child labour as a state intervention 'artificially' restricting entry into the labour market, whereas many Third World capitalists (and indeed the capitalists in the now-OECD economies in the late 19th and the early 20th centuries) regard it as just that. In developed countries, the rights of the children not to toil but to be educated are totally accepted, and have been incorporated into the structure of (property and other) rights and obligations underlying the labour market (as the right to self-ownership has been, since the abolition of slavery); they are *not* a matter of policy debate (i.e. there is no debate on whether the ban on child labour is 'efficient' in some sense). In contrast, in the developing countries (of today and yesterday), such rights of children are not so totally accepted, and therefore state action regarding child labour is considered an 'intervention', whose impact on 'efficiency' is still a *legitimate* subject of policy debate.

To give another example, many environmental standards (e.g. automobile emission standards), which were widely criticized as unwarranted intrusions on business and personal freedom when they were first introduced in the OECD countries not so long ago, are these days rarely regarded as 'interventions'. Therefore there would be few people in the OECD countries who would say that their country's automobile market is *not* a 'free' market because of these regulations. In contrast, some developing country exporters who do not accept such stringent environmental standards as 'legitimate' may consider them as 'invisible trade barriers' that 'distort' the market.

In yet another example, many neoclassical economists who criticize minimum wages and 'excessively' high labour standards in the advanced countries as unwarranted state interventions that 'artificially' set up entry barriers into the labour market, do not even regard the heavy restrictions on immigration that exist in these countries as a state intervention (not to speak of supporting it), although immigration controls set up an 'artificial' entry barrier into the labour market as much as the above-mentioned 'interventions' do. This contradictory attitude is possible only because these economists believe in the right of the existing citizens of a country to dictate the terms of the non-citizens' participation in 'their' labour market, without explicitly stating their 'political' position on this matter.

The examples can go on, but the point is that, depending on which rights and obligations are regarded as 'legitimate' by the members of the society, the same action could be considered an 'intervention' in one society and not in another. And once something is not even considered to be an 'intervention' in a particular society at a given time (e.g. the ban on child labour or slavery in the OECD countries), debating their 'efficiency' becomes politically unacceptable – although there is no God-given reason why this should be the case. The corollary is that, depending on the rights-obligations structure, the same market with the same state 'intervention' in the same area – for example, regarding child labour – can be seen as 'free' (from state intervention) in one society and not in another.

So, therefore, if we want to decide whether a particular market is 'free' or not, we need to understand the underlying institutions which define the rights-obligations structure for the participants in the relevant market (and indeed certain non-participants, when it involves 'externalities'). The institutions that need to be understood in this context will include, among other things: (i) the formal and informal rules that govern the way in which interests are organized and exercised (e.g. rules on political associations, rules on incorporation, rules on lobbying); (ii) the formal and informal 'ideologies' relating to notions such as 'fairness' and 'natural rights' that prevail in the society (e.g. rights for everyone to self-ownership, rights for children to education); (iii) the formal and informal institutions that determine how the rights-obligations structure could be changed (e.g. procedures for legal changes, social customs about when and how some *de facto* rights/obligations can become 'legitimate', if not necessarily legalized).

Thus, the apparently simple exercise of defining what is a 'free' market (and what constitutes 'state intervention') is not so obvious any more – and this is, to repeat, even before we can discuss whether some markets are 'failing' and therefore state intervention may make them 'more efficient'. From the institutionalist perspective, we may even say that defining a free market is at the deepest level a pointless exercise, because no market is in the end 'free', as all markets have some state regulations on who can participate in which markets and on what terms. It is only because some regulations (and the rights and the obligations that they are creating) can be so totally accepted (by those who are making the observation as well as by the participants in the market) that some markets appear to have no 'intervention' and therefore be 'free'.

3.1.2 How do we measure state intervention and why does it matter?

For the purpose of international and historical comparison, people have used some quantitative measures of state intervention. At one level, this seems a straightforward exercise. However, how good a measure of state intervention is depends on the theory (of state intervention) that underpins it. Therefore, we need to look beyond the 'numbers' that are supposed to measure the extent of state intervention and analyse the theories that lie behind those numbers. Let us explain what we mean by this.

Traditionally, the most popular measures of the degree of state intervention have been the total government budget as a ratio of GDP and the share of the public enterprise (PE) sector in GDP (or total investment). It may be true that these measures give us as good an idea of how 'big' the state sector is but it is not true that they are good indicators of the degree of state intervention. This is because a 'big' government is not necessarily a more 'interventionist' government. The point is very well illustrated by the East Asian countries of Japan, Korea, and Taiwan.

On the basis of these traditional measures, until recently many people believed that we could 'objectively' establish that the East Asian countries are 'non-interventionist' (e.g. World Bank, 1991, p. 40, Table 2.2). And except for the (conveniently ignored) fact that Taiwan has one of the largest PE sectors in the non-socialist, non-oil-producing world, this observation does not seem to be too far from the truth – that is, as far as we accept that the 'vision' of the role of the state that lies behind these measures correctly reflects the actual role of state intervention in these countries.[5] However, the mode of state intervention in East Asia has been quite different from what is envisaged in the 'vision' that lies behind these traditional measures, and thus they 'wrongly' measure the extent of state intervention in East Asia.

In the 'traditional' vision, the state exercises its control basically through the ownership of the means of production, which is (wrongly) equated with the control over its use, and the reallocation of resources via taxes and subsidies, for example, in the manner prescribed in welfare economics. However, state intervention in East Asia has been conducted less through state ownership and budgetary outlays, but more through measures which need little state ownership or budgetary outlays. They include: (i) regulatory measures (on entry, capacity, price, technology, etc.); (ii) the state's influence on bank lending decisions (especially in Korea and Taiwan, the majority of the banks have been state-owned); and (iii) various 'informal' channels of influence on the business sector (a manifestation of what Evans describes as the 'embeddedness' of these states; see Evans, 1995).

The example does not, in fact, stop in East Asia. For example, some commentators point out that the US federal state, despite its *laissez faire* rhetoric, has strongly influenced the country's industrial evolution through defence procurement programmes and defence-related R&D contracts – especially in industries like computers, telecommunication, and aviation (Johnson, 1982).[6] So, again, the prevailing vision of the role of the state, where 'defence' is accepted as one of the 'minimum' functions of the state (almost shading into 'non-intervention'), makes people underestimate the importance of the US federal government in the country's industrial development.

The point that we are trying to illustrate with the above examples is that how we measure state intervention matters, because the particular measures that we use embody a particular vision of the role of the state which may not be universally applicable, because the institutional assumptions behind that vision may not hold in contexts other than the one from which that vision emerged. Unless we recognize that different measures of state intervention are based on different theories of the role of the state, which embody different assumptions about the institutions and political economy of state intervention, our empirical investigation of the role of the state will be constrained by the limitations of the theoretical perspective that lies behind the 'measures' of intervention that we use.

3.2   What does Market Failure Mean and How much does it Matter? 'Rival Views of Market Society'

3.2.1   When does the market fail?

The term 'market failure' refers to a situation when the market does not work in the way expected of the 'ideal' market. But what is the ideal market supposed to do? Given the current domination of neoclassical economics, the ideal market is usually equated with the 'perfectly competitive market' in neoclassical economics. However, the neoclassical theory of the market is only one of the many legitimate theories of how the market works (and therefore what we can expect from the ideal market and therefore when we can say a market has 'failed') – and not a particularly good one at that. In other words, there are, to borrow Hirschman's phrase, many different 'rival views of market society' (Hirschman, 1982a). Therefore, the same market could be seen as 'failing' by some people while others regard it as 'normal' or even 'succeeding', depending on their respective theories of the market. Let us illustrate this point with some examples:

1. Many people think that one of the biggest 'failures' of the market is to generate 'unacceptable' levels of inequality (whatever the criteria for 'acceptability' may be). However, in neoclassical economics, this is not a market 'failure', because the 'ideal' neoclassical market is not assumed to generate equitable income distribution in the first place. This is not to deny that many well-intentioned neoclassical economists may dislike the income distribution prevailing in, say, Brazil, and may support some 'non-distortionary' lump-sum income transfers, but to point out that even they would argue that an equitable income distribution is simply not something that the market should be expected to generate and therefore the issue is beyond economic 'science'.

2. A 'non-competitive' market is one of the most obvious examples of a 'failing' market for neoclassical economics, while the Schumpeterian theory (and before it the Marxist theory) argues that the existence of 'non-competitive' (in the neoclassical sense) markets is an inevitable, if secondary,[7] feature of a dynamic economy driven by technological innovation. Thus, a classic example of market failure in the neoclassical framework, namely, the non-competitive market, is regarded as an inevitable feature of a 'successful' dynamic economy, according to the Schumpeterian perspective.[8] Or to put it differently, a market which is 'perfect' in the neoclassical sense (e.g. no participant in the market has any market power) may look like an absolute 'failure' to a Schumpeterian because it lacks technological dynamism.

The point that we have just tried to illustrate with our examples is that, when we talk about 'market failures', we need to make it clear what we think the 'ideal' market is capable of doing. Otherwise, the concept of market failure can become so elastic that it means a hundred different things to a hundred different people. Thus, where one person sees 'perfection', another person can see a miserable 'failure' of the market, and *vice versa* (the above example about monopoly illustrates this point very well). Only when we make our 'theory of the market' clear, can we make what we mean by 'market failure' clear.

3.2.2 How much does market failure matter?

Now, how much does 'market failure' matter, however we may define it? The short answer is that it would matter greatly for the neoclassical economists, while it may not matter so much for other people, especially the institutionalist economists. Neoclassical economics is an economics about the market or more precisely not even that – it is really about the barter exchange economy, where there are, to borrow Coase's analogy, 'lone individuals exchanging nuts and berries on the edge of the forest' (Coase, 1992, p. 718). In neoclassical theory, even the firm exists only as a 'production function', and not as an 'institution of production'. Other forms of institutions that make up the modern capitalist economy (e.g. formal producer associations, informal 'networks', trade unions) figure, if they do, only as 'rigidities' that prevent the proper functioning of markets (for a criticism of the view of non-market institutions as 'rigidities', see Chang, 1995, whose Spanish translation appears in Chang, 1996).

Therefore, for the neoclassical economists, for whom 'the market' is essentially 'the economy', if the market fails, the economy fails. And if the economy fails, the state has to step in, as no intermediate institutions or organization have a legitimate place in their scheme. In contrast, for the institutionalist economists, who regard the market as only one of the many institutional mechanisms that make up the capitalist economic system, market failures may not matter as much, because they know that there are many institutional mechanisms other than markets through which we can organize, and have organized, our economic activities. In other words, when most economic interactions in the modern industrial economy are actually conducted within organizations, and not between them through the market (Simon, 1991), the fact that some (or even many) markets are 'failing' according to one (that is, neoclassical) of many possible criteria, may not really make a big difference for the performance of the capitalist system as a whole.

For example, in many modern industries where there are high incidences of monopoly and oligopoly, the market is 'failing' all the time according to the neoclassical criterion, but at the same time these industries were often very 'successful' in the Schumpeterian sense in that they generated high productivity growth and consequently high standards of living. Such an outcome was due to the 'success' of modern business organizations which enabled the coordination of a most complex division of labour – so, where neoclassical economists see a 'market failure', other economists may see an 'organizational success' (Lazonick, 1991). And if this is indeed the case, state intervention in these markets, especially of the neoclassical anti-trust variety, may not be very necessary, and indeed under some circumstances may actually harm the economy.

The point is not that market failures do not exist or that they do not matter at all – on the contrary, the real world is full of market failures even by neoclassical standards (see section 2.2.) and they do matter. The real point is that the market is only one of the many institutions that make up what people call 'the market economy', or what we think is better called 'capitalism'. The capitalist system is made up of a range of institutions, including markets as institutions of exchange, firms as institutions of production, and the state as the creator and regulator of the institutions governing their relationships. Thus, focusing on the market (and market failure), as neoclassical economics does, really gives us a wrong perspective in the sense that we lose sight of a large chunk of the economic system and concentrate on one part only.[9]

3.3 'In the Beginning, There Were Markets': The Market Primacy Assumption

One thing that distinguishes even the most enlightened and open-minded neoclassical economists from the truly institutionally-conscious economists is their belief in what I call the market primacy assumption. In their view, 'in the beginning, there were the markets' (Williamson, 1975, p. 20),[10] and state intervention, organizations, and other institutions are seen as man-made substitutes which emerged only after the defects in the market ('market failure') became unbearable (Arrow, 1974, is the most sophisticated example of this view).

The most obvious example of this market primacy assumption is the Contractarian 'explanation' of the origin of the state. In this view, the state has emerged as a solution to the 'collective action problem' of providing the 'public good' of law and order (especially the security of property), which is seen as necessary (and often sufficient) for markets to function at all (Nozick, 1974; Buchanan, 1986). Thus, in this view, even the very existence of the state is explained according to the logic of 'market failure' in the sense that it is seen as having emerged only after the market has failed to provide law and order due to the 'public goods' problem – an explanation which is obviously contrary to historical truth and therefore can only be seen as an 'ideological' defence of an 'unjust' system (for a criticism, see Chang, 1994a, chapter 1).

At this point, we must emphasize that the fact that someone attributes institutional primacy to the market does not necessarily mean that he/she endorses a minimal state view, as the problem here is not really about where the right 'boundary' between the state and the market should lie. There are many who start (at least implicitly) from the market supremacy assumption but are keenly aware of the failings of the market and willingly endorse a relatively wide range of interventions. Indeed, as we pointed out earlier (section 2.2), if these open-minded neoclassical economists began to take their own logic to the limit, they could end up endorsing all kinds of state intervention.[11] However, they would still see state intervention, or for that matter any other solution based on non-market institutions (e.g. hierarchical organizations like firms), as 'man-made' substitutes for the 'natural' institution called the market.

The point is that, in the beginning, there were not markets. Economic historians have repeatedly shown us that, except at the very local level (in supplying basic necessities) or at a very international level (in luxury trade), the market mechanism was not an important part of human economic life until recently. In fact, although even Joseph Stiglitz, one of the most enlightened neoclassical economists of our generation, says that 'markets develop naturally' (Stiglitz, 1992, p. 75), the emergence of markets was almost always deliberately engineered by the state, especially in the early stage of capitalist development.

Karl Polanyi's classic work shows how even in the UK, where the market economy is supposed to have emerged 'spontaneously', state intervention played a critical role in the process. He argues that:

> [t]he road to the free market was opened and kept open by *an enormous increase in continuous, centrally organised and controlled interventionism* [italics added]. To make Adam Smith's 'simple and natural liberty' compatible with the needs of human society was a most complicated affair. Witness the complexity of the provisions in the innumerable enclosure laws; the amount of bureaucratic control involved in the administration of the New Poor Laws which for the first time since Queen Elizabeth's reign were effectively supervised by central authority; or the increase in governmental administration entailed in the meritorious task of municipal reform . . . . (Polanyi, 1957, p. 140).[12]

Also in the case of the US, the early intervention by the state in establishing property rights, providing critical physical infrastructure (especially railways and telegraphy), the funding of agricultural research, and so on, were critical for its success in early industrialization (Kozul-Wright, 1995; even the World Bank now recognizes this – see the World Bank, 1997, p. 21, Table 1.2). Most importantly, the US was the home of the idea of infant industry protection (Freeman, 1989), and was indeed the most heavily protected economy among the industrial countries for around a century until the Second World War (see World Bank, 1991, p. 97, Table 5.2; Kozul-Wright, 1995, p. 97, Table 4.8).[13]

Moving beyond the UK and the US, we realize that there is virtually no country, except Hong Kong, which achieved the status of an industrialized country without at least some periods of heavy state involvement in the development effort. The exact forms of intervention varied – the 'pre-emptive' welfare state in Bismarckian Germany, postwar French industrial policy, early Swedish state support of research and development, the transformation of the Austrian manufacturing sector since the Second World War through the public enterprise sector, the well-known state-led developments of the East Asian countries – but the fact remains that all successful development efforts involved substantial state intervention. So if virtually all now-advanced countries, with the possible exceptions of Britain at certain phases and Hong Kong, developed in some 'unnatural' way which involved heavy state intervention, it seems questionable whether there is any point in calling the market a 'natural' phenomenon.

What we have just discussed is not simply of historical interest. Whether or not we accord primacy to the market institution makes a critical difference to the way we design development policies. For example, many former Communist countries which opted for a 'big bang' reform have experienced severe economic crises during the last several years; this is one striking example which shows how the establishment of a well-functioning market economy is impossible without a well-functioning state (see Chang & Nolan, 1995, whose Spanish translation appears as Chang & Nolan, 1996). In fact, if markets evolve so 'naturally' as the neoclassical economists believe, these countries would not be in such trouble now. Likewise, the developmental crises that many developing countries have gone through during the last two decades or so also show how dangerous it is to assume the primacy of market institutions and believe that a market will naturally develop as long as the state does not 'interfere' with its evolution. The assumption of market primacy has a lot more serious implications than are first apparent.

3.4   Can We Rid the Market of Politics?
The Disguised Revival of the Old Liberal Politics

One major assumption behind neo-liberal doctrine is the belief that politics allows 'sectional' interests to 'distort' the 'rationality' of the market system and therefore this is something that has to be purged from the market. Criticizing the naivety of welfare economics which assumed the state to be the all-knowing, all-powerful social guardian, the 'new political economy' of neo-liberalism tried to demonstrate how politics is an inevitably corrupting force on the economy. The neo-liberal political economists have argued that we need therefore to 'depoliticize' the economy by restricting the scope of the state and by reducing the room for policy discretion in those few areas where it is allowed to operate, for example, by strengthening the rules on bureaucratic conduct and by setting up 'politically independent' agencies bound by rigid rules (e.g. independent central banks, independent regulatory agencies).

There have been many powerful criticisms of neo-liberal political economy, and we do not feel that this is a place to go into the details (e.g. see, in chronological order, Toye, 1987; King, 1987; Gamble, 1988; Toye, 1991; Chang, 1994a and 1994b; Evans, 1995; Chang & Rowthorn, 1995a and 1995b, both of whose translations appear in Chang, 1996). However, we want to point out some basic issues in order to highlight some fundamental problems in the neo-liberal (and indeed old liberal) view of politics.

3.4.1   All prices are 'political'
First of all, the establishment and distribution of property rights and other entitlements that define the 'endowments' that neoclassical economics take as given is a highly political exercise. The most extreme example will be the various stories of 'original accumulation' such as the Great Plunder or the Enclosure in the early days of British capitalism or the 'shady' deals that dominate the privatization process in many ex-Communist countries these days; however, the continuous political campaigns that established environmental and consumer rights as legitimate rights at least in the OECD countries are less dramatic but perhaps equally important examples.

Moreover, there are practically no prices in reality which do not have some 'political' element in them. To begin with, two critical 'prices' which affect almost every sector, namely, wages and interest rates, are politically determined to a very large degree. Wages are affected not only by minimum wage legislation, but also by various regulations regarding labour standards, welfare entitlements, and most importantly immigration control. Interest rates are also highly political prices, despite the guise of 'de-politicization' that those who support central bank independence want to give to the process of interest rates determination. The recent debate in Europe on the relationship between political sovereignty and autonomy in monetary policy, which was prompted by the approaching European Monetary Union, shows this very clearly. When we add to them those numerous regulations in the product markets regarding safety, pollution, import content, and so on, there is virtually no price which is 'free from politics'.[14]

Of course, all these are not to deny that a certain degree of de-politicization of the resource allocation process may be necessary. For one thing, unless the resource allocation outcome is at least to a degree accepted as 'objective', the political legitimacy of the market-based system itself may be threatened. Moreover, an enormous amount of 'transaction costs' would be incurred on search and bargaining activities if every allocational decision was regarded as negotiable, as it was in the case of the ex-Communist countries. However, this is not to say that no price under any circumstances should be subject to political negotiations, because in the final analysis, there is no price which is really free from politics.

3.4.2 De-politicization: the disguised revival of old liberal politics

If what appear to be 'objective' outcomes of 'impersonal' markets are in the end the results of certain (explicit and implicit) 'political' decisions about property rights, entitlements and prices, the neo-liberal proposal for 'de-politicization' of the economic policy-making process as a means to restore 'economic rationality' also cannot be taken at its face value.

One basic problem with the neo-liberal proposal for de-politicization is that the 'rationality' that such an exercise wants to 'rescue' from the corrupting influences of politics can only be meaningfully defined with reference to the existing institutional structure, which is itself a product of politics (Vira, 1997, for a further exposition of this point). So when the basic institutional parameters of the economy have been, and can only be, set through an 'irrational' political process, a call for de-politicization of the economic process on 'rationality' ground rings hollow.

Another problem with the neo-liberal proposal for de-politicization is that its politics is not what it pretends to be. The call for de-politicization is often justified in populist rhetoric as an attempt to defend the 'silent majority' from greedy politicians and powerful interest groups. However, the diminution of the legitimate domain of politics that de-politicization will bring only serves to further diminish what little political influence these underprivileged people have in modifying the market outcomes, which, we repeat, are heavily influenced by politically-determined institutional parameters. Thus seen, the neo-liberal call for the de-politicization of the economy aims to revive the old liberal politics in a disguised form (Bobbio, 1990, provides an excellent anatomy of the old liberal politics). Like the neo-liberals, the old liberals believed that allowing political power to those who 'do not have a stake' in the existing institutional arrangements would inevitably result in the modification either of such arrangements or of their outcomes mediated through the market. However, unlike the old liberals, who could openly oppose democracy, the neo-liberals cannot do that, so they try to do it by arguing against 'politics' in general and making proposals which ostensibly seek to reduce the influence of those 'untrustworthy politicians' but ultimately aim to diminish democratic control itself (e.g. proposals for 'independent' central banks or regulatory agencies).

The last, but not least, problem with the call for de-politicization is that it may not be a politically feasible recommendation. For good or bad reasons, all countries have accumulated politically organized groups and have developed certain (at least implicitly accepted) ways to modify 'politically' certain market outcomes.[15] Some of these, of course, could be easily eliminated, but others may be so entrenched that they may be eliminated only at very high political and economic costs. Hence the apparent paradox that radical economic liberalization frequently requires harsh authoritarian politics, in order to achieve the high degree of de-politicization that is required for such policy, as graphically exemplified by the liberalization attempt by the Pinochet regime in Chile (also see Gamble, 1988). But the truth is that, however harsh the political regime which may have been pursued, de-politicization has never been, nor can be, complete in practice, and may even backfire.

4. CONCLUSION: TOWARDS AN INSTITUTIONALIST POLITICAL ECONOMY

After pointing out some internal fault lines and indeterminacy in the neo-liberal intellectual agenda, we critically examined some of its basic concepts and assumptions from the institutionalist point of view. As we have repeatedly emphasized, the real point of our criticism is not that neoclassical theory is too little (or for that matter too much) interventionist. As we have pointed out repeatedly, a full-blooded neoclassical economist can legitimately endorse anything from a minimal state to socialist planning, depending on his/her assumption about technological conditions (and implicitly property rights). What we are really trying to argue is that the way in which the relations between the state and the market (and other institutions on those rare occasions when they feature) are envisaged in neoclassical economics prevents an adequate understanding of some fundamental issues surrounding the role of the state. We propose that an approach which may be called 'institutionalist political economy' should be the way forward, and suggest some elements of this theory.[16]

Our starting point should be to reject the assumption of market primacy that underlies neoclassical economics. As we pointed out earlier, neoclassical economics sees the market as a 'natural' institution (if it is ever acknowledged that it is an institution) which spontaneously emerges, but sees other institutional arrangements, be they state institutions or firms (or 'hierarchies'), as emerging only when the market 'fails'. However, saying that the market emerged as a result of the failure of 'planning' (not necessarily by the state, but also by other organizations) or 'hierarchy' is probably closer to the historical truth, which of course is much more complex. We should see the market as an institution which, both logically and historically, has no primacy over other institutions; it is therefore as 'natural' (or, for that matter, as 'artificial') as other institutions. Only when we do that, will we be able to see the relations between market, state, and other institutions in a balanced and historically more accurate way.

Secondly, we should remember that there is more than one view of what the 'ideal' market can do, and that the neoclassical view is only one of many plausible views – and not a particularly good one at that. Accordingly, it becomes possible that the same market may be seen as failing by some with one 'theory of the market' and as succeeding by others with another theory. Only when an economist makes his/her own theory of the market explicit, will we be able to judge the merit of his/her view that the market is 'failing' (or not) and thus to accept or reject the 'solution' to the problem, whether it is some kind of state intervention or the establishment of some non-market institutions and/or organizations.

Thirdly, we need to realize that the neoclassical theory is essentially a theory of the market (and a very schematic and misleading one at that). However, capitalism, as a socio-economic system, is more than a collection of markets, and is made up of many institutions; these include, among others, firms as institutions of production, markets as institutions of exchange, the state as an institution for addressing collective interests politically, and various producer and consumer groupings (e.g. conglomerations of firms, producer associations, trade unions, purchasing cooperatives, and subcontracting networks). Thus seen, market failure becomes, somewhat paradoxically, less of a problem in the institutionalist framework than in the neoclassical framework, because in the former framework even widespread and severe market failures would not necessarily suggest that the whole 'economy' is failing, whereas the latter framework would see it as just that.

Fourthly, we need to understand that the market is a fundamentally political construction. A market cannot be defined except with reference to the specific rights/obligations structure that underpins it. And since these rights and obligations are determined through a political process, and not by any 'scientific' or 'natural' law as neoclassical (and other neo-liberal) commentators want us to believe, all markets have a fundamentally 'political' origin. Therefore, it is impossible to decide whether a market is 'free' or not, without specifying the position of the person(s) making that statement regarding the legitimacy of the current rights/obligations structure. Added to this is the more explicit control of prices found in many markets through price caps, price ceilings, state setting of certain prices, and quantity controls. While some prices may be more politically administered than others in a given context, ultimately no price is free from politics.

This brings us to our fifth element in the institutionalist theory on the role of the state, namely, the need to build a theory of politics which takes a much more broad, balanced, and sophisticated view of politics than what is offered by neo-liberalism. Neo-liberal thinkers see politics as a market-like process, where material benefits are exchanged for political support, but as a process that ulti-mately corrupts the 'rationality' of the market, because of the discretionary powers that it confers upon those who can make and/or influence political deci-sions. However, this is a fundamentally jaundiced view of politics. The main problem with this view is that the 'rationality' that it wants to preserve through 'de-politicization of the economy', which is in fact a euphemism for emascu-lating democracy, makes sense only in relation to the underlying rights/obliga-tions structure, which is a fundamentally political construction. Thus, we need a theory of politics which is not merely an extension of market logic.

Lastly, we need to pay attention to the institutional diversity of capitalism (Albert, 1991; Berger & Dore, 1996; Chang, 1997).[17] Unfortunately, neoclassi-cal economics has little to say about the issue of institutional diversity, because it is a theory of an abstract market economy, or rather of an 'exchange economy' based on barter, as we have pointed out earlier. Partly for this reason, the neo-liberal economists have found it difficult to admit that there are many ways for the state to intervene other than through taxes/subsidies and public ownership, thus misrepresenting, although for somewhat different reasons, cer-tain countries as being much less interventionist than they actually are (e.g. Japan, Korea, the US; see section 3.1.2.). In discussing this issue of institu-tional diversity, understanding the role of the state is critical, not simply be-cause the international differences in the mode of state intervention are a major source of this diversity, but also because the exact institutional forms of, say, corporate governance or labour representation, will have to be legitimized in the eyes of the (current and prospective) market participants, either through formal legislation by the state or through informal support from the state.

Constructing an institutionalist political economy which satisfies all the above criteria (and I am sure that there are more important criteria that I have not thought of) is surely a tall order. However, without a radical restructuring of the ways in which we conceptualize the market, the state, and politics, and the ways in which we analyse the relationships between them, we will not be able to overcome the neo-liberal world view, which has dominated the political and intellectual agenda of our time, in my view with many negative consequences.

NOTES

1. A Spanish translation of Chang & Rowthorn (1995b) appears in Chang (1996).
2. This point is best illustrated by the experiences during the early days of 'reform' in the former Communist countries. What captured people's imagination in those days was the Austrian-Libertarian languages of freedom and entrepreneurship, and *not* the arid neoclassical languages of Pareto optimality and general equilibrium. However, when the post-Communist governments in these countries chose their foreign economic advisers, it was largely according to how high a standing they had in the Western academic 'hierarchy', which was determined by how good they were in handling the concepts and tools of neoclassical economics.
3. Friedman's list of legitimate functions of the state is as follows: maintenance of law and order; definition of property rights; service as a means whereby people modify property rights and other rules of the economic game; adjudication of disputes about the interpretation of the rules; enforcement of contracts; promotion of competition; provision of a monetary framework; engagement in activities to counter technical monopolies and to overcome 'neighbourhood effects' [his term for externality] widely regarded as sufficiently important to justify government intervention; supplementation of private charity and the private family in protecting the irresponsible, whether madman or child (Friedman, 1962, p. 34).
4. A well-known neo-liberal economist, Robert Lucas, reviewing Krugman's book with Helpmann, asked why they had written the book in the first place if they were going to say in the end that the interventionist policies that follow from their models cannot be recommended because of the political dangers that they carry. See Lucas (1990).
5. The ratio of government expenditure to GDP for Japan in 1985 was 33%, far lower than those in other industrial nations except the US (37%). Corresponding figures include 47% for Germany, 48% for the UK, 52% for France, and 65% for Sweden (World Bank, 1991, p. 139, Table 7.4). In the case of Korea, the ratio of *central* government expenditure to GNP in 1989 was 16.9%, a figure substantially lower than those for other semi-industrialized countries. Corresponding figures were 21.2% for Mexico, 30.6% for Brazil, 32.5% for Chile, and 33% for South Africa (World Bank, 1991, pp. 224–5, Table 11). Comparable data for Taiwan is not readily available. As of the mid-1970s (1974–77), the share of public enterprise output in GDP in Korea was around 6.4% and that in Taiwan around 13.6%. The average for developing countries was 8.6%. Korea, then, was somewhat less interventionist than the average on this account (but higher than Pakistan (6.0%), the Philippines (1.7%), Argentina (4.8%), which are all regarded to be cases of failed state intervention), and Taiwan substantially above-average interventionist. The corresponding figure for Japan is not available, but on the basis of the share of the public enterprise sector in gross fixed capital formation, Japan (11.6%) as of the mid-1970s was of about average interventionism amongst industrialized countries – the average being 11.1% (see Short, 1984, Table 1). A more recent estimate by the World Bank puts the share of public enterprise sector in GDP for the 1978–91 period at 6.9% for Taiwan and at 10.6% for Korea, when the unweighted average of the corresponding figures for 40 developing countries in the sample was 10.9% (World Bank, 1995, Table A.1). However, in the light of other qualitative evidence, the World Bank figure seems to underestimate grossly the importance of public enterprises in Taiwan. In my view, this may be due to the fact that there are many 'public' enterprises that are owned by the ruling Kuomintang Party, which may be officially classified as 'private' enterprises. Unfortunately, I have not been able to acquire any systematic data on this.
6. The most recent and striking example of this comes from the aviation industry. The repeated rejections by the US federal government of applications from McDonnell Douglas for a number of critical defence projects have damaged the latter's profits so badly that it had to merge with its major rival, Boeing, changing the fate of the country's, and indeed the world's, civil aviation industry.
7. Recall Schumpeter's famous metaphor that the relationship between the efficiency gains from competition through innovation and that from (neoclassical) price competition was 'as a bombardment is in comparison with forcing a door' (Schumpeter, 1987, p. 84).

8. This, needless to say, does not exclude the possibility (which is often realized) that an economy may be full of monopolies but undynamic.

9. More recently, the neoclassical economists have started to discuss the workings of non-market institutions, especially the firm (transaction cost economics, e.g. Williamson, 1975) and the state (the 'government failure' literature, e.g. Krueger, 1990). However, these analyses have important shortcomings as these institutions are analysed as 'quasi-markets' ultimately based on voluntary contracting (see Vira, 1997).

10. Williamson defends this starting assumption on the ground of 'expositional convenience', arguing that the logic of his analysis would be the same even if the starting assumption was that 'in the beginning, there was central planning' (pp. 20–1). However, as we shall see below, this apparently innocuous assumption has a lot of important theoretical ramifications and policy implications.

11. Lange's defence of socialist planning may be an extreme example, but Schotter's argument for state provision of basic goods (on the ground that an inadequate amount of consumption of such goods can create 'externality' in the form of crime), which we cited earlier, is a less extreme example of how the logic can be carried much beyond where most neoclassical economists are currently willing to take it.

12. And he continues: 'Administrators had to be constantly on the watch to ensure the free working of the system. Thus even those who wished most ardently to free the state from all unnecessary duties, and whose whole philosophy demanded the restriction of state activities, could not but entrust the self-same state with the new powers, organs, and instruments required for the establishment of *laissez-faire* [italics original]' (p. 140).

13. During this period, few countries had tariff autonomy either because of outright colonial rule or because of 'unequal treaties' – for example, Japan got tariff autonomy only in 1899 when all its unequal treaties expired. Of the countries with tariff autonomy, the US had by far the highest tariff rates. Its average tariff rates since the 1820s were never below 25%, and usually around 40%, when those in other countries for which the data are available, such as Austria, Belgium, France, Italy, and Sweden, were rarely over 20%. For detailed figures, see World Bank (1991, p. 97, Table 5.2).

14. We were reminded of this clearly in the British coal crisis in the early 1990s, when the British coalminers were told to accept the logic of the 'world market' and face mine closures with grace. However, the world market prices, which the then British government argued to be beyond political negotiation, turned out to be determined by the 'political' decisions of the German government to give subsidies to their coal, of the French government to allow the export of their subsidized nuclear electricity, and of the many developing country governments to allow, at least *de facto*, child labour in their coal mines.

15. We should also note that political activities are often ends in themselves and people may derive value from the activities *per se* as well as from the products of such activities (see Hirschman, 1982b, pp. 85–6).

16. I have attempted to develop this theory in a number of my previous works. See Chang (1994b, 1995), Chang & Rowthorn (1995b), and Chang (1997).

17. The issue has been discussed in various areas, including: the organization of finance (capital-market-based vs. bank-led vs. state-dominated); corporate governance (U-form vs. M-form; H-firm or A-firm vs. J-firm); wage bargaining structure (centralized vs. decentralized); union organization (centralized vs. industrial vs. company vs. craft); mode of state intervention (Anglo-American, East Asian, Scandinavian, etc.); industrial policy (general vs. selective). For more details, see Chang (1997).

BIBLIOGRAPHY

Albert, M. (1991), *Capitalism vs. Capitalism*, New York: Four Wall Eight Windows.

Arrow, K. (1974), *The Limits of Organisation*, New York and London: W. W. Norton and Company.

Baumol, W. (1965), *Welfare Economics and the Theory of the State*, 2nd ed., London: London School of Economics.

Berger, S. and R. Dore (eds) (1996), *National Diversity and Global Capitalism*, Ithaca and London: Cornell University Press.

Bobbio, N. (1990), *Liberalism and Democracy*, London: Verso.

Buchanan, J. (1986), 'Contractarianism and Democracy', in *Liberty, Market and State*, Brighton: Wheatsheaf Books Ltd.

Chang, H.-J. (1994a), *The Political Economy of Industrial Policy*, London and Basingstoke: Macmillan.

Chang, H.-J. (1994b), 'State, Institutions, and Structural Change', *Structural Change and Economic Dynamics*, **5** (2), pp. 293–323.

Chang, H.-J. (1995), 'Explaining "Flexible Rigidities" in East Asia', in T. Killick (ed.), *The Flexible Economy*, London: Routledge.

Chang, H.-J. (1996), *El Papel del Estado en el Cambio Económico*, Mexico City: Editorial Planeta Mexicana.

Chang, H.-J. (1997), 'Markets, Madness, and Many Middle Ways: Some Reflections on the Institutional Diversity of Capitalism', in P. Arestis, G. Palma and M. Sawyer (eds), *Essays in Honour of Geoff Harcourt – Volume 2: Markets, Unemployment, and Economic Policy*, London: Routledge.

Chang, H.-J. and P. Nolan (1995), 'Europe versus Asia – Contrasting Paths to the Reform of Centrally Planned Systems of Political Economy', in Chang, H.-J. and P. Nolan (eds), *The Transformation of the Communist Economies – Against the Mainstream*, London: Macmillan.

Chang, H.-J. and P. Nolan (1996), 'La Transición en Europea Oriental y en Asia: Caminos Contrapuestos, Políticas Económicas Diferentes', *Revista de Estudios Asiaticos*, (3), pp. 11–34.

Chang, H.-J. and R. Rowthorn (1995a), 'Introduction', in H.-J. Chang and R. Rowthorn (eds), *Role of the State in Economic Change*, Oxford: Oxford University Press.

Chang, H.-J. and R. Rowthorn (1995b), 'Role of the State in Economic Change – Entrepreneurship and Conflict Management', in H.-J. Chang and R. Rowthorn (eds), *Role of the State in Economic Change*, Oxford: Oxford University Press.

Coase, R. (1992), 'The Institutional Structure of Production', *American Economic Review*, **82** (4), pp. 713–719.

Deane, P. (1989), *The State and the Economic System*, Oxford: Oxford University Press.

Elster, J. (1983), *Sour Grapes*, Cambridge: Cambridge University Press.

Evans, P. (1995), *Embedded Autonomy – States and Industrial Transformation*, Princeton: Princeton University Press.

Evans, P., D. Rueschemeyer and T. Skocpol (eds) (1985), *Bringing the State Back In*. Cambridge: Cambridge University Press.

Freeman, C. (1989), 'New Technology and Catching-up', *European Journal of Development Research*, **1** (1), pp. 85–99.

Friedman, M. (1962), *Capitalism and Freedom*, Chicago and London: The University of Chicago Press.

Gamble, A. (1988), *The Free Economy and the Strong State: The Politics of Thatcherism*, London and Basingstoke: Macmillan.

Hall, P. (ed.) (1989), *The Political Power of Economic Ideas: Keynesianism Across Nations*, Princeton: Princeton University Press.

Hayek, F. (1949), *Individualism and Economic Order*, London: Routledge & Kegan Paul.

Hirschman, A. (1958), *The Strategy of Economic Development*, New Haven: Yale University Press.

Hirschman, A. (1982a), 'Rival Views of Market Society', *Journal of Economic Literature*, **48** (4), pp. 1463–1484.

Hirschman, A. (1982b), *Shifting Involvements*, Princeton: Princeton University Press.

Johnson, C. (1982), *MITI and the Japanese Miracle*, Stanford: Stanford University Press.

King, D. (1987), *The New Right: Politics, Markets and Citizenship*, London and Basingstoke: Macmillan.

Kozul-Wright, R. (1995), 'The Myth of Anglo-Saxon Capitalism: Reconstructing the History of the American State', in H.-J. Chang and R. Rowthorn (eds), *Role of the State in Economic Change*, Oxford: Oxford University Press.

Krueger, A. (1990), 'Government Failure in Economic Development', *Journal of Economic Perspective*, **4** (3), pp. 9–23.

Lavoie, D. (1985), *Rivalry and Central Planning*, Cambridge: Cambridge University Press.

Lazonick, W. (1991), *Business Organisation and the Myth of the Market Economy*, New York: Cambridge University Press.

Lucas, R. (1990), 'Review of *Trade Policy and Market Structure* by E.

Helpman and P. Krugman (1989, Cambridge, Massachusetts, MIT Press)', *Journal of Political Economy*, **98** (3), pp. 664–667.

Marglin, S. and J. Schor (eds) (1990), *The Golden Age of Capitalism*, Oxford: Clarendon Press.

North, D. (1994), 'Economic Performance Through Time', *American Economic Review*, **84** (3), pp. 359–368.

Nozick, R. (1974), *Anarchy, Utopia and the State*, Oxford: Basil Blackwell.

Pagano, U. (1985), *Work and Welfare in Economic Theory*, Oxford: Basil Blackwell.

Polanyi, K. (1957), *The Great Transformation*, Boston: Beacon Press.

Schotter, A. (1985), *Free Market Economics – A Critical Appraisal*, New York: Saint Martin's Press.

Schumpeter, J. (1987), *Capitalism, Socialism and Democracy*, 6th ed., London: Unwin Paperbacks.

Scitovsky, T. (1954), 'Two Concepts of External Economies', *Journal of Political Economy*, **62** (2), pp. 143–151.

Shonfield, A. (1965), *Modern Capitalism*, Oxford: Oxford University Press.

Short, R. (1984), 'The Role of Public Enterprises: An International Statistical Comparison', in R. Floyd, C. Gary and R. Short (eds), *Public Enterprises in Mixed Economies: Some Macroeconomic Aspects*, Washington, D.C.: International Monetary Fund.

Simon, H. (1991), 'Organisations and Markets', *Journal of Economic Perspectives*, **5** (2), pp. 25–44.

Stiglitz, J. (1992), 'Alternative Tactics and Strategies in Economic Development', in A.K. Dutt and K. Jameson (eds), *New Directions in Development Economics*, Aldershot: Edward Elgar.

Toye, J. (1987), *Dilemmas of Development*, Oxford: Blackwell.

Toye, J. (1991), 'Is there a Neo Political Economy of Development?', in C. Colclough and J. Manor (eds), *States or Markets?: Neo-liberalism and the Development of Policy Debate*, Oxford: Oxford University Press.

Vira, B. (1997), 'The Political Coase Theorem: Identifying Differences Between Neoclassical and Critical Institutionalism', *Journal of Economic Issues*, **31** (3), pp. 761–779.

Williamson, O. (1975), *Markets and Hierarchies*, New York: The Free Press.

World Bank (1991), *World Development Report 1991*, New York: Oxford University Press.

World Bank (1995), *Bureaucrats in Business*, New York: Oxford University Press.

World Bank (1997), *World Development Report 1997*, New York: Oxford University Press.

2. Evolutionary economics and the economic role of the state

Leonardo Burlamaqui

1. INTRODUCTION

> We shall suggest that (Schumpeter's) central theme in Capitalism, Socialism and Democracy is ... the role of institutions in the economy. As we know, Schumpeter felt that economic theory should deal with 'economic mechanisms' and economic sociology with economic institutions. (Swedberg, 1991b)

> A context of deliberately created stability achieved by risk-spreading mechanisms °
> can facilitate industrial deepening, export expansion, and political compromises to share adjustment costs. ... Unassisted entrepreneurs may not have either the foresight or the access to capital to follow long-term prospects. Their decisions may lock in the country into a specialization in industries with inferior prospects. (Wade, 1990)

> What we need today is the same kind of pragmatic approach to public policy problems that Keynes offered in his own days. (Rodrick, 1997)

What kind of economic theory is more suitable to give meaning to the empirical fact that the state is a crucial player in the economic system? Given that, which roles should it play, and why? Those are our subjects in this chapter.

Despite the resurgence of the neo-utilitarian (or 'public-choice') perspective on the relationship between state and economy in the eighties (Buchanan, Tollison and Tullock, 1980; Buchanan, 1986), with its 'Hayekian' normative preaching that states and bureaucracies are intrinsically inefficient and should shrink, so as to be able to function properly, there are two facts that should be taken very seriously before one can start an empirically grounded analysis:

1. both states and bureaucracies continue to grow and to play a crucial role in the economy, as *The Economist*'s recent survey points out very clearly (cf. data in *The Economist*'s special survey on 'The Visible Hand', 26 September 1997; and also Johnson, 1982 and 1995; Hall, 1986; Wade, 1990, Evans; 1995);

2. no relevant entrepreneurial decision is taken without close attention to that institution called the state and to its policies and prescriptions.

On the other hand, it is also well known that *the* most spectacular event in the transformation of the international division of labour during the last three decades was exactly the ascendance to a position of 'first class producers' by Japan and its Asian followers: South Korea, Taiwan, Singapore – followers that are themselves now being followed by a wave of 'late-late comers', of which China, Indonesia, Thailand, and Malaysia are the most prominent players.

From an analytical perspective, and again despite the critiques of the 'old public administration' by 'new public management' advocates (Osborne and Gaebler, 1992; Dunleavy and Hood, 1994), it is now easily arguable that this extremely successful development strategy had/has in its core a very aggressive and bold degree of state involvement, which has been translated into a diversified set of government policies (Johnson, 1982, 1995; Amsden, 1989; Gereffi and Wyman, 1990; Abegglen, 1994; Chang, 1994; and Cho and Kim, 1994). In fact, the World Bank itself has increasingly come to embrace these facts.

In 1991, at the annual meeting of the World Bank/IMF, Attila Karaosmaoglu, Vice-President and Manager of the former, made the following statement: 'The East Asian NICs and their successful emulators are a powerful argument that a more activist, positive governmental role can be a decisive factor in rapid industrial growth. ... What is replaceable and transferable must be brought to light and shared with others' (Karaosmaoglu, quoted in Evans, 1995, p. 21). More recently, Joseph Stiglitz, currently Senior Vice-President and Chief Economist of the World Bank, in a lecture about the Asian crisis given to the Chicago Council on Foreign Relations, came back to the same point:

> The crisis in East Asia, an area that was previously viewed as the most successful developing region in the world, has had a profound effect on our thinking about development strategies, the international financial system, and the role of international institutions. Many have seen in the crisis a confirmation of their favorite theories. Some have come away with the lesson that the crisis was the inevitable result of government interference in the economy, and that by destroying once and for all the so-called 'East Asian model,' the crisis has proved that free market capitalism is the only viable economic system. Others have seen the crisis as deliberately engineered by the West to restrain development in East Asian economies and pressure them to open their markets, a step these critics see as benefiting the West at the expense of East Asia ...
> I think that both of these views are wrong. It is hard, in particular, to reconcile the first view with the success of East Asia, the understanding of the lessons of that success, and the benefits that success has brought, not only to the people in the re-

gion but also to the world more generally. Government played an important role in the success of East Asia. But so did an outward orientation and trade policies, both promoted by the government itself. Also, neither of those extremes is consistent with my own and most other people's interpretation of the crisis. I will argue that, although we do not and are not likely to have a complete theory of what precipitated the crisis, there are certain characteristics of the economy and certain government policies that have increased those countries' vulnerability to a crisis and amplified its aftershocks. On the crucial question of the role of government in the crisis, I will argue that the crisis was caused in part by too little government regulation (or perverse or ineffective government regulation) in some areas, and too many or too misguided government administrative controls in other areas. (Stiglitz, 1998, p. 1, our emphasis)

Before we proceed to identify the main propositions of evolutionary economics and connect them to the economic role of the state and to institutional arrangements within it, let us note that according to neoclassical economic theory, those facts – the systematic and cumulative growth of state involvement in both Western and Eastern economies (cf. *The Economist*'s survey, pp. 7–8) – should indicate either the systematic and cumulative growth of market failures (and therefore, the state would be acting to correct them) or the systematic and cumulative erosion of the economies' performance as a whole. Empirical evidence does not confirm the second hypothesis, and as for the first, which is more theoretical in nature, should it be true it would have a more Marxist or – even more so, – a Schumpeterian flavour, indicating progressive socialization as an outcome of the normal operation of market forces.

On the other hand, if the same process – systematic and cumulative growth of state involvement in the economy – were to be evaluated and analysed from the public-choice perspective, it would again have to turn itself into an(other) explanation of systematic and cumulative erosion of the economies' performance as a whole; according to that theoretical approach, strong bureaucracies and big governments are intrinsically inefficient (indeed, 'State interventionism leading to rent-seeking, stagnation and decline' is exactly the thesis of Buchanan and Wagner, as well as the main argument of their critique of Keynes's political legacy. (Buchanan and Wagner, 1977, parts 1–2)).

So, bigger governments and growing bureaucracies should inevitably cause the system's performance to deteriorate. If this kind of approach is accepted, both the 'golden age' of capitalism after the Second World War and even more so the East Asian development explosion from the seventies through October 1997 clearly do not fit in with this hypothesis. Our claim here is therefore that, by way of construction, neither the neoclassical nor the public-choice theoretical perspectives are capable of giving a consistent explanation for the connection between the persistence (and expansion) of government and the outstanding performances of capitalism in the West (1948-74) or in the East (from 1948–50 to September 1997, in the worst case). The main reason for this is that both perspectives are much more normative than positive accounts of capitalism (Stiglitz, 1994; Udehn, 1996, part 1; and Chang, 1997). On the other hand, evolutionary economics is fully capable of providing this missing explanation.

2.   THE EVOLUTIONARY PERSPECTIVE IN ECONOMICS: BASIC PROPOSITIONS AND THEIR IMPLICATIONS.

The task confronting economics today may be characterized as a need to integrate Schumpeter's vision of a resilient intertemporal capitalist process with Keynes's hard insights into the fragility introduced into the capitalist accumulation process by some inescapable properties of capitalist financial structures. (Minsky, 1986)

The Arrow-Debreu model, which ... provides the most well-articulated summary of the neo-classical paradigm and which provides the basis of the widespread belief in the efficiency of competitive markets, explicitly assumes that technology is given. There is no scope for innovation. (Stiglitz, 1994)

By now, 58 years after Schumpeter's *magna carta* of evolutionary economics (or the 'anti-equilibrium manifesto' if you like), it is possible to state some basic principles – or axioms – and to indicate very briefly their – radical – implications for economic analysis; it should be clear by now that they are the building blocks of a completely new paradigm:

* Capitalism is a historical process in which change (and not equilibrium) is the most relevant feature. 'Change', therefore, should be the object of investigation in an evolutionary research programme.
* Economic agents are creative, and firms – the main agents – are agents of transformation.
* Competition, understood as rivalry among firms and as a selection mechanism, is the engine that propels economic change.
* Innovations, understood as applications of new ideas and/or methods to the economic sphere, are the main fuel of that engine.
* Money is an asset and markets are sets of financial interrelations and cash flows in which production and distribution are embedded.
* The main causal chain in the operation of the economic system runs from the entrepreneurial decisions – expenditure decisions bound to financial commitments and directed to an unknown future – to the determination of the aggregate levels of investment, production, demand, and employment.

- Money and innovations function both as 'levers of riches' and as uncertainty creators; their interplay is at the root of the system's twin operating features: progress and conflict.
- Profit rates tend to differentiate (not to equalize), and no 'proportionality law between investments and profits' applies.

Given those 'fundamental propositions', we can very briefly sketch the operation of an 'entrepreneurial economy', a term that both Schumpeter and Keynes used to characterize capitalism. Let us begin with a statement made by Matsushita Konosuke, the creator of an industrial empire in Japan that is known throughout the world by its *Panasonic* trademark: 'Business has become terribly complex (and) survival is very uncertain in an environment filled with risk, the unexpected, and competition' (Matsushita, 1988, quoted in Best, 1990, p. 1). From a theoretical perspective, Matsushita's dictum 'fits like a glove' into evolutionary economics.

Within the evolutionary/Schumpeterian approach, competition is conceived of as the interaction and rivalry among firms in environments where they try to create competitive advantages in order to increase their market shares and realize surplus profits (Schumpeter, [1942] 1992, chapter 7; Penrose, 1959; Nelson and Winter, 1982; Porter, 1985; Lazonick, 1991; Rumelt, Schendel and Teece, 1995). Success – or failure – in these strategies always results in asymmetries and conflicts among firms. Some of them grow and/or strengthen their technological and organizational capabilities, while others disappear or begin to perform marginal activities in the economic system.

Competition is therefore the struggle for survival and growth in a structurally uncertain environment. It is a process of selection that irons out equilibrium tendencies and brings in (cost and price) variety and diversity, which are themselves the causes of the surplus profits pursued by the firms. In this context, the monopolization of market opportunities is not something opposed to competition, but rather the temporary result of the competitive process itself.

By means of competitive strategies, firms pursue monopolistic positions which are capable of converting themselves into sources of cumulative profits and growth potential. Their aim is to create barriers to protect themselves and their markets from 'invasion' by known and unknown competitors, barriers whose robustness – excepting those that are politically maintained – springs as a fruit of successful chains of innovations. Surplus profits can therefore be seen as a consequence of the competitive advantages created by entrepreneurial strategies (Moss, 1981; Rumelt, Schendel, and Teece, 1995).

Surplus profits, however, are temporary, since competition itself means a threat to them, either through the imitation strategies of other firms or through their innovative behaviour, which supplies the substratum for continuous product differentiation and productivity increases. In that framework we have a dynamic connection between innovations, market structures and business strategies – a framework whose main traces can be condensed into the Schumpeterian idea that new products and methods compete with old ones in superior conditions, which may mean the death of the latter; and that 'to avoid destruction all firms are obliged – more or less quickly – to follow the example and invest' (Schumpeter, [1942] 1992, chapter 7).

This, in turn, implies the perception that competition occurs not only in existing markets and among firms operating in the same sectors, but also among firms located in different sectors or industries, and in 'future markets' whose roots are already present only in the firms' innovation strategies and technological expectations. In Schumpeter's words:

> It is not necessary to point out that the kind of competition that we have in mind acts not only when *it actually exists*, but also when *it is merely an omnipresent threat. Businessmen feel in a competitive situation even when they are alone in their market* or even if not being alone they hold such a position that government experts [in antitrust legislation – L.B.] cannot see any effective competition between them and any other firms in the same or neighboring areas. (Schumpeter, [1942] 1992, p.115, our italics)

The main idea to be retained here is that innovations and technical progress are permanently destroying and rebuilding the entry barriers, which become fluid across historical time. This implies a relation of cross-causality between innovation strategies and the reshaping of market structures.

On the other hand, although innovation strategies and investment expenditures certainly leave financial trails, all firms can use financial markets to protect themselves against uncertain asset returns, whether or not they undertake investment expenditures. Financial uncertainty then gets into the picture (Dymski and Pollin, 1992, p. 30). It can show up in at least two ways: first, for firms financing asset positions, as default risk, that is, the risk of a return on investment projects below the expected return. The second is market risk, the risk of loss from adverse price movements in financial markets. Generally, as Dymski and Pollin put it: 'firms which turn to the financial markets to limit their exposure essentially exchange one form of uncertainty for another – they reduce default risk by increasing market risk' (Dymski and Pollin, 1992, p. 31). On top of that, financial markets carry forward the accumulated contractual obligations of all past investment decisions. They therefore become the conduit through which disappointed expectations transmit instability to the economy as a whole (Minsky, 1982, chapters 8–9).

Summing up, in 'evolutionary', 'creative destruction' environments, firms are heterogeneous administrative structures that select and combine material, financial, and human resources with unique strategies and learning mechanisms (Penrose, 1959). Innovative strategies are able to differentiate each firm from all its competitors and, by doing so, create Ricardian rents that are 'organization-based' but 'innovation dependent' to become sustainable (Winter, 1995; and Teece, Pisano, and Shuen, 1992, for the concept of Ricardian rents and its application to firm behaviour). Pricing is also a strategy subject to uncertain expectations, multiple rationalities, and financial commitments. That is, prices are set up within the competitive process and result from different entrepreneurial visions, which are themselves subjectively conditioned and path-dependent. In this kind of environment, markets and competition are not adjustment devices, but rather dynamic forces pushing for change and therefore creating, as we already noted, conflict and instability, not harmony and equilibrium.

Instability, which manifests itself through continuous fluctuations in economic activity, unemployment, bankruptcies, and structural transformations, is an endogenous feature of the normal operation of the economic system. Stability, therefore, is not an inherent property of the system, but the result of a socially and institutionally constructed process. Institutions – both subjectively understood as 'conventions' and objectively taken as 'organizations' – are the constituent elements of all economic transactions. Within evolutionary economics, the economic structure itself has to be analysed as an 'inter-institutional system', and an 'institutional approach' is a methodological requirement for theoretical work. North gives a brief account of the role of institutions, which can be used as a 'link' connecting institutional analysis to evolutionary economics:

> Institutions exist to reduce the uncertainties involved in human interaction. These uncertainties arise as a consequence of both the complexity of the problems to be solved and the problem-solving software . . . possessed by the individual. . . . It is sufficient to say here that the uncertainties arise from incomplete information with respect to the behavior of other individuals in the process of human interaction. (1990, p. 25)

On the other hand, however, the existence of institutions is not a sufficient condition for uncertainty reduction and complexity management. As Powell noted, following Schumpeter's main thesis in *Capitalism, Socialism and Democracy*:

> the benefits associated with familiarity may easily outweigh the gains associated with flexibility. Altering institutional rules always involves high switching costs, thus a host of political, financial and cognitive considerations mitigate against such changes. Success is frequently the enemy of experimentation. (1991, p. 192)

At this point we can recast the main proposition of this paper: from an evolutionary point of view, the unstable and 'conflict-led' dynamics of finance, competition, firm behaviour and institutions require, in order to attain stability, the presence of a robust and active state and of both horizontal and selective public policies. Our contentions here are that (a) all relevant entrepreneurial decisions are heavily conditioned by public policies, and (b) the state, when properly structured and operated, is extremely effective, to paraphrase Minsky's inspired title (1986b), to 'stabilise an unstable economy'. On the other hand, when not properly structured and operated, the state can become a 'problem' instead of a 'solution', as Peter Evans perceptively puts it (Evans, 1995). In the next sections we will try to develop these propositions.

3.   EVOLUTIONARY ECONOMICS AND THE ECONOMIC ROLE OF THE STATE : SCHUMPETER'S APPROACH

> Fiscal measures have created and destroyed industries, industrial regions, even where this was not their intent, and have in this manner contributed directly to the construction (and distortion) of the edifice of the modern economy. (Schumpeter, [1918] 1991)

Schumpeter's admission of the importance of state intervention to encourage and 'frame' industrial activity dates back to at least the year 1918, when he published an essay entitled *The Crisis of the Tax State*, where he made the above statement. At that time, however, his admission did not involve approval and surely did not spring organically from his economic theory: the 'business cycle model' in which the author operated – until 1942 – was basically self-regulating, that is, it cancelled, by way of construction, the opportunity for systematic developmental interventions by the state. In the 1920s, however, Schumpeter's ideas started to change (Allen, 1991, vol. 1, chapter 10).

Yet, in the 1930s, his book of 1912, *Theory of the Economic Development*, suffered a substantive revision in order to be published in English. The translated version was issued in 1934, and its last pages contain a consideration that shows that a new view was already in course of development. In referring to the process of 'abnormal liquidation' brought about by the depressions and the possible measures towards mitigation of their predatory effects, Schumpeter writes the following:

> But [instead of a policy of indiscriminate credit restriction] a *credit policy* is also conceivable – on the part of the individual banks as such, but still more on the part of the *Central Banks,* with their influence upon the private banking world – which

would differentiate between the phenomena of the normal process of the depression, which have an economic function, and the phenomena of the abnormal process, which destroy without function. It is true, such a policy would lead far into a *special variety of economic planning* which would infinitely increase the influence of political factors upon the fate of individual and groups ... Theoretically, it is of interest to establish that such a policy is not impossible and is not to be classed with chimeras or with measures which are by nature unsuited to attain their ends. (Schumpeter, [1934] 1997, p. 254, our italics)

In fact, what is being raised by the author is the functionality – and theoretical support – of a selective credit policy, orchestrated by the central bank and intended to differentiate the 'new' from the 'old' so as to prevent innovations from undergoing the unselective destruction process produced by depressions: a selective intervention, although not systematic and basically defensive. It is obviously an exaggeration to construct the above-mentioned quotation as a selective industrial policy *stricto sensu*, but it is also evident that Schumpeter's thoughts here show a change as to his appraisal of the design and limits of the public-private relation. In our view, his turning point regarding this matter is his book of 1939, *Business Cycles*.

However, this is not noticeable in the theoretical sections of the book, but rather in his analysis of the 'state-directed economy of Germany' in the period between 1933 and 1937. It should be stressed that this analysis refers to the German economy under a National-Socialist administration, and not yet under the war economy that took place starting from the years 1936–7, when Göring took over as 'Plenipotentiary Planning Minister'. At the time indicated, the German economy was operating with almost full capacity and its investments were filled with innovations (Landes, 1969, chapter 6).

That chapter of *Business Cycles* permits a very interesting test of our argument, inasmuch as it places us before Schumpeter's interpretation of a state-led capitalism in whose administration was included an industrial policy agenda. His first statement concerning this process as a whole is the following:

The outstanding feature is the rapid progress, practically without relapse, toward full employment of resources in general and labor in particular, in fact more than that: unmistakable symptoms of overemployment in our sense. ... In many industries, shortage of labor. (Schumpeter, 1939, vol. 2, p. 971)

In his attempt to diagnose the nature and effects of the 'government leadership and control' (Schumpeter, 1939, vol. 2, p. 972), Schumpeter focuses on the state's leadership towards a self-sufficient economy and on the measures for undertaking its operations by analysing them through the lenses of their dynamic impact upon the introduction of innovations. In his words, 'A large part of the new investments in industry was for the development of resources that were to replace imported materials ... But that was not all. New things were done involving the distinct entrepreneurial act that constitutes *creative adaptation*'. To which he adds a note specifically referring to the role of the state:

> It gave leads. It exerted pressure. It helped in various ways in financing and promoting ... This active leadership was, of course, something very different from mere *control* or *regulation*, and also from mere *conditioning*. (Schumpeter, 1939, vol. 2, p. 973, our italics)

Schumpeter's argument concerning this matter is subtle but extremely relevant for our discussion. The crucial point in his interpretation does not concern government control or expenditure policies alone, but their operation under the framework of the fundamental Schumpeterian parameters, namely industrial rationalization, productivity increases, and innovation. Therefore, expenditures should be selective and directed to maintaining the innovative process.

In a similar way, anti-trust policies aiming to 'correct market failures' according to a neoclassical 'perfectly competitive' normative standard could result, from a Schumpeterian perspective, in market structure instability and even in discouragement of the innovative process. State intervention could thus also have a side-effect that would jeopardize the system's performance: it could produce a conflict between public bureaucracy and private managers, bringing about a situation of reciprocal distrust which, according to Schumpeter, would neither be useful nor efficient. This argument is the basis of the author's rejection of what he used to call an anti-business bias of the *New Deal* policies, as well as of his implicit approval of the selective and 'business disciplining' policies targeting productivity increases and innovations in the National-Socialist administration, in whose roots was an industrial policy strategy.

In this regard, Schumpeter writes:

> It is reasonable to attribute [such success] to the manner in which it was done in this case, and to concomitant policy .... Creation of purchasing power was an incident but it was not pursued as an end. Speculation was not encouraged, infraction of social discipline was discouraged. No attempt was made to raise costs .... Saving and accumulation were encouraged ... and in many instances, enforced. (1939, vol. 2, p. 975)

To which he adds in a footnote:

> Compulsion to invest in some lines frequently implied prohibition to invest in other lines, but these prohibitions were no longer dictated by the recovery purpose and carry a different meaning. (ibid.)

Summing up: selective intervention, entrepreneurial leadership, encouragement of investment cartels, and industrial rationalization by the state were the elements stressed by Schumpeter in his (positive) account of German economic policy in the thirties, the same policy that, according to Joan Robinson, caused the German economy 'to eliminate unemployment when Keynes was still concerned about explaining its causes' (Robinson, quoted in Garvy, 1975). It does not require a lot of cleverness to perceive that there is a great similarity between this scenario and the institutional frame responsible for the 'development boom' experienced by Japan, South Korea, and Taiwan in the post-Second World War era. All those are clear examples of – successful – state-led transformation strategies based on bold industrial policy agendas and robust institutional networks (Johnson, 1982; Dore, 1986, 1987; Amsden, 1989; Weiss and Hobson, 1995).

The crucial point is Schumpeter's positive evaluation on this redesign of the frontiers between public and private environments. It should be stressed that his opinion is not grounded on the political regime in course, but rather on the position of the state *vis-à-vis* long-term economic rationality. In Schumpeter's words: 'The strength of the Fascist State as against group interests [rested in] its fundamental attitude to economic life [which] facilitated a behavior in accordance with the rules of long economic rationality' (1939, vol. 2, p. 976). Based upon this diagnosis, Schumpeter makes a consideration that recalls our attention to the relationship between structural change and macroeconomic stability:

> Theoretically it is possible so to plan the sequence of innovations as to iron out cycles: but after strenuous periods of advance there will be recessions even in the corporate State: most of the symptoms of *depressions*, however, need not occur at all. (1939, vol. 2, p. 977)

The elaboration on this argument would only be done, however, in his 1942 book. In *Capitalism, Socialism and Democracy*, Schumpeter is already fully operating, as we have seen, on the concepts of creative destruction and competition via innovations, which are connected with his theory of corporate capitalism, where the big companies and oligopolistic market structures shape the typical economic structure. In this context, there is a whole set of industrial policy measures which acquire their substantive rationality only within this theoretical frame. Cartel policies, as instruments of stabilization and/or speeding technical progress, are fully understandable only under this theory of competition as a creative destruction process filled with technological and financial uncertainties, cut-throat price competition, and the possibility of bankruptcies and involuntary unemployment.

> Restraints of trade of the cartel type, as well as those consisting only of tacit under-standings about price competition *may be effective under conditions of depression. As far as they are, they may in the end produce not only steadier but also greater expansion of total output* than could be secured by an entirely uncontrolled rush that cannot fail to be studded by catastrophes. ([1942] 1992, p. 91, our italics)

Its counterpart would be, however, a cartel-monitoring set of measures designed in order to guarantee their 'efficiency commitment' and encourage entrepreneurial strategies concerning technological creativity and organizational rationalization.

> It is certainly as conceivable that an all-pervading cartel system might sabotage all progress as it is that it might realize, with smaller social and private costs, all that perfect competition is supposed to realize. *That is why our argument does not amount to a case against state regulation proposition against State regulation. It does show that there is no general case for 'trust-busting' or the prosecution of everything that qualifies as a restraint of trade.* Rational as distinguished from vindictive regulation by public authorities turns out to be an extremely delicate problem, which not every government agency ...can be trusted to solve. ([1942] 1992, p. 91, our italics)

However, as already mentioned, Schumpeter's most effective support of a bold 'competitiveness policy agenda' is not contained in the second part of his 1942 book concerning the analysis of capitalism, but rather in the third part, where he discusses and compares the potential efficiency of corporate capitalism to an eventual 'socialist project' of economic administration. His argument is that just as corporate capitalism represents an acceleration of potential growth and economic rationality *vis-à-vis* Adam Smith's type of capitalism, a 'socialist economy' might as well surpass corporate capitalism by means of these same criteria. Here two issues must be clarified: (i) what Schumpeter understood as a socialist economy, and (ii) what his reasoning was to support its potential superiority.

The Schumpeterian definition of socialism is not focused on statization of the means of production nor on the eradication of private property, but rather on its socialization, which involves essentially the redesign of the frontiers between private and public in the economic sphere. In the author's words, socialism is defined as '... an institutional pattern ... where the economic issues of society belong to the public sphere', but '...where almost all liberty of action should be permitted to the administrators' (Schumpeter, [1942] 1992, p. 216). This statement is fundamental inasmuch as it evidences that Schumpeter's concept of socialism can be reconstructed as an institutional variety or pattern of capitalism embedded in a higher degree of socialization. Our contention here is that this 'institutional pattern' has its empirical counterpart in contemporary European countries such as Sweden, Belgium, and Norway, and in East Asian countries such as Japan, South Korea, Taiwan, and Singapore (Bosworth and Rivlin, 1987; Dore, 1987; Vasil, 1992; Chang and Rowthorn, 1995; and Burlamaqui, 1995). This re-reading of the Schumpeterian discourse about both state structures and government policies allows us to state a few points:

In the first place, the socialized economy envisaged by Schumpeter would be economically more rational with regard to information diffusion, on the basis of which more consistent decisions about production and investment could be taken. In his own words:

> Those determined solutions of the problems of production are rational or optimal from the standpoint of given data, and anything that shortens, smoothens or safeguards the road that leads to them is bound to save human energy and material resources and to reduce the costs for which a given result is attained. Unless the resources so saved are completely wasted, the efficiency ... should necessarily increase. (Schumpeter, [1942] 1992, p. 194).

Secondly, the innovative process could be *co-ordinated* taking into account timing and locational considerations. In the process of creative destruction, creation could be performed in a co-ordinated manner and destruction by means of exit policies. In his own words:

> the planning of progress, in particular the systematic co-ordination and the orderly distribution in time of new ventures in all lines, would be incomparably more effective in the prevention of bursts ... and of depressive reactions ... than any automatic or manipulative variations of the interest rate or the supply of credit can be ... And the process of *discarding the obsolete*, that in capitalism – specially in competitive capitalism – means paralysis and losses that are in part functionless could be reduced to what *discarding the obsolete* actually conveys to the layman's mind *within a comprehensive plan providing in advance for the shifting to other uses of the non-obsolete complements of the obsolete plants or pieces of equipment*. (ibid., p. 195, our italics)

Thirdly, the relation between technological change and employment could be also rationalized by coordination policies so that it would be possible to 're-direct the men to other employments which, if planning lives up to its possibilities at all might in each case be waiting for them' (ibid, p. 196). Finally, the resistance to changes could be 'strongly discouraged', and consequently the promotion of innovations would be operated in a quicker and more rational way. The reader can note that all these propositions are grounded on both a concept and a scope of economic policy that are radically distinct from those coming either from neoclassical or public-choice theories.

Summing up: what Schumpeter considered as possibilities of a 'socialist economy' – measures whose implementation would render it more rational and efficient than corporate capitalism itself – are, in our view, crucial elements of the competitiveness policy agenda tied to a different type of capitalism: although rejected on an a priori basis by mainstream economic theory, and therefore largely absent from Anglo-American market-capitalism, they are the 'bread and butter' of the German-Scandinavian-East Asian pattern of 'alliance' capitalism. Its central elements are grounded exactly on the ideological acceptance of state involvement in the economic sphere besides a non-individualist economic culture (even if compatible with a high degree of individual freedom, as the European and Scandinavian countries unmistakably show), and on an economic and institutional structure marked by a substantively higher degree of socialization. It should be stressed that this is our interpretation of Schumpeter's ideas, although the author appears to be pointing in the same direction when he states that:

> the whole of our argument might be put in a nutshell by saying that *socialization* means a stride beyond big business on the way that has chalked out by it or, what amounts to the same thing, that socialist management may conceivable prove as superior to big-business capitalism has proved to be to the kind of competitive capitalism of which the English industry a hundred years ago was the prototype. (Schumpeter, [1942] 1992, p. 196)

The crucial point to be underlined here is the author's definition of 'socialism' as 'an institutional pattern ... where the economic issues of society belong to the public sphere'. There should not be any doubt that the issue this definition really addresses is the centrality of the economic role of the state, to which we now turn.

4. STATE STRUCTURES, EMBEDDED AUTONOMY AND PUBLIC POLICIES: AN EVOLUTIONARY-INSTITUTIONALIST APPROACH

> Situations emerge in the process of creative destruction in which many firms may have to perish that nevertheless would be able to live on vigorously and usefully if they could weather a particular storm ... there is certainly no point in trying to conserve obsolescent industries indefinitely; but there is a point in trying to avoid their coming down with a crash and in attempting to turn a rout, which may become a center of cumulative depressive effects, into orderly retreat. (Schumpeter, [1942] 1992)

At the core of the success of market economies are competition, markets, and decentralisation. It is possible to have these, and for the government to still play a large role in the economy; indeed, it may be necessary for the government to play a large role if competition is to be preserved. (J. Stiglitz, 1994)

Given the above, and despite the current (sometimes enraged) neo-liberal statements that view state action and bureaucracies as always ineffective (or at best irrelevant), the reason seems to remain with Karl Polanyi (for whom 'The road to free markets was opened and kept by an enormous increase in continuous, centrally organised and controlled interventionism' [(1944) 1980, p.127]) and with Max Weber (whose statement that 'Capitalism and bureaucracy found each other and belong intimately together' is as true today as when it was written, in the beginning of the century [1968, p.1395, n. 14]).

As we dive into the last years of the 20th century in which state initiatives, public bureaucracies, and government agencies have never stopped growing, the relevant issues to be discussed are not about more or less state intervention, but about (i) what kind of state structures and (ii) which policy agendas are more conducive to increase 'development power' and competitiveness for firms and nations, as well as employment security and 'work quality' for the labour force. Some comments on each item are in order.

The first essential distinction to be made when dealing with state structures and government policies is between 'strong state' and 'big government'. The confusion between them is responsible for much of the noise that surrounds discussions on the matter. A 'strong state' means the possession of an executive power capable of coordinating and shaping the strategies of big business groups, a bureaucracy with an autonomous core, able to negotiate priorities in the nation's agenda and having the necessary respectability to be heard, and – last but not least – a sound financial capacity to support both those features. It differs sharply from 'big government' in the sense that strong states do not imply state-owned productive enterprises, and welfare systems can be quite small.

The second critical issue to be discussed is the relationship between state structures, business groups, and structural transformation. This will bring us to the concept of embedded autonomy, which we will use following Granovetter ([1985] 1992) and Evans (1995). Concerning the internal organization of the state, the 'Weberian approach' – a highly selective, meritocratically recruited bureaucracy with long-term career rewards that create professional commitment and a sense of corporate coherence – seems to be a necessary condition for achieving 'development power', i.e. the bureaucratic 'autonomy' indispensable to the pursuit of collective action.

A second condition, however (one that was not discussed by Weber and whose roots are in Polanyi and Granovetter, and which is clearly stated in Evans, 1995), seems to be that 'autonomous' state structures and bureaucracy cannot be *insulated* from society (as Weber himself suggested they should be), but must, on the contrary, in order for the state to be able to act as a developmental state, be 'embedded' in a concrete set of social ties that bind the state to society and provide institutionalized channels for the continual negotiation and renegotiation of goals and policies.

A state that is only autonomous would lack both sources of intelligence and the ability to rely on decentralized private entrepreneurial activities. On the other hand, dense connecting networks without a robust internal structure would leave the state incapable of resolving 'collective action' problems, of transcending the individual interests of its private counterparts. Only when embeddedness and autonomy are joined together can a state be called – according to this perspective – developmental (Evans, 1995, pp. 12–13). The combination of corporate coherence and connectedness, or embedded autonomy, provides the underlying structural basis for successful state involvement in structural transformation. A historical illustration should help clarify this issue.

At the end of the Second World War, Britain had a potential competitive advantage in the computer industry which was surpassed only by the United States (Flamm, 1987, p.159; Evans, 1995, p. 99). In the early 1990s, British production was completely erased from the computer industry landscape, when its last major company (International Computers Limited) was purchased by Fujitsu. In the same period, Acer from Taiwan and Samsung from South Korea had converted themselves into major players in the same industry, both competing world-wide and capturing markets from Japanese and American companies.

At first glance, one might think that the British case tells a story of state non-involvement in industry, while Japan, Korea, and Taiwan reflect the opposite. It is our contention, following – among others – Wade, Best, and Evans, that the subject is a little bit more complicated. The difference was not between involvement or its absence, but rather between state structures, therefore between patterns of involvement. The British state had, at least until the Blair administration, a political 'credo' of correcting market failures – a strategy that works mainly *ex-post*, and the British Government conceived of the computer industry mainly as a defence industry, and not as a commercial one (Flamm, 1987, 1988). The Japanese, South Korean, and Taiwanese states embraced a political 'credo' of governing the market – an *ex-ante* strategy (Wade, 1990) – and their governments conceived of the same industry as mainly a commercial one.

Until recently, the Japanese economic history told an ideal-type story in that respect. The strong Japanese state is the result of a long history that goes back to the centralized feudalism of the Tokugawa period (Anderson, 1974, Appendix A) and the restoration of the Meiji era, passing through the years of military government between 1931 and 1945, until the emergence of bureaucracy as the 'Hercules' of the immediate post-war period and the 'head' of the 'turn-around' of the fifties (Lockwood, 1968, chapter 10; Johnson, 1982, *passim*).

With respect to this last step – the reconstruction of the fifties – the legislation approved between 1949 and 1950, was a clear example of 'institutional building', and was of great importance. It allowed bureaucracy, especially within the MITI and the Ministry of Finance (MoF), a substantial discretionary power in the disbursement of resources, as well as in the use of the credit system as an instrument 'par excellence' of an industrial policy designed to push heavy industry and to catch up with the United States and Western Europe (Miazaky, 1967; Eads and Yamamura, 1987, pp. 434–435).

Those two ministries, plus the Economic Planning Board (EPB), appeared then as the main coordinators of Japanese industrial advance. However, it should be stressed that the autonomy initially obtained in a semi-coercive manner and backed by an authoritarian intervention was soon replaced by a continuous process of consultation and meetings with the leaders of the *Keiretsu* (large business groups) and with representatives of the *Keidaren* (Federation of Economic Organisations), where coercion rapidly gave way to persuasion and the search for a consensus (Okimoto, 1988, pp. 312–313). In other words, the autonomy obtained by law became an embedded autonomy, via reciprocal interactions and mutual respect among those ministries, the *Keiretsu,* and the other members of *Keidaren.*

From the above discussion we can extract the hypothesis that both macroeconomic stability and structural transformation are (a) best achieved when assisted, (b) best assisted by public policies designed by taking an evolutionary perspective as a theoretical background, and (c) best achieved when policies are implemented by state structures that are strong but socially embedded.

5. CONCLUSION

We are now able to conclude by connecting the former discussion about evolutionary economic theory and the role of the state with the latter comments on state structures and government policies. In the 'playing field' conceived by evolutionary theory, where finance, technology, and competition are always pushing towards unexpected outcomes and unpredictable possibilities, let us submit that government policies to assist structural transformation are a permanent necessity dictated by the market's behaviour rather than by its failures.

Consequently, their formulation must be based upon the identification of the characteristics that, under this framework, define a capitalist economy: finance as its 'headquarters', competition as turmoil, the endogeny of technical progress, entrepreneurial strategies conceived to differentiate each firm from its competitors, irreversible decisions ('crucial decisions', in G. Shackle's catch-phrase), and, above all, several types of uncertainties (technological, financial, and competitive).

On the other hand, the perception of economic progress under capitalist conditions as turmoil, where new and old assets, firms, and sectors coexist and compete, allows for the introduction of the concepts of sunrise and sunset industries, as well as potential and effective conflicts between them. On the other hand, the perception of the economic environment as a Darwinian-Lamarkian arena where survival does not necessarily belong to those with better technologies or productivity potential, but rather to those with best adaptation skills, enables the defence of sector-based and selective policies targeting the future competitiveness of the system as a whole (a task that each separate sector has no means to anticipate or even map). All the above makes room for policies designed to manage the creative destruction process, and whose aims are investment coordination, innovation diffusion, and conflict management. The overall desired policy result is to decrease the system's structural instability.

In the light of the aforesaid – and in contradistinction to neoclassical theorizing – in an evolutionary environment, market signals (current prices and short-term expectations) should be taken as relevant data concerning mainly current production. They cannot, however, be relevant for providing the necessary information upon which entrepreneurial decisions that involve long-term strategies, are based. Examples here concern long-run investment projects (involving a high degree of asset specificity and sunk costs), choice of technologies, innovation policies, or human resources management for future utilization (for similar statements, see the brilliant anticipations by Richardson, [1960] 1990; Weiss and Hobson, 1995; Chang and Rowthorn, in Chang and Rowthorn, 1995).

For the accomplishment of all those purposes, we claim that there is a strong need for institutions provided with 'beyond-market rationality', in order to coordinate, across time, the decisions to be made now towards an unknown future. In fact, what is being suggested here is the functionality – and the theoretical support – of a selective policy set orchestrated by the state, although negotiated with private sector agencies, intended to cope with the fundamental evolutionary variables: uncertainty, novelty, learning, structural transformation, and instability.

In an evolutionary environment, 'competitiveness policies' should therefore be considered as instruments whose purpose is the attainment of compatibility between macroeconomic stability and technological change in a context of multiple uncertainties and volatile expectations. Based on these premises, we can conceive of structural transformation policies as a set of measures for promoting co-operation among and within public and private institutions in order to encourage and enforce economic competitiveness, and having the preservation of macroeconomic stability and the administration of technological change as their crucial backbones.

This definition leads to our next consideration, regarding specifically the role of government in coping with economic change. Following our previous work, and in line with Schumpeter, Richardson, Nelson, Johnson, Amsden, Wade, Weiss and Hobson, and Chang and Rowthorn, (see Amsden, 1989; Wade, 1990; Richardson, [1960] 1990; Weiss and Hobson, 1995; Chang and Rowthorn, 1995; Burlamaqui, 1991 and 1995, chapter 5; Nelson, 1996), let us suggest that this role should be concentrated in three major areas:

1. *Entrepreneurial stimuli and investment coordination*, that is, uncertainty reduction by means of designing and negotiating investment strategies aimed to match complementary investments, and therefore stabilize and stimulate long-term expectations.
2. *Creative destruction management*, that is, buffering the problems associated with structural change (for instance, providing the financial resources to fund the restructuring – and monitoring – of declining industries, or designing and managing 'learning policies' to enhance work-force skills, and especially to provide new skills for those whose abilities are becoming obsolete due to technological and organizational innovation.
3. *Institutional building* and *bridging,* that is, shaping both regulatory and developmental policy frameworks and building co-operative organizational capabilities where the former tasks (1. and 2.) could take place, which is to say: helping to construct predictabilities by means of institutionally created regularities (institutional trajectories may be a good shortcut concept for that) and institutional coherence.

Having said that, let us now say a word about the instruments and scope of structural transformation policies. There are no theoretical obstacles to the use of any economic policy measures as instruments to assist structural transformation – for instance, competition monitoring, complementary investment coordination policies, exchange rate and capital flow controls, fiscal holidays, import selection, export promotion, bridging public and private institutions to absorb and generate technology, patent legislation, and so on. In addition to all that, educational and trade policies should support, at every step, a structural transformation strategy. The point to be stressed here is that its toolbox includes all types of economic policy instruments and its scope comprises the whole productive structure (see Porter, 1990, chapter 12; Best, 1990 for similar suggestions).

This, in turn, shows a mistake frequently present in the discussions concerning specifically industrial policies: the dichotomy between horizontal and sector-oriented measures, as well as a preferential option for the former. From an evolutionary perspective, such dichotomy is theoretically irrelevant and operationally inappropriate. In those 'creative destruction' contexts, we understand that structural transformation policies have several dimensions or access channels. Their broad conceptual basis – co-ordinating strategies via institutions – necessarily involves both 'horizontal' and sector measures that are therefore complementary, rather than mutually exclusive.

For instance, the volatility of finance and the structural uncertainties inherent in speedy growth processes require institutions functioning horizontally to encourage – and monitor – optimistic long-term expectations *vis-à-vis* investment decisions, in order to minimize eventual bursts of defensive behaviours and sudden shifts towards liquidity preference. On the other hand, the specificity of the finance and funding needs of different sectors and firms, as well as the distinct peculiarities of the expansion process of each industry, usually requires selective measures to support them.

Conversely, the specific technological peculiarities of each industrial sector recommend a selective treatment concerning their analysis and promotion policies. However, the previous argument does not deny the importance of a general policy intended to develop basic research or labour skills that targets their improvement across the entire productive sphere (e.g. 'horizontal' measures again, just to stress the point).

Another important remark concerns one of the crucial dimensions of the structural transformation strategy: employment policies. High rates of unemployment are an element of macroeconomic – as well as of political – instability and their permanence is a threat to the harmony of the social structure. Technological change, on the other hand, is frequently among the causes of higher rates of unemployment. In the light of the above, the management of this potential trade-off should evidently be one of its main purposes. Having said this, it should be stressed that it is imperative to maintain the connections between the purposes of employment maintenance and the promotion of competitiveness in the economy, that is, it is necessary to exclude strategies concerned exclusively with rates of employment and which consider its maintenance as an end in itself.

An employment policy disregarding the competitive dimension inherent in 'creative destruction environments' will almost certainly become, in the medium and the long run, a self-defeating one: a form of preserving the old – obsolete jobs that are no longer needed or, worse still, that are responsible for productivity decreases – which becomes an institutional obstacle to the new. Consequently, the exclusive concern of employment policies with employment rates in the short term may become a source of inefficiency and of future unemployment in the economic system, thus jeopardizing both its stability and its competitiveness. In other words, the maintenance of 'present jobs' as an end in itself carries the danger of 'future jobs elimination'.

Structural transformation strategies should thus incorporate instruments to facilitate the adaptation of the economic system, especially the work-force, to changes introduced by a continuous flow of innovations. From this viewpoint, permanent programmes for training the labour force and improving management quality are most valuable instruments for industrial transformation policies. As the potential of the work-force depends upon its permanent training, the educational system ought to be incorporated in the core strategy of an evolutionary agenda for the economic role of the state. It should be clarified that in this conceptual frame educational policies are core instruments of structural transformation policies.

Summing up, from an evolutionary theoretical perspective the economic role of government concerning the economic system should be based on a vision incorporating the following elements: (i) that market forces are important although insufficient to accomplish the task of managing the conflicting objectives of stability and structural transformation (or, according to an old German axiom, 'the market is a good servant, but a bad master'); (ii) that the state is a fundamental partner in the economic arena, but it must act fundamentally as a network builder and as a 'big push strategist'; (iii) that the possibility of 'playing' both roles is directly related to the presence of the aforementioned embedded autonomy rooting state agencies to the private sector; (iv) that those traces should be connected, in the private sector, with institutions designed to encourage the exchange of information among firms in order to introduce co-operative structures into their competitive strategies.

The last aspect to be mentioned concerns the necessarily manifold ('protean') and institutionally grounded nature of industrial transformation policies. Their design, instruments, and concrete measures should change across time and space and reflect the stage of the economic system regarding its developmental process, historical conditionings, political structure, and organizational resources, as well as its international insertion.

As was repeatedly stressed throughout this paper, such a perspective on the relationship between the role of the state and a 'creative destruction' environment is not compliant with the mechanistic, deterministic, and devotedly attached creed of the (always assumed, but never demonstrated) self-regulating power of markets, on which basis lie the highly abstract axioms of general equilibrium analysis. It is, on the other hand, the necessary institutional counterpart of an evolutionary theoretical perspective.

BIBLIOGRAPHY

Abegglen, J. (1994), *Sea Change*, New York: Free Press.

Albert, M. (1993), *Capitalism vs. Capitalism*, New York: Four Walls Eight Windows.

Allen, R. L. (1991), *Opening Doors. The Life and Work of Joseph Schumpeter*, 2 vols, New York: Transaction Books.

Amsden, A. (1989), *Asia's Next Giant*, Oxford: Oxford University Press.

Anderson, P. (1974), *Lineages of Absolutist State*, New York: New Left Books.

Berger, S. and R. Dore (eds) (1996), *National Diversity and Global Capitalism*, Ithaca, NY: Cornell University Press.

Best, M. (1990), *The New Competition*, Cambridge, MA: Harvard University Press.

Bosworth, B. and A. Rivlin (eds) (1987), *The Swedish Economy*, Washington, D.C.: Brookings Institute.

Brenner, R. (1987), *Rivalry: in Business, Science, among Nations*, Cambridge: Cambridge University Press.

Buchanan, J. (1986), *Liberty, Market and State*, New York: New York University Press.

Buchanan, J., R. Tollison and G. Tullock (eds) (1980), *Towards a Theory of a Rent-Seeking Society*, Texas: A&M University Press.

Buchanan, J. and R. Wagner (1977), *Democracy in Deficit – The Political Legacy of Lord Keynes*, New York: Academic Press.

Burlamaqui, L. (1991), 'Socio-Political Determinants and Industrial Policy in South Korea', *Transactions of the International Conference of Orientalists in Japan*, **36**, Tokyo.

Burlamaqui, L. (1995), *Organized Capitalism in Japan, a Schumpeterian-Keynesian-Polanyian Perspective*, Doctoral Thesis, Institute of Economics, Federal University at Rio de Janeiro.

Carlsson, B. and R. Henriksson (eds) (1991), 'Development Blocks and Industrial Transformation', *The Dahmènian Approach to Economic Development*, Stokholm: Almqvist & Wiksell.

Chang, H.-J. (1994), *The Political Economy of Industrial Policy*, New York: Macmillan Press.

Chang, H.-J. (1997), 'An Institutionalist Perspective on the Role of the State'. Paper presented at the International Seminar 'Institutions and Economic Development', Rio de Janeiro, November.

Chang, H.-J. and R. Rowthorn (eds) (1995), *The Role of the State in Economic Change*, Oxford: Oxford University Press.

Cho, L. and Y. Kim (eds) (1994), *Korea's Political Economy*, New York: Westview Press.

Collins, R. (1986), *Weberian Sociological Theory,* Cambridge: Cambridge University Press.

Crotty, J. (1994), 'Are Keynesian Uncertainty and Macrotheory Compatible? Conventional Decision Making, Institutional Structures, and Conditional Stability in Keynesian Macromodels', in C. Dymski and R. Pollin (eds), *New Perspectives in Monetary Macroeconomics,* Michigan: Michigan University Press.

Dore, R. (1986), *Flexible Rigidities,* Palo Alto: Stanford University Press.

Dore, R. (1987), *Taking Japan Seriously*, Palo Alto: Stanford University Press.

Dore, R. (1997), 'National Diversity and Global Capitalism'. Paper presented at the International Seminar 'Institutions and Economic Development', Rio de Janeiro, November.

Dunleavy, P. and C. Hood (1994), 'From Old Public Administration to New Public Management', *Public Money and Management*, July-September, pp. 9–16.

Dymski, G. and R. Pollin (1992), 'Minsky as a Hedgehog', in S. Fazzari and D. Papadimitriou (eds), *Financial Conditions and Macroeconomic Performance: Essays in Honor of Hyman P. Minsky*, London: Sharpe.

Dymski, G. and R. Pollin (eds) (1994), *New Perspectives in Monetary Macroeconomics,* Michigan: Michigan University Press.

Eads, G. and K. Yamamura (1987), 'The Future of Industrial Policy', *in* K. Yamamura and Y. Yasuba (eds), *The Political Economy of Japan, Vol. 1: The Domestic Transformation*, Palo Alto: Stanford University Press.

The Economist (1997), 'The Visible Hand ', Special Survey, 27 September, pp. 6–48.

Evans, P. (1995), *Embedded Autonomy*, Princeton: Princeton University Press.

Flamm, K. (1987), *Targeting the Computer*, Washington D.C.: Brookings Institute.

Flamm, K. (1988), *Creating the Computer*, Washington D.C.: Brookings Institute.

Freeman, C. and L. Soete (1994), *Work For All or Mass Unemployment*, London: Pinter.

Garvy, G. (1975), 'Keynes and the Economic Activists of Pre-Hitler Germany', *Journal of Political Economy*, **83**, pp. 391–405.

Gereffi, G. and D. Wyman (eds) (1990), *Manufacturing Miracles*, Princeton: Princeton University Press.

Gorz, A. (1989), *A Critique of Economic Reason*, London: Verso.

Granovetter, M. [1985] (1992), 'Economic Action and Social Structure: The Problem of Embeddedness', in M. Granovetter and R. Swedberg (eds), *The Sociology of Economic Life*, New York: Westview Press.

Hall, P. (1986), *Governing the Economy: the Politics of State Intervention in Britain and France*, Cambridge: Polity Press.

Hirschman, A. [1945] (1980), *National Power and the Structure of Foreign Trade*, Berkeley: University of California Press.

Hirschman, A. (1961), *A estratégia do desenvolvimento econômico*, México: Fondo de Cultura.

Hirschman, A. (1985), *A Bias for Hope – Essays on Development and Latin America*, New York: Westview.

Hodgson, G. (1996), 'Varieties of Capitalism and Varieties of Economic Theory', *Review of International Political Economy*, 3 (3), Autumn.

Hodgson, G. (1997), 'From Micro to Macro: The Concept of Emergence and the Role of Institutions'. Paper presented at the International Seminar 'Institutions and Economic Development', Rio de Janeiro, November.

Inoguchi, T. and D. Okimoto (eds) (1988), *The Political Economy of Japan, Vol. 2: The Changing International Context*, Palo Alto: Stanford University Press.

Johnson, C. (1982), *MITI and the Japanese Miracle*, Palo Alto: Stanford University Press.

Johnson, C. (1989), 'MITI, MPT and the Telecom Wars: How Japan Makes Policy for High Technology', in J. Zysman, C. Johnson and L. Tyson (eds), *Politics and Productivity: How Japan's Development Strategy Works*, Ballinger.

Johnson, C. (1995), *Japan: Who Governs?*, New York: Norton.

Keynes, J. M. [1936] (1983), *Teoria geral do emprego, do juro e da moeda*, Rio de Janeiro: Atlas.

Landes, D. (1969), *The Unbound Prometheus*, Cambridge: Cambridge University Press.

Lazonick, W. (1991), *Business Organization and the Myth of the Market Economy*, Cambridge: Cambridge University Press.

Lockwood, W. (1954), *The Economic Development of Japan*, Princeton: Princeton University Press.

Lockwood, W. (ed.) (1968), *The State and Economic Development in Japan*, Princeton: Princeton University Press.

Miazaky, Y. (1967), 'Rapid Econmic Growth in Post-War Japan', *The Developing Economies*, June, 5 (2), pp. 788–801.

Minsky, H. (1986a), 'Money and Crisis in Schumpeter and Keynes', in H.J. Wagener and J. W. Drukker (eds), *The Economic Law of Motion of Modern*

Society: A Marx-Keynes-Schumpeter Seminar, Cambridge, MA: Cambridge University Press

Minsky, H. (1986b), *Stabilizing an Unstable Economy*, New Haven: Yale University Press.

Moss, S. (1981), *An Economic Theory of Business Strategy, an Essay in Dynamics Without Equilibrium*, New York: John Wiley & Sons.

Nelson, R. (1996), *The Sources of Economic Growth*, Cambridge, MA: Harvard University Press.

Nelson, R. and S. Winter (1982), *An Evolutionary Theory of Economic Change*, Cambridge, MA: Belknap/Harvard University Press.

North, D. (1990), *Institutions, Institutional Change and Economic Performance*, Cambridge: Cambridge University Press.

Okimoto, D. (1988),'Political Inclusivity: the Domestic Structure of Trade', *in* T. Inoguchi and D. Okimoto (eds), *The Political Economy of Japan, Vol. 2: The Changing International Context*, Palo Alto: Stanford University Press.

Okimoto, D. (1989), *Between MITI and the Market*, Palo Alto: Stanford University Press.

Osborne, D. and Gaebler, T. (1992), *Reinventing Government*, New York: Plume.

Penrose, E. (1959), *The Theory of the Growth of the Firm*, Oxford: Blackwell.

Polanyi, K. [1944] (1980), *The Great Transformation*, New York: Rinehart.

Porter, M. (1985), *Competitive Advantage*, New York: Free Press.

Porter, M. (1990), *The Competitive Advantage of Nations*, New York: Free Press.

Powell, W. (1991), 'Expanding the Scope of Institutional Analysis', in W. Powell and Di Maggio (eds), *op. cit.*

Powell W.W. and P.J. Dimaggio (eds) (1991), *The New Institutionalism in Organization Analysis*, Chicago: The University of Chicago Press.

Richardson, G. [1960] (1990), *Information and Investment*, Oxford: Oxford University Press.

Rodrick, D. (1997), *Has Globalization Gone Too Far?* Washington: Institute of International Economics.

Rumelt, R., D. Schendel and D. Teece (eds) (1995), *Fundamental Issues in Strategy*, Cambridge, MA: Harvard Business Press.

Schumpeter, J. [1918] (1991), *The Crisis of the Tax State,* in R. Swedberg (ed.), *Joseph. A. Schumpeter – The Economics and Sociology of Capitalism*, Princeton: Princeton University Press.

Schumpeter, J. [1934] (1997), *The Theory of Economic Development*, Cambridge, MA: Transaction Publishers.

Schumpeter, J. (1939), *Business Cycles* (2 vols.), New York: McGraw Hill.

Schumpeter, J. [1942] (1992), *Capitalism, Socialism and Democracy*, Routledge.

Stiglitz, J. (1994), *Whither Socialism?*, Cambridge: MA: MIT Press.

Stiglitz, J. (1998), *The Role of International Financial Institutions in the Current Global Economy*, Address to the Chicago Council on Foreign Relations, Chicago, 27 February.

Swedberg, R. (ed.) (1991a), *Joseph A. Schumpeter – The Economics and Sociology of Capitalism*, Princeton: Princeton University Press.

Swedberg, R. (1991b), *Schumpeter, a Biography*, Princeton: Princeton University Press.

Teece, D., G. Pisano and A. Shuen (1992), *Dynamic Capabilities and Strategic Management*, Berkeley: Haas School of Business.

Udehn, L. (1996), *The Limits of Public Choice*, New York: Routledge.

Vartiainen, J. (1995), 'The State and Structural Change: What Can Be Learnt from the Successful Late Industrializers ', in H.-J. Chang and R. Rowthorn (eds), *The Role of the State in Economic Change*, Oxford: Oxford University Press.

Vasil, R. (1992), *Governing Singapore*, Singapore: Mandarin Press.

Wade, R. (1990), *Governing the Market: Economic Theory and the Role of Government in East Asian Industrialization*, Princeton: Princeton University Press.

Weber, M. [1919] (1974), 'Parlamento e Governo numa Alemanha Reconstruída', in *Os Pensadores*, Rio de Janeiro: Editora Abril, pp. 7–92.

Weber, M. [1922] (1968), *Economy and Society*, n. 14, Berkeley: Berkeley University Press, p. 1395.

Weiss, L. and Hobson, J. (1995), *States and Development*, Cambridge: Polity Press.

Wilks, S. and Wright, M. (eds) (1991), *The Promotion and Regulation of Industry in Japan*, New York: St Martin's Press.

Winter, S. (1995), 'The Four R's of Profitability', in C. Montgomery (ed.), *Resource-Based and Evolutionary Theories of the Firm*, Boston: Kluwer Press.

Yamamura, K. and Yasuda, Y. (eds) (1987), *The Political Economy of Japan, Vol. 1: The Domestic Transformation*, Palo Alto: Stanford University Press.

Zysman, J., C. Johnson and L. Tyson (eds.) (1989), *Politics and Productivity: How Japan's Development Strategy Works*, Cambridge, Mass: Ballinger.

3. Disorderly coordination: the limited capacities of states and markets

Fred Block

The last years of the twentieth century have not been kind to existing models for the management of national economies. One after the other, all of the credible models have been either abandoned or severely discredited. The most dramatic case is the collapse of state socialism between 1989 and 1991 in both Eastern Europe and the former Soviet Union. The few countries that have not explicitly abandoned state socialism – China, North Korea, Vietnam and Cuba – are either in severe crisis or have changed their economic course dramatically by expanding the role of markets. The social democratic model that reached its highest development in Sweden, Norway and Austria has also been in crisis since the end of the 1980s. Social democratic governments have found it increasingly difficult to achieve simultaneously price stability, full employment and continuing economic growth, and they have been forced to restrict the growth of state spending and tolerate levels of unemployment that were previously considered unthinkable. The result is that social democracy has lost its aura as the natural form of economic management and the guarantor of the future. More recently, the Asian model of state-business co-operation that produced spectacular economic results in Japan, South Korea and Taiwan has also become unglued. Throughout the 1990s, Japan has been mired in recession in the aftermath of the bursting of its asset price bubble in real estate and the stock market. The largest Japanese manufacturing firms continue their extraordinary successes in global markets, but there are few voices today urging emulation of the Japanese model. And since the broader Asian financial crisis that began in July 1997 has critically weakened economies across the region – including the greatest recent success story, South Korea – the idea of an alternative Asian economic model has been discredited.

To be sure, neo-liberalism with its emphasis on privatization, deregulation and retrenchment of state spending appears to have emerged victorious from the crises of its would-be challengers. And it is certainly true that the most powerful actors in the international economy – the U.S. Treasury, the International Monetary Fund and international currency traders – are continuing to force the neo-liberal model on the rest of the world. Yet the legitimacy of neo-liberalism has fallen sharply since the era of Reagan and Thatcher. For one thing, both the U.S. and England have elected centrist figures who are committed to 'neo-liberalism with a human face.' More importantly, the accumulated costs of neo-liberal policies have generated widespread doubts about their ability to deliver the goods of economic security and prosperity. Some of the former socialist countries that have tried 'shock therapy' to make a rapid transition to the market have so far failed to establish viable economies. Moreover, the negative experiences of Mexico, Thailand, Indonesia and South Korea with economic liberalization have also cast grave doubts on the neo-liberal model. Neo-liberals insist that nations that make themselves attractive to international capital flows will prosper and experience higher rates of economic growth. However, each of these countries has experienced the downside of reliance on international capital flows; a sudden loss of confidence by international investors leads to massive outflows of capital with devastating consequences for the domestic economy. It is an important indication of weakness of the neo-liberal model that an increasing number of mainstream economists have begun to question whether complete freedom for international short-term capital flows is really desirable (Scharpf, [1987] 1991; Crouch and Streeck, 1997; Gray, 1998, chapter 4; Garrett, 1998).

This crisis of the existing economic models means that policy makers and intellectuals have been left without persuasive roadmaps for thinking about how to manage and structure economies in this period. The purpose of this paper is to suggest that the perspective of 'market reconstruction' that derives particularly from the writings of Karl Polanyi can serve as a starting point for developing a new and more effective economic model that could be used in both developed and developing societies (Block, 1994, pp. 691–710; Unger, 1998). 'Market reconstruction' insists that there is no single way to organize particular markets or even systems of interlocking markets. Since markets are social constructions, they could be reconstructed in ways that produce both 'efficient' outcomes and other desirable social goals, such as greater equality, democracy and human freedom. This view represents a direct challenge to many widely accepted ideas about the functioning of markets, but it also forces a reconsideration of some of the 'statist' assumptions of much of the political left.

This paper will proceed in six parts. The first will briefly recapitulate the critique of the idea of self-regulating markets that lies at the core of neo-liberalism. The second will explain some of the differences between the market reconstruction perspective and Marxism. The third elaborates the market reconstruction critique of state building as the best reform strategy. The fourth will discuss an alternative way of conceptualizing the relationship between states and markets – disorderly coordination. The fifth will discuss the nature of the structural obstacles to pursuing these alternative policies. The sixth is a brief conclusion.

THE LIMITED CAPACITIES OF MARKETS

Karl Polanyi (1886–1964) was a Central European refugee intellectual whose masterpiece, *The Great Transformation* was published in 1944.[1] The book is a powerful critique of free market ideology, but one of its key arguments has not been sufficiently appreciated. This is the analysis of the foundational role of 'fictitious commodities' in the policies and ideology of economic liberalism. Polanyi argued that the effort to establish a self-regulating market requires that land, labour and money be treated as though they are commodities. However, by definition a commodity is something that is produced for sale on a market. Since this is not how land, labour or money have come to exist, it is obvious that they are not true commodities. But the project of creating a market system requires an act of collective imagination in which these three items are treated 'as if' they are true commodities. Polanyi used this argument to drive home the point that there was nothing at all natural about the 'market system'. On the contrary, its artificiality is proven by the fact that it rests on a fiction or a collective delusion to gain the appearance of rationality.

There are important echoes of Marx in Polanyi's analysis of fictitious commodities. Polanyi's footnotes indicate that he was familiar with the German edition of Marx's rediscovered early writings that were not translated into English until the 1960s, so he knew that Marx's critique of capitalism began from the idea that the sale of labour for a wage alienated humans from their 'species being'. Polanyi also well understood the centrality of the distinction between labour and labour power for Marx's mature analysis in *Capital*. In fact, Polanyi was worried enough about the similarity between his concept of fictitious commodities and Marx's famous analysis of the 'fetishism of commodities' to take pains to differentiate them in a footnote (p. 72).

However, Marx's analysis of capitalism's crisis tendencies assumed that the system was working in the way that it was supposed to work – that it had successfully commodified land, labour and money. Polanyi, in contrast, believed that the market system was unworkable from the start. It is worth quoting at length on this point:

> To allow the market mechanism to be sole director of the fate of human beings and their natural environment, indeed, even of the amount and use of purchasing power, would result in the demolition of society. For the alleged commodity 'labor power' cannot be shoved about, used indiscriminately, or even left unused, without affecting also the human individual who happens to be the bearer of this peculiar commodity. Robbed of the protective covering of cultural institutions, human beings would perish from the effects of social exposure; they would die as the victims of acute social dislocation through vice, perversion, crime, and starvation. Nature would be reduced to its elements, neighborhoods and landscapes defiled, rivers polluted, military safety jeopardized, the power to produce food and raw materials destroyed. Finally, the market administration of purchasing power would periodically liquidate business enterprise, for shortages and surfeits of money would prove as disastrous to business as floods and droughts in a primitive society. (p. 73)

This is not simply an argument that it is morally wrong to treat land, labour and money as though they are commodities, but it is also an empirical argument that market self-regulation cannot work properly with fictitious commodities. Since they are not produced for sale on a market, the price mechanism cannot adequately equilibrate supply or demand or protect these precious resources from destructive exploitation.

Polanyi's insight about fictitious commodities has belatedly entered mainstream economic analysis in the form of arguments about information asymmetries. In analysing labour markets, it is increasingly common for economists to recognize that employers purchase the labour time of their employees, but the intensity of employee work effort can vary greatly. While employers can attempt to increase work effort by close supervision, such monitoring efforts are costly. Hence, employers tend to pay 'efficiency wages' that are higher than the market clearing wage in order to induce higher levels of work intensity. Yet this divergence between actual wages and the market clearing wage means that the labour market will not clear and that significant amounts of involuntary unemployment are to be expected (Akerlof and Yellen, 1986).

In a parallel argument, the credit market is also hampered by informational problems. Lenders face considerable uncertainty in determining whether particular borrowers would make good use of borrowed funds. The strategy of simply allowing the price of loans – the interest rate – to rise until the demand for loans and the supply of capital equilibrated is not a solution because of adverse selection. The more sober entrepreneurs would be unlikely to borrow at high interest rates, so that the loans would go exclusively to those willing to take the largest risks. Instead, lenders have no choice but to ration credit – deciding at a given interest rate which borrowers are more or less deserving. But here again, the inevitability of credit rationing means that the anticipated endpoint of market self-regulation – the automatic mobilization of all available economic resources – is never actually reached (Stiglitz, 1994, chapter 12).

In the case of the final fictitious commodity – land, it has long been known that the simple reality of location means that a particular square block located closer to other relevant economic activities and inside relevant political boundaries will have a value very different from a square block away from the city centre. In short, the markets in none of these fictitious commodities can 'clear' through simple variations in prices. Hence, the ideal of an interlocking system of self-regulating markets cannot possibly be achieved. There is no alternative to the creation of regulatory regimes that establish rules for structuring particular markets and for shaping the ways that these particular markets will interconnect. While different regulatory regimes will have very different economic and social consequences, there is no reason – other than simple political prejudice – to believe that a regulatory regime that most closely approximates the ideal of market self-regulation will produce the best economic results.

While this critique of market self-regulation directly challenges neo-liberal claims, it also conflicts with certain important strands of the Marxist analysis of capitalism. In particular, Marxism attributes a fundamental coherence to the system of interlocking markets built around the pursuit of profit by private firms. While Marx recognized the crisis tendencies built into that system, he had no doubts about its coherence – as exemplified in his many references to the logic of capitalism. Yet if different societies make different choices as to how they structure the critical markets for land, labour and money, how could it be that all those societies are subject to the identical 'laws of motion' of capitalism? In short, just as market reconstruction challenges the essentialism of market self-regulation, it also rejects the essentialism of a singular capitalist mode of production always driven by the same inner logic.

RECONCEPTUALIZING SYSTEMIC PRESSURES

The challenge for the market reconstruction approach is whether it can help us to understand the systemic forces at work in contemporary market societies. The strength of Marxism has been that it provides a powerful explanation of such familiar processes as the pressures to expand the market system globally, the forces at work to make the state operate as a 'capitalist state', and the continued reproduction of exploitative class relations at the workplace. If one jettisons the central idea of a 'capitalist mode of production' with a singular logic, is it still possible to understand the systemic pressures at work in market societies?

For Marx, systemic pressures are irreducibly economic. Individual firms are compelled to seek profit because they are located in a competitive environment that is unforgiving; firms that fail to earn adequate profits are unlikely to survive. Individual capitalists have no choice as to the intensity with which they exploit labour; firms that fall behind their competitors will disappear. This is the same image of market competition as a nearly perfect disciplinary device that lies at the heart of neoclassical economics as well (Block, 1996b, pp. 46–57). Marx relies on this imagery to derive the systemic forces at work in the capitalist mode of production; the struggle by individual firms for profit is the foundation for the class-wide efforts of the bourgeoisie to shape the entire society to meet their shared interests.

The Polanyian perspective has a different starting point. There are also individual firms struggling to make a profit, but they exist in markets where competition is generally imperfect. Differences in technology, in product specifications, in location and in a firm's connections to other firms, all work to give individual firms more room to manoeuvre than is allowed in models of markets as perfect disciplinary devices.[2] This is why empirical studies show vast differences in productivity among firms in the same industry (Womack, Jones and Roos, 1991). Furthermore, some firms go through periods in which they are unable to produce any profits, but they are able to survive in business by drawing down family funds or by borrowing through formal or informal mechanisms. In economy-wide economic downturns, this kind of unprofitable survival often becomes the norm even while the very weakest firms are forced to dissolve.[3]

From this starting point, it is not so easy to elaborate systemic dynamics that are purely economic. At any given point in time, there are likely to be very large differences among firms – even in the same industry – in labour practices, in wage levels, and in profitability. Hence, firms are likely to diverge in their perceptions of their own economic interests. But it will also routinely happen that some firms or some entrepreneurs will see future profit opportunities that depend on dismantling existing barriers to the expansion of their own markets. This might involve pursuing sales or investments in foreign markets, drawing on a previously untapped labour pool, eliminating regulations that limit certain types of competition, or dismantling barriers to entry to a market segment that is controlled by a public or private monopoly. In short, there will always be firms that see significant advantages to themselves in advancing what Polanyi called, 'the movement for *laissez-faire*' – the effort to expand the scope of self-regulating markets.

However, the strength of this 'movement for *laissez-faire*' is not constant; it varies considerably over time depending on the number and size of firms that see advantages in market-expanding strategies, perceptions by business of the political terrain, and the popularity of free market ideas. But when a campaign for dismantling barriers has the support of large firms in a variety of industries within a particular country, the movement for *laissez-faire* can be very strong, and its power is magnified by two additional factors. Firstly, large firms generally have ample resources to commit to exercising political influence. Secondly, those who manage the state are dependent on the maintenance of business confidence, so they are often quick to respond to business pressure. This is the constellation of factors that lay behind the global revival of neo-liberalism that began in the United States in the Reagan era with the roll-back of corporate taxes and government regulation and which has continued with systematic efforts to force other countries to restrict state spending, privatize state firms and eliminate barriers to free mobility of goods and capital. Similarly, the pursuit of overseas profit opportunities by critical segments of British business was the source of that country's efforts to impose free trade and the gold standard on the rest of the world in the nineteenth century.

But the market reconstruction perspective emphasizes that as strong as these systemic pressures can be, their triumph is neither necessary nor inevitable. On the contrary, since the ideal of market self-regulation is based on a series of fictions, victories by the 'movement for *laissez-faire*' can often produce economic instability that must then be countered by political actions at the national or global levels. But such pressures can also be defeated before they are victorious because the survival of particular firms rarely depends on market-expanding measures. For example, a large domestic industrial firm might imagine huge profit opportunities if certain foreign tariff barriers were eliminated, but even if foreign opportunities were to be closed off completely, the firm might well be able to expand into other domestic product lines or even survive quite well on the limited domestic market. Since even the largest firms have the opportunity to pursue a range of alternative profit-making strategies, the result is an economy in which there is no systemic necessity behind any specific instance of market expansion. It is often argued, for example, that Britain in the nineteenth century had to expand outward aggressively in search of foreign profit opportunities. However, we also know that in the final third of the century, the City of London was so oriented towards foreign lending opportunities that it neglected the financing needs of domestic industry. Hence, had foreign investment opportunities been less available, the City of London might have actually increased its investments in domestic firms with positive consequences for British long-term industrial competitiveness.

The contingent and variable nature of these structural pressures also helps explain the flexibility with which global market expansion is pursued. If there

were a purely 'economic' logic at work, one would expect that particular nations that violated international free trade rules in specific ways would be subject to severe sanctions. However, in the period since the Second World War,
the intensity of the pressures on countries to open their markets have clearly
been mediated by geo-political factors. The most successful East Asian indus-
trializing countries – Japan, South Korea and Taiwan – pursued development
strategies that gave the state a far larger role in the economy than was consistent with the post-World War II 'rules of the game' (Wade, 1990). However,
since each of these countries was close to the central geo-political fault line of
the Cold War, these deviations were largely ignored by both U.S. foreign policy
and the international institutions created to police the system. Similarly, in recent years, the eagerness of Western and Japanese businesses to invest in China
has created the ironic situation in which some businesses are now lobbying
their home governments against subjecting China to the 'normal' pressures to
obey the international rules governing trade, capital flows and intellectual
property. In short, there are powerful pressures on nations to conform to certain
rules for governing international economic transactions, but enforcement of the
rules is highly uneven.

It is the ideology of economic liberalism that makes the contingent and variable pressures for market expansion appear to be far more systematic and invariant. The ideology provides a cover of seeming coherence and logic to the
episodic and variable efforts of business firms. When business groups wage
campaigns to dismantle one or another set of barriers to market expansion, it is
the idea of a globally integrated system of self-regulating markets that makes
their efforts seem to be more than the pursuit of selfish self-interest. The ideology makes the dismantling of a tariff barrier here or a regulatory barrier there
seem not simply logical but necessary for the effective functioning of the
economy. But when such campaigns are defeated – as they often are – those
same businesses usually find other ways to prosper.

In this respect, the period from 1978 to the present has been unusual in the
history of actually existing market societies. Not since the early part of the
nineteenth century has there been such a sustained period in which 'the movement for *laissez-faire*' has moved so relentlessly from one market expanding
triumph to the next. If one looked at this period alone, it would be easy to
believe that the viability of market societies depends upon steady progress towards a globally integrated market system. However, it is important to remember two things. Firstly, that the great post-World War II economic expansion
occurred under very different political and economic circumstances. Business
flexibility in dealing with labour had been greatly reduced in the U.S. and Europe because of strong unions and government welfare provisions, many coun-

tries had seen substantial nationalizations of previously privately-held firms and international capital movements were severely restricted. Nevertheless, business activity expanded at unprecedented rates. In fact, there can be little doubt that on such key economic indicators as rate of economic growth and levels of unemployment, many developed countries were in better shape in the 1950s and 1960s than they had been in the era of neo-liberalism. Secondly, even with the victories of neo-liberalism, the current global regime falls far short of the ideological claims of market self-regulation. There are still elaborate regulatory mechanisms at the national, regional and global levels that are very different from market self-regulation and that continue to be necessary to make the global economy work.

In sum, the market reconstruction perspective recognizes the same systemic pressures to expand the scope of market society that Marxism has identified. However, it sees those pressures as being contingent, political and vulnerable to organized resistance because actually existing market societies can remain economically viable with a wide range of different institutional configurations.[4]

THE LIMITED CAPACITIES OF STATES

The main traditions of the democratic left in the twentieth century have embraced strategies of political transformation based on the expansion of the powers and capacities of the central state. This strategic approach was solidified in response to the global economic crisis of the 1930s. Theorists of the democratic left saw capitalism as an economic system that was governed by its own powerful inner logic. If the economy were gripped by powerful deflationary pressures, these were understood as being almost like actual physical forces. If these pressures were to be resisted or reversed, one needed to be able to push back with a comparable level of force. The central government was seen as the only institution capable of mobilizing the appropriate level of force. It is as though one lived near a large river that overflowed its banks on a regular basis, producing devastating floods. It would seem obvious that one needed to create an elaborate flood control system that was capable of containing the raging waters. The development of a centralized state with extensive regulative and planning capacities appeared to be the logical counterforce needed to contain the inevitable natural disasters produced by a capitalist economy.

Some of those who embraced this 'counterforce strategy' were persuaded that capitalism could not be controlled or contained even with powerful central states, but they saw the building up of the counterforce as part of a long and gradual transition to socialism. They hoped that while the counterforce strategy was controlling capitalism's worse defects, the public might be persuaded that the only route to stability was to eliminate private ownership of the means of production. Others believed that building up the strength of the state might produce some type of a 'mixed economy' that would be both productive and stable. However, the hopes of both groups have been disappointed; the counterforce strategy has neither facilitated a transition to socialism nor created a stable 'mixed economy'. To be sure, social democratic regimes compiled an extraordinarily successful record of economic management through the 1950s, 1960s and 1970s, but over the last two decades, the social democratic model has slipped into crisis. A number of important gains – including the institutionalization of full employment – have been reversed and confidence in the ability of the social democratic state to counter the pressures of the global economy has been eroded.

The problem with the counterforce strategy is that it depends on a level of state capacities that is difficult to sustain over a long period of time. The great popularity of 'planning' in the first half of the twentieth century led counterforce theorists to exaggerate the ability of state planners to make high quality decisions with any consistency. To be sure, neo-liberal arguments are equally exaggerated in the opposite direction; their presumption is that decisions by private economic actors are almost always superior to decisions made by state actors. It is, however, possible to reject this neo-liberal privileging of market processes and still have a healthy respect for the limitations of state capacities (Offe, 1996).

There are three important processes that tend to undermine the quality of state decision making. The first is the shifting, unreliable and contested nature of the technical knowledge on which decisions must be based. The most obvious recent case of this was the disastrous commitments that a number of nations made to nuclear power generation based on inaccurate estimates of the costs and benefits of that technology. Moreover, anyone who has participated in decisions about what kind of computer system should be purchased for an office is aware of the multiple difficulties of making 'good decisions' in the midst of rapid technological change.

It is extraordinarily easy to place one's bets on a technology that will quickly be orphaned or to overlook an alternative option that will turn out to be the foundation for future development. These same difficulties are multiplied many times when government decisions have the potential to encourage or discourage particular types of technological development.

A second process is rooted in the problem of economic uncertainty. Rates of private business investment tend to be highest when uncertainty is in some intermediate range (Block, 1996b, pp. 81–83). When uncertainty is too high, businesses refuse to invest because the risks of losing money are simply too great. However, when uncertainty becomes too low, firms are also likely to avoid new investments because they seem to be guaranteed an adequate rate of profit. Firms that are in a monopoly situation, for example, face little uncertainty and often have little incentive to make new investments. Their role in reducing uncertainty means that government policies are often initially successful in creating a climate for new private investment. However, over time, the new policy can succeed too well, so that it reduces uncertainty too far, creating a context in which firms are content to extract the rents that the government policies made possible. To be sure, this difficulty can be overcome by a reflexive approach to policy making that subjects all policies to continuous review and updating. However, this is different from historic notions of planning that emphasized the value of predictable and stable long-term patterns.

The third process has to do with cultural changes that tend to undermine the moral foundations of govenment social policies while simultaneously making it more problematic to generate consensus around alternative policies. For example, the 'universality' of the social democratic welfare state was based on a particular pattern of social life – a male wage earner who moved through the life course on a predictable and linear path. Processes of social and cultural pluralization have transformed this pattern of social life; in some countries, women are almost as likely to be wage earners as men and the linear life course has given way to more fluid and irregular patterns of adulthood. As the fit between existing social policies and the needs of certain social groups diminishes, accusations rise that people are 'gaming the system' – using social programmes in completely unintended ways. At the same time, others are likely to experience the social policy regime as unfairly constraining their life choices. In fact, it is typical that existing social policies will create too much uncertanty for some groups and too little for others. And yet, it becomes ever more difficult to create political consensus around reforms that would be 'fair' because pluralization has increased the heterogeneity of life strategies (Offe, 1996, chapter 9).

The common thread of these processes is that they all place limits on the effectiveness with which expert knowledge is exercised in government agencies. Hence, the central task of classical state building – creating state agencies staffed with officials with expert knowledge who are effectively insulated from civil society – becomes increasingly problematic. This is, of course, one of the central points that Peter Evans makes in *Embedded Autonomy* (1995). He insists that the state can play an extremely positive and important role in industrial development, but this requires a significant reconstruction of state-society relations. The classical processes of state building will no longer produce the desired results.

DISORDERLY COORDINATION

With a proper appreciation of the limited capacities of both market self-regulation and state planning, the path is open for strategies of reform based on disorderly coordination. Embedded autonomy, state-society synergy (Evans, 1997) and disorderly coordination are all ways of expressing the same idea – that while both states and markets have limited abilities to produce desirable results when they operate according to their own logics, it is possible to combine their sometimes divergent logics to produce positive outcomes. However, as the idea of disorderly coordination suggests, this process is unlikely to be smooth and stable; policies need continuous adjustment and reconsideration.

But in arguing for these alternative approaches, it is easy to be misunderstood. Most reforms based on this perspective still require action at the level of central government. A strong and effective central government is indispensable for social and economic reform. And there is still considerable room in many countries for completing the historical task of state building – establishing effective tax collection and minimum standards of honesty and efficiency in the public service. Moreover, even with the invention of policies that shift power and authority to lower levels of government, the taxing and borrowing powers of the central government will remain indispensable.

But there is a fundamental distinction to be made between the counterforce strategy and what can be termed a leverage strategy. The counterforce strategy rests on the assumption that capitalism is a coherent and powerful system whose logic can only be overcome through systematic offsetting force exerted by the state. The alternative view is that the coherence of the system is an illusion; there are actually multiple interlocking markets – each of which has been partially shaped by state action. Strategic action by the state to alter the ground rules for particular markets can have unexpectedly large effects on how those markets work and on the outcomes that they produce. Hence, a small amount of leverage can produce very large changes.

In contrast to the counterforce strategy, the leverage strategy is not as dependent on high quality decisions by state actors. Leverage policies always involve an interaction between state action and the choices made by real people operating in market situations. If there are positive consequences, it is because of the interaction between state action and the decisions made by actual people. Hence, those who manage leverage policies must constantly monitor the impact of their efforts and be prepared to alter policies if they are not having the intended effects.

The distinction between these two strategies can be seen by looking more closely at the New Deal in the United States. Two of the most enduring achievements of economic reform in the New Deal are far closer to the leverage strategy than to the counterforce approach. The National Labour Relations Act (Wagner Act) and the Social Security Act were both passed in 1935. These initiatives did not require a huge amount of centralized state capacity or a highly trained staff with very developed analytic skills. On the contrary, these agencies were able to provide specific services – the monitoring of union elections, the adjudication of unfair labour practices and the provision of old age insurance with relatively small staffs and modest budgets. Yet the impact of these agencies was huge because they restructured the labor market. By providing legal protections for the right to organize and to strike, the National Labour Relations Board shifted the balance of power between employers and employees, particularly in heavy industry. In the case of the Social Security Administration, changes came more gradually because the programme was phased in and incrementally expanded over a long period of time. But the Act rescued the elderly from the painful choice between poverty and continued work and it altered the labour market by universalizing the concept of retirement after a lifetime of work. By creating common interests among the elderly as beneficiaries of the same programme, the Act also facilitated the emergence of older Americans as a powerful political force, which laid the basis for later reforms.

In short, these measures did not rely for their effectiveness on the skill or expertise of government bureaucrats; they had much of their effect by empowering citizens. At the same time, reform efforts in the New Deal that were linked to the counterforce strategy were far less successful. Those on the left of the Roosevelt Administration consistently fought for full employment with the government as the employer of last resort and for a unified government agency that would plan and oversee much of the society's public sector infrastructure spending. Both of these initiatives required a very significant expansion in state capacities. However, the Right – even at the lowest point of its political support in the United States – was able to block these initiatives by rallying popular distrust of the state. This is yet another obvious advantage of the leverage strategy. By separating reform efforts from the project of building up the capacities of the central state, the prospects for political success might be considerably enhanced.

Two brief examples should suffice to indicate how disorderly coordination based on the leverage strategy might approach long-standing problems of social and economic policy. Instead of fighting for 'full employment' through public sector job creation as the way to combat poverty and improve the economic bargaining power of low wage workers, the alternative is to provide a negative income tax that would be available to all individuals and households that fall below a certain level of income. In contrast to the positive income tax, the negative income tax provides a tax rebate to those whose income falls beneath a certain level, and this income supplement can be paid out on a weekly or monthly basis. If the support level were high enough, this measure could serve to empower poor individuals and enhance their bargaining power with employers (Block and Manza, 1997).

Instead of trying to centralize infrastructure planning in one central government agency, the alternative would be to use the taxing power of the central government to finance initiatives at the local and state levels. In the U.S., for example, the Federal Government might borrow $50 billion a year in new money at an interest rate of 6 per cent. The money would then be made available to a series of regional infrastructure banks that would reloan the money to localities or nonprofit agencies at subsidized interest rates that would vary depending on the social value of the particular project. Low income housing loans might be provided at a 3 per cent interest rate, environmental reclamation projects might borrow at 4 per cent, and particularly poor regions might be able to finance a range of different projects at only 2 per cent. The costs to the Federal Treasury would be relatively small on an annual basis, and if the funds were invested effectively the costs should be more than offset by increased tax revenues. To be sure, the regional banks would have to screen projects carefully and would have to be insulated from local political interests that sought to use loans simply for patronage purposes. But the general idea is that the government's ability to borrow could leverage large amounts of public infrastructure spending that could have significant social and economic consequences.

These examples are only for purposes of illustration. The task of mapping out a full strategy of economic and social reform based on the concepts of market reconstruction and disorderly coordination remains to be done. Moreover, such strategies cannot be cut from a single cloth; they will vary considerably depending upon the specific economic and political structures of each society. The point here is simply to lay out the argument that there is an alternative set of assumptions that can be the basis for a new family of economic models.

STRUCTURAL OBSTACLES

Even policies based on disorderly coordination face structural obstacles. For example, even a highly decentralized strategy that restructures the labour market in ways that will advantage low wage workers is bound to encounter resistance from those who insist that the resulting increase in wages at the bottom will be inflationary and highly disruptive to the nation's position in the world economy. Moreover, in an era of rapid capital movements and floating exchange rates, such predictions of disaster can be instantly transformed into self-fulfilling prophecies. Currency speculators begin to sell the nation's currency and the resulting financial crisis invariably forces the government to announce a series of policy initiatives that dramatically weaken the bargaining position of most working people. The current world system has powerful disciplinary mechanisms that punish nations that attempt to diverge from economic orthodoxy – regardless of whether their policy choices resemble the counterforce or the leverage strategy.

Yet, it must also be stressed that the current system of almost unlimited short-term capital movements and daily currency transactions in excess of $1.2 trillion per day is profoundly irrational and unstable. While it does operate as a powerful disciplinary mechanism to keep countries from diverging too much from neo-liberal orthodoxy, it has also forced the world to forget the critical lessons of the 1930s. The result is a global economy that is now extremely vulnerable to a deflationary crisis in which currency after currency is subjected to speculative pressures, forcing governments to impose austerity measures that will, in turn, lead to a collapse of global demand. My own view is that this dangerous experiment with global market self-regulation will be abandoned over the next five to ten years, and there will be the restoration of controls over short-term capital flows and the creation of a more stable system of exchange rates (Block, 1996a).

In the meantime, the ultimate success of reform efforts within nations requires a simultaneous international effort to reshape the global rules of the game to provide nations with greater insulation from capital flight and speculative crises. Under the global regime of 'embedded liberalism' in the 1950s and 1960s (Ruggie, 1982), some nations had far greater room to manoeuvre in pursuing domestic economic reforms than they have now, and it should be a paramount goal to recapture that capacity for national level experimentation for both developed and developing nations.

But there may also be ways for nations to recapture some greater freedom to manoeuvre even before reforms have been won at the global level. While theorists of neo-liberalism continually suggest that there is nothing complicated about opening a national economy to international market forces, the reality is that it is extremely complex. Precisely because money is a fictitious commodity, public agencies have to regulate the growth of the domestic money supply. This means that national financial institutions inevitably play a critical intermediary role between global capital flows and domestic economic activity, and even neo-liberals recognize that these financial institutions must be brought under a regulatory regime that assures that financial intermediaries are reloaning funds prudently and minimizing certain types of fraud and corruption. It is possible that relatively small variations in these regulatory regimes could end up significantly weakening the disciplinary power of global finance.

Some nations have successfully held on to restrictions on their own citizens' rights to shift capital abroad, and there is reason to believe that these measures do reduce a nation's vulnerability to currency crises. Financial regulators can also attempt to limit the domestic financial system's vulnerability to hot money flows from abroad through a variety of mechanisms. For example, rules can require that some percentage of foreign bank deposits be held in special illiquid accounts to reduce the threat of mass withdrawals of foreign funds. Similar restrictions might be placed on larger holdings of equity shares, so that foreign investors would not have the option of liquidating their entire position over-night. While such measures might discourage some foreign investment, it is actually rational for nations to discourage hot money flows that will quickly be reversed (Velasco and Cabezas, 1998).

Many of these financial regulatory decisions are highly technical and usu-ally take place at some distance from party politics and the public spotlight. This has served generally to enhance the influence of IMF advisers and foreign financial interests, but it also provides an opportunity for reformist political forces. If reformers are able to gain expertise on these arcane issues, bring them into the sphere of politics and make effective alliances with certain segments of business, it might be possible to make considerable gains. While even the best system of domestic financial regulation will not eliminate the danger of politi-cally disastrous capital flight, it could significantly raise the threshhold before such flight occurred.

But the idea of market reconstruction is built around this type of incremen-talism. The key idea is not to transform the economy immediately but to make gradual but durable improvements in the bargaining position and living stan-dards of people on the bottom. These reforms become durable precisely be-cause they come to be built into the calculations of business. Knowing that wages at the bottom are going to be rising at a certain predictable rate, firms increase their investments in labour saving technologies, so that their rising labour costs are offset by productivity gains. But this rising productivity ex-pands total wealth and gives the reformist regime more space to carry out other types of reforms.

CONCLUSION

The perspective of market reconstruction and disorderly coordination repre-sents a break with utopianism in several ways. Firstly, both Marxism and economic liberalism have insisted that if the institutional arrangements are just right, the tiresome business of politics will either disappear or will be effectively walled off from the economy. Disorderly coordination, in contrast, begins from the recognition of the continuing inevitability of politics, political conflict and an ongoing process of political shaping of the economy. This is one reason why coordination is likely to be disorderly; it will be subject to the twists and turns of democratic politics. Secondly, disorderly coordination is an incrementalist approach that believes that a reform process must occur step-by-step, rather than through some abrupt kind of transformation.

However, this approach to reform does not require an abandonment of the Enlightenment ideal of creating a more rational social order built around democracy, equality and liberty. While reforms must begin from the realities that we currently face, there is no reason to posit any pre-given limits to how far those reforms could go over the next century. The dream of a society without vast inequalities of wealth, without the dominance of politics by powerful economic interests and without the systematic oppression of any social group, can still provide the inspiration for the reconstruction of market societies.

NOTES

1. References, however, are to the later edition, 1957.
2. This point is emphasized in the literature on corporate strategy that emphasizes that firms are not simply passive receivers of market signals (Montgomery, 1995).
3. Moreover, some firms have found ways to use the legal status of bankruptcy as a survival strategy (Delaney, 1998).
4. This argument converges with analysts who stress the 'varieties of capitalism' (Berger and Dore, 1996; Crouch and Streeck, 1997).

BIBLIOGRAPHY

Akerlof, George and Janet Yellen (eds) (1986), *Efficiency Wage Models of the Labor Market*, Cambridge: Cambridge University Press.

Berger, Suzanne and Ronald Dore (eds) (1996), *National Diversity and Global Capitalism,* Ithaca: Cornell University Press.

Bhagwati, Jhagdish (1998), 'The Capital Myth: The Difference between Trade in Widgets and Dollars', in *Foreign Affairs*, May–June, pp. 7–12.

Block, Fred (1994), 'The Roles of the State in the Economy', in Neil Smelser and Richard Swedberg (eds), *The Handbook of Economic Sociology*, Princeton: Princeton University Press, pp. 691–710.

Block, Fred (1996a), 'Controlling Global Finance', in *World Policy Journal,* Fall, pp. 24–34.

Block, Fred (1996b), *The Vampire State and Other Myths and Fallacies about the U.S. Economy,* New York: New Press, pp. 46–57.

Block, Fred and Jeff Manza (1997), 'Could We End Poverty in a Postindustrial Society? The Case for a Progressive Negative Income Tax', in *Politics & Society,* **25** (4), December, pp. 473–511.

Crouch, Colin and Wolfgang Streeck (eds) (1997), *Political Economy of Modern Capitalism,* London: Sage Publications.

Delaney, Kevin (1998), *Strategic Bankruptcy: How Corporations and Creditors Use Chapter 11 to Their Advantage,* Berkeley: University of California Press.

Evans, Peter (1995), *Embedded Autonomy.* Princeton: Princeton University Press.

Evans, Peter (ed.) (1997), *State-Society Synergy: Government and Social Capital in Development,* Berkeley: University of California at Berkeley, International and Areas Studies.

Garrett, Geoffrey (1998), *Partisan Politics in the Global Economy,* Cambridge: Cambridge University Press.

Gray, John (1998), *False Dawn: The Delusions of Global Capitalism,* London: Granta, chapter 4.

Krugman, Paul (1999), *The Return of Depression Economics,* New York: Norton.

Montgomery, Cynthia (ed.) (1995), *Resource-based and Evolutionary Theories of the Firm: Towards a Synthesis,* Boston: Kluwer.

Offe, Claus (1996), *Modernity and the State: East, West,* Cambridge, Mass.: MIT Press.

Polanyi, Karl (1957), *The Great Transformation,* Boston: Beacon Press.

Pontusson, Jonas (1997), 'Between Neo-Liberalism and the German Model: Swedish Capitalism in Transition', in Crouch and Streeck (eds), *Political Economy of Modern Capitalism,* London: Sage Publications.

Ruggie, John (1982), 'International Regimes, Transactions, and Change: Embedded Liberalism in the Postwar Economic Order', *International Organization,* **36** (2), Spring, pp. 379–415.

Scharpf, Fritz [1987] (1991), *Crisis and Choice in European Social Democracy,* translated by Ruth Crowley and Fred Thompson. Ithaca: Cornell University Press.

Stiglitz, Joseph (1994), *Whither Socialism?* Cambridge, Mass.: MIT Press, chapter 12.

Unger, Roberto Mangabeira (1998), *Democracy Realized: The Progressive Alternative,* London: Verso.

Velasco, Andres and Pablo Cabezas (1998), 'Alternative Responses to Capital Inflows: A Tale of Two Countries', in Miles Kahler (ed.), *Capital Flows and Financial Crises*, Ithaca: Cornell, pp. 128–157.

Wade, Robert (1990), *Governing the Market: Economic Theory and the Role of Government in East Asian Industrialization,* Princeton: Princeton University Press.

Womack, James P., Daniel T. Jones and Daniel Roos (1991), *The Machine that Changed the World: The Story of Lean Production,* New York: Harper.

4. Conventions and institutions:[1] rethinking problems of state reform, governance and policy

Michael Storper

1. INTRODUCTION

Consider the following examples of institutional change in economy and society:

- On January 4, 1914, Henry Ford announced an extraordinary increase in the regular wage to $5 per day. In so doing, he inadvertently started a chain reaction of wide temporal and spatial extent, the outcome of which was, much later, described as a new period in the development of capitalism, that of mass production-based industrialism (Wagner, 1994).
- When, in the early 1980s, Luciano Benetton, aided by his advertising firm, decided to carry out a politically-relevant form of advertising ('United Colors of Benetton') he very probably did not dream that this would, in a certain sense, lead to a complete recuperation of the spirit of social movements and 'street culture' by the profit-making economy and obliterate the distinction between mainstream culture and cultural rebellion 'against' it. In so doing, Benetton may have fundamentally altered the relationships of production, consumption and popular culture in contemporary capitalist societies.
- American Black Power activists in the 1960s, coming from so far outside the mainstream and suffering from severe legal and illegal repression, nonetheless asserted a way of seeing the individual in relationship to society which set into motion a redefinition of citizenship (Taylor, 1992) – the relationship between individual identity and group identity – in the Anglo-American Western nations, when they demanded affirmative group recognition and not merely equal procedural treatment.

- Richard Nixon's abandonment of the Bretton Woods international monetary system in 1971 set into motion a chain of events which ultimately led not only to the creation of international money markets and the current international financial system, but also radically transformed the international trade system and the production techniques and organization of many important industries. New forms of economic uncertainty and risk were generated by this profound destabilization of the market environment; in response, new forms of governance of firms, production systems, and regional economies subsequently made their appearance.

Social science has many kinds of stories it tells about these transformations. Most of the mainstream accounts of institutional emergence – especially those coming from, or drawing heavily on, economics – do not have satisfactory approaches to this question of the individual. They are frequently weighed down by heavy and unrealistic assumptions about the nature of interests and the rationality of actors and hence about the necessity and functionality of the transformations which come about.

In both economics and sociology, however, much effort has been devoted in recent years to addressing these problems, on a variety of levels, including approaches to rules, strategic action and group interaction. They have also advanced the micro level considered here, by developing alternative notions of rationality, action and coordination. This paper will be concerned with similar issues, most especially how individual behaviour – perception, calculation, decision making and action – becomes collective action, and hence underpins the emergence and functioning of institutions. We outline a way into institutions, and hence the state, which has developed recently in France. Its central analytical concept is that of the convention in social and economic life (a body of work referred to henceforth in this paper as the SSC, for 'social science of conventions'). The SSC holds that institutions, whether those of the state or of the society, whether formal or informal, are necessarily underpinned by conventions which coordinate the actions of individuals. There are many processes which set into motion the emergence of institutions, but all of them involve the 'social labour' of generating conventions. This point is illustrated by comparing different conventional relationships between states and societies to be found in the West today, and in the light of the ways that experiments in new forms of governance and policy making presuppose new conventional bases for coordinating individuals.

2. SOME RECENT ADVANCES IN THINKING ABOUT ACTION, COLLECTIVE ACTION AND INSTITUTIONS, AND WHAT WE CAN CONTRIBUTE TO THEM

In much contemporary social science, there is a sort of compromise that hides an unsolved theoretical problem. Time and again it is repeated that institutions are both constructed in human interaction and pre-exist the individuals whose actions they shape. As a general statement, this is surely valid. To stop here, however, would mean consolidating a basic cleavage between theories about interaction and the constitution of sociability on the one hand, and theories about social structures which shape or constrain individuals, on the other (Giddens, 1984; Joas, 1996).

This is undoubtedly why the 'old institutionalism,' in both sociology and economics, generated a great deal of dissatisfaction.[2] Even at its best, in struggling with organizations and institutions as complex relations between individuals and the collective, it reproduced the basic cleavage. Institutionalists rejected standard versions of utilitarianism via the notion of interest aggregation in organizations, and documented the existence of unanticipated consequences at the collective level. But they essentially collapsed the individual into the collective through notions such as values, norms and attitudes, imprinted on the individual through socialization. This forced them into an impoverished vision of change, as stemming almost exclusively from the interactions of conflicts of interest and vested interests.

In economics and political science in recent decades, there have been powerful developments in institutional analysis which are based precisely on a reformulation of the role of individual action. Two schools which have received great attention are, respectively, the New Institutional Economics (with its roots in transactions costs economics) and contemporary analytical political economy, which embraces the positive theory of institutions, and spills over into recent analytical economic history (North, 1981; Williamson, 1985). These two schools, for all the very important analytical advances they have made, have certain deep problems. One is of course their underlying model of rationality, which has been much remarked in the critical literature. The other is their starting point. Put simply, both hold that the incompleteness of social life is necessarily problematic. When actors find themselves in concrete situations where everything is not known or clearly demarcated, whether it be 'information' or 'property rights', then we are at risk of coordination failures, due to cheating or free riding. Such incompleteness, it is held, leads institutions – such as firms (Loasby, 1991; Langlois and Foss, 1997),[3] political parties or rules – because markets can no longer function correctly. But where we are in institutions, individual interests suffer from the 'impossibility' of principal-agent relations and other difficulties of interest aggregation. Thus, institutions are always a second-best form of social life. Institutions are second-best because they are fundamentally incompatible with the atomistic nature of human preferences, and are generally hampered because they are not subject directly to the market's disciplining force of exit.[4]

If incompleteness is not inherently so problematic, however, then their conclusions do not follow. And indeed, that is precisely what we shall argue: incompleteness is not always a problem;[5] in social life, it is frequently part of the solution (Favereau, 1993), the starting point for the social labour of coordination through convention. In this vein, there are developments in economics – such as the institutionalism of Hodgson (1997) – which use starting points compatible with that outlined in this paper. Hodgson is inspired by some of the early institutionalist economists, such as Frank Knight (1921), who identified uncertainty as a fundamental condition, but not as a crippling problem, in economic life. Much of this notion that uncertainty – incompleteness – is a foundation for coordination 'solutions', i.e. for the work of creating institutions, has been lost. Nonetheless, if one reviews the economic literature, it pops up again from time to time, as in Alchian (1950), Arrow's (1972) ongoing reflections on what we do in the presence of changing information and learning and Loasby's (1991) notion that incomplete contracts are the basis for firm learning and hence key to certain forms of successful collective action. Similar starting points can also be found at the heart of recent work in evolutionary economics (Dosi *et al.*, 1997).

Sociology – especially economic sociology – has made great strides in overcoming the theoretical cleavages alluded to above in recent years. One thinks of the ways that Granovetter (1995) and Swedberg (1993) have reinvigorated Polanyi's vision of the economy as an institutionalized process.[6] 'Neo-institutionalism' in sociology has addressed the problem of how and why actors act in relationship to collective processes. In contrast to the old institutionalism, the process of building institutions does not concern only narrowly-defined, formal organizations, but fields or sectors of social practices. The theory of action (not just a theory of interest aggregation) is at the centre of research into the complex outcomes of action, and at its centre are its taken-for-granted, unreflective dimensions (and not just unanticipated consequences of rational interest pursuit). These are linked to the outside world through various forms of cognition (not solely through values, norms and attitudes) and become the basis for collective order, in the form of the habits of practical forms of action. Much of the new institutionalism shares with the SSC a concern with the cognitive basis of what actors do, as well as an emphasis on pragmatics.

Much of this reformulation of the theory of action has come in reaction to Parsonian action theory (Powell and DiMaggio, 1991, pp. 1–40). For most card-carrying sociologists, the ultimate goal of the new institutionalism is to find a replacement for the Parsonian map of the social order, but not to abandon the notion that we can map it in a comprehensive way (Powell and DiMaggio, 1991). This project can be found, with very different foundations, in Giddens's theory of structuration (Giddens, 1984), in Collins's use of Durkheim and Goffman (Collins, 1989; Bourdieu, 1990; Parsons, 1951, 1960; Alexander, 1983), or Bourdieu's more formalized notion of habitus as the cornerstone of a hierarchical social order. This is where the SSC parts company with the new institutionalism. The SSC sees the micro-level as leading to a much greater potential variety of forms of coordination than has heretofore been envisaged, and hence views the detailed composition of the social order itself as potentially much more diverse and changing than imagined by either Parsons or those seeking to replace him. We should perhaps no longer be guided by their goal of always finding the roles that the resulting institutions play in some overarching social order. Many contemporary entrepreneurs seem know this, as they now almost self-consciously try to build whole new markets, demands and social practices, a part of 'reflexive modernization'. Most academics and policy makers, guided by notions of coherence, may be slow to recognize the relative openness and diversity of forms that coordination can take in modern society and economy.

It is to this subject, the production of coordination between agents in the presence of incompleteness or uncertainty, to which we now turn.

3.　WHY DO PEOPLE DO WHAT THEY DO? WHAT DOES IT MEAN TO 'ACT'?[7]

The point of departure for the SSC is in essence a pragmatic turn, in the sense that in order to get beyond classical presuppositions – such as individualism/ atomism versus collectivism/holism; utilitarianism versus normativism; the economic versus the sociological – the SSC takes concrete behaviours as time- and space-specific social facts rather than as universal social laws. We do not accuse, for example, the notion of the optimizing market or that of a socially-integrated society as being overly formal abstractions and hence unrelated to the real world. Instead, the very existence of such constructions in social theory is evidence of a social reality worthy of being analysed. But these constructions cannot be taken as positive scientific laws; instead, they are something like different rules of agreement by which real actors attempt to coordinate their actions, and they are justifications given by people for what they do. Social

science errs in transforming them into social laws of a scientific nature. As
Peter Wagner puts it, in drawing on the work of Thévenot and Boltanski
(Wagner, 1994; Thévenot and Boltanski, 1989), 'the task is to dissolve their
disciplinary codifications and recommence the analysis of social action in conceptually more open terms'.

Intellectual History: Elements of a Problem(atic)

One could argue that any of the social transformations referred to at the beginning of this paper – the advent of Fordism; the transformation of contemporary
culture by the market; the rise of new forms of corporate organization and governance; the transformation of identity and citizenship – can be traced back to
acts (Ford's $5 per day strategy; Nixon's abandonment of the gold standard,
etc.) which in turn were elements of strategy. To take just one of our examples:
most current theories would try to explain why Ford did what he did or why his
strategy succeeded. Yet the systematic consequences of Ford's strategy were
that new forms of collective action and institutions were generated. The question becomes how such forms of collective action were produced in the wake of
the shock caused by Ford's strategic rupture. Existing theories might show that
rational workers took the jobs, and that Ford's enterprise ultimately took the
market. But these are just shells of an explanation, for ultimately a whole new
industrial way of life emerged – from the shop floor to the showroom, to the
household and the landscape, from the skilling/training system to the wage
structure, and including the entire cognitive framework by which industrial
technology was conceived and improved, even including aesthetics and symbolic processes. Somehow, all of these new regularities, which go well beyond
Ford's action and direct reactions to it, have to be explained.

The research strategy which motivates the social science of conventions is
essentially to start 'from the bottom up'. Who did what? What were the resources and competences of actors who set change into motion? What were the
controversies which led to transformation of the existing way of doing things?
The SSC emerged out of research on controversies or strategic ruptures which
appeared, at the outset, to be individual reactions to changing circumstances,
attempts to reinterpret reality and find new ways of coping with it. Some such
apparently minor re-evaluations or re-interpretations of 'what is to be done'
end up having large-scale ramifications or effects on collective patterns of action; their effects seem – in conventional sociological parlance – to move 'upward' and 'downward' in society.[8]

Methodologically, the SSC is motivated by the desire to re-situate, bring back
down to the actor, the explanation of what happened, and this means using in the

analysis as few categories as possible which have not been introduced by the actors themselves. This notion of a 'scarcity of presuppositions' is based on a pronounced scepticism with regard to structuralist and functionalist sociology, as well as to neoclassical economics and its social scientific offshoots, all of which are presupposition-rich in their conceptualizations. But this is also where the SSC is sceptical of certain aspects of the new institutionalism: the SSC attempts to get even closer to the categories of action deployed by the actors themselves.

But this does not mean a social science of 'face value'. Quite the contrary: even when actors describe their own actions in terms of laws (as in the everyday use of the language of the market, or reference to collective identity, or reference to procedural rationality) our theories neither have to accept those descriptions as lawful, nor dismiss them as irrelevant falsehoods. Instead, we need to ask where these descriptions come from and how they affect what people do.

Reformulating the Theory of Action

Action is motivated principally by the desire to make effective the action one undertakes. This motivation imparts two fundamental characteristics to action. On one hand is its particularity: actions are inherently associated with objects, circumstances and persons, whose varied and heterogeneous nature make for complex and particular synergies. This particularity is a central aspect of the SSC, what it calls the situation of pragmatic activity. For example, in production, the situation of the actor is fundamentally defined by the product or service s/he is trying to produce. Associated with each output there are relevant tools, persons, institutions (such as markets, governments) and physical environments. The question is how the actors effectively act (produce a given kind of product) given the constraints and possibilities of the particular kind of situation attached to that pragmatic field of activity.

On the other hand, action has a fundamentally collective character: most actions in this world can only be pragmatically effective if what one person does is met with certain kinds of mutually compatible actions by other persons upon whom s/he is dependent. In turn, since virtually all action is both collective and situational, it is associated with a fundamental kind of uncertainty, in the sense that we can not know precisely what the others upon whom we are dependent will do. This is true even in the presence of rules, norms, traditions; none of them eliminates the fundamentally calculating, strategizing nature of the individual, and hence the possibility that a rule, norm or tradition will not be followed in a given situation. One of the main tasks of research in the SSC is to discover how the actor identifies the situation and the specific forms of uncertainty with which it is associated.

The SSC's central 'equation' thus consists of the following terms: in order to proceed with action, which is inherently collective, the uncertainty which is specific to a given kind of situation must be overcome. The actor must be equipped with the means to interpret or understand the situation in which s/he finds him/ herself, in the sense that s/he must be able to identify the aspects of the situation in a way which agrees with the identification made by other actors upon whom s/he is dependent, so that each of them take actions which are mutually compatible (Polanyi, 1958). When this identification process happens so as to allow coordination, it is because mutual expectations have been aligned.

For example, if I, as lender of money, decide to put you in foreclosure when you do not pay me on time, this may be met with a mutually compatible act, acquiescence in liquidation, in California; but if I do it in the context of Hong Kong family capital lending, it may be met with outrage followed by censure, in which case I have failed to identify the situation correctly. By contrast, when the participants in a situation identify it in a common way, we can say that interpretations have led to a sort of 'agreement' about what is to be done. Such agreement, specific to the pragmatic situation at hand, is required for example between buyers and sellers of a commodity, between input supplier and purchaser, between one worker and another on the shop floor, between manager and worker, between states; without it, collective mutually interdependent activity cannot go forward. Contracts and rules cover a remarkably small proportion of the critical situations in economic, social and political life, or skim on the surface of what really goes on in those they do cover.

This is not an 'agreeement' in the sense of a formal contract or explicit rule, but rather in the sense of a common context; a set of points of reference which goes beyond the actors as individuals but which they nonetheless build and understand in the course of their actions. These points of reference for evaluating a situation and coordinating with other actors are essentially established by conventions between persons. Nor is this an agreement in the Panglossian sense of something which the parties necessarily consider good or optimal: it is a sort of concrete convergence of their expectations around what they think can be done.

4.   PROCEDURAL RATIONALITY IS SITUATED, NOT UNIVERSAL IN NATURE

Convention

Conventions emerge both as responses to and as definitions of uncertainty. Conventions resemble 'hypotheses' formulated by persons with respect to the relationship between their actions and the actions of those on whom they must depend in order to realize a goal. When interactions are reproduced time and again in similar situations, and when particular courses of action have proved successful, they become incorporated in routines and we then tend to forget their initally hypothetical character. Conventions thus become an intimate part of the history incorporated in behaviours. Notice that the theory accepts as central the tension between action and structure that people live with in the course of social and economic life, and does not see this incompleteness as something for theory to explain away.

The formal notion of convention stems from the work of analytical philosopher David Lewis (1969).

> A regularity, R, in the behavior of members of a population, P, when they act in a recurrent situation, S, is a convention, if and only if, for each example of S, for the members of P:
> Each conforms to R;
> Each anticipates that all others will conform to R;
> Each prefers to conform to R on the condition that others do so. Since S is a problem of coordination, the general conformity to R results in a coordination equilibrium.

Lewis's definition supposes that each member of a defined population identifies, at least for herself or himself, R as a regularity, as well as the nature of the situations S, their recurrent character, and the relationship between S and R. His definition, which requires some modifications, is nonetheless a good starting point.[9]

Procedural Rationality

Nothing that has been said here implies abandonment of the notion that actors are procedurally rational, but it does suggest that the procedures they use are quite different from those assumed to exist by much social science. The standard parable about rationality holds that individual, self-interested action is ubiquitous and dominant; that the consequences of making rational choices generally allow the intentions governing those choices to be realized; hence, that collective action is exceptional, since collective situations generally impede realization of individual goals in one way or another. Collective action is said to be blocked because of such widely present circumstances as divergent or partially-divergent interests (leading to principal-agent problems which, it is assumed, can never be worked out); bounded rationality or important transactions costs; differences between probable pay-offs to actors or groups (distributional conflicts are assumed to be not amenable to resolution by agreement); and uncertainty about or difficulty in predicting the future. All, in other words, are the specific analytical versions of the incompleteness or uncertainty considered by much social science to be a grave problem for rational actors.

Undoubtedly, these circumstances are widespread and it is to the credit of much analytical political economy and sociology to have been able to understand them. But they are not universal; they are particular conventional outcomes of situations identified by particular groups of actors. Actors have both more and less freedom than this mainstream view of procedural rationality suggests. They have more freedom in the sense that upstream of action is a moment of interpretation, what we have called identification of the situation, a moment in which the actor puts forth (mostly implicitly) something like a rebuttable hypothesis about the nature of the situation. Much of this, s/he does on the basis of precedent. But such precedents, and hence the hypotheses involved, do not have to treat uncertainty, distributional differences, transaction costs and so on, in the one single way suggested by the mainstream. That is, what we are now calling the procedure of identifying the situation is a form of 'labour' not considered by the standard models because they assume that mere identification of the problem calls forth a single, determinate and optimal solution for a given situation.

Yet, this standard 'solution' encompasses only half of the actor's procedure; the other half is upstream, and consists of identifying what other actors are likely to do in view of that circumstance. This, we maintain, is not universal but context-dependent and it does not reduce merely to the nature or quantity of information about the situation which is available. It comes from an interpretative procedure which depends on social life and collective experience (and all the ways of transmitting that experience, including norms, rules and so on), as much as it does from deep universal psychology. Norms, to take an important example, must be identified insofar as they apply to particular pragmatic problems and then applied in specific situations, and their application must be justified (whether to ourselves or others). Norms are in important measure specific to the situation in which they are applied and this interaction between the procedure and its situation is critical to how norms affect the course of action.

Indeed, not only does the rationality of procedures include reference to the specific possibility sets for coordination which exist in particular situations (as we noted above), it may also involve the justifications (Thévenot and Boltanski, 1991) we furnish for doing something. The relationship of what we do and how we justify it is conventionally constructed. There is no inherent reason to get behind the back of the actor and to distinguish categorically the reasons furnished by people for what they do, from why they really do it. If such justifications are widely shared, they actually become means of coordination through their effect of abating uncertainty. The corollary of this is what certain philosophers and historians have captured as the fundamental incommensurability of traditions: we can compare our behaviour with those of others who are within our system of action, according to the conventions we share; but between different systems of justification, there is no fruitful comparison to be made, and the rationality used to get to a conclusion can only be judged with respect to its internal consistency, i.e. as an internal property of the system of which one is a member (MacIntyre, 1988).

One could address this issue at other levels, as some of the institutionalist literature has done. For example, conflicts can be engendered by a wide variety of processes, such as changes in technology or prices. These changes might upset existing relationships and one could imagine situations where the actors find themselves trying to resolve conflicts through an existing institution, such as the courts. Are the procedures entirely set in advance? Obviously not. Precisely what the actors do, how they attempt to frame the issues in the conflict relative to the overarching set of procedures and precedents, and how the courts adjudicate are all highly context-sensitive and involve the system of downstream coordination between actors which we have described above. In a sense, the cases which can be brought before a given court are the results of what kinds of 'skilled' social actors exist to do so, but this in turn is a product of existing conventional understandings of the situation at hand.

To take another example, certain production systems are coordinated by interpersonal relationships; the industrial districts of the Third Italy are the oft-cited cases. The standard account would always say that such relationships work because reciprocity is 'policed' by reputation effects, and because both lower transactions costs. But upon reflection, we can see that this is no explanation at all of how such a mode of coordination comes about. It is just an after-the-fact and *ad hoc* description of some of its qualities and some of its efficiency attributes. The interesting issue is how actors establish such interpersonal conventions in the first place and then institutionalize them through precedent and learning. And here, the standard explanations have no way of not being simply circular: people do it because it is efficient and because they fear doing otherwise, but they fear doing otherwise because other people do it.

Other examples of this reasoning applied to economics are: Loasby's theory of the firm (Loasby, 1991); Alchian's demonstration that uncertainty poses no significant problem either to the attainment of positive profits or to selection, but where decision makers are not omniscient, nor is the system (Alchian, 1950), recent work in evolutionary economics (Dosi and Orsenigo, 1985).

5. CONVENTIONS, INSTITUTIONS, CULTURE, POWER

The word 'convention' is commonly understood to suggest at one and the same time: a rule which is taken for granted and to which everybody submits without reflection; the result of an agreement, such as a contract; or a founding moment, such as a Constitutional Convention. Convention thus refers to the simultaneous presence of three dimensions: the rules of spontaneous individual action; constructing agreements between persons; and institutions in situations of collective action. Each of these three has a different spatio-temporal extent, and they overlap in complex ways at any given moment or situation. Identifying them is one of the major tasks of empirical research within the SSC paradigm.

The SSC shares with the new institutionalisms in both sociology and economics the notion that social action requires some form of communication and understanding between human beings. But it departs quite radically from other explanations of the social order in that it does not presuppose such an order and instead turns the production of agreement and coordination into the key issue. There are three main consequences of such a revision of the objective:

Firstly, it means that the main analytical task – as is noted above – is to specify under which conditions, for what issues and in what intensity, such a need for agreement and coordination exists. Walkers in a park need an agreement, but it is qualitatively different from and probably less intense than, say, that between buyers and sellers of certain kinds of commodities, between citizens in political decision making, or between parents over the raising of a child. The institutionalist literature has identified the existence of different 'organizational fields' – relatively durable linkages between groups of actors and groups of organizations. Our reading of this, through the micro-lens of the SSC, is that the overall institutional 'map' of society is of an infinite complexity and variety. Hence, from the standpoint of the SSC, society is not an encompassing social order in the traditional sense, but rather an assemblage of multiply-produced agreements, as well as persistent disputes, of highly varying spatio-temporal extents and contents. Social life is organized, but is also pervaded by uncertainty and incompleteness.

Secondly, there is not as strong a tendency for reproduction of such institutional fields, as is held by many neo-constructivist approaches (Giddens, 1984), nor even through the processes of coercion, mimesis or transmission of norms (Powell and DiMaggio, 1983). All these exist. But coordination is not reached simply by the application of pre-existing or unequivocal rules, resources or powers. Instead, there is ongoing social labour involved in interpreting and identifying situations, mutually adapting interpretations and determining modes of coordination. In this sense, a key question for social science becomes the competences or capacities (skills) that agents bring to a situation, whether it be for reproduction or transformation.

Thirdly, and perhaps most importantly, this means that there is a critical quality (in the sense of 'crisis' or radical openness) to each situation, defined by its uncertainty. The result of a process of coordination cannot be derived from the nature of the situation, nor from the social positions of the persons involved. We cannot even derive the nature of the controversy of interpretation and identification. What is to be expected is a plurality of criteria and approaches to determine what the situation is and a process of selecting the appropriate criteria for response. This definitional work is part of the attainment of coordination.

The SSC, therefore, has two principal ways of approaching social research. The first is analytical: the variability of requirements for coordination, i.e. the analytical dissection of the situation, including its objective dimensions, the interpretative activity of people involved and the plurality of results. The second is historical, genealogical, thick description, mostly investigations of critical moments or controversies, where old conventions broke down or where conflict was resolved via the formation of new, temporarily stable worlds of coordination. In both cases, however, it is deeply sceptical of any functionalist readings of institutions, whether a priori or ex posteriori.

Equivalence: or, the Genesis of Institutions

Thus far, one could be reminded of studies in symbolic interactionism or even ethnomethodology with their inability to move beyond the particular or ideographic. It could be objected that social life looks plural and diverse only as long as the more extended and solid constraints of human action by stable or more efficient institutional forms (including power and culture)[10] are not brought into view. Specificities are interesting, one might say, only if we do not even bother to search for potentially general features; without this, we are advancing a simplistic, voluntarist view of the world.

But actually the main project of the SSC is to inquire into the emergence of ensembles of conventions that have wide spatio-temporal extent.[11] We can call attention to three means by which actors identify situations so as to coordinate with other actors, going from narrower to wider spatio-temporal extent.

1. In some cases, the identification of a situation and the persons and objects involved in it is done via a familiar gesture, i.e. through interpersonal familiarity.
2. In others, it involves a communicable judgement, presupposing some understanding of what is common.

3. Finally, some situations are coordinated via a *generalizable judgement*, i.e. through conventions that make a certain judgement about the situation widely available, without specific instance-to-instance communication about it. This is especially important, in that it involves drawing analogies between very different situations, objects and actions, a kind of ongoing social labour of creating 'equivalences' between situations – a kind of abstraction – on the part of the actor.

For example, the SSC argues that what economists call 'occupational-wage structures' are highly conventional and historical in origin, and only secondarily shaped by market clearing processes of wage determination. This is an argument which has been made in other terms by a number of prominent economic sociologists (Granovetter, 1993). But the SSC goes a bit further than they have. Wage structures are said to express the value that the market puts on skills, giving rise to the wage hierarchy. The problem is that 'skill' is a highly abstract notion, covering extremely heterogeneous categories of real work. In order to call, for example, the work of the electrician and that of the car mechanic 'skilled', one has to find some kind of abstract equivalence between the two. The market does not give us these abstract equivalences through the law of supply and demand. Nor can the frequently-cited notion of the schooling required to carry out a kind of job. Indeed, diplomas are precisely what the SSC calls a form (in this case an institutional form) which is created, like money, to represent two concretely very different skills as containing similar quantities of this common currency (schooling), which is then translated into another currency, that of money. Once we begin to look at the wage and salary structure this way, we see that behind it is a conventionally-constructed system of equivalences between heterogeneous things, and that the market is then the result of the trading – supplying and demanding – of these equivalences, not the other way around. Studying such equivalences makes it possible to move from studies of specific interactions to social and economic regularities of wide spatio-temporal extent.

This work of creating equivalences is ongoing, and they may be unstable. Equivalences may also be challenged and broken by certain kinds of actors, whether they be charismatic leaders, 'policy entrepreneurs', leaders of social movements, or other skilled social actors (Fligstein, 1990). This scepticism about the stability of institutions resembles that which can be found in the pessimism of the New Institutional Economics and its political science offshoots. But unlike the latter, existing structures of rationality or interest are not seen as inherently impeding institution formation: it is impossible to know, a priori, what kinds of equivalences may be created among them by active human actors. Thus, the SSC rejects any notion of the unity or cohesion of a group solely as the product of a substantive pre-definable similarity between its members and an objectively shared interest. Instead, our attention centres on the immense social labour which is necessary to unite disparate beings around the same system of representation, to constitute the reality of such a heterogeneous ensemble, and to embody it in actions, persons and objects. It is for this reason that coordination cannot be reduced to the mere functional maintenance of an order. Once in place, of course, institutions of a certain coherence may allow us to use notions such as normality or even rationality, but without any of the baggage which these terms usually carry. Normality is the ability to deal with uncertainty about the future, and rationality becomes the coherence of an adjustment to a situation. It has nothing inherently to do with separation of procedure from substance, nor with separation of motivations from procedures.

In spite of these differences at the extreme micro-level, there are many aspects of the SSC's institutional analysis which cover the same ground as that of much contemporary institutionalism. Six such points of contact can be cited: (1) emphasis on institutions as networks; (2) the chief content of networks is practices,[12] transmitted via and interpreted through conventions; (3) it is the intermediate forms of governance – coordination in 'small' action situations – which are most important; (4) the dynamic of most interest is how actors learn convention, and how they modify convention through crises, conflicts and the establishment of new precedents for action; (5) the evaluation of structure turns on the notion of relationship between groups of conventions around pragmatic action situations, and how 'bigger' institutions bring those pragmatic fields together under one roof; and (6) networks of actors and their conventions and practices tend to have path dependencies.[13]

Culture versus Convention

If we accept the definition of culture as a set of transitive, informal rules or guidelines for action, which have a coordinative effect and are applied in specific kinds of situations, the question arises as to how the notion of culture relates to that of convention. The rules that constitute a culture are those which no longer have a hypothetical character. They go so far back in time (or are so generalized over space) that the equivalences they represent can no longer be excavated, no longer rendered specific to a situation; they are not incomplete or tendential. Hence, the conventions which constitute culture often work at the level of metaphor or generalized custom. They do affect interpretation and justification, but when it comes to the kinds of action situations we are considering here, culture has to be re-concretized in the form of conventions whose hypothetical character is nearer to the action to be taken than is culture. Culture's relationship to the situation is too metaphorical or too general to resolve the uncertainty. In this sense, culture does not have a determining effect on the formation of convention, and so the problem of coordination cannot be successfully resolved by the mere reference to culture. Both concepts are necessary, but cover different aspects of reality.

Power and Convention

The emphasis on how 'agreement' is produced in the SSC does not imply equality of the parties or non-existence of power relations. The standard categories for analysing power, however, have persistent and deep problems. Why do people sometimes submit to the powerful and at other times revolt? Why does the control of resources – economic, physical, means of violence – sometimes enable the powerful to get their way and at other times not? Why do sanctions sometimes work and at other times not work? These are the classical questions posed in the theoretical debates about power. Because the standard bases of power work sometimes and then do not work at others, they fail as the bases of a satisfactory theory of power. Intermediate explanatory factors must be found. Certain others are invoked as candidates, especially ideology and hegemony. But it is just as strange to call upon psychological processes to determine the effectiveness of the material, as it is to reduce the mental to the material. And the question of how they relate, or what it is that they do when they take the form that we label ' power' is simply begged.

For the SSC, power is essentially the asymmetric ability to affect the construction of equivalences. This approach extends the SSC's emphasis on uncertainty, incompleteness, interpretation, and spatial and temporal unevenness. It does not answer all of our questions about the origins of power, but suggests that the variables cited in the power literature, both mental and material, have or do not have their effectiveness with respect to this labour of constructing equivalences. In this way, once again, the standard categories are lightened of the theoretical burdens they have shown themselves unable to bear. They are no longer determinants, nor are they mere 'factors' in a multi-factoral soup of potential bases of power, but resources which can be used in the construction of conventions of power as a form of social coordination.

6. FORMAL INSTITUTIONS: THE STATE AND GOVERNANCE OF THE ECONOMY

Formal institutions have a special status in all this, in that they try to stabilize certain equivalences between persons and things in the forms of rules and institutional fields. Perhaps the key formal institution is the state. The state, like other institutions, presupposes conventions between persons. Unlike other institutions, in Western democracies all state conventions are also based on normative representations of the 'common good' for their societies. Whereas non-state institutions and conventions may be constructed by actors in pursuit of their particular common interests, as efforts to resolve particular problems of coordination, the state is formally assigned the role of creating the conditions that maximize the possibility of attaining a general common good. There are many possible definitions of the common good in a democracy; hence, the ways that each democracy concretizes its notions of the common good as enforced by its state is through the social labour of creating equivalences of the 'good'.

Conventions of the state are widely mobilized, like other conventions, in situations of economic action. In western capitalist countries, we can observe three general conventions of the state with respect to economic coordination. In some societies, each person expects the state to intervene in the economy from a position outside and above the situation of action – this is the convention of the 'external state' which is particularly strong in France. In other societies, each person expects the state to be absent from situations of economic action, and for individuals to work out coordination between themselves – this convention of the 'absent state' is particularly marked in the United States. A third possibility is that the persons involved in economic action (including representatives of the state) operate on the premise that the state participates in economic coordination but as an equal, neither superior nor absent. We call this the convention of the 'situated state,' adapting slightly the concept from contemporary political philosophy, which terms this the 'subsidiary state'. All these conventions have strong effects on how their societies are able to experiment with new forms of governance of their economies today and illustrate well the ways that conventions shape and translate the impacts of external forces for change on the institutional regularities that result.

Example 1: The Objective Common Good of the External State

In France, post-war economic planning in particular and economic interventionism in general have been rooted in a widespread expectation that the state will insert itself from outside and above society to supply elements of coordination assumed to be essential to meeting common goals of national independence and full employment. The state is not defined in opposition to the popular will, as in Anglo-American liberalism, but as the embodiment of it. This convention between actors allows the state to intervene in the economy, applying monetary, fiscal, budgetary, industrial, and employment and training policies intended to maximize the common good.

Our purpose is not to judge the veracity of this idea of the state as external to economy and society, but to emphasize the powerful real effects this notion can have when it operates as a convention between persons. According to this convention, the state is the flux that allows the solder to hold; it covers the gaps and eliminates failures in the coordination of economic activity. Each person is thus aware of, and anticipates gaps in coordination (for example, a shortage of necessary resources) or failures (for example, to meet commitments); and each person thus expects that the state representatives authorized to intervene in the particular situation at hand will take corrective or complementary action. Most importantly, each person defines his or her action on the basis of this premise and thus holds back to some extent from fulfilling commitments to action or mobilizing resources. As a result, the convention becomes part of a self-fulfilling prophecy: in the final analysis, the state appears to be truly necessary to economic efficiency.

Both the successes and the limits of French industrial policy can be interpreted in the light of these conventions (Storper and Salais, 1993). Post-war policy used forced concentration to modernize certain sectors. Its success was not principally because of the scale it imposed on production, as many traditional analyses claim, but because centralization allowed the state to eliminate the coordination gaps which existed in a more fragmented system. Other methods of coordination, such as are to be found in Germany, did not work in France, precisely because actors in France counted on the state to step in. Hence, when the state did so in the big industrial sectors, it was able to impose a certain form of coordination. That coordination worked best when the state was not only the investor, but also client, and when a certain isolation from immediate market processes could be achieved, as in large-scale infrastructural goods, systems engineering, or basic industrial inputs. Rationalized, bureaucratic forms of coordination, subject to public scrutiny, work less well in other kinds of sectors, however.

Many current attempts to reform state intervention in the French economy centre precisely on the needs of other kinds of sectors in today's knowledge-intensive economy, which require a great deal more agility and flexibility. In this context, the tendency of certain private-sector actors to expect the state to resolve their coordination gaps, and to resolve them in a universalizing, rationalist way, has slowed down progress towards meeting contemporary competitive conditions, and this is the case even when the state has been rather clear about its intention no longer to supply coordination in the old way. This has often generated contradictions in the state's interventions: when coordination failures come about and threaten the economy as a whole, the state is forced to step back in and this reinforces the pre-existing conventional expectations of how it will act.[14]

Thus, while not arguing that more standard institutionalist arguments about these kinds of situations should be rejected, our point is that they are incomplete if they do not consider the conventional bases of coordination and coordination failures.

Example 2: 'States versus Markets'

The convention of the absent state takes the form of opposing the 'state' to the 'market'. In the United States, for example, the common good is defined, first and foremost, as a structure of opportunities which maximizes for each person the chance to pursue her particular interests; this is assumed to act as a powerful incentive which leads to the greatest possible economic growth and full employment, and thereby allows people (according to their different and unequal efforts and talents, of course) to enjoy upward social and economic mobility. The general common good, then, is defined as the result of maximizing the interests of particular persons. External (interventionist) action is criticized by those within this framework on the grounds of its supposed effects: by hindering market action, it blocks actors from realizing their individual potential and hence works against the common good. Actors subscribing to this convention hold that the state, and all forms of non-market coordination, are inherently worse than the market because they inhibit human agency; paradoxically, even when these actors use the state, they tend to be more critical of it than they would be of the market and its failures.

This argument is blind to its central paradox: a direct effect of the convention is that for the state to be really absent from each situation of action, the state itself must enforce this particular conception of the common good, since in reality there can be no such thing as a completely self-regulating market. The state thus becomes what it claims not to be, an activist in the name of continually 'effacing' barriers to the market.

In the external-and-absent 'Anglo-American' state, then, each person expects the state to impede collective action, except that which follows market principles; this pushes actors to expect that other actors will conduct themselves according to market principles. Actors then deploy strategies to protect themselves from the 'moral hazards' of the market (cheating, opportunism, universal self-interest) while profiting from its transitory opportunities. This is the universe described by, and normatively defended in, the new institutional economics and its political science extensions.

Most neo-institutionalist analyses would see the underlying tendency for the US to favour market-oriented solutions to policy problems as evidence, variously, of the rationality of certain interest blocs, the institutional fields they dominate, ideologies, concentrated corporate power, political division and disenfranchisement of those whose interests are damaged by policies, or skilled actors in favour of liberal policies, and so on. These arguments, in our view, go only part of the way. The propensity of different groups to question the fundamental efficiency of the state, and to incorporate this into their behaviours, leads to real effects that make certain non-state and non-universalist approaches to problems more rational in real terms. For example, in response to problems in public schools and growing income gaps in the society, there has been withdrawal by upper-income groups. Other groups, such as certain parts of the African-American population, also challenge public schools. They argue that such schools fail their children not only through a failure of universalism (a poor version of the basic education proposed), but more recently, because the universal model, they say, is not the right one for them. There are real behaviours that come from these critiques, notably withdrawal and gradual weakening of the universality of the education system's goals. Both have led, in concert with deeply reduced funding favoured by the Right, to widespread questioning of the value of state-supplied public education. There is now a growing coalition, consisting of these strange bedfellows, for more market forces in education policy (vouchers and private-public competition).

Such responses would be almost inconceivable in most European contexts; the elites use the public systems to educate their children and other populations aspire to this same achievement and their demands are formulated as those of perfecting the delivery of the universal, not questioning its value, even when there are grave problems. In other words, the actors in the two situations have fundamentally different expectations about how a problem of coordination is to be resolved and hence about who is to resolve it. The American situation of a self-fulfilling prophecy of questioning the state's ability to deliver is unlikely to come about in Europe in the first place, in spite of similar social processes that place pressure on the school systems there.

Example 3: Contemporary Experiments with Governance via 'Situated States'

All the Western democracies are currently facing major questions of state reform. There are big policy areas which fit poorly with standard forms of state organization and state-society relations, whether it be centralization in Europe or even top-down bureaucratic rationality as a method for implementing liberal programmes in the Anglo-American world.

In Western Europe and North America, for example, there are enormous efforts to find more satisfactory, and less costly, forms of the welfare state. In the US, for the time being, these efforts have taken the form of dramatic reduction in benefits, coupled to a discourse which extols the virtues of context-sensitive (more local) administration, determination of benefit levels, and eligibility rules. In Western Europe, the strains on the post-war system are apparent, but the reform efforts go in a rather different direction, which might be termed 'context-sensitive universalism'. The guarantee of protections is rarely questioned; but it is widely admitted that they often do not reach their targets. So there are attempts to find more diverse ways of getting them to their recipients, based on the notion that rigid substantive rationalism in programme administration is no longer well-adapted to the wide variety of situations of need.

The notion of a 'situated' state is entirely different from the concepts of external and absent states. It views the general common good as a situation in which actors have autonomy of action. Autonomy is defined, not with respect to the individual's procedural rights, as in liberal-contractual theory, but (in addition to those rights) with respect to collective action and the right of groups to deploy different action frameworks in coordination with each other. The state's role is to ensure that these frameworks of action and practices of coordination are treated with respect. If, as we have shown, economies are built on a diverse mix of potential efficient frameworks of action and coordination, then a 'democratic' state will respect and support the autonomy of actors, individually and collectively, to draw on such frameworks. The general common good, in other words, is directly linked to the extent to which the state and its policies grant actors the freedom and resources needed to draw on diverse possible frameworks of efficient economic action.

The autonomy of both individual and collective actors must be respected through the presumption that their resources and, most importantly, their frameworks of action, all deserve equality of consideration, and are not excluded up front by abstract criteria for defining appropriate means or the ends of action in the economy. Concretely it means that all-purpose formulae, such as economic liberalism or statism are inappropriate; instead, there are different, highly context-dependent ways to coordinate an economy that must be respected, at least as starting points, in any reform project. In conventions of situated states, each person acts to the best of his or her ability, and the state fills in only as a last resort when there are problems of coordination; the state is neither parent nor policeman, but handmaiden. There remain issues of universal needs in a society, such as those described by Rawls (1971), which only a state can guarantee. But the ways in which most social and economic goals can be reached are very diverse and must be situated.[15]

No such states currently exist, but perhaps they are the direction that certain kinds of governance experiments are currently taking. One of these is the European Union, which is based on a delicate compromise between transnational rules and group specificities. Economic policy at the regional level is another area in which new models of the situated state seem to be evolving (Piore and Sabel, 1984; Scott *et al.*, 1999). With the advent of production systems which must respond rapidly to changing circumstances – knowledge-based production, technological innovation, global competition, shorter product cycles – the old system of supports for firms in Europe has shown itself to be too slow and too centralized to react well, while American hands-off attitudes allow market and system failures to flourish. In both places, a wide variety of experiments in context-sensitive, regionally-coordinated assistance to private sector actors has evolved over the last two decades. Rules and resources drawn from a variety of traditional levels of policy making and geographical scales are blended in a pragmatic and highly flexible way.

Another area in which situated forms of governance appear to be emerging can be seen in experiments in multi-cultural group compromise at the municipal level in certain American cities, and in some Anglo-American political philosophy. We should be clear that much so-called 'multiculturalism' at the societal or national level in the United States is essentially taking the form of a super-liberalism, where group injuries and group claims are grafted on to individual procedural rights (Taylor and Gutman, 1992). In contrast, certain versions of big city municipal politics in the US seem to be experimenting with the possibility of group recognition within a framework of territorial cooperation (something like a municipal version of the European Union!) (Kayden, 1997). For example, in a number of big American cities, there have been successful 'living wage' campaigns recently. In Los Angeles, an election confirmed that city government would now have to pay a minimum hourly wage considerably higher than the federal minimum, corresponding better to local costs of living and to the existence of a huge, exploited immigrant population. These experiments are interesting for the ways they seem to be resituating certain types of state functions in concrete contexts and elaborating more complex approaches to the governance of the labour market.[16]

In all these areas, there is some evidence – however preliminary, of processes of coordination emerging which are different from those underlying the external state and the absent state.

The Problem of State Reform

This analysis has a strong implication for any attempt to reform state insitutions. What we have described here is essentially an endless circularity between convention and institutions. Institutions have a strong effect, by generating regularity and precedent, in the formation of conventions that people employ to cope with pervasive uncertainty. But by the same token, formal organized institutions can only function successfully if the rules, procedures, incentives and sanctions they establish are integrated into the conventions that guide people's behaviour.

Reform projects, or institution-building projects in general, have somehow to cut into this circularity. They cannot parachute from above, as in the 'external' conception of the state so favoured by, for example, most international institutions (e.g. IMF) in dealing with nation-states.[17] Most of those projects of the international elites are, in any case, based on a kind of minimalism with respect to states, consisting of economic liberalism and basic rules about procedural transparency (based on the so-called Western model of doing private business).[18] Reform projects need to cut into circularity in a 'situated' way, using devices that can create precedents and build confidence that are appropriate not only to a given ending point, but more importantly, with reference to the situation of the actors and their existing conventions and expectations (Storper, 1997, chapter 10). To put it in a single phrase: state reform is about building new precedents that would lead to new conventions; to do this, they need to involve the actors, which requires talk among the actors so that they might ultimately build confidence in new patterns of mutual interaction, which is the prerequisite of new sets of mutual expectations which are, in effect, convention.

Thus, there will be many different state reform projects, not one optimum result or one correct procedure. Surely they will all share certain results which are common to democracy, such as transparency and fairness, and which are necessary to capitalism, such as resource mobility, but beyond that, it would be a grave mistake to believe that external or absent states can bring most societies forward where they want to go. Situatedness may sound like a vague and complicated recipe, and convention-building a very soft goal, and they are, but they are probably the only practical choices.

This by no means replaces other kinds of analyses that could be done of the problem of institutional reform or change. The problems identified in the wider literature on this subject – interests (as we have redefined them), inertia, leadership, transition costs, coalitions, etc. – are essential dimensions of thinking about changing institutions to respond to new policy dilemmas. The present analysis insists, however, that these other dimensions need to be viewed in relationship to the possibilities for establishing new conventional bases of coordination. In considering the construction of new forms of governance in Europe or the US, or the reform of states in Latin America, rich insights could come from considering this dialectic of the meso-level of fields and practices which has been so well developed by various forms of new institutionalism, and the conventions which underpin institutions.

NOTES

1. This paper was initially prepared for presentation to the Seminario Internacional, *Instituições e Desenvolvimento Econômico: Perspectivas sobre a Reforma do Estado*, 12-14 November 1997, Rio de Janeiro. Earlier versions of this paper were presented to the Institute of International Studies, University of California, Berkeley, in March 1998, to the Political Economy/ Economic Sociology workshop at the University of Wisconsin, Madison in May, 1998, and to the Franco-American colloquium on 'Action, Institutions and Rationality', Château de la Bretesche, Brittany, September 1998. I thank those present for their comments. I particularly thank Patrick LeGalès for his detailed and critical comments, which enabled me to revise the paper substantially.

    The paper draws upon work I have carried out together with Robert Salais (Storper and Salais, 1997). It has also drawn liberally from the work of scholars who work on conventions, especially Peter Wagner's article (1994). See also J. Wilkinson (1997). None of these individuals is, however, responsible for the content of this paper.

2. Giddens's major project was motivated precisely by the impasse created by the old institutionalism and its underlying social theory.

3. The notable exception in the theory of the firm is that of Brian Loasby and the work it has inspired.

4. Robert Salais and I develop this critique of the New Institutional Economics and New Institutional Analysis in detail in chapter 12 of our book, *Worlds of Production: the Action Frameworks of the Economy* (Storper and Salais, 1997).

5. Incompleteness is *sometimes* a problem. We do not wish to deny that, in some circumstances, incompleteness leads to market failure and to forms of institutionalization which have the problems described in these literatures. Our point, however, is that what happens in the face of incompleteness does not have to take the determinate forms identified by those theories, and that when it does take those forms (e.g. firms), they do not always operate in the ways described by those theories. This is because the resulting types of coordination are conventional, not deterministic.

6. In another very different vein, which is somewhat related to the concerns of this paper, in the recently developed field of 'critical social science', the emphasis is on showing how institutions are reflections of power relations, and on showing how representations of institutions that are constructed using the language of positive or analytical social science are themselves part of the construction and reproduction of power relations because they mask power behind such notions as rationality, interest-seeking behaviour, and so on. One inspiration for this came from philosophers and linguists who stress the importance of context, the textuality of social life, and the way that discourse creates and not just conveys meaning (Flyvberg, 1998). Another strand from sociology and anthropology is the actor-network theory of Callon, Law and Latour, who hold that actor networks exert power and hold networks in place through organizations and the translation of embodied texts, machines, objects and money (Callon, Law and Rip, 1986; Latour, 1987).

    These approaches have the merit of trying to make the social scientist more conscious of the circle of meanings of which her/his own discourse is a part, as well as sensitizing us to the ways that social and economic phenomena are represented by those who have the control over the means of representation: think tanks, academia, media, opinion makers etc. But it still reduces almost everything to a game of power, and reduces virtually all notions of knowledge or truth to mere reflections of the interests of the powerful. By throwing the baby of structure, rationality and interaction out with the bathwater of neutrality and determinism, it reproduces the divide between the critical and the positive.

7. Many of the observations in this section are owed to Peter Wagner (1994), and to Robert Salais, but they are not responsible for the interpretation advanced here.

8. Early work began by looking at the effects of the emergence of the statistical category, 'unemployment' at the end of the 19th century, showing how an ostensibly simple statistical innovation was part of a thorough and categorical reordering of modern economic life, around the notions of what it is to be employed or not employed (Salais, Baverez and Reynaud, 1986). Moreover, the notion that this phenomenon was generated directly from the 'objective' realities of urbanization and economic cycles is shown to be wrong. By investigating the controversies over interpretation of the situation, it is shown that both the situation and the solutions were actively defined by the actors themselves and subsquently routinized and institutionalized into the now seemingly-natural categories we call 'employment' and 'unemployment'.

9. There are critical differences between our use of convention and the way Lewis and other analytical philosophers deploy it. Convention does not emerge automatically under specific external conditions, 'in a given situation', such that whenever such a situation exists, the convention will automatically be called forth. A situation may itself be identified (interpreted) by the actor in many different ways, and thus it may lead to quite different actions from one moment to another. It follows that coordination among actors depends not on correct application of unambiguous decision rules, but on interpretation in the course of action. Even though in daily life we proceed as if certain things were agreed upon, there is no structural guarantee of this.

Our conception differs from that which can be found in contemporary game theory as well. The assumptions necessary to do game-theoretic analysis are too restrictive, the definition of the actor's 'interest' typically too narrow and the role of interest too preponderant, and the equilibrium solutions are too far from reality, as well as having too great a role in determining the questions which can be asked.

10. These issues are taken up below.

11. Just to give a flavour of some of the work that has been done within the SSC: Boltanski's work on the formation of the managerial classes (1982); Desrosières on the emergence of statistical categories (1993); Thévenot has reconstructed the emergence of Taylorism as a set of conventions of production, work and management and their diffusion; Boyer has adapted the SSC to the Regulationist school of economics, looking at how Ford's wage policy transformed modern industrial production (Boyer, 1997); and Salais and others have looked at the invention of the modern concept of unemployment and its impacts on state-economy interactions over the last century (Salais, Baverez and Reynaud, 1986). Salais and I have looked comparatively – intersectorally and inter-nationally – at economic organization in our work on worlds of production and extended it to contemporary problems of economic specialization, competitiveness and the negotiation of economic change (Storper and Salais, 1993; Storper and Salais, 1997).

12. And note, in contrast to many theories of networks, that the content is not information *per se.* The informational content of networks is relevant insofar as it attaches to the transmission of expectations about how to act in a given kind of situation, i.e. convention.

13. But the stress on interpretation and radical uncertainty are fundamentally different from formal network analysis in sociology (White, 1992).

14. One thinks of the truckers' strikes of the 1990s in this regard, which forced the state to protect the drivers while enabling the sector to continue in its inefficient, uncoordinated way.

15. An excellent example of this is furnished by François Ascher. He cites the French post-war experience with territorial planning, noting that most of its current deficiencies come from its

insistence on applying abstract formulae to the problem of development. Using statistical analyses of departures from norms (growth, density, income levels, distribution of public services, etc.), the programmes pushed by the DATAR cannot respond to what is the real diversity of developmental needs and possibilities. Ascher advocates much greater context-sensitivity through making DATAR's efforts (Ascher, 1997) more situated.

16. Though, as we know, there are also tendencies for compromise to break down, as in the fights over school curricula in many American cities, or the simple devolution of community economic development policies into *de facto* quota systems for each group present (each ethnic group gets its share of the project).

17. The height of what might be called 'universalist hubris' came recently when Wall Street leaders claimed credit for 'bringing democracy to Indonesia', via their sanctioning of the Suharto regime. *Los Angeles Times,* Business Section, 27 May 1998.

18. The problem comes because 'external state' meta-principles frequently contradict or cannot co-exist with other possible conventions of social action. They brook no diversity. Wade (in this volume), for example, shows that the Western, IMF-led treatment of the 1997–98 Asian debt crisis was based on a fundamental error of this type. All Asian network- and family-based lending systems were lumped together as if they were all equivalent to Indonesian crony capitalism. It can easily be demonstrated that the family- and network-based systems for channelling high amounts of savings into the economy are not associated with high degrees of corruption and cronyism in places such as Taiwan. The vulnerability of the formal banking systems in many countries is indeed a problem when much saving does not go through these institutions, and policies are needed so that liquidity can be generated without excessive indebtedness of the formal institutions, something which a number of countries did not understand. Moreover, a number of observers have pointed out that even in the Indonesian case, and even with its astounding corruption, that country made more significant progress in reducing poverty than any Latin American country in recent times. Yet the international monetary authorities, with their rigid conventions of state intervention, are not prepared to act with context sensitivity and some experts even suspect them of deliberately trying to weaken Asian network-based savings and investment systems (Wade, 1998).
Jeffrey Sachs accuses the IMF of the same rigid externalist approach with respect to Russia and Eastern Europe. *Los Angeles Times,* Metro Section, 4 June 1998.

BIBLIOGRAPHY

Alexander, J. (1983), *The Modern Reconstruction of Classical Thought: Talcott Parsons,* Berkeley: University of California Press.

Alchian, A. (1950), 'Uncertainty, Evolution and Economic Theory', *Journal of Political Economy,* **58**, pp. 211–221.

Arrow, K.J. (1972), *The Limits to Organization,* New York: Norton.

Ascher, F. (1997), *La République contre la Ville,* Paris: Odile Jacob.

Boltanski, L. (1982), *Les Cadres: la Formation d'une Groupe Sociale,* Paris: Les Editions de Minuit.

Bourdieu, P. (1990), *The Logic of Practice,* Stanford: Stanford University Press.

Boyer, R. (1997), *After Fordism,* London: Macmillan.

Callon, M., T. Law and A. Rip (eds) (1986), *Mapping the Dynamics of Science and Technology,* Basingstoke: Macmillan.

Collins, R. (1989), 'The Micro Contribution to Macro Sociology', *Sociological Theory*, **6**, pp. 242–253.

Desrosières, A. (1993), *La Politique des Grands Nombres: Histoire de la Raison Statistique*, Paris: La Decouverte.

Dosi, G., F. Malerba, O. Marsili and L. Orsenigo (1997), 'Industrial Structures and Dynamics: Evidence, Interpretations, and Puzzles', *Industrial and Corporate Change*.

Dosi, G. and L. Orsenigo (1985), *Order and Change: An Exploration of Markets, Institutions and Technology in Industrial Dynamics*, Brighton: SPRU Discussion Paper no. 32.

Favereau, Olivier (1993), *L'Incomplétude n'est pas le Problème, c'est la Solution*. Communication au colloque de Cerisy, 5–12 June, 'Limitations de la Rationalité et Constitution du Collectif'.

Fligstein, N. (1990), *The Transformation of Corporate Control*, Cambridge, MA: Harvard University Press.

Flyvberg, B. (1998), *Rationality and Power*, Chicago: University of Chicago Press.

Giddens, Anthony (1984), *The Constitution of Society: Outline of the Theory of Structuration*, Cambridge: Polity Press.

Granovetter, M. (1993), *Getting a Job: A Study of Contacts and Careers*, Cambridge, MA: Harvard University Press.

Granovetter, M. (1995), *Getting a Job: A Study of Contacts and Careers*, 2nd ed., Chicago: University of Chicago Press.

Hodgson, G. (1997), 'From Micro to Macro: The Concept of Emergence and the Role of Institutions'. Paper presented at the Rio seminar, *Instituições e Desenvolvimento Economico: A Reforma do Estado*.

Joas, Hans (1996), *The Creativity of Action*, Chicago: University of Chicago Press.

Kayden, Xandra (1997), 'Governance and Leadership for the Region's Future'. Unpublished paper, delivered to the Pacific Council on International Relations project meeting on Los Angeles in the Global Economy, 3 June.

Knight, Frank (1921), *Risk, Uncertainty and Profit*, New York: A.H. Kelly.

Langlois, R. and N. Foss (1997), *Capabilities and Governance: The Rebirth of Production in the Theory of Economic Organization*, Aalborg, Denmark: Danish Research Unit on Industrial Dynamics, Working Paper 97-2.

Latour, B. (1987), *Science in Action: How to Follow Scientists and Engineers through Society*, Cambridge, MA: Harvard University Press.

Lewis, D. (1969), *Convention: A Philosophical Study*, Cambridge, MA: Harvard University Press.

Loasby, Brian J. (1991), *Equilibrium and Evolution: An Exploration of Connecting Principles in Economics*, Manchester: Manchester University Press.

MacIntyre, Alasdair (1988), *Whose Justice? Which Rationality?* Notre Dame: University of Notre Dame Press.

North, D. (1981), *Structure and Change in Economic History,* New York: Norton.

Parsons, T. (1951), *The Social System,* Glencoe: The Free Press.

Parsons, T. (1960), *Structure and Process in Modern Societies,* Englewood Cliffs, NJ: Prentice-Hall.

Piore, M. and C. Sabel (1984), *The Second Industrial Divide*, New York: Basic Books.

Polanyi, M. (1958), *Personal Knowledge*, Chicago: University of Chicago Press.

Powell, W.W. and P.H. DiMaggio (1983), 'The Iron Cage Revisited: Institutional Isomorphism and Collective Rationality in Organizational Fields', *American Sociological Review*, **48**, pp. 147–160.

Powell, W.W. and P.H. DiMaggio (eds) (1991), *The New Institutionalism in Organizational Analysis,* Chicago: University of Chicago Press.

Rawls, J. (1971), *A Theory of Justice,* Cambridge, MA: Harvard/Belknap.

Salais, R., N. Baverez and B. Reynaud (1986), *L'Invention du Chômage, Histoire et Transformation d'une Catégorie en France des Années 1890 aux Années 1980,* Paris: Presses Universitaires de France.

Scott, A.J., J. Agnew, E. Soja and M. Storper (1999), *Global City-Regions.* Paper prepared for the Global City-Regions Conference, Los Angeles, October.

Storper, M. (1997), *The Regional World: Territorial Development in a Global Economy*, New York and London: Guilford Press, chapter 10: 'Institutions of the Learning Economy'.

Storper, Michael and Robert Salais (1993), *Les Mondes de Production,* Paris: Editions de l'Ecole des Hautes Etudes en Sciences Sociales (2nd ed., 1998).

Storper, Michael and Robert Salais (1997), *Worlds of Production: the Action Frameworks of the Economy,* Cambridge, MA: Harvard University Press.

Swedberg, R. (ed.) (1993), *Explorations in Economic Sociology*, New York: Russell Sage Foundation.

Taylor, C. (1992), *Multiculturalism and the Politics of Recognition*, Princeton, NJ: Princeton University Press.

Taylor C. and Amy Gutman (1992), *Multiculturalism and the Politics of Recognition*, Princeton, NJ: Princeton University Press.

Thévenot, L. and L. Boltanski (1989), *Les Économies de la Grandeur,* Paris: Presses Universitaires de France.

Thévenot, L. and L. Boltanski, (1991), *De la Justification*, Paris: Gallimard.

Wade, R. (1998), 'The Asian Debt-and-Development Crisis of 1997-? Causes and Consequences'. Paper delivered to the UCLA Center for Social Theory and Comparative History colloquium, 12 March.

Wagner, Peter (1994), 'Dispute, Uncertainty, and Institutions in Recent French Debates', *Journal of Political Philosophy,* **2** (3).

White, H. (1992), *Identity and Control: A Structural Theory of Social Action,* Princeton, NJ: Princeton University Press.

Williamson, O. (1985), *The Economic Institutions of Capitalism,* New York: The Free Press.

Wilkinson, J. (1997), 'A New Paradigm for Economic Analysis: Recent Convergences in French Theory and an Exploration of the Conventions Approach', *Economy and Society,* **26** (3).

5. From micro to macro: the concept of emergence and the role of institutions

Geoffrey M. Hodgson

1. INTRODUCTION

These days, mainstream economists seem to wonder less and less about the conceptual and philosophical foundations of their subject – and about the reality with which it is meant to engage – and more and more about their own individual prowess at mathematical gymnastics. Yet the fundamental problems of theory and application will not go away. No matter how hard mainstream economists pursue their *a priorist* and formalistic programme, some basic questions of assumptions and methodology are inescapable.

In this respect we can learn a great deal from the attempt to place macroeconomics on 'sound microfoundations'. Let us briefly put this in historical perspective. From the 1870s to the 1930s, mainstream economics in the English-speaking world was almost entirely microeconomics. Despite earlier, nineteenth-century developments in macroeconomic theory – by Friedrich List, Karl Marx and others – macroeconomics proper did not really get off the ground until after the publication in 1936 of the *General Theory* by John Maynard Keynes. In fact, the word 'macroeconomics' itself did not come into use until 1939.[1] From the 1940s to the 1960s there was an uneasy synthesis in the mainstream economics textbooks – exemplified in Paul Samuelson's best-selling *Economics* – between a neoclassical microeconomics and a bowdlerized and sanitized version of Keynesian macro-theory.

However, the life of a relatively autonomous macroeconomic theory was short. There was increasing unease with even the limited version of 'Keynesianism' that had made its way into the mainstream. Consequently, the neoclassical fundamentalists mounted a counter-attack. Emanating from Chicago and elsewhere, this assault was well under way by the 1970s. 'Keynesianism' was attacked on both methodological and policy grounds. In policy terms, the limited justification of state intervention in the textbook

'Keynesian' system was rejected. In methodological terms, theories based on supposed aggregate behaviour were regarded as scientifically unsound and *ad hoc*. The reductionist idea of explaining wholes in terms of individual parts had long been seen by many as the *sine qua non* of all science. Confidence in the necessity of reductionism in science reached the point that the Nobel Laureate James Tobin (1986, p. 350) wrote that:

> This [microfoundations] counter-revolution has swept the profession until now it is scarcely an exaggeration to say that no paper that does not employ the 'microfoundations' methodology can get published in a major professional journal, that no research proposal that is suspect of violating its precepts can survive peer review, that no newly minted Ph.D. who can't show that his hypothesized behavioral relations are properly derived can get a good academic job.

'Scientific' credentials were claimed for the microfoundations enterprise. Jon Elster (1983, pp. 20–4) expressed and endorsed a very widespread view when he wrote:

> The basic building block in the social sciences, the elementary unit of explanation, is the individual action guided by some intention. ...Generally speaking, the scientific practice is to seek an explanation at a lower level than the explanandum. ...The *search for micro-foundations*, to use a fashionable term from recent controversies in economics, is in reality a pervasive and omnipresent feature of science.

Applying such notions to economics, Nobel Laureate Robert Lucas (1987, p. 108) wrote:

> The most interesting recent developments in macroeconomic theory seem to me describable as the reincorporation of aggregative problems such as inflation and the business cycle within the general framework of 'microeconomic' theory. If these developments succeed, the term 'macroeconomic' will simply disappear from use and the modifier 'micro' will become superfluous. We will simply speak, as did Smith, Ricardo, Marshall and Walras, of *economic* theory.

Mainstream economics took the veracity of its reductionist research programme for granted. It attempted to build up a composite picture of the economic system from atomistic, individual units, just as the particle forms the elemental unit in Newtonian mechanics. The attempt was to explain the whole through its analytical reduction to its presumed microfoundations and component parts.

Yet we may note in passing a strange dissimilarity between the reductionist project in other sciences and that in economics. Reductionists in the physical sciences try to explain all phenomena in terms of their fundamental units or components. Strictly, this procedure should carry on until we reach the most fundamental sub-atomic particle: the basic constituent of all matter, whatever it may be. By contrast, reductionists in the social sciences seem content to stop with human individuals. This approach is widely described as 'methodological individualism'. But if reductionism is a worthy and worthwhile project, why stop with the individual? If we can reduce explanations to individual terms, why not further reduce them to the biological genes, and then on to the sub-atomic particles of physics?

In fact, both the microfoundations project in economics and methodological individualism carry reductionist flags but always involve a partial analytical reduction only. They thus fail to succeed in full reductionist terms. As philosophers of biology David Sloan Wilson and Elliott Sober (1989) argued, for the reductionist to settle on the individual involves an inconsistency. Adequate reasons why explanation should be reduced simply to the level of the individual, and stop there, have not been provided. The same general arguments concerning explanatory reduction from the macro to the micro – or from groups to individuals – apply equally to explanatory reduction from individual to gene, gene to molecule, and so on. If we can reduce explanations to individual terms, why not further reduce them to the terms of genes? Or molecules? To avoid this 'double standard' one must either accept multiple levels of analysis, each with their own partial autonomy, or reduce everything to the lowest possible level as the biological reductionists in the social sciences – such as Herbert Spencer in Britain and William Graham Sumner in America – attempted in the late nineteenth century.

A reductionism that suggests that wholes must be explained in terms of parts must take the parts as given. To take a contrary view would suggest an infinite regress, in which each part has to be explained in terms of its relations with other parts, and so on, without end. The reductionist injunction assumes that which must eventually reach the basic, imperturbable and irreducible parts or individuals where the analysis can come to a stop (Hodgson, 1988, 1993a, 1998a).

The reasons why the most zealous of reductionists in the social sciences are incomplete in the application of their own reductionist canon are too complex to concern us here. In part they involve the rift in the early twentieth century between the social and the biological sciences (Degler, 1991; Hodgson, 1999a). This legitimized an (untenable) explanatory barrier between the natural and the social world: allegedly a barrier that no theorist need, or should try, to cross. The reasons for an incomplete and individual-centred reductionism also relate to the tenacious influence of an individualistic political ideology in the social sciences.

What does concern us here is the reason why reductionism in general, and the microfoundations project, in particular, have failed. Furthermore, we are concerned to examine the rudiments of an alternative approach.

Section 2 of this essay notes the failure of the microfoundations project in mainstream economics. In a more general vein, section 3 goes on to examine the limits of reductionism in science. The critique of reductionism is linked to the concept of emergence in section 4. Section 5 examines the development of the concept of emergence in more detail. Section 6 examines the old institutionalist approach to macroeconomics, and sketches a possible line of argument, using institutions rather than individuals as units of analysis. Section 7 concludes the essay.

2. THE FAILURE OF THE MICROFOUNDATIONS PROJECT AND THE CRISIS OF MAINSTREAM THEORY

Mainstream theory has been engaged in a long-lasting attempt to place economics on secure and individualistic microfoundations. However, it was eventually realized that assumptions of diversity among individuals threatened the feasibility of this project. Many types of interaction between the individuals have to be ignored to make the analysis tractable. Indeed, it was not easy to develop a composite picture from the assumption of a diversity of types of individual agent.

Even with the standard assumptions of rational behaviour, and its drastic psychological and epistemological limitations, severe difficulties are faced. As Nobel Laureate Kenneth Arrow (1986, p. S388) has been led to declare: 'In the aggregate, the hypothesis of rational behaviour has in general no implications.' Consequently, in a desperate attempt to deduce something in the macro-sphere from the micro-tenet of individual rationality, it is widely assumed that all individuals have an identical utility function. Apart from ignoring obvious differences in individual tastes, this denies the possibility of 'gains from trade arising from individual differences' (p. S390).

Typically, the textbook macroeconomics that is spun out of neoclassical microeconomic theory goes well beyond the confinement and rigour of general equilibrium theory, to make bold and general claims concerning the relationship between wages and unemployment, and inflation and the money supply. Only the more honest and careful neoclassical theorists have questioned such bold macroeconomic derivations from microeconomic assumptions. For instance, Arrow (1986, p. S386) stated that he knows 'of no serious derivation of the demand for money from a rational optimization'. In an extensive examination of orthodox, textbook, macroeconomic theories, John Weeks (1989, p. 236) showed that they 'suffer from serious flaws of internal logic. Accepting these models and proceeding as if they were analytically sound is essentially an act of politically-motivated faith.' As Donald Katzner (1991) has argued, it is not possible to aggregate from individual supply and demand functions to such aggregated functions at the level of the market if considerations of ignorance and historical time are taken into account.

However, let us leave aside the more incautious textbook statements and concentrate on the more considered propositions of the theoretical pioneers. The fact is that, several years ago, the microfoundations project reached insurmountable difficulties and it essentially collapsed due to the weight of its own internal problems. This truth is not widely broadcast. Nevertheless, starting from the assumption of individual utility maximization, Hugo Sonnenschein (1972, 1973a, 1973b), Rolf Mantel (1974) and (Nobel Laureate) Gerard Debreu (1974) showed that the excess demand functions in an exchange economy can take almost any form. There is thus no basis for the assumption that they are downward sloping. This problem is essentially one of aggregation when individual demand functions are combined. As Alan Kirman (1989) has reiterated, the consequences for neoclassical general equilibrium theory are devastating. As S. Abu Turab Rizvi (1994a, p. 363) put it, the work of Sonnenschein, Mantel and Debreu is quite general and is not restricted to counter-examples:

> Its chief implication ... is that the hypothesis of individual rationality, and other assumptions made at the micro level, gives no guidance to an analysis of macro-level phenomena: the assumption of rationality or utility maximisation is not enough to talk about social regularities. This is a significant conclusion and brings the microfoundations project in [general equilibrium theory] to an end.

In general, research into the problems of the uniqueness and stability of general equilibria have shown that they may be indeterminate and unstable unless very strong assumptions are made, such as the supposition that society as a whole behaves as if it were a single individual. Again, this demolishes the entire microfoundations project (Lavoie, 1992, pp. 36–41; Screpanti and Zamagni, 1993, pp. 344–53). Facing such profound problems, Kirman (1992, p. 118) wrote: 'there is no plausible formal justification for the assumption that the aggregate of individuals, even maximizers, acts itself like an individual maximizer'. He concluded: 'If we are to progress further we may well be forced to theorize in terms of groups who have collectively coherent behavior. ... The idea that we should start at the level of the isolated individual is one which we may well have to abandon' (Kirman, 1989, p. 138).

The theoretical implications of these uniqueness and stability results for general equilibrium theory are devastating. A fundamental consequence is the breakdown of the types of analysis based on individualistic or atomistic ontologies.

The indeterminacy and instability results produced by contemporary theory lead to the conclusion that an economy made up of atomistic agents has not structure enough to survive, as its equilibria may be evanescent states from which the system tends to depart (Ingrao and Israel, 1985, 1990; Kirman, 1989).

Fabrizio Coricelli and Giovanni Dosi (1988, p. 126) argued that 'the project of building dynamic models with economic content and descriptive power by relying solely on the basic principles of rationality and perfect competition through the market process has generally failed'. Attempts to base macroeconomics on neoclassical microfoundations involve faith in the 'invisible hand' and in the substantive capabilities of individuals to calculate endlessly and make supremely rational choices. Yet the results of this theoretical endeavour show no more than a very crippled hand, incapable of orderly systemic coordination even in relatively simple models:

> Moreover, note that these results are obtained despite an increasing attribution of rational competence and information processing power to individual agents. Certainly ... the attempt to 'explain' macroeconomics solely on the basis of some kind of 'hyper-rationality' of the agents ... and the (pre-analytical) fundamentals of the economy (i.e. given technology and tastes) has failed. (Coricelli and Dosi, 1988, p. 136)

Hence it is no exaggeration to say that the microfoundations enterprise has effectively disintegrated, and for reasons well known to and understood by the leading theorists of the genre.

As Rizvi (1994b) pointed out, it was this partially-hushed-up-crisis in general equilibrium theory in the 1970s that led to the adoption of game theory in the 1980s. Today, game theory has largely replaced the general equilibrium approach that was found to be non-viable in the 1970s. However, Rizvi (1994b, pp. 23–4) argued that game theory does not save mainstream economics from its core problems:

> Game theory does not solve the arbitrariness problem which led to the halting of the general equilibrium research programme and its replacement by game theory methods. Instead, the fact that such arbitrariness appears so significantly in both the general equilibrium and the game theory settings is strong evidence that the approach of making (even strong) rationality assumptions on individual agents considered individually and then expecting system-wide outcomes to be orderly or usefully arrayed is badly flawed. Moving from one micro-rational system to another does not seem to improve matters at all.

In a related vein, Roy Radner (1996) argued that the game-theoretic analysis of institutions is thwarted by problems of uncertainty about the logical implications of given knowledge, and by the existence of multiple equilibria. Cristina

Bicchieri (1994, p. 127) notes that what is missing in most game theoretic models is 'a description of the players' reasoning processes and capacities as well as a specification of their knowledge of the game situation'. This amounts to the observation that the processes of cognition and learning are absent from much of game theory.

Far from leading the mainstream to salvation, theoretical work in game theory has raised questions about the very meaning of 'hard core' notions such as rationality. Yanis Varoufakis (1990) surveyed some of the recent results concerning the problems of rational decision making in the circumstances where a limited number of other actors are believed to be capable of 'irrational' acts. Such 'irrationality' need not stem from stupidity; it is sufficient to consider the possibilities that rational actors may have incomplete information, limited computational capacities, slight misperceptions of reality, or doubts concerning the attributes of their adversaries. Agents do not have to be substantially irrational for irrationality to matter. Irrational behaviour may emerge simply where some people are uncertain that everybody else is rational.

The problems in the mainstream approach go further. After the neglect of decades, mainstream theorists now, albeit in a limited fashion, admit discussion of problems of imperfect or asymmetric information and even 'bounded rationality'. While these are welcome developments, they have created havoc with orthodox presuppositions. For instance, as Joseph Stiglitz (1987) has elaborated, where prices signal quality to the consumer, standard demand analysis and the so-called 'law of demand' get overturned.

In addition, the intrusion of chaos theory into economics has put paid to the general idea that economics can proceed simply on the criterion of 'correct predictions'. With non-linear models, outcomes are oversensitive to initial conditions and thereby reliable predictions are impossible to make in regard to any extended time period. In particular, chaos theory has confounded the rational expectations theorists by showing that even where most agents know the basic structure of the economic model, in general they cannot derive reliable predictions of outcomes and thereby form any meaningful 'rational expectations' of the future (Grandmont, 1987).

Mainstream economic theory is in fact in a profound crisis. Its attempts to explain real economic phenomena in terms of given individuals by using reductionist methods have failed. The gravity of this crisis is not widely appreciated, however. The means by which this crisis has been concealed has been to turn economics into a branch of applied mathematics, where the aim is not to explain real processes and outcomes in the economic world, but to explore problems of mathematical technique for their own sake. By this method, the failure of mainstream economics to provide a coherent theoretical apparatus to explain real phenomena is obscured. Seemingly, explanation is no longer the goal, and reality is no longer the object of reference. Economics is thus becoming a mathematical game to be played in its own terms, with arbitrary rules chosen by the players themselves, unconstrained by questions of descriptive adequacy or references to reality.

However, those who are concerned to save economics from this plight have an opportunity. Not only has the microfoundations project in economics failed, but also philosophers of science are increasingly questioning the reductionist imperative. These philosophical developments provide an opportunity for those that may be dissatisfied with mainstream theory. It is to these philosophical issues that we now turn.

3.   THE NATURE AND LIMITS OF REDUCTIONISM

Reductionism sometimes involves the notion that wholes must be explained entirely in terms of their elemental, constituent parts. More generally, reductionism can be defined as the idea that all aspects of a complex phenomenon must be completely explained in terms of one level, or type of unit. According to this view there are no autonomous levels of analysis other than this elemental foundation, and no such thing as emergent properties (see below) upon which different levels of analysis can be based.

In social science in the period 1870–1920, reductionism was prominent and typically took a biological form. Accordingly, attempts were made to explain the behaviour of individuals and groups in terms of their alleged biological characteristics. By the 1920s, biological reductionism was largely abandoned in Anglo-American social science, although it has reappeared in the 1970s in the controversial form of socio-biology (Wilson, 1975).

Reductionism is still conspicuous in social science today and typically appears in the special form of methodological individualism. This is defined as 'the doctrine that all social phenomena (their structure and their change) are in principle explicable only in terms of individuals – their properties, goals, and beliefs' (Elster, 1982, p. 453). It is thus alleged that explanations of socio-economic phenomena must be reduced to the properties of constituent individuals and relations between them. Allied to this is the attempt discussed above to found macroeconomics on 'sound microfoundations'. There are other versions of reductionism, however, including versions of 'holism' that suggest that parts should be explained in terms of wholes.

It should be pointed out at the outset that the general idea of a reduction to parts is not being overturned here. Some degree of reduction to elemental units is inevitable. Even measurement is an act of reduction. Science cannot proceed without some dissection and some analysis of parts.

However, although some reduction is inevitable and desirable, a complete analytical reduction is both impossible and a philosophically dogmatic diversion. What is important to stress is that the process of analysis cannot be extended to the most elementary sub-atomic particles presently known to science, or even to individuals in economics or genes in biology. A complete reduction would be hopeless and interminable. As Karl Popper has declared: 'I do not think that there are any examples of a successful reduction' to elemental units in science (Popper and Eccles, 1977, p. 18). Reduction is necessary to some extent, but it can never be complete.

In the social sciences, methodological individualism carries similar problems of intractability. Indeed it has never been fully carried out in practice. Lars Udéhn (1987) has argued convincingly that not only is methodological individualism flawed, but also because of the problems of analytical intractability involved, it is inoperable as a methodological approach. The reductionist explanation of all complex socio-economic phenomena in terms of individuals is over-ambitious, and has never succeeded. In practice, aggregation and simplification are always necessary.

Notably, the adoption of an organicist ontology implies that the reductionist and methodological individualist project to explain all social and economic phenomena in terms of given individuals and the relations between them is confounded. The adoption of an organicist ontology means precisely that the individual is not given (Winslow, 1989). Organicism obstructs the treatment of individuals as elemental or immutable building blocks of analysis. Exponents of organicism argue further that both the explanatory reduction of wholes to parts and parts to wholes should be rejected. Just as society cannot exist without individuals, the individual does not exist prior to the social reality. Individuals both constitute, and are constituted by, society. Unidirectional modes of explanation, such as from parts to wholes – and vice-versa – or from one level to another, are thus thwarted. There is both 'upward' and 'downward' causation.[2]

Reductionism is countered by the notion that complex systems display emergent properties at different levels that cannot be completely reduced to or explained wholly in terms of another level. Anti-reductionists often emphasize emergent properties at higher levels of analysis that cannot be reduced to constituent elements. It is to the concept of emergence that we now turn.

4.   THE CONCEPT OF EMERGENCE

The idea of emergence has an established history in biology and other disciplines and has made rare appearances in economics. Emergence refers to the idea that novel properties may 'emerge' in a complex system that are not reducible to constituent micro-elements at a 'lower level'. The concept of emergent properties is typically prominent in critiques of reductionism. In particular, concepts like consciousness and purposeful behaviour may be regarded as an emergent property of the complex human nervous system (Sperry, 1991).

The philosopher of science Paul Feyerabend (1965, p. 223) has provided a useful example. Consider the relationship between the movements of molecules, at one level, and the concept of temperature, on another. Feyerabend asserts that although the concept of temperature can be associated with statistical mechanics and the movements of molecules, the kinetic theory cannot 'give us such a concept' as temperature, which relates to an interactive level above and beyond the combined movements of molecules.

Earlier examples are found in the *Rules of Sociological Method* ([1901] 1982, pp. 39–40) written in the late nineteenth century by Emile Durkheim (although he himself did not use the word emergence):

> The hardness of bronze lies neither in the copper, nor the tin, nor in the lead which have been used to form it, which are all soft or malleable bodies. The hardness arises from the mixing of them. The liquidity of water, its sustaining and other properties, are not in the two gases of which it is composed, but in the complex substance which they form by coming together. Let us apply this principle to sociology. If, as is granted to us, this synthesis *sui generis,* which constitutes every society, gives rise to new phenomena, different from those which occur in consciousness in isolation, one is forced to admit that these specific facts reside in the society itself that produces them and not in its parts – namely its members.

There are other examples. The meteorologist Lewis Fry Richardson (1922) wrote a famous paper showing that the wind has no specific velocity or direction. The wind is a turbulent flow of tiny eddies: the atoms move in all different directions and at different speeds. Wind speed and direction are thus emergent properties of a much more complex system.

Jack Cohen and Ian Stewart (1994, p. 232) ask: Are carbon atoms black, or sulphur atoms yellow? No.

> The colors are not present, not even in a cryptic or rudimentary form, in the atoms from which the chemical is made. ... The collective structure of bulk matter reflects light at certain preferred wavelengths; those determine the color. Color is an emergent phenomenon; it only makes sense for bulk matter.

The concept of self-organization in complex systems is also related to the concept of emergence. Ilya Prigogine and Isabelle Stengers (1984) developed the idea of order emerging from chaos some time ago. They showed that order and structure can develop through the interaction of elements such as cells or molecules. This idea has been developed by Stuart Kauffman (1993, 1995) and his co-workers at the Santa Fe Institute in the United States.

In general, as Tony Lawson (1997, p. 176) explained: 'an entity or aspect is said to be emergent if there is a sense in which it has arisen out of some "lower" level, being conditioned by and dependent upon, but not predictable from, the properties found at the lower level'. Furthermore, as Margaret Archer (1995, p. 9) elucidated: 'What justifies the differentiation of strata and thus use of the terms "micro" and "macro" to characterize their relationship is the existence of *emergent properties* pertaining to the latter but not to the former, even if they were elaborated from it'.[3]

5. THE EMERGENCE OF EMERGENCE

The idea of emergence is perhaps foreshadowed in the 'dialectic' of Georg Hegel, with the idea of the transformation of quantity into quality. The philosopher Auguste Comte (1853, vol. 2, p. 181) wrote of irreducible properties: 'Society is no more decomposable into individuals than a geometrical surface is into lines, or a line into points'. The notion of emergence was further hinted at by John Stuart Mill (1843, bk. 3, ch. 6, para. 2) with his idea of 'heteropathetic' causation. The word 'emergent' in this context was first suggested by the philosopher George Lewes (1875, chapter 3, p. 412). Subsequently, the philosopher of biology C. Lloyd Morgan (1927, 1933) wrote extensively on the topic. Following Mill and Lewes, Morgan defined emergent properties (1927, pp. 3–4) as 'unpredictable' and 'non-additive' results of complex processes. He saw such properties as crucial to evolution in its most meaningful and creative sense, where 'the emphasis is not on the unfolding of something already in being but on the outspringing of something that has hitherto not been in being. It is in this sense only that the noun may carry the adjective "emergent"' (Morgan, 1927, p. 112). For Morgan, evolution creates a hierarchy of increasing richness and complexity in integral systems 'as new kinds of relatedness' successively emerge (Morgan, 1927, p. 203). Also for Morgan, the 'non-additive' character of complex systems must involve a shift from mechanistic to organic metaphors: 'precedence should now be given to organism rather than to mechanism – to organization rather than aggregation' (Morgan, 1933, p. 58). When elements enter into some relational organization in an entity, and this entity has properties which could not be deduced from prior knowledge of the elements, then the properties of the entity are said to be 'emergent'.

Morgan visited Chicago in 1896 and the institutional economist Thorstein Veblen was crucially influenced by his ideas (Dorfman, 1934; Hodgson, 1998b; Tilman, 1996). However, although Veblen arguably incorporated the concept of emergence into his thinking, he did not dwell upon or further refine the idea. One of the few economists to take note of the concept of emergence in the interwar period was the institutional economist John A. Hobson. In his book *Veblen,* Hobson (1936, p. 216) wrote in one short passage: 'Emergent evolution brings unpredictable novelties into the processes of history, and disorder, hazard, chance, are brought into the play of energetic action'.

Despite Morgan and Hobson, the idea of emergence was largely submerged in the positivistic and reductionist phase of Anglo-American science in the interwar period (Ross, 1991). Sir Karl Popper and others rediscovered the idea of emergent properties some time after the Second World War. As Popper (1974, p. 281) remarked: 'We live in a universe of emergent novelty'; a novelty which is as a rule 'not completely reducible to any of its preceding stages' (Popper, 1982, p. 162).

The existence of emergent properties at each level means that explanations at that tier cannot be reduced entirely to phenomena at lower levels. Philosophers Roy Bhaskar, Arthur Koestler, Alfred Whitehead and others have proposed that reality consists of multi-levelled hierarchies. The existence of emergent properties at each level means that explanations at that tier cannot be reduced entirely to phenomena at lower levels. As the biologist Ernst Mayr (1985, p. 58) put it:

> Systems at each hierarchical level have two characteristics. They act as wholes (as if they were a homogeneous entity), and their characteristics cannot (not even in theory) be deduced from the most complete knowledge of the components, taken separately or in other partial combinations. In other words, when such systems are assembled from their components, new characteristics of the new whole emerge that could not have been predicted from a knowledge of the components. ... Perhaps the two most interesting characteristics of new wholes are that they can in turn become parts of still higher-level systems, and that they can affect properties of components at lower levels (downward causation) ... Recognition of the importance of emergence demonstrates, of course, the invalidity of extreme reductionism. By the time we have dissected an organism down to atoms and elementary particles we have lost everything that is characteristic of a living system.

James Murphy (1994, p. 555) developed a similar argument:

The theory of emergence ... is a nonreductionist account of complex phenomena. ... The notion that from complexity emerges new phenomena that cannot be reduced to simpler parts is at the center of modern biology ... Complex systems very often have a hierarchical structure, and the hierarchical structure of living systems shares some important features with our hierarchy, one being that higher levels can affect properties of components at lower levels.

This implies 'downward causation' (Sperry, 1969; Campbell, 1974), which means that outcomes at a higher level can react upon and transform lower-level components. In economics an obvious example, emphasized by the institutional economist John K. Galbraith (1958), would be the effect of advertising and fashion in reconstituting individual preferences. The fact that structures or elements on one level can essentially reconstitute those at another level confounds reductionism. Although reductionism is still prominent, both in biology and in the social sciences, in biology strong and influential voices can be found against it, reflecting the history of the concept of emergence in that subject.

Emergence has been linked to chaos theory. Working on non-linear mathematical systems, chaos theorists have shown that tiny changes in crucial parameters can lead to dramatic consequences, known as the 'butterfly effect – the notion that a butterfly stirring the air today in Peking can transform storm systems next month in New York' (Gleick, 1988, p. 8). There are parallels here with the account of 'bifurcation points' in the work of Prigogine and Stengers (1984). After behaving deterministically, a system may reach a bifurcation point where it is inherently impossible to determine which direction change may take; a small and imperceptible disturbance could lead the system into one direction rather than another.

Chaos theory suggests that apparent novelty may arise from a deterministic non-linear system. From an apparently deterministic starting point, we are led to novelty and quasi-randomness. Accordingly, even if we knew the basic equations governing the system we would not necessarily be able to predict reliably the outcome. The estimation of 'initial conditions' can never be accurate enough. This does not simply undermine the possibility of prediction; in addition the idea of a reductionist explanation of the whole in terms of the behaviour of its component parts is challenged. As a result, the system can be seen to have emergent properties that are not reducible to those of its constituent parts. Chaos theory thus undermines the ideas that science is largely about prediction and reductionism. Furthermore, it can sustain a concept of emergence.

In recent years much work has been done with complex, non-linear computer systems, attempting to simulate the emergence of order and other 'higher-level' properties. Reviewing the modelling of such 'artificial worlds', David Lane (1993, p. 90) wrote that a main thrust 'is to discover whether (and under what conditions) histories exhibit interesting *emergent properties'*. His extensive review of the literature in the area suggests that there are many examples of artificial worlds displaying such attributes. This lends credence to the idea that emergence is important in the real world.

The notions of emergence and downward causation are used in critiques of methodological individualism and of the reductionist idea that macroeconomics can only be built on 'sound microfoundations'. If socio-economic systems have emergent properties – by definition not entirely explicable of constituent elements at a basic level – then the ideas of explaining the macro-behaviour of socio-economic systems in terms of individuals and individual actions (methodological individualism) or, more generally, completely in terms of microeconomic postulates (the microfoundations project), are confounded. Furthermore, in explaining complex systems we may be forced to rely on emergent properties at a macro level.

6. INSTITUTIONALISM AND MACROECONOMICS

The suggestion here is that, by reference to the concept of emergence, the relative autonomy of macroeconomics and the idea of the workability of aggregates can be re-established. This idea was partially developed by the American institutionalists long ago. In his 1924 Presidential Address to the American Economic Association, the institutional economist Wesley Mitchell (1937, p. 26) argued that economists need not begin with a theory of individual behaviour but with the statistical observation of 'mass phenomena'. Mitchell (1937, p. 30) went on: 'The quantitative workers will have a special predilection for institutional problems, because institutions standardize behavior, and thereby facilitate statistical procedure'. Subsequently, Rutledge Vining (1949, p. 85) noted how 'much orderliness and regularity apparently only become evident when large aggregates are observed' and noted the limitations of a reductionist method in economics. Modern computer simulations and other studies of complex systems seem to underline similar points (Cohen and Stewart, 1994; Chiaromonte and Dosi, 1993).

Mitchell and his colleagues in the US National Bureau for Economic Research in the 1920s and 1930s played a vital role in the development of national income accounting and suggested that aggregate, macroeconomic phenomena have an ontological and empirical legitimacy. Arguably, this important incursion against reductionism in economics created space for the Keynesian revolution. Through the development of national income accounting, the work of Mitchell and his colleagues helped to establish modern macroeconomics and influenced and inspired the macroeconomics of Keynes (Mirowski, 1989, p. 307).

In defending Mitchell's approach against the reductionist criticisms of Tjalling Koopmans (1947, 1949a, 1949b), Vining (1949, p. 79) argued that

> we need not take for granted that the behavior and functioning of this entity can be exhaustively explained in terms of the motivated behavior of individuals who are particles within the whole. It is conceivable – and it would hardly be doubted in other fields of study – that the aggregate has an existence apart from its con- stituent particles and behavior characteristics of its own not deducible from the behavior characteristics of the particles.

Here the institutionalist Vining hints unknowingly at the concept of emergent properties, then regrettably a relatively unknown concept in the circles of both the natural and the social sciences.

The 'old' institutional economics did not attempt to build up a picture of the whole system by moving unidirectionally from given individuals. Instead there is the idea of interactive agents, mutually entwined in durable and self-rein- forcing institutions. This provides a quite different way of approaching the problem of theorizing the relationship between actor and structure.

The 'old' institutionalism saw institutions as connected to individual habits. Indeed, an institution was defined by institutionalists in the old tradition as 'a way of thought or action of some prevalence and permanence, which is embed- ded in the habits of a group or the customs of a people. ... Institutions fix the confines of and impose form upon the activities of human beings' (Hamilton, 1932, p. 84). Habits both reinforce and are reinforced by institutions. Through this circle of mutual engagement, institutions are endowed with a stable and inert quality, and tend to sustain and thus 'pass on' their important characteris- tics through time. Further, institutions play an essential role in providing a cog- nitive framework for interpreting sense-data and in providing intellectual hab- its or routines for transforming information into useful knowledge. The strong influence of institutions upon individual cognition provides some significant stability in socio-economic systems, partly by buffering and constraining the diverse and variable actions of many agents.

A rigorous and detailed exposition is lacking, but we may sketch out a pos- sible argument along the following lines. The institutionalizing function of in- stitutions means that macroeconomic order and relative stability are reinforced alongside variety and diversity at the microeconomic level. Ironically, by as- suming given individuals, the microfoundations project in orthodox economics had typically to assume, furthermore, that each and every individual was iden- tical in order to attempt to make the analysis tractable. The concept of an institution, properly handled, points not to a spurious supra-individual objectivity, nor to the uniformity of individual agents, but to the concept of socio-economic order, arising not despite but because of the variety at the micro-level. Without such micro-variety there would be no evolutionary development of the processes of conformism and emulation that can sustain order.

A slightly different, but complementary, argument is suggested by work carried out by Gary Becker in 1962 and more recently by Dhananjay Gode and Shyam Sunder (1993). These authors have constructed models where systemic constraints prevail over micro-variations. For example, Becker demonstrated that an 'irrational' mode of behaviour, in which agents are ruled by habit and inertia, is just as capable of predicting the standard downward-sloping demand curve and the profit-seeking activity of firms. Becker showed how the negatively inclined market demand curve can result from habitual behaviour. Actors 'can be said to behave not only "as if" they were rational but also "as if" they were irrational: the major piece of empirical evidence justifying the first statement can equally well justify the second' (Becker, 1962, p. 4). Kenneth Arrow (1986) has also accepted the possibility of an alternative approach based on habit. Gode and Sunder go on to show that experiments with agents of 'zero intelligence' produce predictions that differ little from those with human traders. Two conclusions follow. First, the 'accuracy of the predictions' or other familiar criteria for theory selection do not give outright victory to rational choice models. Second, these models suggest that ordered and sometimes predictable behaviour can result from institutional constraints, and may be largely independent of the 'rationality', or otherwise, of the agents.

Generally, institutions fill a key conceptual gap in social and economic theory. Institutions simultaneously constitute and are constituted by human action. Institutions are sustained by 'subjective' ideas in the heads of agents and are also 'objective' structures faced by them (Searle, 1995). Choosing institutions as units of analysis does not necessarily imply that the role of the individual is surrendered to the dominance of institutions. Both individuals and institutions are mutually constitutive of each other.

The institutionalist John Commons (1934, p. 69) noted that: 'Sometimes an institution seems analogous to a building, a sort of framework of laws and regulations, within which individuals act like inmates. Sometimes it seems to mean the "behavior" of the inmates themselves.' This dilemma of viewpoint persists today. For example, Douglass North's definition of institutions as 'rules of the game ... or ... humanly devised constraints' (1990, p. 3) stresses the restraints of the metaphorical prison in which the 'inmates' act. In contrast, Veblen's definition of an institution as 'settled habits of thought common to the generality of men' (1919, p. 239) seems to start not from the objective constraints but from 'the inmates themselves'. However, as Commons himself concluded, the thrust of the 'old' institutionalist approach is to see behavioural habit and institutional structure as mutually entwined and mutually reinforcing; both aspects are relevant to the full picture. A dual stress on both agency and structure is required.

What is significant is the relative invariance and self-reinforcing character of institutions: to see socio-economic development as periods of institutional continuity punctuated by periods of crisis and more rapid development. The fact that institutions typically portray a degree of invariance over long periods of time, and may last longer than individuals, provides one reason for choosing institutions rather than individuals as a bedrock unit. Hence the institution is 'a socially constructed invariant' (Mirowski, 1987, p. 1034n). As a result, institutions can be taken as the units and entities of analysis. This contrasts with the idea, in mainstream economics, of the individual as the irreducible unit of analysis.

However, the proposed alternative is not a crude holism. Complete explanations of parts in terms of wholes are beset with problems of equivalent stature to those of the inverse procedure. Just as structures cannot be adequately explained in terms of individuals, individuals cannot adequately be explained in terms of structures. Fortunately, there are sophisticated alternative approaches in philosophy and social theory (Archer, 1988, 1995; Bhaskar, 1979; Bourdieu, 1990; Giddens, 1984; Kontopoulos, 1993; Lawson, 1997; White, 1992) that emphasize the structured interaction of parts with wholes, and eschew single-level explanations.

7. IN CONCLUSION

The literature on complex systems and emergent properties lends support to the 'old' institutionalist idea that the economy can and must be analysed at different levels. There is a valid and sustainable distinction between the 'micro' and the 'macro', without reducing the former to the latter, or vice-versa. The concept of an institution provides a key conceptual bridge between the two levels of analysis. It connects the microeconomic world of individual action, of habit and choice, with the macroeconomic sphere of seemingly detached and impersonal structures. While analyses at each level must remain consistent with each other, the macroeconomic level has distinctive and emergent properties of its own.

Accordingly, there is a role for the kind of macroeconomics that was prominent in the 1940s and 1950s, when notions of 'Keynesianism' were at the zenith of their reputation. Today, such 'old fashioned' macroeconomics is confined to the unfashionable quarters of Post Keynesianism and institutionalism. It is said to be founded on *ad hoc* assumptions, while ignoring the necessary microfoundations. The suggestion here, however, is that the quest for microfoundations can never be completed, and the assumption of the microeconomic unit of the given individual is as *ad hoc* as any other. Keynesian and institutionalist macroeconomics was thus abandoned in haste. Much of it can be rehabilitated.

Such alternative approaches – of which only a most rudimentary and preliminary sketch has been provided here – do not always lend themselves to formal modelling. Complexity itself imposes limits on mathematical modelling and formal theory. The adoption of more modest formal aims and the shifting of the balance of economic theory away from mathematics may be a necessary outcome. Indeed, the problems faced by the microfoundations project in mainstream economics suggest that there are limits to the deductivist conception of theory that has dominated economics for the last 50 years. As Frank Hahn (1991, p. 50) has conjectured: 'Not only will our successors have to be far less concerned with ... grand unifying theory ... [but also] less frequently for them the pleasures of theorems and proof. Instead the uncertain embrace of history and sociology and biology.' We must face and enjoy this embrace.

NOTES

1. According to Samuelson (1997, p. 157) the word 'macroeconomics' was first used by Lindahl (1939).
2. For a development of the idea of downward causation see Hodgson (1999b).
3. See also Lane (1993, p. 91) and Kontopoulos (1993, pp. 21–3).

BIBLIOGRAPHY

Archer, Margaret S. (1988), *Culture and Agency: The Place of Culture in Social Theory,* Cambridge: Cambridge University Press.

Archer, Margaret S. (1995), *Realist Social Theory: The Morphogenetic Approach,* Cambridge: Cambridge University Press.

Arrow, Kenneth J. (1986), 'Rationality of Self and Others in an Economic System', *Journal of Business,* **59** (4.2), October, S385–S399. Reprinted in Hogarth and Reder (1987), *Rational Choice: the Contrast Between Economics and Phsychology,* Chicago: University of Chicago Press and in John Eatwell, Murray Milgate and Peter Newman (eds) (1987), *The New Palgrave Dictionary of Economics,* 4 vols, London: Macmillan, vol. 2.

Becker, Gary S. (1962), 'Irrational Behavior and Economic Theory', *Journal of Political Economy*, **70** (1), February, pp. 1–13. Reprinted in Bruce J. Caldwell (ed.) (1993), *The Philosophy and Methodology of Economics*, vol. 1, Aldershot: Edward Elgar.

Bhaskar, Roy (1979), *The Possibility of Naturalism: A Philosophic Critique of the Contemporary Human Sciences*, Brighton: Harvester.

Bicchieri, Cristina (1994), *Rationality and Coordination*, Cambridge and New York: Cambridge University Press.

Bourdieu, Pierre (1990), *The Logic of Practice,* translated by Richard Nice, Stanford and Cambridge: Stanford University Press and Polity Press.

Campbell, Donald T. (1974), '"Downward Causation" in Hierarchically Organized Biological Systems', in Francisco J. Ayala and Theodosius Dobzhansky (eds) (1974), *Studies in the Philosophy of Biology*, Berkeley and Los Angeles: University of California Press, pp. 179–86.

Chiaromonte, Francesca and Giovanni Dosi (1993), 'Heterogeneity, Competition, and Macroeconomic Dynamics', *Structural Change and Economic Dynamics*, **4** (1), June, pp. 39–63.

Cohen, Jack and Ian Stewart (1994), *The Collapse of Chaos: Discovering Simplicity in a Complex World*, London and New York: Viking.

Commons, John R. (1934), *Institutional Economics – Its Place in Political Economy*, New York: Macmillan. Reprinted 1990 with a new introduction by M. Rutherford, New Brunswick, NJ: Transaction.

Comte, Auguste (1853), *The Positive Philosophy of Auguste Comte*, 2 vols., translated by Harriet Martineau, London: Chapman.

Coricelli, Fabrizio and Giovanni Dosi (1988), 'Coordination and Order in Economic Change and the Interpretative Power of Economic Theory', in Giovanni Dosi, Christopher Freeman, Richard Nelson, Gerald Silverberg and Luc Soete (eds) (1988), *Technical Change and Economic Theory*, London: Pinter, pp. 124–47. Reprinted in Hodgson (1993b).

Debreu, Gerard (1974), 'Excess Demand Functions', *Journal of Mathematical Economics*, **1** (1), March, pp. 15–21.

Degler, Carl N. (1991), *In Search of Human Nature: The Decline and Revival of Darwinism in American Social Thought*, Oxford and New York: Oxford University Press.

Dorfman, Joseph (1934), *Thorstein Veblen and His America*, New York: Viking Press. Reprinted 1961, New York: Augustus Kelley.

Durkheim, Emile (1982), *The Rules of Sociological Method*, translated from the French edition of 1901 by W.D. Halls with an introduction by Steven Lukes, London: Macmillan.

Elster, Jon (1982), 'Marxism, Functionalism and Game Theory', *Theory and*

Society, **11** (4), pp. 453–82. Reprinted in John E. Roemer (ed.) (1986), *Analytical Marxism*, Cambridge: Cambridge University Press.

Elster, Jon (1983), *Explaining Technical Change*, Cambridge: Cambridge University Press.

Feyerabend, Paul K. (1965), 'Reply to Criticism', in Robert S. Cohen and Max W. Wartofsky (eds) (1965), *Boston Studies in the Philosophy of Science*, New York: Humanities Press, pp. 223–61.

Galbraith, John K. (1958), *The Affluent Society*, London: Hamilton.

Giddens, Anthony (1984), *The Constitution of Society: Outline of the Theory of Structuration*, Cambridge: Polity Press.

Gleick, James (1988), *Chaos: Making a New Science*, London: Heinemann.

Gode, Dhananjay K. and Shyam Sunder (1993), 'Allocative Efficiency of Markets with Zero-Intelligence Traders: Market as a Partial Substitute for Individual Rationality', *Journal of Political Economy*, **101** (1), February, pp. 119–37.

Grandmont, Jean-Michel (ed.) (1987), *Nonlinear Economic Dynamics*, New York: Academic Press. Reprint of October 1986 issue of the *Journal of Economic Theory*.

Hahn, Frank H. (1991), 'The Next Hundred Years', *Economic Journal*, **101** (1), January, pp. 47–50.

Hamilton, Walton H. (1932), 'Institution', in Edwin R. A. Seligman and A. Johnson (eds), *Encyclopaedia of the Social Sciences*, New York: Macmillan, vol. 8, pp. 84–9. Reprinted in Hodgson (1993b).

Hobson, John A. (1936), *Veblen*, London: Chapman and Hall. Reprinted 1991 by Augustus Kelley.

Hodgson, Geoffrey M. (1988), *Economics and Institutions: A Manifesto for a Modern Institutional Economics*, Cambridge and Philadelphia: Polity Press and University of Pennsylvania Press.

Hodgson, Geoffrey M. (1993a), *Economics and Evolution: Bringing Life Back Into Economics*, Cambridge, UK and Ann Arbor, MI: Polity Press and University of Michigan Press.

Hodgson, Geoffrey M. (ed.) (1993b), *The Economics of Institutions*, Aldershot: Edward Elgar.

Hodgson, Geoffrey M. (1998a), 'The Approach of Institutional Economics', *Journal of Economic Literature,* **36** (1), March, pp. 166–92.

Hodgson, Geoffrey M. (1998b), 'On the Evolution of Thorstein Veblen's Evolutionary Economics', *Cambridge Journal of Economics,* **22** (4), July, pp. 415–31.

Hodgson, Geoffrey M. (1999a), *Evolution and Institutions: On Evolutionary Economics and the Evolution of Economics*, Cheltenham: Edward Elgar.

Hodgson, Geoffrey M. (1999b), 'Structures and Institutions: Reflections on Institutionalism, Structuration Theory and Critical Realism', University of Hertfordshire, mimeo (unpublished).

Ingrao, Bruna and Giorgio Israel (1985), 'General Economic Equilibrium: A History of Ineffectual Paradigmatic Shifts', *Fundamenta Scientiae*, **6**, pp. 1–45, 89–125.

Ingrao, Bruna and Giorgio Israel (1990), *The Invisible Hand: Economic Equilibrium in the History of Science*, Cambridge, MA: MIT Press.

Katzner, Donald W. (1991), 'Aggregation and the Analysis of Markets', *Review of Political Economy*, **3** (2), April, pp. 220–31.

Kauffman, Stuart A. (1993), *The Origins of Order: Self-Organization and Selection in Evolution*, Oxford and New York: Oxford University Press.

Kauffman, Stuart A. (1995), *At Home in the Universe: The Search for Laws of Self-Organization and Complexity*, Oxford and New York: Oxford University Press.

Kirman, Alan P. (1989), 'The Intrinsic Limits of Modern Economic Theory: The Emperor Has No Clothes', *Economic Journal (Conference Papers)*, **99**, pp. 126–39.

Kirman, Alan P. (1992), 'Whom or What Does the Representative Individual Represent?', *Journal of Economic Perspectives*, **6** (2), Spring, pp. 117–36.

Kontopoulos, Kyriakos M. (1993), *The Logics of Social Structure*, Cambridge: Cambridge University Press.

Koopmans, Tjalling C. (1947), 'Measurement Without Theory', *Review of Economics and Statistics*, **29** (3), August, pp. 161–72.

Koopmans, Tjalling C. (1949a), 'Identification Problems in Economic Model Construction', *Econometrica*, **17**, pp. 125–44.

Koopmans, Tjalling C. (1949b), 'Methodological Issues in Quantitative Economics: A Reply', *Review of Economics and Statistics*, **31** (2), May, pp. 86–91.

Lane, David A. (1993), 'Artificial Worlds and Economics, Parts I and II', *Journal of Evolutionary Economics*, **3** (2), May, 89–107, and **3** (3), August, pp. 177–97.

Lavoie, Marc (1992), *Foundations of Post-Keynesian Economic Analysis*, Aldershot: Edward Elgar.

Lawson, Antony (1997), *Economics and Reality*, London: Routledge.

Lewes, George Henry (1875), *Problems of Life and Mind*, 2 vols, London: Trubner.

Lindahl, Erik R. (1939), *Studies in the Theory of Money and Capital*, London: Allen and Unwin.

Lucas, Robert E., Jr (1987), *Models of Business Cycles*, Oxford: Basil Blackwell.

Mantel, Rolf R. (1974), 'On the Characterization of Aggregate Excess Demand', *Journal of Economic Theory*, **12** (2), pp. 348–53.

Mayr, Ernst (1985), 'How Biology Differs from the Physical Sciences', in David J. Depew and Bruce H. Weber (eds), *Evolution at a Crossroads: The New Biology and the New Philosophy of Science*, Cambridge, MA: MIT Press), pp. 43–63.

Mill, John Stuart (1843), *A System of Logic: Ratiocinative and Inductive, Being a Connected View of the Principles of Evidence and the Methods of Scientific Investigation*, 1st ed., 2 vols, London: Longman.

Mirowski, Philip (1987), 'The Philosophical Bases of Institutional Economics', *Journal of Economic Issues*, **21** (3), September, pp. 1001–38. Reprinted in Philip Mirowski (1988), *Against Mechanism: Protecting Economics from Science*, Totowa, NJ: Rowman and Littlefield.

Mirowski, Philip (1989), *More Heat Than Light: Economics as Social Physics, Physics as Nature's Economics*, Cambridge: Cambridge University Press.

Mitchell, Wesley C. (1937), *The Backward Art of Spending Money and Other Essays*, New York: McGraw-Hill.

Morgan, C. Lloyd (1927), *Emergent Evolution*, 2nd ed. (1st ed. 1923), London: Williams and Norgate.

Morgan, C. Lloyd (1933), *The Emergence of Novelty*, London: Williams and Norgate.

Murphy, James Bernard (1994), 'The Kinds of Order in Society', in Philip Mirowski (ed.) (1994), *Natural Images in Economic Thought: Markets Read in Tooth and Claw*, Cambridge and New York: Cambridge University Press, pp. 536–82.

North, Douglass C. (1990), *Institutions, Institutional Change and Economic Performance*, Cambridge: Cambridge University Press.

Popper, Sir Karl R. (1974), 'Scientific Reduction and the Essential Incompleteness of All Science', in Francisco J. Ayala and Theodosius Dobzhansky (eds) (1974), *Studies in the Philosophy of Biology*, Berkeley and Los Angeles: University of California Press, pp. 259–84.

Popper, Sir Karl R. (1982), *The Open Universe: An Argument for Indeterminism*, from the *Postscript to the Logic of Scientific Discovery*, edited by William W. Bartley, III, London: Hutchinson.

Popper, Sir Karl R. and John C. Eccles (1977), *The Self and Its Brain*, Berlin: Springer International.

Prigogine, Ilya and Isabelle Stengers (1984), *Order Out of Chaos: Man's New Dialogue With Nature*, London: Heinemann.

Radner, Roy (1996), 'Bounded Rationality, Indeterminacy, and the Theory of the Firm', *Economic Journal*, **106** (5), September, pp. 1360–73.

Richardson, Lewis Fry (1922), *Weather Prediction by Numerical Process,* Cambridge: Cambridge University Press.

Rizvi, S. Abu Turab (1994a) 'The Microfoundations Project in General Equilibrium Theory', *Cambridge Journal of Economics,* **18** (4), August, pp. 357–77.

Rizvi, S. Abu Turab (1994b) 'Game Theory to the Rescue?', *Contributions to Political Economy,* **13**, pp. 1–28.

Ross, Dorothy (1991), *The Origins of American Social Science,* Cambridge: Cambridge University Press.

Samuelson, Paul A. (1997), 'Credo of a Lucky Textbook Author', *Journal of Economic Perspectives,* **11** (2), Spring, pp. 153–60.

Screpanti, Ernesto and Zamagni, Stefano (1993), *An Outline of the History of Economic Thought,* Oxford: Clarendon Press.

Searle, John R. (1995), *The Construction of Social Reality,* London: Allen Lane.

Sonnenschein, Hugo F. (1972), 'Market Excess Demand Functions', *Econometrica,* **40** (3), pp. 549–63.

Sonnenschein, Hugo F. (1973a), 'Do Walras's Identity and Continuity Characterize the Class of Community Excess Demand Functions?', *Journal of Economic Theory,* **6** (4), pp. 345–54.

Sonnenschein, Hugo F. (1973b), 'The Utility Hypothesis and Market Demand Theory', *Western Economic Journal,* **11** (4), pp. 404–10.

Sperry, Roger W. (1969), 'A Modified Concept of Consciousness', *Psychological Review,* **76**, pp. 531–36.

Sperry, Roger W. (1991), 'In Defense of Mentalism and Emergent Interaction', *Journal of Mind and Behavior,* **12** (2), pp. 221–46.

Stiglitz, Joseph E. (1987), 'The Causes and Consequences of the Dependence of Quality on Price', *Journal of Economic Literature,* **25** (1), March, pp. 1–48.

Tilman, Rick (1996), *The Intellectual Legacy of Thorstein Veblen: Unresolved Issues,* Westport, Connecticut: Greenwood Press.

Tobin, James (1986), 'The Future of Keynesian Economics', *Eastern Economic Journal,* **13** (4).

Udéhn, Lars (1987), *Methodological Individualism: A Critical Appraisal,* Uppsala: Uppsala University Reprographics Centre.

Varoufakis, Yanis (1990), 'Conflict in Equilibrium', in Yanis Varoufakis and David Young (eds) (1990), *Conflict in Economics,* Hemel Hempstead: Harvester Wheatsheaf, pp. 39–67.

Veblen, Thorstein B. (1919), *The Place of Science in Modern Civilisation and Other Essays,* New York: Huebsch. Reprinted 1990 with a new introduction by W. J. Samuels, New Brunswick, NJ: Transaction.

Vining, Rutledge (1949), 'Methodological Issues in Quantitative Economics', *Review of Economics and Statistics*, **31** (2), May, pp. 77–86.

Weeks, John (1989), *A Critique of Neoclassical Macroeconomics*, Basingstoke: Macmillan.

White, Harrison C. (1992), *Identity and Control: A Structural Theory of Social Action*, Princeton: Princeton University Press.

Wilson, David Sloan and Elliott Sober (1989), 'Reviving the Superorganism', *Journal of Theoretical Biology*, **136**, pp. 337–56.

Wilson, Edward O. (1975) *Sociobiology: The New Synthesis*, Cambridge, MA: Harvard University Press.

Winslow, Edward A. (1989), 'Organic Interdependence, Uncertainty and Economic Analysis', *Economic Journal*, **99** (4), December, pp. 1173–82.

PART TWO

Policy Perspectives

6. National diversity and global capitalism

Ronald Dore

It is doubtful whether 'globalization' as such is a sensible object of study. It certainly seems to be considered by publishers to be a good way of selling books. Already by 1996 the Harvard catalogue had 188 titles which included the word globalization, about a half of them published in the previous two years; from the globalization of the defence industry and the globalization of innovation to the globalization of poverty, of theological education and of the Jakarta stock exchange. Some titles clearly suggest that it is a good thing, some that it is a bad thing; some express scepticism as to whether it is happening at all. 'Globalization is globaloney' is the title of one polemic[1] which seeks to 'send up' the whole notion and the hype surrounding it.

This paper is concerned, not with globalization in general, nor 'the spread of global capitalism', but the spread of a particular kind of capitalism – stock-market-centred Anglo-Saxon capitalism. But first a few remarks about globalization in general, primarily to make the point that the variety of trends in different institutional spheres listed below have one thing in common. They all derive their appearance of inexorable inevitability from a single source. They are all in some sense a consequence of technological progress and the enormous cheapening of transport and communications. Herewith a non-exhaustive list.

1. The first is the internationalization of product markets, markets in goods and services – a product both of the communications revolution and of the steady efforts to reduce trade barriers. World trade as a ratio of GNP is a dicey figure since the one is a market value figure and the other a value added figure, but the differential growth rates of the two must surely mean that more and more of the world's production crosses frontiers between producer and consumer. The World Bank estimates those growth rates for the period 1970–92 at 3.0 per cent for world GNP and 4.9 per cent for merchandise trade – a nearly 2 per cent difference.[2]

2. The second is the internationalization of financial markets, which has gone further and faster than that of any other type of market and has come to dominate all others. At what one might call the sober, serious end are the markets in long-term capital, for example, Eurotunnel getting its finance from loans from Japanese banks, Sony floating bonds in Zurich, Daimler-Benz getting itself access to cheaper funds by seeking a quotation on the New York stock exchange. At the pure casino end are the 24-hour-a-day foreign exchange markets on which speculators shift money across the exchanges in volumes a hundred times those required by international trade. But both ends are joined in a seamless web; long-term investors cannot but be interested in the exchange value of the currency in which they take their interest or profits; traders do need some hedging of their foreign currency risks.

It is glaringly obvious that the volume of such hot money slopping around the world – several times the total reserves of national central banks – imposes severe restraints on the monetary and fiscal policies of national governments. In countries with relatively stable floating exchange rates it makes the control of inflation a universally dominant objective of monetary policy in order to keep it that way. Where unwise attempts are made to maintain a particular rate, the punishments 'the markets' deliver can be severe. Once the initial shock is absorbed the subsequent growth effects can be benign – as in Italy and Britain after 1992 and later in Mexico. It remains to be seen whether the same salutary effects of surgery are obtained when the domino effect spreads the disruption widely enough to have an appreciable effect on the world economy – as in Asia 1997–8.

It does have to be said, however, that improved cheap communications do not inevitably bring about these effects. They inevitably make controls over capital flows much harder to administer. But the reimposition of capital controls, though advocated by such mainstream economists as Dornbusch, never appears on the agendas of international meetings. Attempts to do so are weakened by the world-wide ideological dominance of free trade doctrine, and easily defeated by resolute opposition from the US, the nation with the biggest financial power and, arguably, the nation in which government policy is most completely deferential to the interests of the finance industry.

3. The third process is the growth of multinational firms. Again, this is an accelerating process. In the 1960s direct investment of firms in overseas countries was increasing twice as fast as world GNP; in the 1980s it grew four times as fast; an acceleration partly due to the removal of national controls over capital flows. The growth of the global corporation is partly a matter of cross-border ownership and control, partly of the internationalization of the

process of production itself. The Ford cars assembled in Valencia and Saarlouis contain parts supplied from all over Europe, North America and Japan. The growth of the multinational firm is intimately related to the growth of world trade, of course. According to some estimates, 40 per cent of America's foreign trade is intra-enterprise trade.

Even if one excludes corruption – the non-transparent transactions between policy makers, especially those in poor countries, and rich multinationals – the contribution of multinationals to the erosion of national sovereignty, the constraints they pose on the autonomy of national economic policy, are fairly obvious. Their ability to choose their investing locations gives rise to regime competition. Worker protection legislation? Curbs on dismissal? Privileges for trade unions? Thank you, we will go elsewhere. Though if you give us a ten year tax holiday...

It is a paradox that the more intense product market competition becomes and the more national governments are concerned about national 'competitiveness' – in Britain, for example, a key term of British political discourse only for the last 20 years – the more the growth of multinationals serves to blunt some of the industrial policy measures which might enhance that competitiveness.

In Europe, of course, there is the special factor of creeping political integration in the European Community. Industrial policy to foster British or Italian 'national champion' firms has had largely to give way to European policies to promote European firms. Europe-wide research consortia like Eureka promote co-operative arrangements for long-range, 'blue sky', so-called precompetitive research designed to help European firms beat the living daylights out of their competitors in the US and Japan. But what is a European firm? With IBM-Europe taking part in Eureka; IBM-US taking part in the American counterpart organization Sematech, and IBM-Japan taking part in Japan's research co-operatives, who is helping whom to defeat whom?

So far, the weight of such genuine multinationals in what are still predominantly clubs of domestically-based firms is not such as to reduce that effectiveness to zero, but it soon might. And we are not likely to get the United Nations Industrial Development Organization running a world industrial policy until we find one of those other planets to fight a star wars with.

4. Which brings me to the fourth process, which is the growth of transnational governance. This has both an economic and a political aspect. It is partly a matter of the steady accumulation of rules and conventions governing the operation of international markets and the creation of international bodies to monitor conformity to those rules – most recently, after some fifty years, the creation of the last of the originally proposed Bretton Woods organizations,

the World Trade Organization. It is partly also a matter of the global concentration of military power. The Pax Britannica of the nineteenth century was sustained outside Europe and North America by gunboat diplomacy. Under today's Pax Americana, the United States, with its far more extensive information-gathering machine of spy satellites and AWACs, can react far more quickly and deliver much more overwhelming force at any point on the globe. But at the same time, it is far more constrained than ever Britain was by international rules and procedures. America was careful to get the backing of Security Council resolutions at every stage of its action against Iraq during the Gulf War. It has become more unilateralist since then, but its failure for five years and more to topple Saddam Hussain, shows, not just, like its earlier defeat in Vietnam, the limitations on its power to deal with popular nationalisms, but also the extent to which the international system is no longer just a system of power balances, but also an embryonic world community in which it makes sense to talk, not just of power, but also of legitimate authority.

5. The fifth process is the emergent awareness of problems which are, in the nature of the case, global problems. Environmental hazards which affect neighbouring countries are not new: acid rain and radioactive fallout have long since been no respecters of frontiers. But global warming and the destruction of the ozone layer, the reduction of biodiversity through the disappearance of species, the use of the limited resources of the global commons – the oceans and space – and the overall Malthusian population/food balance, are obviously of a different order. What the citizens of any one country do can affect everybody else. The need, in such matters, for concerted action to establish universal common rules is increasingly accepted, even if the willingness to accept the constraints of such rules is not so apparent.

6. Sixth comes the growth of transnational ties which are neither economic nor political – cross-border communities, or organizations, of chess-players and astronomers, of Jehovah's Witnesses and gay rights activists, athletes and paedophiles. Some of these do form international organizations which are properly called *inter*national because their members see themselves as taking part as representatives of their nation; the Olympic Committee, for example, which promotes a benign form of international warfare. Some, however, are better called *trans*national because their members participate as indididuals; nationality is more or less irrelevant, though language is not. Economists are a good example; they do have organizations, the International Economic Association, for example, but rather more important for globalization is the sense in which economists, particularly those who read and write English, form something like a world community which provides

its members with their primary reference group; in many of the contexts in which they spend their daily lives, they are economists first and Americans or Brazilians or Japanese second.

One thing, paradoxically, that enhances the sense of membership in that community is that it is riven by factional disputes like any other community. A member of the neoclassical mainstream can feel more fellow-feeling towards another mainstreamer from a different country than towards a fellow-countryman given to institutionalism or evolutionism or other perverse forms of deviation. For all the hype surrounding it, the Internet is almost bound to accelerate the formation of these transnational professional quasi-communities.

One other community of particular importance for the global spread of American capitalism is what Huntington calls the exponents of 'Davos culture' – the managerial power elite who gather annually at the World Economic Forum in Switzerland to listen to the wisdom of, among others, some of the more prominent gurus of the economics profession's mainstream.

7. And perhaps that requires enumeration as a separate trend, since ideas move on paper as well as in people. The factionalism of quasi-communities like those of economists is an important symptom of the gradual establishment of world-wide orthodoxies which become the orthodoxies not only of the professionals themselves, but of wider intellectual communities the world over – orthodoxies of the world's chattering classes (to use a British expression which seems to me worth giving global currency). 'Democracy' is such a powerful part of that orthodoxy that even the most repressive military government is likely to claim that it is only preparing the way for eventual elections. That inflation control should be *the* dominant objective of economic policy, more important than growth or employment, is another example of an orthodoxy of growing strength. Over the last 20 years the annual G7 summit meetings have played an important role in crystallizing and diffusing such orthodoxies.

8. And finally there is the homogenization of popular cultures, the process which we used to call cocacolonization in recognition of the fact that although Milan fashions, pizzas and spaghetti bolognese, Scotch whisky and the Beatles may have a part, it is predominantly American popular culture which is becoming the world norm – even the pizzas are most often Chicago-style deep-dish pizzas. It is certainly American culture that the Taliban and other Islamic fundamentalists seek to keep out as the devil's corruption, and American films whose television time the French and the Canadians want to limit. Again satellite TV will add a new dimension to this process over the next decades.

GLOBALIZATION = CONVERGENCE?

Two things to note about these processes. First, they are not always mutually reinforcing. Sometimes they may operate contrarily; it is often obstacles to trade – tariffs or the threat of tariffs or dumping duties – which provide the motive for foreign direct investment. That was certainly the case when the Japanese automobile companies moved into the United States and Europe, for instance.

Secondly, one should not exaggerate their extent. Much of the talk about 'our global village' is fanciful rhetoric. Most so-called global firms still have a strong national colouring and a strong national base, and a board of directors of one predominant nationality. It is only a few firms, like the oil companies, and Swiss firms like Nestlé and ABB with a tiny home market, which have more than half their employees abroad.

Nevertheless these trends are by and large interacting and mutually reinforcing, and probably, if one could find proxy quantitative measures for them, accelerating. And they all threaten to erode the sovereignty of nation states; to diminish the control which governments can exercise over what goes on in their territories.

But, a more intriguing question, do they necessarily promote institutional convergence? How far do all these trends lead to a progressive homogenization of national – political and social as well as economic – institutions?

The subsidiary questions are almost as important. In so far as convergence *is* taking place, how far does it operate through the unwilled cumulative effect of the choices of private actors responding to market signals, and how far through government action? How much of the government action involved is unilateral and designed to promote the conditions for economic advancement, and how much through international agreement designed for mutual advantage?

There is also the personal political question. When there really is an alternative to global conformity, what political criteria – i.e. value criteria, ethical, moral criteria – should one adopt for judging how far the homogenization process should be allowed to go; how much should one seek to preserve national distinctiveness? What are the criteria which would be adopted, say, by a *persona per bene*, neither a rabid nationalist nor a rootless cosmopolitan, neither a free trade demagogue nor a total believer in consumer sovereignty, nor yet an introverted protectionist?

JAPAN'S DISTINCTIVE FORM OF CAPITALISM

Such questions have a particular relevance to Japan, whose economic organization clearly differs from that of the US or the UK. In 1990, one might have said without much fear of contradiction, that it was different and more successful in world market competition. But much has changed in seven years. In 1997 the dominant view – shared, indeed, by the majority of articulate Japanese – seems to be that it is distinctive and less successful.

Whether the loss of overall competitive advantage is temporary or long-lasting; whether, if long-lasting; the solution is to adopt American patterns; or whether, even if it is less successful, distinctively Japanese structures and institutions are worth preserving for their own sake because of their social – or moral – superiority, are matters of much debate in contemporary Japan.

And cross-cutting these differences about the desirability or otherwise of change, is a difference about the feasibility of not changing. Can Japan, if it should wish to, really manage to stay different, in a world dominated by the Anglo-Saxon form of capitalism?

Before sampling that debate, a brief summary of the major characteristics which make the Japanese form of capitalism distinctive from that of the UK and the US – to which one might add, to offer justification for the general label 'Anglo-Saxon' – Canada, Australia and New Zealand.[3]

1. The major corporations are managed, not primarily in the interests of share-holders, nor of the managers who run them, but primarily for the benefit of those who have been, as it were, admitted to membership of the firm community – its regular employees.

- Dividends are treated as a fixed charge, and have rarely in recent decades, exceeded 1 per cent of current share prices.
- Shareholder pressure is minimized by greater use of debt and equity cross-holdings, which eliminate the fear of takeovers.
- Boards of directors are made up of senior managers who, in the words of one of the most perceptive of studies of comparative corporate governance, are the products of 'the slow slog and patient development of a business career' in which they become infused with the company's culture.[4] They see themselves not as servants of shareholders, but as elders of the firm community, with responsiblity for its reputation and its long-term future as well as its current profits. Their salaries are only modestly higher than those of their middle-manager juniors.
- 'Lifetime employment' for the regular labour force: i.e., only in dire emer-

gencies will employees be made redundant, though they may be asked to accept well-compensated early retirement or transfer to other firms.

- For both managers and blue collar workers there is a 'rate for the person' wage system, not a 'rate for the job'. Pay is on seniority-plus-merit incremental scales, only loosely connected to promotion through job functions. There is a reliance on social and long-term career motivation, not objective-measurement pay-performance links.
- There are enterprise unions (including young university graduates, future top managers). Wage bargaining is centred on 'what the company can afford given investment needs'.

To illustrate in concrete terms what some of these characteristics mean, Japan Steel, one of Japan's largest companies, has a Board of Directors of 50 men. Only one of the 50 has not spent the whole of his business career in the company – the former President of the Japan Development Bank who recently became the Chairman of the Audit Committee in his mid-seventies – the chief guarantor to the outside world of the honesty of the company's accounts. All the other 49 were appointed to the Board between the ages of 52 and 56, after a career in which they gradually rose through the management ranks, but a little bit faster than their contemporaries. One exception is the man who became a director at the age of 51, a real high flyer who is now the company's president. Every one of these appointments to the Board was made in June of an odd-numbered year, the time for a general reshuffle of all managerial posts in the company.

What difference does it make that the directors see themselves as elders of a community of employees, rather than (as Japanese law actually defines them) agents of shareholder principals? A big difference. For the last seven years the economy has been stagnating in recession. Yet nobody in Japan Steel has simply been dismissed. There have been voluntary retirement schemes, which doubtless involved occasionally unwelcome persuasion. And, until recently some 15 000 workers, still on Japan Steel's payroll, were temporarily or semi-permanently 'leased out' to other firms, at some cost to Japan Steel, which received in 'rental' less than it was paying out in wages. Meanwhile a lot of the board's energies have been devoted to attempts at diversification aimed primarily at giving employment to surplus employees – into computer software production, silicon wafer production or tourism using abandoned steel mill sites.

It may be worthwhile to put the point about the motivations of Japanese top managers in terms of the Brazilian debate about the reform of federal administration. According to an extremely interesting paper by the Minister on his concept of the social-liberal state,[5] at the core of his plans for the creation of 'agencies' is a perceived contrast between the bureaucratic and the managerial – perhaps better described as market-managerial – form of organization. Put starkly, in ideal-type terms, it goes as follows. Bureaucracies recruit people at the start of their careers through a rigorous competitive selection process. They have tenure and can be dislodged only for serious misdeeds. Their career progress is constrained by seniority, but how far and how fast they go is determined by their performance. Pay is determined only by seniority and functional rank, and the incremental scales are seamless; the people at the top get only a little more than those just below the top and so on down. Within what is often called 'the service', people are expected to serve. That is to say the organization trusts in their wanting to do a good job. Although there *are* self-interest incentives – getting faster promotion – a dominant motive for doing good work is expected to be a sense of responsibility to the society which employs one, backed by pride in one's membership of an elite. If that is further supported by the pleasure of exercising power or of solving problems, so be it, but in such organizations' own definitions of their ethos, it is usually the responsibility to respond to society's trust that is stressed.

In the managerial system, by contrast, the employment contract is a job contract, not a career contract, or, if one likes to put it that way, it is a market contract rather than a membership contract. The organization may use the external labour market to fill posts, though it often makes every effort to fill vacant posts internally; however, this is still, usually, by open internal competition. Wages and salaries are a function of the positions occupied; the rate for the job is the dominant principle. Incentives for high-quality performance are provided; usually, in order to eliminate frictions which might be caused by invidious subjective judgements of merit, pay or bonuses are tied to some sort of objective indicators – output, profits or movements of the share price. People do not have to be trusted to be loyal or to identify with the organization and its future; they just have to have a sense of responsibility to fulfil their contracts. Beyond that, self-interest should be sufficient to secure efficient performance.

The Brazilian plan, as I understand it, proposes to confine the bureaucratic system to the diplomatic corps, financial administration and general planning. Everything else – education and health as well as driving licences and prisons – will be run by executive agencies, mostly not for profit, on the managerial rather than the bureaucratic system, with the elite tenured self-motivated bureaucratic planners setting the targets for each agency – both financial and output – by which the monetary incentives for good work are created.

The point of this digression is this: the same 'bureaucratic' system of career structuring, the same pattern of 'organizational loyalty' motivation – which in Brazil is thought to be likely to 'work' only for a few hundred core civil servants – is in Japan the dominant pattern, not only of the whole government bureaucracy, but of the whole of private sector management as well.

2. Contrary to neo-liberal doctrine, the state is believed to have a positive and varied role to play in the economy: (a) promoting economic growth by curing the imperfections of the market, coordinating investment plans, (marginal) priority allocation of credit, etc.; (b) arbitrating between producer and consumer interests (permitting a refinery industry cartel in return for a particular socially desirable price structure for its various products); (c) securing distributional equity (e.g. subsidizing declining industries like steel or textiles so that they can be run down with minimal social dislocation, or making the efficient, highly capitalized oligopoly whisky producers stick to their whisky and not invade the market of the small-firm producers of traditional sake rice wine).

3. Also reducing the importance of competitive markets, particularly in intermediate goods, is the predominance of relational contracting. Supplier-customer relationships tend to be stable over time, and to involve extra-contractual obligations which lead to an exchange of not precisely costed services only roughly balanced out over the long term.

4. As compared with the Anglo-Saxon economies, the financial sector dominates – constrains the activity of – the industrial and commercial sector to a much lesser degree; within that financial sector, impersonal markets – the stock market, bond market, insurance market and their derivatives – are less important than relational transactions between lenders and borrowers who acknowledge only implicitly contractual relations with each other.

One way of summarily characterizing many of these features is to say that there is a general acceptance of, and a general willingness to assume, moral obligations over and above those to which one is contractually bound. This applies to relationships between shareholding firms and the firms whose shares they hold, to trading relationships between, say, parts suppliers and automobile assemblers, to the relationships between managers and their subordinate employees, and to the quasi-co-operative relationships among competitors within Japan's powerful industry associations.

This is not the place to go deeply into the question whether or not there is an alternative – what Michel Albert dubbed the Rhenish[6] – form of capitalism of which both Germany and Japan are examples, but it is worth noting in passing, that this same characteristic – the acceptance of obligations over and above those imposed by contract to a far greater degree than in the Anglo-Saxon economies – is apparent in the German economy too. There are, to be sure, important differences. The obligations accepted in Japan are, to put it a bit pompously, particularistic – obligations towards particular individuals and groups; those in Germany are seen as more universalistic, duties to the public at large. The German firm, it is often said, is seen as a public institution, rather like a hospital or a school. Secondly, the obligations involved in the German system are to a much greater extent enshrined in law – the obligation to belong to the Chamber of Commerce and to take part in the apprenticeship training system, for instance, and, most important, the system of co-determination which gives workers seats on supervisory boards and works councils. In Japan on the other hand, the whole system is almost completely informal. The Commercial Code is almost entirely Anglo-Saxon in the way it enshrines the principle of shareholder sovereignty, and only a certain amount of case law supports the informal system as it actually exists.

Thirdly, the German system is more overtly adversarial, preserving the class relations of traditional capitalism in the national-level wage bargaining system for instance. Co-determination is socially defined as a means of bringing about management by consensus between shareholder representatives and worker representatives, who are seen as having interests which, though partly coinciding, are also partly at variance. In practice, however, in many of the medium-sized *Mittelstand* firms, particulary those with predominant family ownership, the works council does take on something of the character of the management-union consultation committees in Japanese firms. That is to say, they act less as bargaining forums for 'the two sides of industry' as the British put it, and more as something like community councils – councils of the enterprise community – on the assumption that managers and workers have far more in common than that which divides them. And there is the same preference in Germany, as in Japan, for long-term commitment to a single firm. The statistics for the average length of time people have been in the same job look very much alike in the two countries.

SYSTEM FRAGILITY

Either way, both Germany and Japan are societies in which the individual pursuit of self-interest in free markets is constrained by a variety of obligations which go beyond either the restrictions of law or of formal contracts. Such systems, depending as they do on convention, lacking the reinforcing coercion of the law, have a certain fragility. They are liable to be disrupted by what the games theorists call 'defectors'. People who decide to ignore conventional obligations can often make considerable short-term profits. This example was given recently by a Japanese economist: the American junk bond operator T. Boone Pickens some years ago made a bid for a Japanese firm called Koito. His attempts to buy all the available Koito shares raised the price of those shares on the Tokyo stock exchange by a factor of 10. Sixty per cent or more of the firm's shares were in the hands of other firms with whom Koito did business – Koito's 'stable shareholders' in the Japanese phrase. Any one of them could have sold its Koito shares and made a handsome profit. Yet none of them did. There were no defectors. One can plausibly explain their choice in two ways: as the product of an in-built moral sense of obligation, or as a result of their calculation that by selling they would lose their reputation as people and as companies that can be trusted, and this loss of reputation would involve long-term losses which outweighed the short-term gains. Or it could be interpreted as an unanalysable mixture of the two. The fact remains that there is a big difference between a society in which shareholding generates commitments which one ignores at one's peril, and a society in which failing to take advantage of all profitable opportunities is seen as a sign of incompetence.

When only a few mavericks have an incentive to defect, systems of normative rules can maintain their viability. When defectors grow in number they create the possibility of changing the rules of the system. It is arguable that the forces of globalization are such that, in both Japan and Germany, defectors are growing in number, ceasing to be defectors, and claiming instead to be the bearers of a better theory and a better ideology. The theory is that of neoclassical economics, that allocative efficiency is the most important sort of efficiency and that free markets, minimal commitments and maximal flexibility is a better recipe for national competitiveness than maintaining a system of mutual trust and co-operation. The ideology is partly the nationalism which the talk of competitiveness implies. It is also partly – call it Darwinian if you want to be rude, meritocratic if you wish to be kind – about the market as an impersonal arbiter which awards everyone his just deserts. And thirdly, it is partly about the nature of 'true' capitalism, the system which, in Japan at least, is actually enshrined in its legal system, since the form of the business corporation is prescribed by Japan's Commercial Code. Its definition of the duties of directors, for example, is not so very different from that in Britain and the United States.

THE JAPANESE DEBATE: NECESSITY AND DESIRABILITY OF CHANGE

The potential for defectors to gain legitimacy increases when there is a sense of crisis, and if the scale of the rhetoric frequently employed in current Japanese economic debates is a good indicator, in the seventh year of recession that sense of crisis is certainly there.

The following distillation of the arguments deployed derives from two reports of one of the three major businessmen's associations (which has individual, rather than enterprise membership), the Japan Association of Corporate Executives,[7] and the report of the Deregulation Subcommittee of the Administrative Reform Commission.[8]

There are two main strands to the argument: the argument from necessity under the imperative of intensified world competition and the argument from value premises, the argument for what its proponents consider to be progress.

To take the necessity argument first: hitherto, Japan was able to achieve a remarkable rate of economic growth by virtue of the peculiarly Japanese features of its economy – the lifetime employment system, the bureaucratic, seniority-constrained pay and promotion system, company loyalty, cheap capital that stayed at home and long-standing ties between suppliers and customers. But now the system has changed.

First, the overvalued yen and high wage costs mean that Japan must go global. Its new investment has to be overseas, which means that technological change will simply displace Japanese workers, not give them new tools to work with.

Secondly, the intensification of competition in product markets means that margins are cut back; moreover, the bursting of the asset bubble and the eating up of reserves during the prolonged recession, has meant that firms can no longer find the resources that enable them to carry surplus employees during a downturn; lifetime employment must come to an end.

Thirdly, until recently, firms could grow by catch-up; importing technology produced elsewhere. Now they have caught up; they are at the frontiers, and need not just diligent and loyal employees, they need innovative and creative employees, and they must reward them to keep them; they cannot keep the old system of respecting seniority, and if that means that the wage gap between the talented creative individual and the mere diligent plodder grows, so be it. That cannot be helped; they cannot afford the luxury of an anti-competitive egalitarianism.

Fourthly, the liberalization of capital markets means that Japanese firms have got to compete for capital. Moreover, the population is ageing; life insurance companies and pension schemes are under increasing pressure to earn high returns. The era of cheap capital and low dividends, is over. Nobody buys shares in the expectation of long-run capital gains any more. Return on equity must be made a major criterion of manager performance. Lifetime employment must go if necessary.

Fifthly, Japanese firms competing internationally are hampered by over-regulation. Costs are inflated due to inefficiencies in the non-tradeables sector

– power generation, transport and services. These inefficiencies are attributable to a mass of regulation designed to suppress competition, and the 'convoy system' maintaining cartel-like arrangements – such as the segmentation of the drinks industry, keeping the big-capital whisky firms from invading the markets of the local sake producers.

The value arguments are the standard ones of neo-liberalism backed by neo-classical economics:

- Efficiency is the dominant maximand.
- Giving incentives for efficiency means inequality; so be it.
- Individual self-fulfilment is more important than fraternity/social solidarity; hence equality of opportunity should be the goal, not equality of outcomes.
- Efficiency is best promoted by competition, both domestic and international, both inter-firm and inter-personal.
- Competition cannot be 'excessive' (the loss of sunk capital is always recouped by subsequent efficiency gains) except in the sense that it leads to monopoly which kills competition – which must be prevented.
- Consumer sovereignty is the economic counterpart of political democracy and should be the touchstone of all regulatory policy.
- The expansion of individual choice is as important in the labour market as in consumption; careers should be freed from organizational entanglements.

GLOBAL REINFORCERS

The diffusion in Japan of the ideology of American free-market capitalism and individualistic competition is mediated partly by the spread, through translations and local popularizations, of American management literature. There could well be more books in Japanese with titles including the words 'restructuring' or 're-engineering' than in English. But it is also partly due to flows of people. Large numbers of junior Japanese managers have been sent by their firms to spend a couple of years at American business schools – a flow considerably increased since yen revaluation reduced the costs of doing so. Once, Japanese managers went to American business schools to learn how the American mind ticked, in order to cope better in dealing with Americans in world markets. Now the Japanese manager is more likely to come back brainwashed and convinced of the need for Japanese firms to become as efficient as their American rivals. The influence of these managers – large Japanese corporations now count their MBAs in their hundreds rather than their tens – is reinforced by the growing influence in the media, in business magazines and television commentaries, of economists who acquired their PhD in American graduate schools and are 'true believer' adherents of the free-market-competition-is-the-only-route-to-efficiency doctrines of neoclassical economics.

And nothing serves more effectively to reinforce the belief that 'America has it better' than the contrast between the buoyant American economy and the stagnation which has followed the bursting of Japan's asset price bubble. The brash confidence of late 1980s Japan had been markedly attenuated by the five years of stagnation which followed the crash. By the summer of 1998, when it seemed that nothing could stop the economy from spiralling down into deep recession, it had entirely evaporated.

TOWARDS THE 'SHAREHOLDER SOVEREIGNTY' FIRM

Some of the institutional changes in the last seven years since the Structural Impediments talks have been designed to bring the Japanese financial system closer to American norms. New regulations to curb insider trading have had as their intention the 'rehabilitation' of the stock market, an attempt to clean up its image as a den of gambler cheats which prevented it having the veneer of gentlemanly respectability which history had conferred on London and Wall Street. This was clearly a contribution to the reassertion of shareholder power. This was followed up in 1997 by an onslaught on the major stockbroking firms' links with *yakuza* gangsters, leading to wholesale dismissals and the imprisonment of senior managers of Nomura, Yamaichi, etc. The decision to tackle publicly what has long been widely believed to be a pervasive feature of Japan's financial system is another part of the 'image clean-up' strategy, made urgent by the strong threat from Singapore and Hong Kong to Tokyo's supremacy as Asia's number one financial centre. It seems, too, that this determination to be Asia's leading financial centre – a world market, not a mere 'local market' like Frankfurt as one writer puts it[9] – is the main motive for the wholesale liberalization of financial markets begun in 1998 and planned to end in the year 2000. This nationalist drive – to be number one, to have Asia's, if not the world's dominant stock market – seems to be more important in the 'big bang' decision than any belief that Japan will benefit materially either from the enhanced international competitive power of its own banks, stockbrokers and insurance companies, or from spin-off from the financial business conducted in Tokyo by foreigners.

A second measure – also springing directly from negotiations with the United States, was legislation which makes it much simpler and cheaper for shareholders to sue Boards of Directors for losses caused by negligently inept decisions. Nobody even discussed taking the 'stakeholder' – employee sovereignty – reality seriously and giving enterprise unions similar facilities.

Thirdly, in June 1997, an amendment of company law permitted the payment of directors in part in stock options – which had been legalized some years earlier for the special class of high-risk venture start-ups – to be generalized to all firms. This was a clear attempt to give to directors a sense that they are not so much elders of the employee community as agents of their shareholder principals.

DEFENCE?

To be sure, there is some evidence of an articulate effort to buck the dominant trend and preserve the distinctiveness of the Japanese system. One recent expression is a highly polemical book denouncing those who would accept the United States as the image of Japan's future, by a senior official of Japan's Ministry of Finance. It begins, significantly, with an account of his visit, on a day stolen from trade negotiations in Washington, to the American family with whom he had stayed as a 17-year-old high school student. The school in which he had spent a happy and peaceful year was in the centre of what had now become a no-go area, riddled with gun-toting drug pushers.[10] The irony is that this same official was one of the main architects of the financial liberalization, big bang plan. He claims to be confident that 'Japan can handle it'; Japanese firms can be helped to improve their international competition without the essentials of the system being put in jeopardy.[11]

And yet, it is surprising how little opposition the reformers (proponents of steps which amount to an edging towards the shareholder-sovereign firm on the Anglo-Saxon model) actually arouse. The introduction of stock options is a case in point. There was no battle. A trawl through the major economic newspaper turned up only one clear statement of dissent. The former president, subsequently chairman, of a steel firm described how his firm had been on the verge of bankruptcy but successfully turned around:[12]

> We got back into profit. But that was by group effort. Supposing that my role as flag-waver in the process had been seen as important and I'd been given stock options and exercised them and made a lot of money, I don't think I would have felt too happy about that. And I don't think my colleagues, in the bottom of their hearts, would have accepted the justice of it. In individualistic societies like America and Europe stock option systems may fit in very well, but I really wonder about their suitability for Japan.

It is very different, he goes on, from

> the egalitarian approach to human relations of the Japanese firm. As it is commonly observed, the difference in pay between managers and other employees is far smaller in Japan than in America. And both managers and workers agree that this should be so. A factory director – a member of the Board usually – wears the same overalls and eats in the same canteen as the shopfloor workers and that is taken for granted.
>
> When I read in the newspapers about CEOs in America who lay off large numbers of workers in a restructuring and earn themselves large sums of money from their stock options as a result, I ask myself how that can be psychologically possible. Japanese managers would have given up a part of their salary before they would get to involuntary lay-offs. My own salary at the moment is subject to a cut of ten percent plus. This is not hypocrisy. The saying that sums it up – 'Scarcity is tolerable; inequality is not.' – is a deeply rooted part of the Japanese ethic.
>
> Group-orientation, group-consciousness, backed by this egalitarian ethic, is one of the important factors which have made Japan's growth possible. And in itself is not by any means a bad thing. It is true that the waves of global standards are lapping at the shores of Japan, and we have to appreciate that and deal with that and adapt. That I accept. But should we not also try to preserve those aspects of which we can be proud. People in leadership positions have a duty to look closely at the real facts.

But even his opposition to the innovation was muted. He starts off by saying that he understands that the stock option system has 'already been introduced in the advanced countries of America and Europe' (the taken-for-granted nature of the America-as-model assumption again) and 'if it is necessary to revitalise the economy then the more options there are the better'. He excuses himself for feeling uncomfortable on the grounds that he is only 'an old steel man, drenched in the culture of an historic industry', and old men 'of my generation of Japanese simply cannot free themselves of the feeling that "Fishing for people with the bait of money" is just an ignoble thing to do. That may be one reason why I would drag my feet on this issue.'

He is probably right about the importance of generational change. He and his ilk are men who have vivid memories of the days just after the war when they were struggling to rebuild the economy and they had just as big holes in their shoes and just as shabby clothes as the shopfloor workers with whom they worked shoulder to shoulder. If it is instinctive fellow-feeling and shared hardship that makes for social solidarity and a sense of benevolent responsibility, then they have it. But the young economists on the government committees, and all the MBAs in middle management, have been brought up in affluence. Their smooth career paths have given them no such background of shared experience with those on the receiving end of their advice or their orders – the likely losers from what they propose. For the last twenty years an increasing proportion of them have been siphoned off at the age of 11 into the élite private secondary schools and have no more contact with their less well-off country-men than an Etonian has with his. They will not be quoting proverbs about fishing for men with money.

CONVERGENCE?

If one were to judge only from the debates in the Japanese press, or the reports on corporate governance produced in turn by the major business organizations, one would guess that the eventual outcome is clear. The three-pronged effects of (i) necessity arising from the exigencies of competition in product and finan-cial markets, (ii) direct government-to-government pressures from trading partners and (iii) the 'soft' ideological power of the cultural hegemon, look set to bring about Japan's surrender to the model of Anglo-Saxon capitalism with less resistance than when it surrendered to American armies.

And yet one cannot be sure. If one looks at what Japanese firms have actu-ally done, rather than at what Japanese businessmen say, the shift in institu-tional practices is not all that great – in spite of the sense of crisis brought on by five years of low growth. The pattern of cross-shareholding seems to have held up. Dividend levels have not markedly changed. Some suppliers have taken hard knocks, but where parent firms have shifted production abroad, they have often taken their suppliers with them, and the conventions of supply relations seem little changed. No major firm has embarked on the path of non-negotiable redundancies; wage and salary structures and promotion criteria in most firms have seen only marginal shifts towards merit in the merit/seniority mix.

One thing does, however, seem clear from Japan's modern history. While the Japanese feel more comfortable with their own less ruthlessly competitive and relatively egalitarian economy, and may even believe it to be morally supe-rior, if it does become clear that it involves permanently lower growth rates, the nationalist drive to keep up can provide the momentum for large-scale change.

And about the prospects of future growth rates, there are arguments to counter the superficial triumphalism of the *Wall Street Journal*, but they belong to a different paper.

NOTES

1   S. Hanke, in *Forbes Magazine*, **157**, (i), 1996, p. 56.
2   *World Development Report 1994*, New York: Oxford University Press. The 1995 development report reflects second thoughts on the 1970s, revising the growth figure from 3.4 to 3.6 per cent. It also abandons ambitions to calculate an overall growth figure for merchandise trade.
3   For a more elaborate characterization, see my 'The Distinctiveness of Japan', in C. Crouch and W. Streeck (eds), *Political Economy of Modern Capitalism: Mapping Convergence and Diversity*, London: Sage, 1997.
4   Jonathan Charkham, *Keeping Good Company*, Oxford, OUP, 1995, p. 323.
5   Luiz Carlos Bresser Pereira, *Managerial Reform in Brazil's Public Administration*. Paper presented to the Congress of the International Political Science Association, Seoul, August 1997.
6   In his book *Capitalism contre Capitalisme*, Paris: Editions du seuil, 1991, translated as *Capitalism versus Capitalism*, New York: Four Walls Eight Windows, 1993.
7   *Shijo-shugi sengen: 21-seiki e no akushon-puroguram* (A Marketist manifesto: An action programme for the 21st century), January 1997, and *Sengo Nihon Shisutemu no Sokessan: Ima koso, waga kuni zaisei no arata na gurando dezain o egakiageyo* (Drawing a line under the post-war Japanese system: now is the time for a grand design), April 1997. The former is available in English translation under the title *Manifesto for a Market-Oriented Economy* (which does not capture the 'ism' of the Japanese original). The second is a report of the Assocation's Public Finance and Taxation Committee, and is signed by its 76 members under the Chairmanship of a respected retired insurance company executive.
8   Gyosei-kaikaku Iinkai, Kisei-kanwa shoiinkai (Administrative Reform Commitee, Deregulation Sub-committee), *Soi de tsukuru arata na Nihon (Creativity to build a new Japan)*, 5 December 1996.
9   Madamoto Yashiro, *Yomigaere Nihon Kigyo* (How to give new life to Japanese firms), Tokyo, Nihon Keizai, 1997.
10 *Sakakibara Eisuke, Shimpo-shugi kara no ketsubetsu* (Farewell to progressivism), Tokyo, Yomiuri-shimbunsha.
11 See the conversation with Sakakibara Eisuke in R. Dore, *Nihon o Tou: Nihon ni tou* (Asking Japan: Asking about Japan), Tokyo Chikuma Shobo, 1997.
12 Suzuki Yoshio of Godo Seitetsu, writing in the *Nihon Keizai Shimbun*, 17 July 1997.

7. Gestalt shift: from 'miracle' to 'cronyism' in the Asian crisis

Robert Wade[1]

Was the Asian crisis caused by the build-up of vulnerabilities in the real economy, with panicky investor pull-out as merely the trigger or messenger of a necessary market correction? Or was it caused largely by the normal workings of under-regulated national and international financial markets, the panicky pull-out itself being a prime cause? The short answer is, some of both. The paper describes the double helix-like interaction of real and financial causes. It then outlines a strategy of escape from crisis, including the reintroduction of capital controls and creation of an Asia Fund.

Explanations are about the only thing not in short supply in the Asian crisis. It would be entertaining to plot them on a matrix, with 'actors' on one axis and 'actions' on the other. Even a small sampling has to include:

- The governments of the crisis-affected countries, individually and collectively (corruption, collusion, nepotism, distorted markets, insufficient democracy, excessive democracy, 'crony capitalism', fixed exchange rate regimes, implicit government guarantees to banks and big companies in their foreign borrowing, premature capital account liberalization, lack of regional co-operation).
- Foreign banks (sloppy credit risk analysis, excessive confidence in currency pegs, moral hazard behaviour, Panglossian values, panic).
- Domestic banks (ditto).
- Investors, domestic and foreign (ditto).
- Domestic firms (ditto, plus occult accounting, family control).
- The IMF (pressure for premature financial liberalization, moral hazard, bailout conditionality of excessive austerity and excessive emphasis on structural reforms.
- The US Treasury (pressure for premature financial liberalization, insufficient contribution to bailout funds).

- The Japanese government (insufficient demand stimulus at home, insufficient contribution to bailout funds abroad).
- The Japanese economy (two-thirds of the Asian economy, in its seventh year of stagnation and getting worse).
- 'Globalization', with its free floating responsibility.

This rich diversity reflects, in part, participants' attempts to shift the blame on to others. The main external actors blame national actors, governments blame outsiders and national populations blame everyone but themselves. It also reflects the fact that there is not one Asian crisis, but several countries with different kinds of troubles and backgrounds to which different explanations may apply.

Beyond this, the diversity reflects deeper differences in beliefs about rationality and markets. Those whose wider world view emphasizes rationality, self-adjusting markets and market failure as exceptional except when governments introduce distortions, see the Asian crisis as the result of rational calculations by rational actors in a situation of market-distorting government interventions. Those whose world view stresses nonrationality (or a different kind of rationality than that assumed by neoclassical theory), routine failure of well-working markets, and the need for government interventions to modify market outcomes, see it as the result of nonrational calculations in under-regulated markets.

The debate about the causes has been less a debate than paradigms ('parrot-times') talking past each other. Some hard testing is needed. The problem is that even in one country several different explanations may contain truth and even reinforce each other. But even allowing for country and time differences, 'There are not eighteen good reasons for anything', as George Stigler once said (Lipton, 1998). This paper aims, modestly, not at the necessary hypothesis formulation and testing but at an interpretative account. It gives prominence to the nonrational elements as an offset to the tendency of economists to be much more accepting of stories based on the assumption of rational calculation simply because they are more congruent with neoclassical theory. And unlike other accounts, it encompasses both the crisis *and* the prolonged prior success.

SCALE OF THE CRISIS

Exchange rates and stock prices in East and Southeast Asia changed between June 1997 and late March 1998. The three countries identified as the worst affected – South Korea, Thailand and Indonesia – have had the biggest falls in exchange rates, ranging from 36 per cent to 72 per cent. However, Malaysia and the Philippines, generally regarded as having escaped lightly, have had exchange rate declines of not much less than Thailand and Korea. Adding the fall in the stock market to the fall in the exchange rate to get a broader measure of impact, we have to put Malaysia with the group of worst affected countries, with the Philippines just behind. In short, the conventional understanding that only Korea, Thailand and Indonesia have been badly affected is not true by these measures – Malaysia and the Philippines have been hurt almost as much. Even Japan, Hong Kong and Singapore have taken substantial hits. Taiwan and China look to be least affected.

As of July 1998 it is clear that, except perhaps in the case of Korea, the crisis was not yet in the clearing-up-after-the-storm stage. After a respite in early 1998, a second great wave of capital outflow occurred in May and June, and forecasters resumed chasing the economies downhill. A recent report in the *South China Morning Post* began, 'A cocktail of negative factors is fast unravelling Asian stock markets' first-quarter gains and more losses may be in store as further evidence emerges about the parlous condition of the region's economies' (Lloyd-Smith, 1998). It is not an exaggeration to liken the Asian crisis to the Great Depression of the 1930s in terms of the scale of the falls in output and consumption and the increase in poverty and insecurity. Countries have been pushed back down the hierarchy of world income to where they were ten years ago and more.[2] Meanwhile the international lenders have escaped with at most small losses, disproving once again the adage, 'If you owe the bank $100 000 you have a problem, if you owe the bank $1 billion the bank has a problem'.

THE HIGH DEBT: DEBT DEFLATION STORY

Most commentators agree that the sharp pull-out of funds by investors across the region (domestic as well as foreign investors) was the trigger, and that the pull-out was panicky. The whipsaw movement from capital inflows to capital outflows was on a scale that could not but tear apart the social fabric of countries subjected to it, especially where political structures are only weakly institutionalized. Net private flows to or from the five Asian economies (the ASEAN four plus South Korea) were plus $93 billion in 1996, turning to minus $12 billion in 1997. The swing in one year of $105 billion (with most of the outflow concentrated in the last quarter of 1997) equals 11 per cent of the combined GDP of the five countries. Asia's experience was worse even than Latin America's in the 1980s. The swing between 1981 inflows and 1982 outflows in the three biggest debtors (Brazil, Mexico, Argentina) amounted to 8 per cent of their combined GDP.

An interpretative account has to explain why the inflows were so big, why the outflows were so big and why the contraction of economic activity has continued to be so sharp. It has to link the banking crisis, the currency crisis and the corporate crisis, and the politics with the economics, without becoming so luxuriant as to be obscure.

The Bank-Based High Debt Model

Thanks to relatively equal income distribution, the large majority of Asian households are net savers (in contrast to Latin America). They deposit much of their savings in banks. Banks have to lend, but not to households and not to governments, which are not sizeable net borrowers. Banks have lent largely to firms seeking to borrow in order to invest.

Large Asian firms have tended to finance a large proportion of their investment from bank borrowings, and to carry large amounts of debt relative to equity compared to Western or Latin American firms.[3] High debt/equity ratios allowed them to invest much more than through retained earnings or equity finance alone, and high corporate investment helped to propel the region's fast economic development over several decades.

Corporate sectors with high levels of debt are vulnerable to shocks that cause a fall in cash flow or an increase in fixed payment obligations – systemic shocks such as a fall in aggregate demand, a rise in interest rates, or devaluation of the currency (when part of the debt is foreign) (Wade and Veneroso, 1998).

This bank-based system of financial intermediation encourages close relations between bankers and corporate managers, and is sometimes called 'relationship' banking. The system often includes government incentives to lend to particular sectors or functions. And it includes, importantly, a closed or partially closed capital account, such that financial capital cannot move freely in and out of the country. Local citizens and foreign residents are not permitted to hold accounts with commercial banks abroad; banks are not allowed to extend loans in foreign currencies in the domestic market; non-bank private corporations are not allowed to borrow abroad; foreigners cannot own shares listed by national companies on domestic stock markets; national companies cannot sell securities on international stock and bond markets; and foreign banks are restricted in the domestic market. This apparatus buffers highly leveraged corporate sectors from systemic shocks and from the prudential limits of Western banks, allowing them to sustain levels of investment well above what the risk preferences of equity holders would allow. Very high domestic savings permit the investment to be financed domestically.

At its most fully developed the bank-based high debt model becomes the developmental state. The developmental state was most fully developed in Japan (1955–73), Korea (1961–95) and Taiwan (1955–continuing) (Wade, 1990, chapters 10–11). Amidst the current talk of the death throes of Asian crony capitalism, it is worth recalling that Japan, Korea and Taiwan are the most successful non-city-state developing countries since the Second World War. No other countries have achieved such big gains in the average real wage or the average real wage of the bottom 25 per cent. No other countries have risen so far in their technological capacity. Japan takes out more patents in the US than any other country bar the US itself. In recent years, Taiwan has taken out the 6th largest number, Korea the 7th largest, ahead of the middle-ranking OECD countries like Italy, Ireland, Netherlands, Scandanavia (Patel and Pavitt, 1994, pp. 759–87; Wade, 1996a). No other developing countries come even close. (But the environmental costs of the model have been very high.)

Singapore and Malaysia are closest to developmental states in Southeast Asia; Indonesia is the furthest.

Financial Liberalization

Asian governments, encouraged by the IMF and the World Bank as well as by national business élites, liberalized their financial systems through the 1990s, including the external capital account.[4] Liberalization permitted domestic agents to raise finance on foreign markets and gave foreign agents access to the domestic financial market. Hence locals could open foreign bank accounts; banks could extend credit in foreign currencies in the domestic markets; non-bank financial institutions and private corporations could borrow abroad; foreigners could own shares listed by national companies on domestic stock markets; foreign banks could enjoy wider freedom of entry into the domestic banking sector; and offshore banks could borrow abroad and lend domestically (Islam, 1998). All this took place in the context of a more-or-less fixed nominal exchange rate regime, in which the domestic currency was either fixed to the US dollar or moved in close correspondence with it.

The liberalization of capital movements removed the capacity for governments to coordinate foreign private borrowing. Those who demanded financial liberalization acknowledged the need for *pari passu* strengthening of bank regulation and supervision, but did not constrain their push for liberalization by the pace of regulatory strengthening on the ground.

In Korea, the Kim Young Sam government of 1993 sharply accelerated the process of financial liberalization, including, for the first time, substantially opening the capital account. This was done to meet the conditions for joining the OECD, a primary policy goal of the Kim government. It also happened because the big private firms had by this time high enough credit ratings in international financial markets for them to borrow easily on their own account, and they stopped wanting government support (Chang, Park and Yoo, 1998).

As part of the liberalization, the government licensed nine new merchant banks in 1994 and 15 more in July 1996, in addition to the six that existed before the 1993 liberalization. These inexperienced merchant banks drove the explosive growth of Korea's foreign debt. The debt rose from $44 billion in 1993 to $120 billion in September 1997, most of it private and roughly 65 per cent of it short-term.[5]

The design of the liberalization programme itself encouraged short-term foreign borrowing, because the application procedures for short-term borrowing entailed much lower transaction costs than those for long-term borrowing (Chang, Park and Yoo, 1998). Moreover, the government allowed non-bank firms to borrow abroad on their own account without central coordination. About a third of Korea's total foreign debt is accounted for by these non-bank firms. This borrowing was outside the scope of bank regulation and supervision, yet constituted foreign exchange liabilities for the central bank.

Across Southeast Asia, too, domestic enterprises became free to borrow abroad on their own account with no more public supervision than in Korea. Non-bank firms had an even higher proportion of total foreign borrowing than in Korea: around 60 per cent in Malaysia and more in Indonesia (Bank for International Settlements, 1998a). All this escaped bank regulation.

In Thailand, radical financial liberalization began in 1988 with the country's first fully civilian government, and intensified with the new civilian government of 1992. It included opening to foreign borrowing and the creation of a large number of new finance companies able to compete with the commercial banks.[6] These developments gave politicians plenty of opportunities to raise campaign finance. Political competition undermined any independent monitoring or regulation by the central bank (see below).

In Indonesia, 'the economy's vulnerability to financial collapse can be traced to the mid-1980s, when Indonesia opened the banking industry to competition but never put modern bank regulations in place. "It's as if the Government had gotten rid of the policeman at every corner, but didn't bother to put up stop signs or lights", suggested [an economist at the University of Indonesia]. "The traffic moved faster, but was prone to accidents"' (Passell, 1998, p. A10).

Liberalizing the financial sector and opening the capital account is dangerous when the banks are inexperienced and when non-banks also borrow abroad (Wolf, 1998). It is doubly dangerous in the context of a bank-based financial system and a high debt-to-equity corporate sector. It is triply dangerous when the exchange rate is pegged. When, in addition, the banks and non-banks are essentially unsupervised, a banking-cum-currency crisis is just waiting to happen. In Asia, swift external financial liberalization with unsupervised banks and fixed exchange rates undermined the previous system of industrial and banking cooperation and exposed fragile debt structures to unbuffered shocks.

Inflows

The capital inflow side of the story starts with the extraordinary growth of international capital flows in recent years, that now amount to well over 70 times the volume of world trade. The flows are mostly short-term; 80 per cent of net global foreign exchange transactions have a maturity date of seven days or less (Eatwell [1997], p. 4). The growth of these flows reflects, in part, the efforts of central banks in Europe and Japan to stimulate their economies by means of loose monetary policy.

The growth also reflects the imbalance between savings and investment in Japan. For many years the Japanese, the fastest ageing population in the world, have been saving hard for the approaching years of long retirement. (The average Japanese family saves more than 13 per cent of its income, the average American family 4 per cent) (Schlesinger and Hamilton, 1998, p. A1). The economy is mature, among the richest in the world, and not able productively to utilize enough investment to absorb the savings. The result is an excess of domestic savings over domestic investment that manifests itself in chronic current account surpluses matched by capital exports (Wolf, 1998b).

In the decade 1985 to 1995 the yen appreciated hugely against the US dollar, from about 238 to 80. East and Southeast Asian currencies, linked to the dollar, depreciated against the yen. Real exchange rates moved similarly. At the depreciated exchange rates, East and Southeast Asia provided much more competitive production sites. Japanese capital flooded out to Asia, much of it in export-oriented production aimed at the US. Capital from other core economies joined in. With such high rates of investment, much of it in tradeables, the economies grew at speeds rarely equalied in human history. Thailand had about the highest growth rate in the world in 1985–1994.

Japan's imbalance between saving and investment grew after the early 1990s because of the bursting of the property, stock market and currency bubbles. Japanese banks found themselves with many bad loans. Banks near to insolvency tend to take big risks unless they are recapitalized, merged or forced into bankruptcy. Rather than follow one or other of these solutions the Japanese government decided to allow them to write off the bad loans gradually (to 'trade through'), giving them extra profits via a low bank rate and tax-avoiding declarations of losses.[7] Meanwhile the voracious Japanese appetite for savings continued, the savings going mostly into the banks. The banks had to lend. The 'near to insolvency – high risks' pressure therefore continued.

Japanese banks aggressively sought high returns from foreign lending, much of it in risky loans to Southeast Asia. They found themselves able to borrow both domestically and abroad at low rates. They lent short-term to Southeast Asian banks and firms at appreciably higher rates, confident that Southeast Asian currencies would remain pegged to the US dollar. They thereby earned both an interest gain and (as the yen depreciated against the US dollar after 1995) a currency gain. European banks also lent heavily, especially after the flight from Mexico in the wake of the Mexican crisis of 1994–95. By mid-1997 European banks accounted for the largest share of the region's external bank debt, with 39 per cent. Next came Japanese banks, with 33 per cent.[8]

On the demand side, banks and firms in Korea and Southeast Asia rushed to borrow abroad. Borrowing abroad at roughly half the cost of borrowing domestically and on-lending domestically seemed to be a one-way bet. You could only win. The proviso was that the currency peg to the US dollar be maintained, precluding exchange rate risk. (The higher credit-rated banks and enterprises of Korea not only borrowed abroad and lent domestically, they also on-lent to Southeast Asia.)

At the same time, capital flowed in to accommodate the excess of investment over savings. Gross domestic investment was even higher than gross domestic savings, itself about the highest in the world at well over one-third of GDP.

In short, the inflows were driven both by the need to accommodate the excess of investment over savings (manifested in current account deficits, see below), and by the opportunity, thanks to capital account opening, for foreign creditors to get higher returns and domestic borrowers to borrow more cheaply. They were also driven by the image of 'miracle Asia'. Nobody was paying much attention to the growing imbalances in the banking systems or to other risk factors.[9]

The inflows put upward pressure on the exchange rate. The attention of the monetary authorities and of speculators and investors was on the chances of preventing appreciation of the nominal exchange rate. Nobody was thinking depreciation. Nobody was hedging against a currency sell off.

Real Vulnerabilities

The proximate source of real economy vulnerability was the deterioration in the current account in all the affected countries, especially in 1995 and 1996. The deficits for 1996 ranged from 3.5 per cent of GDP for Indonesia to 8 per cent for Thailand. The most rapid increase occurred in Korea, which went from 1 per cent in 1993–95 to 5 per cent in 1996.

Falling export growth was the main cause of the rising deficits. This reflected, first, a fall in demand for some of the main exports, notably semiconductors in the case of Korea (semiconductors being Korea's biggest single export item). Falling export growth reflected, secondly, declining competitiveness as a result of domestic costs rising faster than productivity. Capital inflows combined with the currency peg caused appreciation of the domestic currency. The real exchange rate appreciated in all five of the most affected countries in 1995–96, choking exports (Kaplinsky, 1998).

Thirdly, the nominal exchange rate rose sharply against the yen from spring 1995 onwards, as the yen fell against the dollar (from a peak of 80 in 1995 to 147 in June 1998). Investments that had been competitive at the earlier exchange rate were now less competitive, especially against Japan and China. Much investment now looked to be 'excessive'. Fourthly, the terms of trade (export prices over import prices) were trending downwards, due especially to competition from China. Fifthly, China gobbled up export markets in the US and Japan over the 1990s, raising its overall share of US merchandise imports from 3 per cent in 1990 to 6 per cent in 1994, and its share of Japanese merchandise imports from 5 per cent to 10 per cent. Its share of US footwear imports rose from 16 per cent to 45 per cent in the same years; its share of Japanese clothing imports rose from 28 per cent to 54 per cent (Kaplinsky, 1998).

As investment surged throughout the region, much of it into a narrow range of sectors, productivity and profits began to suffer. At the margin, companies put more and more investment into non-tradeable speculative ventures, including property and land. Thailand, Malaysia and Indonesia all experienced speculative property balloons inflated by foreign finance. The borrowers received returns in local currency and had to repay in foreign currency. They began to accumulate a massive currency mismatch.

In terms of their structural position in the world economy, the Southeast Asian economies have been much more dependent on foreign expertise and foreign capital than were the East Asian economies at the same average income level. The prospects of them following the East Asian trajectory were always much more uncertain. They have remained in a subcontractor role. They have seriously under-invested in education, resulting in secondary school enrolments in Thailand and Indonesia half or less than half those of Korea and Taiwan at the same per capita income level. They suffer serious infrastructure congestion. These endowment problems, combined with Chinese competition from below and Korean, Taiwanese, Japanese and European competition from above, have pinned them in a medium technology trap.

The advent of democratically-elected civilian governments in Thailand and Korea added to their vulnerabilities. In Thailand this began in the late 1980s with the first democratically-elected government, and intensified under the next civilian government of 1992.[10] These governments began to undermine the previously high level of autonomy and competence of the economic technocracy. Their constituency lay predominently in rural areas well away from Bangkok. Candidates who purchased votes to win parliamentary elections ran up huge obligations. The successful candidates, eyes on their war chests, set about capturing income and power in the state bureaucracy. The first civilian government was popularly known as 'the buffet cabinet' in tribute to its appetite for money. 'To them, and more importantly, to their constituents, the public treasury is a milch cow, and the MPs' central chore is to milk that cow and bring the milk back home to their constituents' (Siamwalla, 1998; see also Doner and Ramsay, 1998; Emmerson, 1998). The finance ministry and the central bank, whose independence and technocratic excellence had helped previous military governments maintain macroeconomic stability, came under their sway. Political appointees went into senior positions and corrupted decisions about economic policy.

In Korea, the first democratically-elected civilian government, under President Kim Young Sam, came to power in 1993 committed to far-reaching liberalization. It abolished the investment coordination superministry (the Economic Planning Board), merging it with the Ministry of Finance. At the same time it allowed some of the *chaebol* to become closer to, more personally involved with, the regime than had its military predecessors since the beginning of the 1960s.

Problems were also building up in Korea's corporate sector. A series of bankruptcies occurred in 1997 that contributed to the November 1997 crash (Mathews, 1998). The bankruptcies were concentrated in the middle-ranking *chaebol* rather than among the biggest. The middle-ranking ones had over the 1990s borrowed the most relative to their equity in order to grow and diversify as fast as possible, seeking to catch up with the leaders. They were able to borrow so much because company accounting practices allowed them to cross-guarantee the debts of one affiliate with promises from other affiliates instead of presenting stand-alone business investment projects independently collateralized. The practice of cross-guarantees between the affiliates of a *chaebol* exposed the whole conglomerate to the default of one of the components. The middle-ranking *chaebol* were also allowed to borrow so much because they bribed the relevant bankers and politicians; and because international banks based in Japan, Europe and the US practically begged them to take the money.

The bankruptcies in Korea revealed serious shortcomings in several institutions, including irregular supervision of the banks, feeble supervision of company accounting practices, and growing dishonesty among public officials. Above all, they illustrated how the *chaebol* dominated the economy, marginalizing small and medium enterprises and robbing Korea of an equivalent to Taiwan's swarms of small, nimble, niche-seeking firms. Indeed, some of the IMF's conditions on such matters as corporate governance – matters that seemed a long way from the solutions to the immediate crisis – were inserted with the encouragement of Korean Ministry of Finance officials, who saw the crisis as a golden opportunity to force through structural changes which they had long wanted but which had been blocked in the Korean political process (Mathews, 1998).

Over and above the condition of each country was the fact that they were fairly highly integrated (roughly half of total trade was intra-regional) *and* moving cyclically rather than countercyclically. Had they been less integrated or less cyclical, the regional multiplier effects would have been much smaller. (Taiwan has survived relatively unscathed partly because it had had its boom and bust in the early 1990s. By the time this crisis hit the region, Taiwan's banks were in relatively good shape) (Wade and Veneroso, 1998). The third vital element in the regional picture, after integration and cyclicality, was the stagnation of Japan; that accounts for two-thirds of the East and Southeast Asian economy.

In short, the vulnerability of the real economy in Asia did increase in the few years before the crisis. Price and investment trends led to growing current account deficits. Also, at least in Thailand and Korea, new civilian democratic regimes corrupted the central policy-making technocracy and lost focus on national economic policies. Government-bank-firm collaboration came to be steered more by the narrow and short-term interests of shifting coalitions. Their experience is bad news for the proposition that more competitive politics yield better policies.

Outflows

Granted that the whipsaw movement of capital inflows and outflows is the main proximate cause of the crisis, could it have happened without serious vulnerabilities in the real economy? Almost certainly, yes. We know from history that financial crises can occur in the absence of *ex ante* signs of rising vulnerability (though any self-respecting analyst can find vulnerabilities *ex post)*. Indeed, when times are good and demand is fast growing, firms tend to assign increased weight to past positive experience and reduce the probability of loss associated with some of their investment projects. They may cut back their cushion of safety (probable cash flow minus probable fixed payments) and thereby become *more* vulnerable to a downturn (Kregel, 1998). This is how, paradoxically, the passage from a sound to a fragile to an unstable financial system can occur even faster after a period of good times than after a period of uncertain times.

Also, we know that bankers and money managers tend to exhibit herd-like behaviour based on the incentive that any individual banker or individual bank will be faulted by management or shareholders for missing out on business that others are getting, but will not be faulted for making losses when everyone else is making losses. The effect is compounded by information cascade, such that the entry (exit) of one prominent actor is interpreted by other actors to signal that the situation is better (worse) than they thought. They then enter or exit for reasons related not to their own independent assessment of risk and reward but to their presumption that the first actor knows something they do not.

The fall in export growth and rising current account deficits by 1995 and 1996 made for mild concern among international banks and money managers, especially about Thailand. But doubts were held at bay by the continuing fast growth and the image of miracle Asia. Then the outlook for speculators and investors in the European and US markets improved in 1997. Interest rates looked set to rise, presenting lenders with opportunities for higher risk-adjusted returns than they had had before. Equity markets soared (Rude, 1998). In Japan, on the other hand, the outlook turned for the worse in the second quarter of 1997. In early May 1997, Japanese officials, concerned about the decline of the yen, hinted that they might raise interest rates. The threat never materialized. But the combination of the threat of a rise in Japanese interest rates in order to defend the yen, plus the worries that were circulating about Thailand's currency, plus the brighter opportunities in the US and Europe, raised fears among commercial bankers, investment bankers and others about the safety of big investment positions throughout the region that were predicated on currency stability.

The Asian crisis proper began as a huge liquidity crisis in Thailand. First the Thai property and stock market bubbles burst in 1995 and 1996 respectively. The property market is a market where small withdrawals can have a big effect on prices and leave the banking system in the sort of danger that makes depositors withdraw their money. The property market crash ripped through the whole financial sector and on into the foreign exchange market as foreign investors saw that a devaluation would render domestic borrowers less able to meet the now more expensive debt service charges on their short-term foreign loans. With a baht devaluation in sight (a breaking of the peg), companies in Thailand, both foreign and domestic, tried to sell their baht for dollars. Foreign banks realized they had large short-term foreign exchange loans to Thai borrowers that were unhedged and perhaps uncovered by Thai reserves. Knowing that the profitability of their loans depended on the currency peg they raced for the exits at the first signs that the peg might not hold. There were runs on the baht in mid-1996 and again in early 1997. The Thai central bank bought baht to prevent the price fall, but eventually gave up as reserves fell to dangerously low levels. It also resorted secretly to borrowing abroad and including the borrowed funds in its officially declared reserves (Wade, 1998c).

With reserves running out, the baht was floated in early July 1997, and sank. The IMF entered Thailand in August 1997 with a support package and conditionality measures that included the freezing of many finance companies. This was the start of what Jeffrey Sachs has called the IMF's screaming fire in the theatre (Sachs, 1998). The freezing of finance companies sent uninsured depositors into a panic. Later the IMF imposed the closure of some domestic banks in Indonesia with the same result (inevitable where deposits are uninsured).

Taiwan's small (12 per cent) devaluation in October, despite its towering foreign exchange reserves, acted as a firebridge from Southeast to East Asia. After Taiwan's unexpected devaluation the Hong Kong dollar and the Korean won suddenly looked set for a catch-up devaluation. As holders of these currencies, too, tried to pull out the crisis grew from a 'Southeast Asian' crisis to an 'Asian crisis'. Between October and December, Japanese, US and European bankers demanded full repayment of interest and principal from their Korean borrowers as short-term loans became due, and the Korean government had no option but to turn to the IMF. The IMF and the Korean government signed a $57 billion rescue package in early December. In mid-December the Koreans revealed that their short-term debt was nearly double what they had said just the previous week, at $95 billion. The gap between $95 billion and $57 billion left scarcely a dry pair of pants in the official community on either side of the Pacific.

A very big rescue package at this point could have stopped the crisis from spreading. Better information about bank and corporate balance sheets might also have checked the panic by enabling investors to discriminate between good and bad assets.

Instead, the perception shifted from 'miracle Asia' to 'Asian crony state capitalism' almost overnight. 'Crony capitalism', originally coined by activists in the anti-Marcos struggle in the Philippines, was now appropriated to convey a told-you-so moral about the dangers of government intervention (Emmerson, 1998).

Debt Deflation and Import Inflation

Once floated, the currencies fell in vicious iteration with domestic bankruptcies (which no amount of developmental state socializing of risk could avoid). As foreign banks that had been routinely rolling over their short-term loans began to demand repayment of not only the interest but also the whole of the principal, highly leveraged firms found their cash flow insufficient to cover their now much higher payment obligations. They started to reduce their cash outflows by delaying payments to suppliers, cutting back on expenditure, raising cash by selling inventories at cut-rate prices, selling assets at whatever they could fetch, and firing employees. In Korea and Southeast Asia the proportion of technically insolvent large companies (unable to pay interest charges out of net cash flow) was expected to jump between 1997 and 1998 from 21 per cent to 32 per cent in Korea; Malaysia, from 11 per cent to 19 per cent; Indonesia, 16 per cent to 46 per cent; the Philippines, 11 per cent to 18 per cent.[11] The calculations date from February 1998. More recent ones would show higher figures for 1998. The tragedy is that many of these insolvent companies were well managed and profitable in competitive markets.

The process fed through from firms to banks as banks wrote off loans and wrote down assets. Their calling in of loans put pressure on their borrowers, and those that went bankrupt put pressure on their depositors. The financial economy and the real economy dragged each other down.

This is 'debt deflation', akin to the Great Depression of the 1930s (Kregel, 1998; Wade and Veneroso, 1998; Wade, 1998b). Debt deflation is a downward pressure on prices of both products and of assets at a time when investment demand is falling, resulting in a rising real value of debt. It is given a vicious twist in Asia by the steep rise in the price of imports, including intermediate goods and medicines. Asia is now caught in the slow, painful unfolding of debt deflation with import inflation. It is all the worse because of Asia's high debt/ equity ratios, that impart a bigger multiplier effect to a given reduction in demand and cash flow. This is how, in the chaos theory metaphor, the butterfly that flapped its wings in Thailand caused a hurricane across Asia.

The IMF's Role

The IMF's interventions in Thailand, Indonesia and Korea (and informally, without funding, in Malaysia) have made things worse than need be, according to this story. Misdiagnosing the problem as a macroeconomic balance of payments problem (the type of problem it is used to dealing with) rather than as a microeconomic debt deflation problem, and as a crisis of excess consumption rather than excess investment, it insisted on a domestic austerity package and on fundamental structural reforms in return for bailout funds.[12] It justified big increases in real interest rates on the grounds that high rates would give incentives for domestic capital to stay at home and foreign lenders to resume lending, which would boost the currency. The currency boost would both make it easier for domestic firms to repay their foreign debts and check the dangers of competitive, 1930s-style devaluations. It insisted upon far-reaching structural reforms, because, as First Deputy Managing Director of the IMF Stanley Fischer says, 'The faster [the underlying structural problems in the financial and corporate sectors are dealt with], the shorter the period of pain, and the sooner the return to growth' (Fischer, 1998; see also Stiglitz, 1998b).

This was the theory. In practice the increase in real interest rates combined with other elements of the austerity package (tax increases, cuts in government expenditure) only depressed firms' cash flow and raised their fixed payment obligations, tipping more and more into insolvency, accelerating the outflows and reducing the inflows. In prioritizing the return of capital flows the Fund forgot that private capital flows are cyclical rather than countercyclical. When a whole economy is sinking and instability abounds, foreign capital will not return whatever the interest rate. Certainly the high real interest rates did not have the effect of reversing the currency falls in Asia. And the cross-country evidence shows no clear relationship between the level of real interest rates and changes in the exchange rate (Stiglitz, 1998a).

A sharp dose of austerity may make sense for a Latin American-style excessive consumption crisis. But the Asian crisis was related to excessive investment (much of it in non-tradeables), not excessive consumption. IMF demand compression worsened already existing problems of excessive capacity.

Similarly, being required to undertake fundamental structural reforms at the height of the crisis worsened confidence, reinforcing the 'cronyism-failure' gestalt. Requiring a sharp rise in bank capital adequacy standards in the midst of the crisis caused a cut in credit, a rise in nonperforming loans and further bankruptcies. The Asian experience confirms that the middle of a liquidity crisis is a bad time to make radical financial reforms.

These various policy mistakes help to explain why the crisis has been so protracted. Their effects are compounded by the high debt/equity ratios of the corporate and financial systems, by the relatively high level of regional integration, the synchronous movement of all the regional economies except Taiwan and by Japan's stagnation. Mexico in 1994 recovered relatively quickly by exporting to the giant in the north, whose political structure was sufficiently institutionalized to accommodate a $20 billion swing in trade balances in one year. Had Japan been expanding it might have played a similar role as the US to Mexico. Fears of further falls in the Japanese yen (even after the steep fall of June 1998 to 147 yen to the US dollar) add to the continuing reluctance to invest and raise fears of competitive devaluations, notably in China and Hong Kong.

THE FUTURE

As of July 1998 governments of the region are beginning to follow an expansionary policy, lowering real interest rates, expanding the monetary base and running bigger fiscal deficits. This represents a considerable change of direction.[13] It sets aside the central bank orthodoxy that has dominated the discussion, according to which very low inflation, restrained demand and high real interest rates are the top priorities. Governments now have to channel credit into export industries, generate an export boom taking advantage of exchange rates and let the profits therefrom reinforce inflationary expectations in reflating domestic demand. Hopefully inventory depletion will be followed by a bounceback in demand.

Governments may have to reintroduce some form of cross-border capital controls for this strategy to be viable. Indeed, it is not obvious why Asia needs to draw capital from the rest of the world (except in the form of foreign direct investment, a small proportion of the total). Its savings are more than enough to support the volume of investment that is productive and profitable without being speculative. Of course, the reintroduction of some forms of capital controls in Asia would be a major setback in the current Big Push for liberalization of capital movements world-wide, and would be fiercely resisted by Western financial interests.[14] If capital controls are not re-established the exchange rate must float. The Asian crisis shows only too clearly the dangers of free capital movements and fixed rates.

The escape from crisis could be much accelerated through regional co-operation between the governments and their central banks. The lack of deliberately concerted regional expansion is one of the most striking features of the whole story. The region has the means to solve the crisis if only it could put them to work: some $700 billion of foreign exchange reserves between China, Hong Kong, Taiwan and Japan, growing current account surpluses in the crisis-affected countries (even if due more to import compression than export expansion), net creditor positions in terms of foreign asset ownership, and huge savings.

These endowments could easily provide the basis for an Asia Fund. The Fund would help member countries in replenishing reserves as soon as signs of distress become obvious, thereby reducing the chance of investor pull-out. It would be designed to be quick disbursing and lightly conditional. Even the first moves towards an Asia Fund might trigger a shift of image from 'failure' to 'recovery' and send Western capital racing to take positions before prices rise – especially if Western stock markets fall from current valuations that are, in the US case, twice the previous historic highs.[15]

The main obstacle is political. Japan's proposal for an Asia Fund, made in mid-1997, was shot down by the US Treasury, which wanted any such thing to be within the IMF. Japan has since exercised negligible leadership, and remains paralysed by the power struggle between big manufacturers, wanting a weak yen, and banks, wanting a strong yen. China has shown a moderate amount of leadership, and emerges from the crisis with its reputation enhanced relative to Japan's. But it is the US Treasury under Secretary Rubin and Under Secretary Summers that has been shaping the overall strategy, both directly and indirectly via the IMF.[16] The US emerges from the crisis with much greater power in the region than it had before. And the US does not want an Asian initiative that would exclude it from a central role.[17] Nor does China want a Japanese-led fund.

Until Asian governments – very much including the Japanese government – adopt expansionary policies, take control of short-term capital movements and co-operate within the region, the crisis is likely to drag on and on, like water torture, bringing poverty and insecurity to hundreds of millions of people and turning parts of Asia into a dependency of the IMF and its number one shareholder.

CONCLUSION

'Real' or 'financial' causes? Rational behaviour, boundedly rational, or nonrational? Individually rational, collectively nonrational, socially suboptimal? Specific and exceptional market failure or well-working markets producing massive economic, political and social failures (as in 'the operation was a success but the patient died')?

The capital inflows were a function of capital account opening, fixed exchange rates, bank supervision inadequate for an internationalized system, depreciation of domestic currencies against the yen (because linked to the falling dollar), and higher returns to financial assets in Asia than in the US and Europe. The outflows were a function of capital account opening, appreciation of domestic currencies against the yen after spring 1995 (because linked to the rising dollar), falling export growth and rising current account deficits, the combination of the last two giving rise to fears of devaluation.

The causation also has another strand relating to herding behaviour, information cascades and the like, that link individual rationality with collective nonrationality or suboptimality. What is striking about the Asian crisis is the abrupt shift of confidence from 'miracle Asia' to 'crony Asia' – a 'gestalt shift' in the language of cognitive psychology. In the famous drawing of a vase or a pair of inturned faces we see either one or the other, not some of one and some of the other, and the shift takes place instantaneously, not by degrees. This is a long way from the idea of rational, weighing-up-risks-and-rewards calculation.

The notion of gestalt shift lends support to the 'panic' story – that the crisis was caused in large part by speculator and investor pull-out from economies that but for the pull-out would have remained viable enough to generate returns within the normal range. The panic, in other words, was not simply the 'trigger' or messenger of a crisis. The panic was a primary cause.

This line of argument suggests that had the massive outflow not occurred in Thailand or had it been reversed in a matter of a couple of months, the Asian crisis would not have happened. One can see several turning points where things might have gone differently. The inflows would have been less large had the countries not opened up the capital account earlier in the 1990s. The Japanese economy might still have been expanding had the Japanese government not made a colossal macro error in the spring of 1997 of raising taxes as the economy was slowing. Had the Japanese government in August 1997 matched its pledge to play a big role in promoting financial stability in the region with a contribution to the Thai bailout of $10 billion rather than $4 billion, confidence might have been restored; this might also have been the case had the US Congress not declined to provide more funds to the IMF in November 1997 because of a dispute about an abortion-related amendment to the country's foreign aid programme. It took an unlikely conjuncture of these and several other events that might easily have been different to produce a crisis on anything like this scale. In this sense the crisis was under-determined.[18] This is to make the contrast with interpretations that stress major vulnerabilities in the real economy as the causes, according to which the crisis was over-determined – a major crisis was bound to happen and any of many events could have triggered it. The real economy trends, notably falling export growth and widening current account deficits, were amplifiers, not prime causes.[19]

China stands as a case in point. It has many characteristics of the crisis countries, pre-crisis, only more so: great dynamism and huge structural problems. Its banking system is in worse shape than Thailand's or Korea's before the crisis. Its escape from a direct hit reflects its closed capital account, implicit government guarantee of deposits and big foreign exchange reserves.

This same line of argument throws doubt on the popular moral hazard argument for why the inflows were so big. It says that lenders lent appreciably more than otherwise because they believed they would be covered by implicit government or IMF guarantees. But the hypothesis is advanced without evidence that, for example, lenders lent more to companies, banks, sectors and countries where there was a stronger *ex ante* presumption of bailout. It is equally plausible that lenders were paying no attention to downside risks, being carried along by the gestalt of miracle Asia and the incentives for herd behaviour. (Life insurance policies are not normally blamed for suicides.)

Much the same point applies to the popular 'lack of transparency' hypothesis about the size of the inflows: that lenders lent more than they would have had they been better informed about balance sheets, foreign exchange reserves and foreign debts. In fact, plenty of relevant information was publicly available; for example, the Bank for International Settlement's commentaries from early 1995 onwards stressed the build-up of short-term foreign debt (1996a, p. 5; 1996b, p. 141). But investors were not reading – until after the crisis hit, at which point they refocused from macro indicators towards the micro indicators of debt maturity structures and the like that they could have been tracking all the while had they a mind to. On the other hand, lack of transparency may have a significant role in explaining the magnitude of the panic, and hence the size of the outflows, for the reason given earlier.

The IMF argues that its far-reaching conditions for austerity and institutional reform boosted confidence as investors saw the governments taking firm action to repair the underlying vulnerabilities. The gestalt shift argument says, in contrast, that the news that a country was negotiating conditionalities with the IMF aggravated the loss of confidence, prompting a bigger rush for the exits; as did the signal that far-reaching institutional reforms were essential for growth to be restored.

The latter argument raises an interesting question of causality. IMF critics have pointed out that no sizeable changes occurred in indicators of national institutional strength in the last year or two before the crisis, and go on to ask how, given this, institutional factors could be assigned a large role. (For example, the ratio of short-term to total debt had been constant since 1993, and not so much above the rising Latin American average.) But weaknesses such as lack of bankruptcy codes and creditor rights may exist for years without causing difficulties provided growth remains high. Once growth falters these same constant weaknesses may help to bring on a crisis and hinder the resumption of growth. The question remains, however, whether the Fund should have insisted on such reforms in the middle of a liquidity crisis.

However the explanation is parsed, capital account opening is central. It exposed domestic financial structures – that had been strong enough to allocate huge domestic savings to generally productive and profitable investments over many years – to unbearable strain (Wade, 1990). Yet the IMF and the US and UK Treasuries now insist that the crisis demonstrates the importance of liberalizing the capital account even more – though in an 'orderly' way. Orderly means with a proper regulatory and supervisory regime in place. The way to create that regime, they say, is to bring in foreign banks and financial services firms to operate in the domestic market. They will demand an effective regime and help to supply the skills to operate it with. In return, they will require freedom to enter and exit as they wish, and national treatment (parity with domestic firms, or better).

Even with a sizeable sector of foreign financial firms, developing an effective regime will take many years. And duration aside, regulation according to whose norms? The norms of a capital-market-based Anglo-American system are very different from those of a bank-based Asian system. The latter reflect the functioning of a system that allows firms to carry much higher levels of debt than consistent with Anglo-American prudential limits. The system has powerful developmental advantages as well as higher risks of financial instability. And it also seems to be a response to very high levels of household savings that are deposited in banks. A regulatory regime based on Anglo-American norms of prudent debt/equity ratios will probably not work in these conditions.

The idea that the way to avoid more Asian-style crises is to integrate national economies even more fully into world capital markets is implausible. As Dani Rodrik remarks,

> Thailand and Indonesia would have been far better off restricting borrowing from abroad instead of encouraging it. Korea might just have avoided a run on its reserves if controls on short-term borrowing had kept its short-term exposure to foreign banks, say, at 30 percent rather than 70 percent of its liabilities. On the other hand, which of the recent blowups in international financial markets could the absence of capital controls conceivably have prevented? (Rodrik, 1998; see also Bhagwati, 1998)

There is little empirical evidence that capital account opening improves economic performance (Stiglitz, 1998b; Rodrik, 1998; Bhagwati, 1998; Quinn, 1997).

The greatest concern about capital account convertibility, however, is that it brings economic policy in developing countries even more under the influence of international capital markets – the influence of a small number of country analysts and fund managers in New York, London, Frankfurt and Tokyo. Even if it were the case that free capital movements do lead to efficiency in the allocation of capital and as such do maximize the returns to capital world-wide, governments have much more than the interests of the owners of capital in view – or ought to have. They want to maximize the returns to labour, to entrepreneurship and to technical progress, and to maximize them within their own territory rather than somewhere else; they want to provide public goods that contribute to the good life. Only blind faith in the virtues of capital markets could lead one to think that maximizing the returns to capital and promoting development goals generally coincide.

At the least we should insist on a linguistic convention. 'Investor' should be used only for someone who allows his money to be used for the production of goods and services in return for a share in the proceeds, including the purchase of new shares. Someone who buys financial assets in secondary markets in the expectation of subsequently selling them at a profit due to exchange rate shifts or asset price shifts related not to dividend flows but to the number of buyers and sellers is properly called a 'speculator'. The distinction helps to avoid assuming that what is good for speculation is also good for investment.

NOTES

1. This paper builds on Robert Wade and Frank Veneroso, 'The Asian crisis: The High Debt Model vs. the Wall Street-Treasury-IMF Complex', in *New Left Review*, no. 228, Mar.–Apr., 1998, and Robert Wade, 'The Asian Debt-and-Development Crisis of 1997-?: Causes and Consequences', in *World Development*, Aug. 1998, to which the reader is referred for more references. The paper benefits from conversations with Nesli Basgoz, Keith Besanson, Jagdish Bhagwati, Manfred Bienefeld, Donald Brash, Robert Brenner, Leonardo Burlamaqui, Alessandra Casella, Ha-Joon Chang, Richard Doner, Ronald Dore, Barry Eichengreen, Peter Garber, Jan Kregel, Stephan Haggard, Barry Herman, Michael Lipton, Arvid Lukauskes, my *ad hoc* research assistant Robert K. Merton, Percy Mistry, Kevin Muehring, Loren Ross, Eric Wanner, David Weiman and especially Frank Veneroso.
2. *Per capita* income measured at current exchange rates.
3. See Wade and Veneroso, 1998, for discussion of the problems of the empirical evidence on debt/equity ratios. Among other problems, the evidence I have seen includes only long-term debt, and in the case of conglomerates it does not properly consolidate debt so as to account for the practice of one affiliate borrowing to buy quasi-equity in another affiliate, thereby spuriously lowering the second one's debt/equity ratio. Evidence on the size of bank intermediation suggests that the ratio of credit to GDP in Asia in 1990–96 ranged from 207 per cent in Japan down to 114 per cent in Singapore (with Hong Kong, Thailand, Malaysia and Korea in between, but Indonesia and Philippines around 63–65 per cent). Colombia, Brazil, Mexico and Argentina ranged from 42 per cent to 18 per cent, with Chile at 70 per cent. The US figure was 58 per cent. Source is Goldman Sachs, elaborated in Pomerleano, 1998.
4. Japan resisted the push for financial liberalization in developing countries. Its conflicts with the World Bank and the IMF on this matter in the Asian context gave the impetus to the World Bank's *The East Asian Miracle* study (Wade, 1996b).
5. Bank for International Settlements, 1998. Korea's figure fell from 68 per cent at end 1996 to 63 per cent at end 1997. Indonesia's figures for the same years were 62 per cent and 61 per cent, Thailand's 65 per cent and 66 per cent. These figures are for lending to the country by foreign banks, where 'to the country' means to any entity in the country, including subsidiaries of foreign firms. The World Bank's figures on total debt and short-term debt in *Global Development Finance* tend to be appreciably different from the BIS figures. The BIS uses creditor statistics (from the loan-extending banks), the World Bank uses debtor statistics (from the debtor governments). The BIS figures cover only bank lending, the Bank also covers non-bank, specifically government or public loans. Yet the Bank's figures are often smaller. The differences reflect first, the poorer quality of debtor statistics (there are many more debtors than creditors, and debtor banks are less well supervised) and secondly, differences in methodology (on such things as treatment of subsidiaries of banks and non-banks, and the entities whose debts are to be included in external debt – all residents, including

subsidiaries of foreign companies, or only nationally-owned debt, including debt of foreign subsidiaries of domestic firms).

6. In March 1993 the Bank of Thailand opened the Bangkok International Banking Facility (BIBF), intending to make Thailand a regional financial hub. In practice it mostly intermediated between Thai borrowers and foreign lenders, all in foreign currency (Siamwalla, 1998).

7. The opprobrium now directed at the Japanese government for not moving earlier to clean up the banking system conceals the point that as of 1996, before the wider crisis, the trading through strategy seemed to be working tolerably well compared to the likely alternatives. And it ignores the point that the US government waited from 1984 to 1988 before it developed a comprehensive wind-up rescue plan with public money to clean up the Savings and Loan crisis. The US's disregard of the wider impacts of its macroeconomic policy choices (as in the Volker interest rate hike, undertaken with no thought to its impact on Latin America, and its reluctance to contribute to the Bretton Woods institutions and the UN) does not qualify it to be self-righteous about Japan's choices. On alternative methods of debt workouts see Wade and Veneroso, 1998.

8. (*The Economist*, 1998, p. 42). The Asian countries in the calculation include South Korea, China, Indonesia, Thailand, Taiwan, Malaysia and the Philippines. US banks accounted for only 8 per cent of external bank debt as of the end of June 1997. However, derivatives complicate the picture. American banks hold a large amount of derivatives contracts with Asian entities, probably more than other banks. For example, J.P. Morgan, which probably has the most at stake of the American banks, had $116 billion total credit risk from derivatives at the end of 1997. A loss of one-tenth of that amount would wipe out its equity. In 1997, 90 per cent of its nonperforming loans were defaults from Asian derivatives counterparties. Derivatives are more likely to be defaulted on than loans, because the counterparty 'can always say [it] didn't understand the derivative or the bank tricked [it] or whatever', and hence 'Companies do not view a default on derivatives as face losing' (financial analyst with Standard and Poor's) (Baumohl, 1998).

9. It will be interesting to read future histories of the World Bank, the IMF and the rating agencies to see how contrary information was kept out of their reports, and what happened subsequently to the responsible managers. See Brauchli, 1998 (thanks to Laura Resnikoff for drawing it to my attention). As an example of the problem, the staff of the World Bank's resident mission in Indonesia prepared a speech for President Wolfensohn to deliver during his visit in the autumn of 1997, praising Indonesia's performance but also containing a strong warning of serious difficulties that needed urgent attention. Wolfensohn himself deleted the passage, substituting an even more fulsome endorsement of Indonesia as an Asian miracle. As another example, the Bank's lead economist for Thailand in 1994 wrote the (confidential) annual report on the economy and the Bank's strategy (the Country Assistance Strategy), and warned of major problems associated with the build-up of foreign debt. His division chief removed most of the bad news. The division chief was promoted, the lead economist left the division. Neither Wolfensohn nor the division chief had independent empirical grounds for reversing the judgement of their subordinates. 'We were caught up in the enthusiasm of Indonesia', said Wolfensohn to critics in Jakarta in early 1998 – with disingenuousness in the 'we'.

10. The first government was headed by Chartchai Choonawan and lasted from 1988 to 1991. After a military interlude the second civilian government was headed by Chuan Leekpai from 1992 to 1995.

11. A comparable calculation for Thailand, for 1996 and third quarter 1997, gives a jump from 12 per cent to 36 per cent. The figures are to be taken as no more than rough approximations. They are based on Goldman Sachs, 1998 and Mako, 1998.

12. The Fund's conditions in Asia are open to the same critique as Mark Blaug makes of economists' advice about the transition problem in Eastern Europe. 'We have not been very good at thinking about the transition problem in Eastern Europe because we have not been thinking about how market economies actually work and what is required to make markets function. So our advice to Eastern Europe has been very wooden...' (Blaug, 1998).

13. The Fund has endorsed some relaxation. It is not clear how much the Fund had a change of mind and how much it is making the best of fait accomplis (Wade, 1998a; Tseng, 1998; Wade, 1998b).
14. Wade and Veneroso, 1998; Wade, 1998. Chris Rude, 1998, emphasizes the ambiguity in the minds of Wall Street money managers about what to do. Wearing their 'market professional' hat they are sympathetic to the idea of various forms of capital controls, temporary or otherwise, because they see – not just in the Asian crisis – that international financial markets can be severely dysfunctional. Wearing their 'businessman' hat, however, they want total freedom and national treatment. This suggests that a serious push for a more regulated international monetary system, complete with potential for capital controls, might not be as strongly opposed from Wall Street as is generally thought.
15. The record-breaking rise in American stocks has been propelled partly by capital coming out of Asia (Fuerbringer, 1998).
16. Weisberg, 1998; Wade and Veneroso, 1998; Wade, 1998c. Note that the State Department, Commerce Department, National Economic Council, National Security Council and CIA have had virtually no role; the Treasury has called all the shots.
17. At the Hong Kong Annual Meeting of the Fund and the World Bank in late September/early October 1997 Eisuke Sakakibara, Japanese Vice-Minister of Finance for International Affairs, called a meeting of senior Asian finance officials without informing the Americans. When word reached Treasury Under Secretary Summers, he left his meeting, entered the room where the Asian officials were gathered, sat down at the table and said, 'Now where were we?' From a source who requests anonymity.
18. The analytical challenge is to marry the contingent aspects of the crisis with the propensity of the world economy to generate rotating credit balloons and investment excesses.
19. The analytical challenge is to marry the contingent nature of the Asian crisis with the propensity of the world economy to generate credit balloons and crashes that rotate from place to place.

BIBLIOGRAPHY

Bank for International Settlements (1996a), *The Maturity, Sectoral and Nationality Distribution of International Bank Lending, First Half 1995*, January, Basle.

Bank for International Settlements (1996b), *66ᵗʰ Annual Report,* 10 June, Basle, p. 141.

Bank for International Settlements (1998a), *The Maturity Sectoral and Nationality Distribution of International Bank Lending, First Half 1997*, Jan., Basle, Table 1, cited in Yilmaz Akyuz, 'The East Asian Finantial Crisis: Back to the Future?', UNCTAD, n.d.

Bank for International Settlements (1998b), *The Maturity, Sectoral and Nationality Distribution of International Bank Lending*, May, Basle.

Baumohl, Bernard (1998), 'Asia Crisis: The Banks' Nuclear Secrets', *Time*, 25 May, pp. 46–47, 50.

Bhagwati, Jagdish (1998), 'The Capital Myth: The Difference between Trade in Widgets and Dollars', *Foreign Affairs,* May.

Blaug, Mark (1998), 'The State of Modern Economics: the Problems with Formalism'. Interview, *Challenge*, May–June, pp. 35–45.

Brauchli, Marcus (1998), 'Speak No Evil: Why the World Bank Failed to Anticipate Indonesia's Deep Crisis', *Wall Street Journal*, 14 July.

Chang H.-J., Park, and C. G. Yoo (1998), 'Interpreting the Korean Crisis', *Cambridge Journal of Economics*, November, pp. 735–746.

Doner, Richard and Ansil Ramsay (1998), 'Thailand: From Economic Miracle to Economic Crisis'. Unpublished paper, Political Science Department, Emory University, January.

Eatwell, John [1997], *International Financial Liberalization: the Impact on World Development*. Discussion paper, Office of Development Studies, UNDP, p. 4.

The Economist, (1998), 'Asia and Europe: Hard Talking', 4 April, p. 42.

Emmerson, Donald (1998), 'Economic Rupture as Political Rorschach: Paradigmatic Aspects of the East Asian Crisis'. Unpublished, Political Science Department, University of Wisconsin, Madison, March.

Fischer, Stanley (1998), 'Year of upheaval: the IMF was right on high interest rates and immediate restructuring', *Asiaweek*, 17 July.

Fuerbringer, Jonathan (1998), 'Markets are bolstered as investors flee rout in Asia', *New York Times*, 14 May.

Goldman Sachs (1998), *Asset Quality for Korean Banks, Part II, Bottom-Up Approach for Estimating NPLs*, 19 February.

Islam, Azizul (1998), *The Dynamics of Asian Economic Crisis and Selected Policy Implications*, Development Research and Policy Analysis Division, UN ESCAP, July.

Kaplinsky, Raphael (1998), '*If You Want to Get Somewhere Else, You Must Run at Least Twice as Fast as That!': The Roots of the East Asian Crisis*. Paper for East Asian conference, Institute of Development Studies, Sussex University, 13–14 July.

Kregel, Jan (1998), 'Yes, "It" Did Happen Again – a Minsky Crisis Happened in Asia'. Unpublished, Jerome Levy Institute, New York.

Lipton, Michael (1998), *The East Asian Crises, Banking, and the Poor*. Paper for 'Asian Crisis conference', Institute of Development Studies, Sussex University, 13–14 July.

Lloyd-Smith, Jake (1998), 'Asia Hunkers Down for Bumpy Journey', *South China Morning Post*, 7 May.

Mako, William (1998), *Thai Corporates: Origins of Financial Distress and Measures to Promote Voluntary Restructuring*.

Mathews, John (1998), 'Fashioning a New Korean Model out of the Crisis', *Cambridge Journal of Economics*, November, pp. 747–760.

Passell, Peter (1998), 'Experts Say Indonesia Can Boom, Long-term', *The New York Times*, 22 May, p. A10.

Patel, Parimal and Keith Pavitt (1994), 'Uneven and Divergent Technological Accumulation among Advanced Countries: Evidence and a Framework of Explanation', in *Industrial and Corporate Change*, **3**, pp. 759–787.

Pomerleano, Michael (1998), *The East Asia Crisis and Corporate Finances: a Micro Story*. Preliminary draft, World Bank, May.

Quinn, Dennis (1997), 'The Correlates of International Financial Deregulation', *American Political Science Review*, **91**, September, pp. 531–551.

Rodrik, Dani (1998), *Who Needs Capital Account Convertibility?*, in S. Fisher *et al.*, *Should the IMF Persue Capital Account Convertibility?*, International Finance Section, Dep. of Economics, Princeton University, February.

Rude, Chris (1998), *The 1997–98 East Asian Financial Crisis: a New York Market-informed View*, Department of Economic and Social Affairs, UN, July.

Sachs, Jeffrey (1998), 'The IMF and the Asian Flu', *The American Prospect*, March–April, pp. 16–21.

Schlesinger, Jacob and David Hamilton (1998), 'The More the Japanese Save for a Rainy Day, the Gloomier it Gets', *Wall Street Journal*, 21 July, p. A1.

Siamwalla, Ammar (1998), *Can a Developing Democracy Manage its Macroeconomy? The Case of Thailand*. Paper for the Asian Crisis conference, Institute of Development Studies, Sussex University, 13–14 July.

Stiglitz, Joseph (1998a), *Knowledge for Development: Economic Science, Economic Policy, and Economic Advice*, Annual Bank Conference on Development Economics, World Bank, Washington DC, April.

Stiglitz, Joseph (1998b), 'Road to Recovery: Restoring Growth in the Region Could Be a Long and Difficult Process', *Asiaweek*, 17 July.

Tseng, Wanda (1998), 'Near-zero Interest Rates are No Panacea for Asia', *Financial Times*, 6 July, letters.

Wade, Robert (1990), *Governing the Market: Economic Theory and the Role of Government in East Asian Industrialization*, NJ: Princeton University Press.

Wade, Robert (1996a), 'Globalization and Its Limits: Reports of the Death of the National Economy are Greatly Exaggerated', in S. Berger and R. Dore (eds), *National Diversity and Global Capitalism*, Ithaca: Cornell University Press.

Wade, Robert (1996b), 'Japan, the World Bank, and the Art of Paradigm Maintenance: *The East Asian Miracle* in Political Perspective', *New Left Review*, 217, May–June, pp. 3–36.

Wade, Robert (1998a), 'Asian Water Torture', *Financial Times*, 23 June.

Wade, Robert (1998b), 'IMF and US Treasury Playing Catch Up on Asia Strategy', letters, *Financial Times*, 14 July.

Wade, Robert (1998c), 'The Asian Debt-and-Development Crisis of 1997: Causes and Consequences', *World Development*, August.

Wade, Robert and Frank Veneroso (1998), 'The Asian Crisis: The High Debt Model vs. the Wall Street-Treasury-IMF Complex', *New Left Review*, no. 228, March–April.

Weisberg, Jacob (1998), 'Keeping the Boom from Busting', *The New York Times Magazine*, 19 July, pp. 24 ff.

Wolf, Martin (1998a), 'Caging the Bankers', *Financial Times,* 20 January.

Wolf, Martin (1998b), 'Saving Japan: a Permanent Cure', *Financial Times,* 7 April.

World Bank (1993), *The East Asian Miracle: Economic Growth and Public Policy*, New York: World Bank.

8. State reform in the 1990s: logic and control mechanisms

Luiz Carlos Bresser Pereira

The great political task of the 1990s is to reform or to rebuild the state. Between the 1930s and 1960s, the state became a significant factor in fostering economic and social development. During that period, and particularly after World War II, we witnessed a time of economic prosperity and an increase in standards of living as never before in the history of mankind. Yet, since the 1970s, because of its distorted growth coupled with the globalization process, the state entered into a crisis and became the main cause for the drop in economic growth rates and the increase in unemployment and inflation rates that have taken place throughout the world. A neo-conservative wave and market-oriented economic reforms were respectively the ideological and political responses to the crisis – reforms which neo-liberals or neo-conservative politicians and intellectuals hoped would reduce the size of the state to a minimum. But in the 1990s, when the neo-conservative proposal of a minimum state proved not to be feasible, the true nature of the reforms was disclosed: the rebuilding of the state was essential for it to undertake not just its classical tasks of assuring property rights and contracts, but also those required to ensure social rights and promote competitiveness in the country.

State reform involves four issues which, although interdependent, may be distinguished as follows: (a) an economic-political problem concerning the size of the state or the delimitation of the areas the state is supposed to actuate; (b) a deregulation question where the degree of state regulation is discussed; (c) an economic-administrative aspect regarding the recovery of governance, i.e. the financial and administrative capacity to implement political decisions taken by the government; and (d) a political issue – the governability problem – i.e. the political capacity of the government to represent and to be an intermediary between different interest groups so as to guarantee legitimacy and political power for the administration's decisions.

In defining the size of the state, three issues gain relevance: privatization of state enterprises, 'publicization' of social and scientific services and outsourcing of support activities. While the delimitation of the size of the state may follow some clear principles that I will try to present in this paper, the deregulation problem is a question of the degree to which the state, that always regulates through the legal system, will regulate a given industry, depending on its degree of monopoly. With respect to governance, several aspects are involved: a financial aspect, overcoming the fiscal crisis; a strategic one, redefining the ways in which the state will intervene in the economic and social spheres; and an administrative one, involving the substitution of a managerial for a bureaucratic kind of public administration, while the bureaucracy itself is strengthened and acquires a relative autonomy from politicians and pressures from its clientele. Finally, governability – the enhanced capacity of the state to govern – covers the following issues: the legitimacy of the administration *vis-à-vis* society, and before that, finding ways to put in place political institutions that promote representation, stimulate social control and serve as intermediaries among diverse interests.

In this paper I shall attempt to analyse the four basic aspects of state rebuilding: setting limits to its institutional scope together with the downsizing processes, establishing a proper framework for its role as a regulator coupled with the deregulation processes, increasing its capacity for governance and enhancing its governability. In all four cases, the objective is not to weaken the state, but rather to strengthen it. At all times it will be assumed that the regime is democratic, not just because democracy is an end value in itself, but also because at the current stage of civilization it is the only system that assures political stability and sustainable economic development. I shall not go into this issue, nor why the crisis of the state arose, and I shall make just a brief reference to the theoretical discussion on market coordination constraints which make it imperative for the state to intervene in a complementary role.

The key issue of this article is the state reform process which was under way in the 1990s, and its practical and theoretical foundations. The analysis will be centred on this reform and on the institutions that stem from it. Behind it, there is a logic of economic and social control, that I will discuss later in this paper. I shall start out from the premise that the state is an essential factor in promoting development, which is something that pragmatists of all ideological orientations uphold. This role may be performed by deliberately enhancing investment combined with substantial expenditure in the social sector, as is the proposal of the social-democratic or social-liberal left; or by limiting the state to guaranteeing property rights and contracts, as the new neo-liberal right desires.

I shall basically use the historical method, which is more appropriate when it undertakes an analysis of macroeconomic and political problems. I shall not examine the crisis of the state and the ongoing reforms in abstract; instead I shall consider the reality of the second half of the 1990s. However, logical-deductive and rather abstract tools will be used whenever they are useful for the analysis. In this manner I shall develop a few models: distinguishing between the activities that belong exclusively to the state and the social and scientific services that the state provides; defining public non-state (or non-profit) property as different from state property and private property; defining the concepts of the new institutions that will characterize the new state that is emerging in the twenty-first century; and identifying a range of controls prevailing in contemporary capitalism, involving legal, market, democratic and administrative controls – the logic behind this range of controls sets the basis for the choice of institutions through which the state must act.

CRISIS AND REFORM

The Great Economic Crisis of the 1980s reduced the growth rate of the developed countries to half compared with what it had been in the twenty years following World War II, caused the per capita income of developing countries to remain stagnant for fifteen years and led to the collapse of centralized state regimes of the Soviet type. When I say that this Great Crisis had as its basic cause the crisis of the state – a fiscal crisis of the state, a crisis of the mode of state intervention and a crisis of the bureaucratic way in which the state is managed – the assumption is that the state has an essential role regarding economic coordination, apart from ensuring internal order, monetary stability and the normal operation of markets.[1] Or, in other words, it is implicit that the coordination of the economic system in contemporary capitalism is not only carried out by the market – as conservative neo-liberalism wishes[2] – but also by the state. The market coordinates the economy through exchanges, the state through transferences to those sectors that the market is unable to remunerate adequately (in the political judgement of society). Thus, whenever there is a significant crisis, its origin must be sought either in the market or in the state. The Great Depression of the 1930s stemmed from a malfunction of the market, while the Great Crisis of the 1980s arose due to the collapse of the social-bureaucratic state that characterized the twentieth century.

The market is the mechanism 'par excellence' for resource allocation, but even in this task its action is limited since there is monopoly power and positive or negative externalities. The modern state, in turn, came into being before the capitalist market, just as Hobbes and his social contract, which legitimated the state, preceded Adam Smith and the principle that, if each one defends his own interests, the collective interest will be assured through market competition.

The modern state comes before the capitalist market because it guarantees property rights and contracts, but it is contemporary and concurrent with markets, because it performs an essential role in directing income distribution, by concentrating it in the hands of the capitalists in periods of primitive accumulation, or by distributing it among the poorest, so as to render viable the emergence of civilized and modern societies, that, apart from being wealthy are supposed to be reasonably fair.

The Great Depression of the 1930s came about from market failures. Keynes explained this with his theory of chronic insufficiency of demand. With the depression, the liberal state collapsed, giving way to the social-bureaucratic state: 'social' because the state assumed the role of guaranteeing social rights and full employment; and 'bureaucratic', because it did that through the direct hiring of bureaucrats. Now, besides judges, tax collectors, policemen and military, the state hired professors, doctors and even artists. The welfare state then emerged in the developed countries, while in the developing countries the state assumed the form of the developmentalist state, actively promoting industrialization through protectionist strategies, and in Russia, China and their satellites, it assumed the form of the Communist state, which attempted to replace the market instead of complementing it.

This last distortion, which reached its peak in the Soviet Union, arose from an overestimation of the role of the bureaucratic middle class in managing contemporary economic systems. In the twentieth century, with the appearance of multinational corporations and the modern state, capitalism was no longer the product of an alliance between the emerging bourgeoisie and the aristocracy – this was the liberal state of the nineteenth century – but the outcome of a new alliance between capital owners and an expanding bureaucratic middle class. This technobureaucracy or new middle class held the monopoly of technical and organizational knowledge – a knowledge that turned increasingly strategic as technological development gained momentum all over the world.[3] Yet it disproved the bureaucratic or statist assumption that it would be feasible to substitute managers for business entrepreneurs, organization for capital or bureaucratic planning for markets. Managers, organization and planning gained space, but never to the point of replacing markets. Instead, what became clear was the need to combine or complement the market and the state, capital and organization, entrepreneurs and (public or private) managers, given the essential roles that these institutions and actors performed in the operation of modern and complex economic systems, and in the consolidation of democratic regimes.

The great thrust of technological development in the second half of this century led the world economic system to deep transformation. With the dramatic drop in transportation and communication costs, the world economy became global, i.e. far more integrated and competitive. Consequently, the nation-states lost autonomy, and the developmentalist economic policies which require relatively closed and autarchic countries, were no longer effective. Soon afterwards it was increasingly clearer that the state intervention strategy could no longer be protection against competition, but would have to become a policy deliberately aimed at stimulating and preparing private enterprises and the country as a whole for international competition. The state and the market would no longer be seen as polarized alternatives but as complementary economic coordination factors.

The world economy faced another great crisis starting in the 1970s and coming to a peak in the 1980s. This was partly due to an inability to recognize and cope with the new technological realities; partly due to a mistaken view of the role of the state as a direct provider of social services; and partly because, as the state grew, fiscal and administrative distortions stemming from rent-seeking became unavoidable, mostly because capitalist development was essentially subject to cycles or waves of prosperity and slow-down. In the first world, growth rates were half of what they used to be in the first two decades after World War II, while unemployment rates rose, principally in Europe, and even the Japanese miracle that was booming in the 1980s was stumbling in the 1990s.[4] In Latin America and East Europe, which refused to engage in a fiscal adjustment in the 1970s, the crisis broke out in the 1980s and was far more violent.

This crisis, however, is no longer the result of the chronic shortage of demand mentioned by Keynes; it is not therefore a market crisis, as was the case in the 1920s and 1930s. Even less can it be attributed to the greater momentum of technological progress, which might cause temporary unemployment, but is in fact the source of growth, not of its failure. The main cause behind the Great Crisis of the 1980s was rather the crisis of the social-bureaucratic state, that stopped being a factor favouring development and began to hinder it, as it grew too much and lost functionality. Only East and Southeast Asia escaped from the economic crisis, precisely because they managed to avoid the crisis of the state. But even there, in the 1990s, economies such as Japan and Korea already showed signs of exhaustion of the state-led development strategy.

The crisis of the state I refer to is not a vague concept. On the contrary, it has a very specific meaning. The state enters into a fiscal crisis as it loses public credit to a greater or lesser degree, and, at the same time, its capacity to generate savings diminishes or even disappears, as public savings, which used to be positive, become negative. Consequently, the capacity for state intervention drops dramatically. The state is rendered paralysed. Added to the fiscal crisis were crises of the mode of state intervention – particularly the direct provision of social services by the state – and of the bureaucratic way of managing government, making the state expensive in a world where globalization and international competition became the rule. Here we have the origins of the slowdown in growth rates, the new surge of unemployment and the increasing concentration of income. The crisis of the state is associated, on the one hand, with the cyclical nature of state intervention, and on the other, with the globalization process that reduced the autonomy of nation-states in defining social and economic policies, particularly in protecting their firms and citizens from foreign competition.

The crisis of the 1930s was a crisis of the market – of a market that was not able to assure employment and an even distribution of income. Hence, when Keynesian macroeconomic policies and ideas in favour of planning appeared in the 1930s they were immediately adopted, and led to a considerable improvement in the performance of the national economies. In the 1950s, the idea of a state that had a strategic role in promoting technical progress and capital accumulation was commonplace, together with the idea that it was responsible for ensuring a reasonable income distribution. However, these successes led to an explosive growth of the state not only in the field of regulation, but also in the social and productive spheres. In order to do this the tax burden, which accounted for 5–10 per cent of GDP at the beginning of the century, increased to 30–60 per cent, the number of civil servants whose tasks had nothing to do with the classic roles of the state increased substantially, and the number and size of state-owned enterprises were multiplied many times. The state became a social-bureaucratic state insofar as it directly hired civil servants such as teachers, doctors, nurses, social workers, artists, engineers, scientists, etc. with the purpose of promoting social welfare, technical and scientific growth and economic development.

As is usually the case when a system or an organization grows, distortions soon started to emerge.[5] State transferences were diverted to meet the needs of special interests of businessmen, the middle-class groups and public bureaucrats. Rent-seeking became increasingly widespread, as economic agents tried to capture the *res publica*. State-owned enterprises, which at first had been a powerful mechanism for achieving forced savings, to the extent that they had monopolistic profits and invested them, soon saw this role begin to wane; at the same time, their performance proved to be inefficient, as they were increasingly subject to bureaucratic control patterns. Bureaucratic public administration, which had proved effective in fighting corruption and nepotism in the small liberal state, now showed themselves highly inefficient in directly providing the large social and scientific services. Classical bureaucracy was fitted to perform the exclusive activities of the state, comprising economic, social and scientific policies, but proved to be inefficient in providing the services that the citizen-customers started to demand in the twentieth century. The ensuing crisis led governments all over the world to substitute a managerial public administration for the bureaucratic one.[6]

Anyway, whether it was due to the capture of the state by private interests, the inefficiency of its administration or the imbalance between the demands of the population and its capacity to meet them, the state came to a crisis; this first, in the early 1980s, took the form of a fiscal crisis and specifically a foreign indebtedness crisis. As public savings become negative, the state lost financial autonomy and was rendered immobile. Consequently, its managerial limitations arose more clearly. The crisis of governance, which in extreme cases took on the form of hyperinflationary episodes, became all-embracing: the state was no longer an agent of development, but an obstacle to it.

On the other hand, another factor that exerted additional pressure in favour of state reform was the globalization process. It was a gradual quantitative shift that in the end became a major qualitative shift. Arising from a considerable drop in the costs of international transportation and communications, globalization led to a huge increase in world trade, international financing and direct investments by multinational corporations. It also meant a rise in international competition to undreamed-of levels, and a reorganization of production at world-wide level sponsored by the multinational corporations. The market gained much more space at a world-wide level and transformed international competitiveness into a condition determining the survival of the economic development of each country. The consequences were, as is always the case when the market prevails, a better resource allocation and an increased productive efficiency. On the other hand, there was a relative loss of autonomy by the state; its ability to protect the economy from international competition also waned. Since markets always act in favour of the strongest, the most capable, income concentration was greater than before, both among countries and among citizens of a single country. Among countries because the more efficient ones were in a better position to impose their interests over the less efficient, and among the citizens of each country because, with the surge of technical progress, the demand for the most efficient and better educated rose more rapidly than for the less-educated. If we take only the workers in poor and rich countries, the advantage was for the former: since their wages were considerably lower, developing countries' exports to developed countries soared, thus depressing the wages of the less skilled workers from the developed countries. Thus, globalization exerted a twofold pressure over the state. On the one hand it represented a new challenge – the role of the state was to protect its citizens, and this protection was now jeopardized, although it continued to be dramatically required; on the other hand, it demanded that the state – which had to be stronger in order to tackle the challenge – also had to be cheaper, carrying out its tasks more efficiently so as to reduce the costs of its private enterprises that had to compete internationally.

The crisis in the state broke out because it was often captured by private interests when it grew too much, and also because of the globalization process that reduced its autonomy. The fiscal crisis was defined by a greater degree of public borrowing and by the growing inability of the state to achieve positive public savings that would have enabled it to finance public policies. The crisis in the way the state intervened was apparent in three forms: the crisis of the welfare state in the rich economies, the exhaustion of import substitution industrialization in most developing countries and the collapse of the centralized state in the Communist countries. The inefficiency of the state bureaucratic manner was revealed in the high costs and low quality of the services provided.

As the crisis was universal, the responses to it also had the same character, given the swift dissemination of ideas and public policies that the new communication systems permitted,[7] but it varied according to the ideological affiliation of each group. In order to describe these responses, I reduced the number of the groups or social actors to four – the archaic (or populist) left, the social-democratic and pragmatic centre-left, the pragmatic centre-right (or the establishment), and the neo-conservative or neo-liberal right; this will enable me to tell a brief and stylized story.

Given the crisis, the archaic and populist left – formed by those who did not accept that the national-developmentalist approach was something of the past – went into a crisis and was paralysed, ceasing to have real proposals to deal with the new problems. It could not have happened otherwise, since its diagnosis of the crisis was erroneous, believing that it was caused by foreign interests: by imperialism in the past, and now by globalization. The pragmatic centre-right – formed by the business, political and bureaucratic establishments – decided, out of Washington and New York, that the countries that were heavily in debt had, first (1982), to follow macroeconomic fundamentals advancing fiscal adjustment, price liberalization and exchange devaluation so as to reduce the current account deficits; and, second (1985, with the Baker Plan), to engage in market-oriented reforms (trade liberalization, privatization, deregulation) to be politically supported by specific compensatory social policies.

The neo-conservative right, which had hopelessly criticized the growth of the state since the 1930s, now gained adepts and adopted a triumphant attitude, as it assumed that a firm alliance had been established with the pragmatic centre-right. It considered that market-oriented reforms would automatically bring about economic development, as long as markets recovered full control of the economy, individuals stopped being monitored or protected by the state, and the minimum state was turned into reality. Now it was necessary to privatize, liberalize and deregulate industries and labour markets; the state would divest itself of all interventionist roles in the economic and social spheres and limit itself to assuring macroeconomic fundamentals, property rights and contracts. Macroeconomic policy should be neutral, the only goals being to achieve zero public deficit and a steady growth of money supply consistent with the GDP growth rate. Industrial policy was ruled out, and so was social policy in the purest version of the neo-conservative credo, given its unexpected and perverse effects.[8]

In the meantime, the pragmatic centre-left, making a transition from a social-democratic to a social-liberal approach, defined the Great Crisis as a crisis of the state, affirmed the need to obey the macroeconomics fundamentals – i.e. fiscal adjustment, tight monetary policies, right market prices, positive interest rates and realistic exchange rates – and supported the market-oriented reforms. But this support did not mean the acceptance of a self-regulating market according to neoclassical general equilibrium theory and ideology, since free markets ensure neither economic development nor social justice. It thus affirmed that market-oriented reforms were in fact needed, but not in the radical form sustained by the neo-conservatives; they were necessary to correct the distortions caused by the excessive growth of the state and to eliminate arbitrary interference in defining relative prices. But to return to the liberal state of the nineteenth century was definitely infeasible. Instead of reducing the state to a minimum, the social-liberal centre-left proposed reforming or more precisely rebuilding the state, giving it governance and governability, so as to enable it – in a new cycle – to once again effectively complement and correct market failures. Rebuilding the state meant recovering public savings; overcoming the fiscal crisis; redefining the ways in which it intervened in the economic and social sphere; substituting a managerial for a bureaucratic public administration; and contracting out non-profit, public non-state organizations to competitively provide education, health care and cultural services. It meant making a transition from a state that directly carried out social services, and even the production of goods and services through state-owned enterprises, to a state that acted as a regulator, facilitator or provider of funds to foster economic and social development through non-profit organizations.[9]

In the mid-1990s, the pragmatic centre-right and, in a broader sense, the international élites, after a brief hesitation, perceived that the neo-conservative approach was neither economically nor politically feasible. The way was open for a political concentration between the centre-left and the establishment on the basis of the above line of action. The thesis of reforming or rebuilding the state turned into an important issue. The World Bank and the Inter-American Development Bank gave priority to loans for state reform. The United Nations promoted a 'resumed general assembly' and there were many meetings on public administration and the reform of the state. Many countries set up ministries or high-level committees in charge of state reform. The 1997 *World Development Report* was originally entitled *Rebuilding the State*.[10] The reform of the state was then the motto of the 1990s, replacing that of the 1980s, which was structural adjustment.

A broad coalition between the centre-left and the centre-right was thus established or re-established. A coalition that led governments in Latin America, Eastern Europe and a large number of developing countries in Asia, apart from the developed countries, to promote state reform in order to make the state smaller and more specifically geared to the activities that belonged to it. This involved raising state capability and making it politically, fiscally and administratively stronger, i.e. empowered with governability and governance, and hence able to promote education and health, technological and scientific development. Instead of simply protecting the national economy, the state is now supposed to assist it in becoming more competitive internationally.

In this way, the state of the twenty-first century began to take shape. It will certainly not be the social-bureaucratic state, since that was that state which went into crisis. It will not be the neo-liberal state dreamt of by the neo-conservatives, since there is no political support nor economic rationale for a return to the liberal state of the nineteenth century. My prediction is that the state of the twenty-first century will be a social-liberal state. It will be social because it will continue to protect social rights and promote economic development. It will be liberal because it will do so using more market and less administrative controls; it will carry out its social and scientific services mainly through competitive public non-state organizations; it will make labour markets more flexible; and it will promote human capital and technological development so as to allow its business enterprises to be more innovative and internationally competitive.[11]

Summing up, I see four basic components of the state reform which took place in the 1990s, that will transfer to the social-liberal state of the twenty-first century:

1. Setting more precisely the limits of state action, by reducing its size; privatizing state-owned enterprises; giving autonomy and transferring to the non-profit sector the social and scientific services while keeping its financing within the state; outsourcing non-core or auxiliary activities.
2. Reducing the extent to which the state regulates the private sector, transforming the state into a promoter of the competitive capacity of the country instead of a protector of the national economy against international competition.
3. Increasing state governance, i.e. its capacity to make government decisions effective, by means of a fiscal adjustment that refunds financial capacity to

the state, and of administrative reform aimed at a managerial public administration (instead of a bureaucratic one).
4. Increasing governability – i.e. the power to govern – through political institutions that ensure a better intermediation of interests and make governments more legitimate and democratic, thus improving representative democracy and opening spaces for social control or direct democracy.

Another way to conceive the current state reforms that are taking place is to understand them as a process of the creation or transformation of institutions with the purpose of increasing governability and governance. In this sense, privatization aims to transform state-owned enterprises into private ones; 'publicization' means transforming state entities into non-profit institutions; and outsourcing is a process through which auxiliary and support services are purchased from the private sector instead of being directly provided by the state. In all these cases we have the creation or transformation of institutions. Within the state *stricto sensu*, where the exclusive activities of the state are carried out, it is possible to distinguish three types of institutions: policy-making departments, executive agencies and autonomous regulatory agencies. Besides these new institutions, understood in the restricted sense of organizational institutions (this is especially true for the institutions devoted to social control), we have in the reform of the state new legal institutions: electoral legislation, reform of political parties, political finance regulation and the increasing involvement of civil society in political decision making.

In a more abstract manner, it is possible to consider state reform on the basis of the principal-agent model, as a strategy of creating incentives and punishments for politicians so that the will of the voters is reflected in the administration. According to this model, in its simplified form, voters would be the principals, the elected politicians their agents and these, in turn, would be the principals of the bureaucrats or civil servants.[12] The main task of the reform would be the creation or the reform of institutions in such a way that the incentives and penalties make the state more democratic and efficient, and the politicians and the bureaucrats more accountable. At this level of abstraction, I find no fault in this approach. Ultimately, it codifies the obvious. However, when authors adopting the rational choice approach, assume that politicians are only motivated by rent seeking and the will to be re-elected, excluding public interest as a third motivation, the model's explanatory capability is lessened. In the same line, when the motivation of civil servants is reduced to rent seeking and the will to be in office, excluding the achievement motivation and the will to promote the public interest, the meaning of the reforms towards a 'new public administration' or a managerial public administration becomes incomprehensible. The radically pessimist view of human nature involved only allows the existence of the classical bureaucratic model, where controls are strict, step by step, and confidence, null.

In the next sections I shall examine these four basic components of state reform: (a) the delimitation of the role of the state that is taking place by means of privatization, 'publicization' and outsourcing; (b) the deregulation process, that involves a question of degree of state intervention, not of delimitation of scope; (c) the effort for increased governance; and (d) the struggle for enhanced governability. Additionally, I will discuss the logic underlying state reform – a reform that involves downsizing, diminished intervention in economic activities, rise in fiscal and administrative capability, and greater political legitimacy within a democratic regime that gradually tends to be more direct, more subject to social control. In so doing I shall concurrently be analysing the main institutions which are at the core of state reform in the 1990s.

LIMITS TO THE STATE DIRECT SPHERE OF ACTION

Reform of the state is often seen as a downsizing process, as its role is redefined. Keeping in view its excessive growth in this century, the high hopes that the socialists had for it, and the distortions that it finally underwent, this perspective is essentially accurate. The state grew in terms of staff and mainly in terms of income and expenditure. In many countries, civil servants (excluding those who work for state-owned enterprises) account today for 10 to 20 per cent of the workforce, when, at the beginning of this century, the corresponding figure was around 5 per cent. State expenditure, in turn, was multiplied by three or four in this century: in the last thirty years the figure doubled and now stands between 30 and 60 per cent of GDP.[13] This growth took place at the same time as the role of the state was enlarged, mainly in the social sphere.[14]

The ratio between the number of civil servants and the economically active workforce is invariably smaller than the relationship between the tax burden and GDP. This in part stems from the fact that civil servants are more skilled and consequently their average salaries are higher than those paid to workers in the private sector, but the main reason is that the state is increasingly financing instead of directly executing social services, and thus requiring fewer civil servants. At the beginning of the twentieth century the state was directly responsible for construction works, support services and social services. But after some time it became clear that outsourcing engineering services, support services and finally, social services, was more efficient. The state reform that took place in the 1990s started from this general vision, that required, above all, defining the role of the state, determining its exclusive tasks, and leaving the private sector or the public non-state sector to execute those activities that do not involve state power.

In order to define clearly the limits or the realm of state direct action it is necessary to start out from the concept of the state and to distinguish three areas of activity that we may find there: (a) exclusive state activities; (b) social and scientific services provided by the state; and (c) the production of goods and services for the market. It is convenient to distinguish, in each of these areas, the core activities from the auxiliary or support ones. Figure 8.1 summarizes these distinctions in a simple matrix. The columns show Exclusive State Activities, Social and Scientific Services and Production of Goods and Services for the Market.

The definition of exclusive state activities comes from the definition of the state. It is the political organization that holds 'extroverse power' over the civil society existing in a given territory. Private organizations and public non-state entities only hold power over their employees, whereas the state has power outside itself: the power of making and imposing law, of taxing and of transferring funds from tax payers. The state holds this power in order to assure domestic order – i.e. to guarantee property rights and contracts, to defend the country against a foreign enemy and to promote economic and social development. In this latter role, the state can be viewed in economic terms as a bureaucratic organization which, through transferences, complements the market in coordinating the economy. Whereas markets operate through the exchange of equivalents, the state does so through transferences financed from taxes.

The state is a monopolistic entity by definition. It was for no other reason that Weber defined it as an organization that holds the legitimate monopoly of violence. Exclusive activities of the state are thus monopolistic activities, in which the power of the state is exerted: the power to make and enforce the laws of the country, to impose justice, to maintain order, to defend the country, to represent it overseas and to collect taxes, to regulate economic activities. These activities are monopolistic because they do not allow for competition. Imagine for instance, a state appointing two ambassadors to represent it in a single country in order to see which one does better... Or allowing two judges to hear a single case concomitantly... Or to give two tax collectors the task of competitively inspecting the same taxpayer... These hypotheses obviously make no sense.

	State Exclusive Activities	Social and Scientific Services	Goods and Services Production for the Market
Core Activities	STATE as Civil Service	↓ publicization	↓ privatization
Support Activities	outsourcing ————————————————→		

Figure 8.1: Setting the Limits for the Sphere of Action of the State

Nonetheless, apart from these activities, which are characteristic of the classical liberal state, there is a series of other activities that pertain exclusively to the state. In essence they are the activities required for policy making in the economic, social and scientific spheres, and for implementing these policies through transferences of funds for education, arts, health care, basic social security and unemployment benefits, besides the enforcement of laws protecting the environment and the cultural heritage. Not all these activities are intrinsically monopolistic or exclusive, but in practice, in view of the large transference of state resources they involve, they are actually exclusive state activities. There is a whole range of reasons for the state to subsidize these activities, but they fall outside the scope of this paper. The main economic argument that justifies them is that these activities, as they involve significant positive externalities, are not properly remunerated by the market.[15] The ethical argument is that they are activities that involve direct fundamental human rights that every society must guarantee for its citizens.

And we also have exclusive state economic activities. The first and foremost of these is to guarantee currency stability. For this purpose, the creation of central banks in this century was fundamental. To assure the stability of the financial system is another strategic activity that falls exclusively upon the state. Regulating monopolistic activities and promoting competition is another one. Investments in infrastructure and in public services are not, rigorously speaking, exclusive state activities as they can be subject to concession to the private sector, but the final responsibility for them belongs to the concessionaire authority.

In state reform, exclusive state activities should remain within the state. Among them we can distinguish the strategic core, where strategic decisions are taken by the parliament, the main tribunals, the president or prime ministers and the ministers, supported by the policy-making secretariats from the executive agencies and regulatory agencies. These institutions will be dealt with in the section concerning governance and the new or managerial public administration.

At the other extreme, as shown in Figure 8.1, we have the production of goods and services for the market. This is an activity which, except for the ephemeral Soviet-type central state system, has always been dominated by private enterprises. Nonetheless, in the twentieth century, the state intervened strongly in this area, mainly in the monopolistic public utilities subject to concession, and in the infrastructure, steel and mining industries, where there were large economies of scale. The basic reasons why the state intervened in this area were practical rather than ideological. They were twofold: the state invested in sectors in which investments were too heavy for the private sector to undertake; and it invested in monopolistic sectors that could turn out to be self-financing because of the extraordinary profits they could yield.[16] The assumption behind the former reason was that the state was able to achieve public savings. When a fiscal crisis of the state broke out, this ceased to be true, and an opposite movement started: privatization. Besides usually being more efficiently run, private enterprises and private capitalists were able to make savings where the state was unable to do so. Since the state was undergoing a fiscal crisis, it was unable to invest, and depended on the resources coming from privatization to reduce its heavy indebtedness. On the other hand it was quite clear that it was not convenient for the state to engage in entrepreneurial business, since it was something that the market could manage better, more efficiently. Apart from the fact that state control is less efficient than market control, private management tends to be more efficient than state management, that is permanently threatened by unacceptable political interests. Another problem is related to objectives: while corporations are supposed to be competitive and make a profit, the state – and the state-owned enterprises – were often required to engage in social policy. For a long time the issues of privatization and nationalization were the subject of a broad ideological debate. Nowadays, this debate no longer exists; there is a quasi-consensus on whether it is necessary to privatize – given the fiscal crisis – or convenient to privatize – given the greater efficiency of the privatized enterprises. The only industries where a legitimate doubt exists about privatization are the natural monopolies. In this case privatization can only be undertaken if autonomous regulating agencies are set up, capable of artificially setting the prices as if competitive markets existed.

Halfway between exclusive state activities and the production of goods and services for the market, there is today, within the state, a series of activities in the social and scientific field that are not exclusive since they are not intrinsically monopolistic and do not involve state power. Included in this category are the schools, universities, scientific and technological research centres, day-care centres for infants, outpatient clinics, hospitals, entities that provide assistance to the needy – mainly children and the elderly – museums, symphony orchestras, art workshops, educational or cultural radio broadcasting stations and television networks, etc. Although the financing of some of these activities are clearly appropriate for the state – it would be very difficult to ensure free universal basic education or universal health care relying only on public charity – and should be included in exclusive state activities, the execution of these services is not in the same situation. Quite the contrary, these are competitive activities that can be financed by the state, and controlled through the use of a managerial public administration, the setting up of quasi-markets, and social control mechanisms.

In this regard, these activities do not have to remain within the state nor be state monopolies, but they do not have to be private – i.e. geared towards profit-making or private consumption – either, since they are often strongly subsidized by the state and the object of private donations. For this reason, the reform of the state in this field does not involve privatization but rather 'publicization' – i.e. its transference to the public non-state sector.[17] The assumption behind this is that there is a third form of property which is relevant in contemporary capitalism: public non-state property. In everyday language only two forms of property are mentioned: public property, seen as synonymous with state property, and private property. This simplification, which has its origin in the dual nature of law – public or private law – leads people to refer to entities whose nature is essentially public, not profit-making, as 'private'.[18] However, if we define as 'public' the organization and property which address the general interest, and as 'private' those which address the interests of individuals and their families, it is clear that the public sphere is not restricted to the state, and that non-profit organizations, which additionally are not geared to the defence of corporate interests (a fourth relevant form of property), but to the general interest, cannot be considered private. The Ford Foundation or the Santa Casa da Misericórdia in São Paulo are not private entities, they are public. But, since they are not subordinated to the government and do not have civil servants on their staff, they are not part of the state. Actually, they are public non-state entities (sometimes known as: third sector entities, non-profit entities, non-governmental organizations, volunteer organizations).

The public sphere is broader than the sphere of the state. In theory, whatever belongs to the sphere of the state is always public, but in practice that is not the case: the pre-capitalistic state was, ultimately, private, since it existed to attend to the needs of a prince; in today's world what is public used to be conceptually separated from what was private, but every day we see attempts at private appropriation of the state. The sphere that belongs to everybody and is for everybody is the public one. A specific form of that space or of the public property is that of the state. The property that is meant for profit-making or for consumption by individuals or groups is private. A foundation, even though ruled by civil law and not by administrative law, is a public institution insofar as it attends to the general interest. In principle all non-profit organizations are or should be non-state organizations.[19] It could be said, in short, that there are still two kinds of property: public and private. However, there are two important distinctions: first, public property is subdivided into state and non-state to avoid confusion with the state sphere in itself; and second, private law institutions addressed to the public interest and not aimed at private consumption are not private, but merely public non-state entities.

The acknowledgement of a public non-state sphere became especially significant when the crisis of the state deepened the dichotomy of the state-private sector, leading many people to imagine that the only alternative was either state property or private property. Privatization is a suitable alternative when an institution has the power to manage all its income from the sale of products and services, and the market is in a position to take over the coordination of its activities. Whenever this is not the case, it is possible for it to operate in the public non-state sphere. On the other hand, whenever the crisis of the state demands a review of the relationships between the state and society, the public non-state sphere may have an intermediation role or may facilitate the appearance of direct control by society and of partnerships, which open up new prospects for democracy. As Cunill Grau observes (1995, pp. 31–32):

> The introduction of 'public' as a third dimension, that overcomes the dichotomic point of view that confronts in an absolute manner what pertains to the state and what is private, is unquestionably linked to the need to redefine the relations between the state and society ... What is public, 'in the state' is not in itself a definite piece of information, but rather a construction process, that in turn supposes the activation of the social public sphere in its task of influencing state decisions.

Manuel Castells declared at a seminar in Brazil (1994) that NGOs are quasi-public institutions, which is true, since they are halfway between the state and society. Public non-state organizations carry out public activities and are directly controlled by society through their administrative boards. There are, however, other forms of direct control by society and these can also be defined as belonging to the public non-state sphere. In Brazil, an interesting experience which started in Porto Alegre was that of participative budgets, by which citizens could be directly involved in the preparation of the municipal budget.[20]

According to Tarso Genro (1996), non-state organizations made it possible for society to find an alternative to privatization. This could be the proper modality of property if a company is in a position to be self-financing in the market. However, whenever the funding for a given activity relies on donations or transferences from the state, this would mean that it is a public activity, and if this activity does not need to be part of the state, it could therefore be performed by a public non-state entity under the control of society itself, which actually finances it and directs it. Then, in a situation in which the market is clearly incapable of undertaking a series of jobs and the state is not flexible or efficient enough to carry them out, there is a place for them to be done by public non-state organizations.[21]

In the second half of the twentieth century, the growth of public non-state entities boomed. Sometimes these organizations were mixed with a fourth type of property pertaining to contemporary capitalism – 'corporatist property' which is characteristic of trade unions, peer associations and clubs.[22] This is only legitimate in the case of grassroots associations that simultaneously represent group interests and undertake community services oriented to the general interest. The growth of entities that represent special or group interests has been considerable in this century, and, as Putnam demonstrated (1993), this growth is an essential factor for the strengthening of civil society and the economic development of the region or country where it occurs; however, the growth of public non-state entities aiming at social control and/or at the production of social services has been just as significant or more so, although not as much studied. This growth was brought about by the greater effectiveness – and hence greater efficiency – shown by this kind of institution in performing social services. These services, which are not naturally monopolistic, can benefit from competition and from the support of society and the state. Since they are directly addressed to the population, they can be effectively controlled by the citizens through social control mechanisms.[23]

The process that led to the expansion of the public non-state sector has two origins: on the one hand, society itself, that continuously creates entities of that nature to perform social control or the production of social services; and on the other, the state, which, in the process of reform, engages in the publicization process of its social and scientific services. Publicization took place particularly in New Zealand, Australia and the United Kingdom. It is likewise taking place in several European countries and more recently in the United States in the field of basic education. The right to free basic schooling is increasingly being met by public non-state schools of a community nature whose operational costs are financed by the state.[24] In Britain, universities and National Health Service hospitals, which used to be part of the state, were transformed in to quangos (quasi non-governmental organizations). In Holland, all national museums were transformed into non-profit organizations. In Brazil, the ongoing publicization programme foresees that state social and scientific services will become 'social organizations' – public entities operating according to private law that are so recognized by the state, enter into management contracts with the government and are consequently financed in part or in full by state funds.

Finally, in analysing the rows of Figure 8.1, we have Core Activities and Auxiliary or Support Activities. Core activities are those that pertain to the state itself, those through which the power of the state is exercised; they include law making, regulating, administering justice, law enforcement, taxation, policy making and fostering social and economic development. But for these roles of the state to be performed, it is necessary for politicians and the high-level state bureaucracy at the strategic core, as well as for medium level public administration,[25] to have the support of a series of auxiliary activities or services: cleaning, security, transportation, catering, technical computer services, data processing, etc. According to the logic ruling the state reform of the 1990s, these services should in principle be outsourced, i.e. they should be awarded by a competitive bidding procedure and contracted with third parties. In this sense, these services, which are marketplace services, are carried out in a competitive manner, enabling the Treasury to benefit from substantial savings.

There can always be exceptions to this outsourcing process; grey areas will always exist. Is it convenient to outsource the work of secretaries? Probably not, although their role has decreased considerably in the modern administration. There are other services such as those, in which, because of their proximity to the exclusive activities, outsourcing is not advisable. Because of that and because there will always be grey areas between what should be the subject of 'publicization' and what should not, it is suitable to consider two legal systems within the state: one governing statutory officials and another governing employees. That is in fact a common practice in developed countries, endowed with developed bureaucracies. The condition of being a statutory civil servant is limited to those who make a career within the state; the other public servants who perform auxiliary activities that are not to be outsourced and that cannot be the subject of 'publicization' are considered employees.

Support services outsourcing, which all modern states are engaged in, is just another chapter in the subcontracting that gained strength in mid-century, when public works were outsourced. At the outset of the twentiwth century, it was still the norm for the state to undertake its engineering projects and works directly. With the appearance of contractors and engineering companies, this practice vanished. Similarly, privatization is in part a process involving a return to the principles of concession of public services.

	State Exclusive Activities	Social and Scientific Services	Goods and Services Production for the Market
Core Activities	State as Staff	Non-State Public Entities	Privatized Enterprises
Auxiliary Activities	Outsourced Enterprises	Outsourced Enterprises	Outsourced Enterprises

Figure 8. 2: Institutions Resulting from State Reform

In state reform, the outcome of this threefold process – privatization, publicization and outsourcing – is that the state, when seen as staff, is limited to just one section in Figure 8.1. In the other sections, as can be perceived in Figure 8.2, we find the Public Non-State Organizations,[26] Privatized Enterprises and Outsourced Enterprises. The first section is described as 'State as Staff' because the state is greater than its staff, insofar as we have a social state and not a liberal state; it is, however, a state that is ceasing to be a social-bureaucratic state that directly performs social services, to become a social-liberal state that contracts out competitive services. The best way to measure the size of the state as compared to the country or nation-state it forms part of is not by considering the ratio of members of its staff related to the total workforce, but by considering the percentage of the state expenditure related to its GDP. In the social-liberal state, the second ratio (expenditure to GDP) will be considerably greater than the former (statutory civil servants to workforce), discounting the fact that the average salary of the civil servants is greater than the national average salary. The social-liberal state of the twenty-first century, just like the social-bureaucratic state of the twentieth century, will continue to be a significant promoter or financing agent of social and scientific activities, except that the execution of those activities will be carried out by public non-state entities. To represent this fact graphically, the 'State as Expenditure' would take up a large portion of the column devoted to social and scientific services, insofar as they are financed in a non-recoverable way by the state budget.[27]

DEREGULATION

Besides setting the limits for the sphere of the state's direct action, state reform involves establishing the limits for its role as a regulator and hence for the deregulation processes that are taking place today. It is one thing to define the institutional scope of the state and know whether the state should undertake a series of activities directly – as in the social-bureaucratic state – or whether it should tend to confine itself to its specific functions, as in the ongoing state reform of the social-liberal state. However, determining the scope of its role as a regulator of private activities is something quite different. It is a specific function of the state, since it enacts the laws that govern social and economic life. But what should be the extent of this regulation, especially with regard to economic activities? As society becomes more complex and the state grows, its regulation will also tend to be more extensive. Yet, regulation has often been excessive. In the United States the state has a tendency to regulate in order to protect social rights, assure quality standards for goods and services and ensure the proper operation of the market in monopolistic areas, and thus it finds it easy to incur excesses; Japan and Germany do something similar, although their purpose is to promote cooperation among companies (Audretsch, 1989). There was a movement in favour of greater regulation towards the end of the nineteenth century, whose main defenders were the consumers and small enterprises in the United States (Audretsch, 1989, chapter 5). Since the 1970s however, these same groups have been going in the opposite direction, towards deregulation. Actually, regulation implies a cost for the economy; it is a kind of tax that is not collected but that the private sector is forced to pay.[28] A cost which is often necessary, but that at other times simply responds to special interests.

The fight against regulatory excesses was always the fight of the liberal economists armed with their neoclassical theory on self-regulatory markets. Rigorously speaking, mainstream economics developed on the basis of the assumption that the market is capable of optimally coordinating the economy and so state intervention is not necessary. But this theory, and the ideology behind it, although long dominant, did not prevent the state from regulating the economy intensively. Given that, one of the neo-liberal founders of the School of Chicago, George Stigler (1975, pp. X–XI), adopted a new approach to the problem: to develop 'the political economy of regulation', i.e. to check who benefited from regulation, based on the principle that there is a political market for regulatory legislation. Who are these beneficiaries? Stigler (1971, p. 114) considers that as a rule, regulation is a demand of the economic sector and is mainly aimed at benefiting it. Based on that approach, Stigler founded a new conservative political economy, that has been extraordinarily developed through the concept of rent seeking (Krueger, 1974) and by the rational choice school headed by Buchanan and Olson.

The purpose of this paper is not to review the abundant literature on regulation and deregulation. It gained momentum in the 1980s, when the privatization process began in the United Kingdom, and then spread out universally. Yet the limits of privatization and deregulation soon became apparent, since the privatized natural monopolies now demanded even greater regulation.[29] The liberal agenda found it therefore necessary to deregulate and regulate simultaneously: deregulate in order to reduce state intervention; regulate to render privatization viable. Whatever the circumstances, the problem of the limits to state intervention in the market persisted. State reform, as it took place in the 1990s, inherited all this debate, at a time when the limits of the neo-conservative proposal in favour of reducing the state to a minimum became clearer.

Instead of summarizing this debate – which is not among the objectives of this paper – I would like to mention the logic underlying the present day reform which I am describing.

Mainstream neoclassical economics, mainly after Coase (1937) and Williamson (1985), assumes that market coordination is in principle more efficient. However, due to transaction costs, it can be more efficient to have certain activities coordinated administratively. That is what leads to the emergence of enterprises, or rather organizations, within which the market does not work; they are submitted externally to the market, but not internally. This theory is appealing; it is one of the most stimulating discoveries that have taken place in the field of economics in this century. It is, nonetheless, a purely economic theory, that may only be applied to a limited extent in the field of politics. Ultimately, it reiterates the issue that the market is the best way to coordinate or control an economic system, and fails to do so only in exceptional cases, depending on transaction costs. In these terms, it does not provide us with a satisfactory explanation, nor does it give us clear criteria to identify the areas in which the state should act and those which should be left to the market.

The regulation process that took place in the twentieth century involved subsidies and fiscal waivers of all kinds. Industrial, agricultural and foreign trade policies became omnipresent, and eventually turned excessive, distorting economic calculus and allowing the private capture of the *res publica*, as it responded to special interests. Yet, this does not lead us to infer that the state can or should withdraw fully from regulating the economy. Regulations generally imply a heavy cost burden for the companies, detracting from their international competitiveness. That is why there is a tendency to reduce them as much as possible. In contrast, subsidies, protectionist measures and fiscal waivers give rise to deep distortions in relative prices, stimulate rent seeking and imply high costs for the state. It is for this reason that state reform aims at reducing them substantially, although realistically speaking, it is not possible to conceive that they can be altogether eliminated. In many areas the state still has an essential role to play as a regulator. Foreign trade policies, for instance, are more active today than ever before. Environmental control policies have never been as significant as they are now. Faced with such a complex problem as this one, Cardoso (1996, pp. 15–16) presents criteria that help us to think about the issue, taking as a starting point the combination of greater efficiency and better income distribution:

> The problem we face is twofold: efficiency and equity ... In this respect, the state-market dilemma is false. The role of the state as regulator when faced with, for instance, ecological issues, has increased constantly. Thus, the correct proposal for us to study is *the role of the state in the market*. The question is how to increase competitiveness (that leads to a rise in productivity and the streamlining of economic activities) and how investment decisions, and those which affect consumption, can be made more public, i.e., how can they become more transparent and liable to be controlled by society ... and not just by bureaucracies (those of the state or of companies). (Italics by the author.)

THE RANGE OF CONTROLS LOGIC

There may not be a general theory aimed at setting the limits to the sphere of action of the state or to the extent of its regulation of the market. Yet, based on the state reform of the 1990s, it is possible to find a logic that helps to distinguish what is supposed to be in the public and in the private sector, and, within the public sector, what is supposed to remain in the state and what should belong to the public non-state sphere. I propose to call this logic 'the range of controls logic'.

In order to coordinate itself, every society uses a series of control and coordination mechanisms besides its traditions, basic values and beliefs. From an institutional perspective, and by a simplification, there are three basic control mechanisms: the state, civil society and the market. The state comprises the legal system, which is made up of the legal rules and the main institutions that govern society. The legal system is the most general control mechanism, practically identifying itself with the state insofar as it establishes the basic principles for other mechanisms to be able to operate. The market, in turn, is the economic control system that is driven by competition. Finally, the third mechanism is civil society, i.e. society structured according to the relative political weight of the different social groups, that organizes itself to protect private interests or special interests of a collective nature, or acts in the name of public interest. No matter which, all of them are essentially control mechanisms.[30]

Instead of the institutional criterion, it is however possible to use a functional criterion, superimposed over it but not the same. According to this view there are also three types of control: hierarchical or administrative control exerted within public or private organizations, democratic or social control exerted in political terms over organizations and individuals, and economic control exerted by the market.

Based on the functional criterion, it is possible to order the control mechanisms which are relevant for our analysis in a range that covers, from one end, the most diffuse, automatic and democratic control mechanism, to the other end, the most focused control mechanisms resulting from decision-making processes; or, in other words, from the most democratic to the most authoritarian disposition. According to this criterion, the following control mechanisms can be identified, besides the legal system which comes before any of them: (1) market, (2) social control (direct democracy), (3) representative democracy, (4) managerial hierarchical control, (5) bureaucratic hierarchical control and (6) traditional hierarchical control.

The principle behind the choice of controls is that the most general, most diffuse and most automatic is the one to be preferred, provided that it is efficient and effective. That is why the market is the best control mechanism, since competition in principle leads to the best results with the lowest costs, not implying the use of power, whether democratic or hierarchical. For that reason the general rule is, that whenever it is possible for the market to control something, it should be the control mechanism of choice. Nonetheless, there are many situations that escape from market control, be it because there are other values at stake apart from the economic one (and the market only controls economic efficiency), or because even in the economic field the market often does not operate properly. This is because of: (a) its own imperfections, and (b) the existence of positive externalities, the ones that have not been adequately remunerated by the market, or of negative externalities, the ones that are not punished by the market. Consequently, it is necessary to consider other forms of control.

Direct democracy or social control is, in this scale model or range, the next most democratic and diffuse control mechanism. Social control enables society to organize itself formally and informally to control not only individual behaviour but also public and private organizations, which is what matters in the context of this analysis. Social control may also take place in the political field by referendum or plebiscite. It may originate in two ways: either from the grassroots up, when society organizes itself politically, aiming to control or to influence institutions over which it does not have formal instruments; or top down, when it takes on the role of guiding public non-state institutions as a deliberate consequence of state reform. Direct democracy is ideal and it is increasingly being used at local level or to control decentralized public services, but it is still not feasible at national level except in a restricted manner, when the people are asked by means of a referendum to confirm or orient the decisions of their representatives about subjects very clearly defined.

In the third place there is representative democracy; by means of this mechanism society is represented by elected politicians who are empowered by society. The legislative branch in modern democracies is organized according to this principle. The parliamentarian system is intended in part to transfer this same principle to the executive branch. Anyway, the limitations of this kind of control are also obvious, insofar as it is only suited to define general laws and not to execute them.

In this respect society depends on the hierarchical type of control, which can be managerial (rational), bureaucratic (rational-legal) or traditional. Weber clearly defined the latter two kinds of domination or hierarchical control. In the administration of the state traditional control corresponds to 'patrimonialism'; bureaucratic rational-legal control to 'bureaucratic public administration', in which objectives and the means to attain them are rigidly defined by law; and managerial control to 'managerial public administration', that will be analysed in greater detail in the next section.

These six types of mechanisms – excluding the legal mechanism that overlies all of them – are generally combined with each other in specific social arrangements. In historical terms, and from an optimistic perspective of history, it can be considered that in primitive societies the prevailing controls were traditional hierarchical and social control. In the complex pre-capitalistic societies, hierarchical traditional control turned dominant and was expressed in patrimonialism. In the liberal capitalistic regimes of the nineteenth century, the dominant types of control were bureaucratic control combined with a representative democracy and with market control. In the social-bureaucratic capitalism of the twentieth century, bureaucratic control combined with a representative democracy and regulated markets prevailed. Last, in the global capitalism that is now emerging as well as in the state reform of the 1990s, a combination of managerial hierarchical control, representative democracy, social control or direct democracy, and market control will be predominant.

In terms of the public and private spheres, both were mixed in primitive society and under patrimonialism; in the times of liberal capitalism, the private sphere was made distinct from the public one and gained autonomy; in social bureaucratic capitalism, the public sphere grew once again as the state; in the capitalism of the twenty-first century, the public sector will increase in size once again, not as the state grows but as the public non-state forms of organization of production and social control grow.

This logic guiding state reform has a historic nature and simultaneously follows a few general principles: basically, the political preference for democracy or for a more spread-out or diffuse distribution of power; the economic preference for greater efficiency and effectiveness; the economic and political preference for automatic controls, and the principle of enlargement of the public non-state sphere.

GOVERNANCE: ADMINISTRATIVE REFORM

Following the above range of controls logic, there is a third essential element of state reform of the 1990s: governance.[31] A government may have governability insofar as its leaders have the necessary political support to rule, but it can at the same time fail to rule properly due to lack of governance. Governance exists in a state when its government has the required financial and administrative conditions to implement the decisions it takes. A state that is undergoing a fiscal crisis, that has a negative public savings rate, and therefore lacks the resources to undertake investments and to finance social and scientific policies, is a state that has been rendered immobile. The crisis of the state in the 1980s was above all a crisis of governance because it first manifested itself as a fiscal crisis.[32] That is why fiscal adjustment policies took priority in that decade. In the 1990s, fiscal adjustment still remains an essential question – actually it is a permanent problem for all countries – but it is now increasingly clear that to adjust is not enough to achieve good governance: the reform of public administration is also required.

The issue of the managerial capacity of the state, and hence of administrative reform, became fundamental in the 1990s. Administrative reforms are a recurring issue. Almost all governments, at all times, talk about the need to have a more modern public administration, a more efficient one. However, there have been only two structural administrative reforms in capitalism. Replacing 'patrimonialist administration', the first reform involved the implementation of the bureaucratic rational-legal public administration; it took place in the nineteenth century in the leading European countries, in the first decade of this century in the United States, and in the 1930s in Brazil. The second, occurring now, is the change towards a managerial public administration. This new public administration had its first manifestations in the 1960s, but only started to be put into effect in the 1980s in the United Kingdom, New Zealand and Australia, and in the 1990s in the United States of America, when the subject caught the attention of the public at large with the publication of *Reinventing Government* and the adoption of the National Performance Review by the Clinton administration. In Brazil it has been implemented since Fernando Henrique Cardoso took office and the *Plano Diretor da Reforma do Aparelho do Estado* (*Master Plan for the Reform of the State Apparatus*) was approved and began to be enacted (1995). Until this date, the two countries in which managerial public administration had been more extensively implemented were the United Kingdom and New Zealand, in the former country under a Conservative government, in the latter initially under a Labour administration.

I do not intend here to repeat what I have been writing recently on managerial public administration.[33] It is important, however, to point out that bureaucratic public administration, described by Weber as a 'rational-legal' form of domination, was characterized by an intrinsic contradiction. A bureaucratic administration is rational, in terms of instrumental rationality, insofar as it adopts more suitable (efficient) means to attain its goals. It is, on the other hand, legal, insofar as it rigidly defines the objectives and the means to achieve them in law. However, in a world that is undergoing a complete technological and social transformation, it is impossible for a manager to be rational if he does not have decision-making capacity, if he cannot use his discretion and judgement, but must, on the contrary, blindly follow the procedures laid down in the law. In the nineteenth century, when bureaucratic public administration replaced the patrimonialist one, this involved a great step forward in putting an end to corruption and nepotism. Nevertheless, in the twentieth century, when the state grew and assumed new roles, and scientific discovery and technological change progressed at an unprecedented pace, the inherent inefficiency of this type of administration became evident. At the same time as the state bureaucracy – i.e. the professional civil servants taken as a whole – experienced a rise in their strategic position in society, it was clear that new forms to manage the *res publica* had to be adopted, forms that were more compatible with technological progress, speedier, decentralized, more aimed at controlling results than at controlling procedures. And they also had to be more in line with the progress of democracy throughout the world, which increasingly required a more direct involvement of society in public management.

I would therefore like to define the main characteristics of the managerial public administration, which is also being called 'new public administration', as follows:

1. The administration is citizen-user or citizen-customer oriented.
2. There is an emphasis on the control of results through management contracts (instead of control of procedures).

3. The state bureaucracy is strengthened and given increased autonomy, particularly the civil servants' bodies that execute the exclusive activities of the state, so that their political and technical role in formulating and following up public policies, together with the politicians and society, becomes apparent and more worthy.[34]
4. The secretariats in charge of public policy making, of a centralized nature, are separated from the decentralized units which execute those same policies.
5. A distinction is made between two types of decentralized units: the executive agencies, which carry out exclusive state activities and are by definition monopolistic, and the social and scientific services that are of a competitive nature, and in which the power of the state is not involved.
6. The above social and scientific services are transferred to the competitive public non-state sector.
7. In order to control these decentralized units, (a) direct social control mechanisms, (b) management contracts in which performance indicators are clearly defined and the results measured, and (c) the formation of quasi-markets in which administered competition takes place are adopted.
8. Auxiliary and support activities that are subject to a competitive bidding procedure in the market are outsourced.[35]

The increase in the autonomy of the state bureaucracy should not be confused with bureaucratic insulation – i.e. the insulation of the state agencies from political influences – which is frequently proposed as a solution to economic populism and clientelism.[36] In democratic societies, the high cadres in public administration are embedded in the political process and are part of it. The ideal type of purely technical bureaucrat does not make sense, in the same way as it does not make sense to assign him the role of ensuring the rationality of public administration and more broadly of government, a rationality that would continuously be threatened by politicians. This is an authoritarian view, which still believes in the enlightened monarch and in the 'good' dictator – it is a point of view that is finally being overcome through the progress achieved by democracy in this century. Peter Evans (1995) proposes that the contradiction between the need for autonomous state bureaucracies and democracy can be overcome by means of the concept of 'embedded autonomy', i.e. through a bureaucracy that is simultaneously autonomous and embedded in society.[37]

In carrying out exclusive state activities, it is necessary to distinguish between three types of institutions: the public policy-making secretariats at the strategic core of the state, together with the ministers and head of the government who are involved in the strategic decisions taken by the government; the executive agencies, which carry out the policies defined by the government; and the regulatory agencies, which enjoy a greater degree of autonomy and try to set prices that would be market prices in a realm of natural or quasi-natural monopolies. The regulatory agencies must be more autonomous than the executive agencies because they do not exist with the purpose of implementing government policies but rather to carry out a more permanent job, i.e. replacing competitive markets and fostering market competition.

In short, governance is achieved and state reform will be successful when the state becomes at the same time stronger and smaller: (a) financially stronger, since the financial crisis of the 1980s has been overcome; (b) structurally stronger, with clearly set limits for its sphere of action, and with a precise distinction between its decision-making strategic core and its decentralized units; (c) strategically stronger, endowed with political élites capable of taking the necessary political and economic decisions; and (d) administratively stronger, with a technically capable and motivated bureaucracy.

GOVERNABILITY: POLITICAL REFORM

Finally, state reform implies a political reform which guarantees its governability. Much has been said in recent years on governability, mainly since the Great Crisis of the 1980s fully hit Latin America and Eastern Europe, but this governability crisis was evidently combined with a governance crisis, since its main cause was the fiscal crisis of the state.[38] Governability and governance are concepts imprecisely defined and frequently mixed up. The political capacity to govern, or governability, derives from the relation of the legitimacy of a state and its administration *vis-à-vis* society, whereas governance is the financial and administrative capacity of an administration to implement policies. It is impossible to have governance without governability, but the latter can be highly deficient even under satisfactory conditions of governability. In the concept of governance can be included, as Reis does (1994), the capacity to add up the different interests, thus establishing a bridge between governance and governability. Good governance, as observed by Frischtak (1994), increases the legitimacy of a government and, consequently, the governability of the country.

If even in advanced democracies, governability problems often arise, what can be said about the recent and imperfect democracies, where political institutions are poorly defined, and governments are unstable, easily losing political support? So, on the problem of governability, the most serious – if not fatal – condition for governments is to lose the support of civil society, since, in practical terms, governability depends on government legitimacy, that is, on the support it has from civil society.

Governability in democratic regimes depends: (a) on strong political institutions, able to make governments representative, and to mediate adequately between conflicting interests; (b) on the existence of mechanisms that make politicians and bureaucrats accountable; (c) on society's capacity to limit its demands, and on the government's ability to respond to the demands which are eventually maintained; and, essentially, (d) on the existence of a basic social contract. It is this basic social agreement, this Hobbesian social contract, that guarantees legitimacy and governability in advanced societies. In developing countries, especially in Latin America, where society is characterized by a deep heterogeneity, this agreement is often absent or imperfect. Thus the relevance of political agreements which are oriented towards economic development. These pacts and the respective economic development projects are always relatively exclusive, as they keep part of the population out of it, but they grant a vision of the future to society, thus making government feasible.[39]

The political dimension of state reform is at the same time the most important, since the state is the political entity 'par excellence', and the least clear, since we can not speak of a state political crisis in the 1990s. Political crisis is a synonym of governability crisis. The government lacks the conditions to govern effectively because it loses legitimacy *vis-à-vis* society or because its institutions are inadequate for exercising political power. We cannot say that democratic governments, both in developed and developing countries, are in crisis because they have lost social legitimacy or because their political institutions have deteriorated. On the contrary, the twentieth century was, in final terms, the century of democracy. In the developed countries, it was consolidated in the first half of the century; in the developing ones, it began to be affirmed in the second half, particularly since the early 1980s, when a wave of democratic transitions took place in Latin America, then in Eastern Europe and more recently, in Asia.[40]

It is only possible to speak of a political 'crisis' if we compare reality with an ideal situation – if we think, for instance, that democratic regimes do not ensure a 'good government', i.e. government which would lead society in an optimal way. Naturally, this is at the core of the concerns of the rational choice school, which dominated North American political science over the last twenty years. It is the fundamental basis of neo-liberal criticism of state intervention since, according to the neo-conservative view, there is no way to ensure that politicians actually rule in the interest of those who are ruled; on the contrary, since they tend to rule in their own interest, good government is almost impossible, and the best alternative is to downsize the state to a minimum, thus reducing the need to govern to what is strictly necessary; markets would take care of every-thing else.

The misconceptions involved in this approach start with the method used. Instead of thinking of politics and policy making as a historical process which evolves over time, going through crisis and transformations, never reaching an optimal status, neo-conservatives see politics and administration as something static and abstract. Supported by the neoclassical microeconomic view, it un-derstands the political process as a frustrated optimization process, as a princi-pal-agent relationship, in which the principals are the citizens and the agent, the government. It would really be very difficult to have good government with selfish politicians, aiming exclusively at satisfying their political ambitions and rent seeking.

Yet this method enables us to discuss certain essential problems, which of-ten remain implicit in analysis based on the inductive/historical approach. Przeworski (1995a), adopting the rational choice method, wrote a fascinating essay on state reform. After summing up the internal criticism of the neoclassi-cal assumption of market efficiency – using for that purpose Stiglitz's analysis (1992, 1993a, 1993b) and his own (1990), he tried to respond to two questions: (1) which are the political conditions enabling a state to intervene efficiently?; and (2) how can state institutions be reformed so that market failures are cor-rected and not made more serious? To answer those questions, Przeworski criti-cizes Chicago's and Virginia's neo-conservative models. Electors may be rela-tively ignorant, but they are 'rationally ignorant'; they are informed on what interests them. On the other hand, the role of political opposition should not be underestimated; opposition keeps voters critically informed of government performance.[41] That is why a good government would be possible – not because politicians were committed to the public interest independently from the elec-toral advantages involved.

This is an internal criticism of the neo-conservative model, which accepts the assumptions of the rational choice school: politicians are exclusively moved by a willingness to be reelected and rent seeking or, in other words, all actions of politicians may be explained by the support they will receive from voters or by the economic gains that they will secure for themselves by making use of the state power to make transferences to given interest groups. When both objectives are not consistent, the ruler will make trade-offs between them. Yet, in spite of the intellectual attractiveness of limiting the critique to internal criticism, this is not always possible and it is certainly not realistic in the present case. Politicians are moved by a third reason: their commitment to their ideological and moral principles, that is, their own assessment of what is the public interest. This type of politician – the good politician – will eventually become a statesman. He also carries out trade-offs, but the basic trade-off is between his desire to be re-elected and his commitment to the public interest. When the existence of this third motivation is assumed, the immediate problem that appears is that related to the objective of political reform. Is it a question of guaranteeing as much as possible that the will of citizens be met by politicians, as stated by Przeworski, or of ensuring that the public interest be met when it conflicts with the electorate's assessment? As Przeworski (1995a, p. 1) observes:

> My argument is that the quality of intervention in an economy depends largely on the effectiveness of the mechanism through which governments are obliged to be accountable to the public for the results of their actions.

Undoubtedly, a main intermediate objective of any democratic regime is to increase the accountability of politicians. Politicians should always be accountable to their citizens. The clearer the responsibility of the politician *vis-à-vis* citizens and their claims, the more democratic the regime is. But this does not mean that all the claims of the citizens should be accepted by politicians. To hold this view implies that the 'imperative mandate' is a requisite of democracy: the politician would be elected exclusively to meet the purposes of his voters, and could lose office in case of conflict with them. The imperative mandate, however, is the result of collective democratism rather than of democracy. According to Bobbio (1984, p. 10):

> Modern democracy, born as representative democracy, as opposed to the democracies of antiquity, should be characterized by political representation, that is, a representation in which the representative who is called to look after the interests of the nation cannot be subjected to an imperative mandate.[42]

The accountability concept already implies the rejection of the imperative mandate.[43] The ruler is not only accountable *vis-à-vis* the electorate; he is also accountable to his own conscience. His republican virtues are also part of the democratic concept. Stokes (1995), acknowledging that this freedom is implicit in the accountability concept, proposed the concept of 'responsiveness' as an additional condition of democracy. The responsive ruler would be the one who faithfully met the wishes or determinations of the citizens. In fact, there is no need for that concept, unless we accept the imperative mandate as a valid democratic institution. If we agree that the imperative mandate is not desirable, there is no need to think of responsiveness; it is sufficient to think of the politician's accountability towards the citizens and himself. Good political institutions, plus a political culture based on democratic and republican values, will enable politicians to be accountable to voters, as they encourage governments to act in accordance with the public interest, rewarding good governance and penalizing bad. In the final analysis, the good politician will be the one who is capable of differentiating the short-term interests of his voters – which they perceive immediately – from their medium and long-term interests, and be loyal to the latter and not the former.[44] This will not make trade-offs impossible for him regarding his re-election objective, but will give him a sense of the priorities.

The imperative mandate is linked to a radical concept of democracy, which makes no sense when we recall that ultimately politics is the art of commitment, a strategy of mutual concessions, a difficult intermediation of interests in conflict. On the other hand, at the opposite extreme, the concept of the statesman as a politician who has the courage and vision to face his electorate and risk his re-election to be loyal to his concept of what is public interest, is associated with the idea of the enlightened monarch, or republican virtues. Greek philosophers preferred monarchy to democracy because they knew about the instability of democracy in those times, and had a clear differentiation between monarchy and tyranny, and they expected the monarch to be enlightened. Now, in the contemporary world in which democratic regimes can be stable because the economic surplus is no longer appropriated by the use of political power but through the market, none of the extremes makes sense – neither the imperative mandate, nor full dependence on the statesman or on republican virtues (or the enlightened monarch).

From the point of view of political reform, there is no doubt that it is necessary to focus attention on institutions which guarantee or even better, which increase politicians' accountability, once this is a matter of degree. To reform the state in order to grant it greater governability is to make it more democratic, to endow it with political institutions enabling a better mediation between the conflicting interests of the different social and ethnic groups and nations of the different regions in the country. While the market is the field where equivalents are exchanged, and may hence be relatively impersonal, from the economic point of view, the state is the realm of transferences. Politics and policy making in contemporary capitalism is largely a struggle for the size of the tax burden and, given the budget, for those transferences, which are often only more-or-less successful rent-seeking attempts. But, in principle, this struggle is legitimate, representing class and group differences which are the very object of politics. The political challenge state reform faces is to have political parties corresponding to ideological orientations; to develop an electoral system which enables representative governments with stable majorities; to have a vigorous opposition fighting within a common field of interests; to have a free and responsible media that better reflects the opinions of the readers, listeners or viewers than those of the media owners or of their advertisers; to have a legal system which not only makes justice among citizens and defends them from the state but which also knows how to defend the *res publica* against the ambition of powerful citizens wishing to capture it; to have a bureaucracy which is less self-referred and abandons the practice of secrecy, managing the public patrimony with transparency; to have a legislative power relatively immune to clientelism; to develop systems for the participation of citizens in the direct control of state and public non-state institutions; to have a more transparent and democratic way of financing electoral campaigns; and finally, to develop accountability systems for politicians and senior public bureaucrats.

CONCLUSION

The state reform we examine in this article is a historical process whose dimension is proportional to that of its crisis. The crisis started in the 1970s and exploded in the 1980s, and led to the resurgence of neo-liberalism and to a deep criticism of state intervention by some eminent intellectuals and a few neo-conservative politicians; few, because politicians are more realistic than intellectuals. It was precisely that realism of politicians and, more broadly, of the ruling classes at world level, which led them in the 1990s to abandon the idea of the minimum state and concentrate their attention on state reform. Since the main cause of the large economic crisis of the 1980s was the crisis of the state, the correct thing to do was to rebuild it instead of erasing it.

In this paper I examined the main lines of that reform. I divided it into four sections: setting the limits of the state's direct sphere of action, deregulation, strengthening of governance and the conquest of governability. To present these four subjects I developed a model based on differentiation between state, public non-state and private organizations, and between exclusive state activities and competitive social and scientific services that the state is supposed to finance. Deregulation was seen as a problem of degree and of cyclical movements of state intervention. Governance was seen as a question of fiscal adjustment and administrative reform towards a managerial public administration. Governability was considered to be the outcome of the development of political institutions which guarantee a better intermediation and representation of interests combined with a democratic culture and republican values. As a basis for the model, I developed a general explanation that I called the range of controls logic, according to which the control mechanisms of contemporary capitalist societies ranged from market control to traditional hierarchical control.

The outcome of the reform that took place in the 1990s will be a more efficient and democratic state, responding to those to whom it definitively has to respond: the citizens. Thus, it will be a state acting jointly with society and according to its desires. It will be a state less centred on protection and more on promoting competition capabilities. It will be a state which will not use state bureaucrats to provide social and scientific services, but which will contract out to public non-state organizations for that purpose and on a competitive basis. It will be what I propose to call a social-liberal state, replacing the social-bureaucratic state of the twentieth century: certainly a democratic state, because the great political feat of the twentieth century was the consolidation of democracy. The democratic regime was able to establish reasonably stable institutions and a sufficiently sound democratic culture, so that its great limitation – political instability – was overcome or prevented. That instability led the Greek political philosophers to prefer a 'good' monarchy and a 'good' aristocracy instead of democracy, knowing that the risk of monarchy was tyranny and that the risk of aristocracy was oligarchy. Today, in view of the economic and political development that has taken place, democratic regimes are far more stable than authoritarian regimes.[45]

The state reform of the 1990s was a reform which presupposed citizens and was devoted to them: citizens less protected or ruled by the state, with greater freedom, inasmuch as the state reduced its paternalistic approach; citizens who combined cooperation and competition; and citizens who were politically more mature. These citizens would probably be more individualistic because they were more conscious of their individual rights, but they would also have more solidarity among themselves (although this may appear to be contradictory), because they were more fit for collective action and, consequently, more willing to organize themselves in institutions oriented to the public interest, and in corporatist institutions oriented towards the protection of group or class interests. This ongoing reform, as I see it, is not based on the bureaucratic premise of a state insulated from society, acting only in accordance with instrumental reason, nor on the neo-conservative premise of a state lacking a society, in which isolated egoistic individuals make decisions on the economic and political markets. That is why it requires the active participation of the citizens; that is why the new state which is emerging will not be indifferent or superior to society. On the contrary, it will institutionalize mechanisms enabling an ever-growing participation by citizens, an ever-growing direct democracy. That is why the ongoing reforms are also the expression of a redefinition of citizenship itself: citizens are expanding their scope, becoming social subjects more aware of their rights and duties within a democratic society in which competition and solidarity will continue to be complementary and contradictory elements.

I am quite aware that this is an optimistic view. It does not deny that poverty and injustice and lack of respect for civil and political, social and republican rights, are still dominant problems all over the world. It just assumes that, although unsatisfactory, progress is taking place, and that the reform of the state is today an essential and strategic step in the right direction.

NOTES

1. I initially studied the crisis of the state in 'Economic Reforms and the Cycles of the State' (Bresser Pereira, 1993a) and in the essays published in *A Crise do Estado* (Bresser Pereira, 1991).
2. I mean economists such as Friedrich Hayek, Milton Friedman, James Buchanan, Mancur Olson and Anne Krueger.
3. My theoretical work on this consists of 'A Emergência da Tecnoburocracia' (Bresser Pereira, 1972) and 'Notas Introdutórias ao Modo Tecnoburocrático ou Estatal de Produção' (Bresser Pereira, 1977a) which were later included in the book *A Sociedade Estatal e a Tecnoburocracia* (Bresser Pereira, 1981); an unpublished paper called 'As Classes Sociais no Capitalismo Contemporâneo' and chapter 10, 'Etapas do Desenvolvimento Capitalista' in *Lucro Acumulação e Crise* (Bresser Pereira, 1986).
4. The sustained growth rate in the United States since 1991 may indicate that this country benefited by the end of the Cold War, which permitted a sizeable fiscal adjustment; it was the first to overcome the crisis and is engaging in a new long wave of growth. Britain, which underwent structural reforms in the 1980s, may be in the same position.
5. These distortions usually have a cyclical character. I examined the cyclical quality of state growth and intervention in Bresser Pereira (1993a).
6. I shall examine the concept of management-oriented public administration later on, in the section concerning governance and administrative reform. To see the subject in greater depth see Bresser Pereira (1996c).
7. See Melo and Costa (1995). The authors analysed the dissemination of neo-liberal policies and more broadly the policy bandwagoning mechanism consisting of the emulation by governments of public policies that were successful in other countries or regions.
8. On the reactionary nature of neo-liberal thinking, see Hirschman (1991).
9. A systematic presentation of this view can be found in Bresser Pereira, Maravall and Przeworski (1993). In practical terms, the shift towards economic policies aimed at fiscal adjustment and state reform in social-democratic governments, that took place in France (1981), Spain (1983) and Brazil (1995), were manifestations of this new stand of the modern social-liberal centre-left.
10. Eventually the WDR was given the title *The State in a Changing World*, but it kept its basic inspiration: the reform or rebuilding of the state. In its introduction, the report affirmed that sustained development – economic and social – demands an effective state. 'Fifty years ago, when people said that the state had a central role in economic development, they meant a development guaranteed by the state; today we are once again seeing that the state has a key role in economic and social development, but mainly as a partner, as a catalyzing and facilitating agent' (World Bank, 1997).
11. Bob Jessop (1994, p.103) affirms that in the twenty-first century the Keynesian welfare state will be replaced by the Schumpeterian workfare state that promotes innovation in open economies and subordinates social policy to the needs of market flexibilization and international competition requirements. There is a clear connection between the concept of a social-liberal state and the Schumpeterian workfare state.

12. To analyse the state reform from this perspective see Przeworski (1996b) and Melo (1996).
13. In measuring the size of the state by its expenditure, the World Bank (1997, p.16) confirmed that in three and a half decades, between 1960 and 1995, the state doubled its size.
14. European states which developed a sophisticated welfare system, ensuring that all their citizens would have a minimum standard of living, are now at the upper limit, whereas countries with an intermediate level of development, and the United States, where inequalities are great and some minimum social rights are not guaranteed, are clustered around the lower limit. As Adam Przeworski wrote (1995b), for a country to be 'civilized', i.e. for it to have less than 10 per cent of its population below the poverty line, it is necessary for the tax burden to be about 45% of GDP. According to this criterion, the United States is not a civilized country, since roughly 18% of its population is poor.
15. There is a huge amount of literature on the economic argument; see particularly Stiglitz (1989, 1993b, 1994) and Przeworski (1990, 1995b, 1996a).
16. In Brazil, state investments in the steel and petrochemical industries can be included among the former; those in telecommunications in the latter; and those in oil and electric energy in both cases. See Bresser Pereira (1977b, chapter 10) and Alves dos Santos (1996).
17. The word 'publicization' was created to distinguish this reform process from that of privatization.
18. In the United States, for instance, universities such as Harvard or Chicago are called 'private', but in fact they are public non-state organizations. The NGOs – non governmental organizations – are another form of public non-state property.
19. I say 'are or should be' because an entity that is formally public and non-profit making may in fact make profits, in which case it is a false public entity. Cases of this type are common.
20. The participative budget was introduced by Mayor Olivio Dutra (1989–1992) and then continued by Mayor Tarso Genro (1993–1996) both from the Partido dos Trabalhadores – Workers' Party.
21. I originally examined this matter in a paper on the transition of formerly Communist enterprises to capitalism. It proposed that large monopolistic utilities should not be privatized, at least at first, but rather transformed into public non-state organizations.
22. Corporatist organizations defend the interests of their members, be it in the political field (trade unions) or for consumption (clubs).
23. In general, however, it is possible to distinguish a public non-state organization clearly from a corporatist organization; it is also easy to distinguish it from a private organization. However, in countries where the state is not well organized, it is possible to find many organizations that present themselves as public non-state ones in order to benefit from fiscal exemptions; in fact they are private, profit-oriented for the benefit of one or more 'owners'. This is just a case of fraud and tax evasion.
24. In Spain, practically one quarter of students go to free community schools which receive from the state the equivalent of that spent in state-run schools. In the United States, 'chartered schools' have recently developed, following the same funding principle.
25. I am using 'public administration', followed by the predicative 'high-level' or 'medium-level', and 'state bureaucracy' as synonyms.
26. Public non-state entities which in Brazil, when subject to 'publicization', are called 'social organizations'.
27. It should be observed that the state can be measured including its state enterprises. In this case, however, we run into a series of difficulties since these enterprises are not financed by tax revenues but from their own sales. Anyway, this issue has lost relevance since the privatization processes became generalized.
28. According to *The Economist* (1996, p. 19), when reporting on the research undertaken by Thomas Hopkins at the Rochester Institute of Technology, the cost the companies had to pay to comply with regulatory laws accounted for $668 billion dollars in 1995, whereas the total expenditure of the Federal Government that year was US$ 1.5 trillion.
29. See Armstrong, Cowan and Vickers (1994), Claudio Frischtak, ed. (1995).

30. In this paper the relative relevance of these three institutional control mechanisms is not analysed. It is clear that the perspective of the neoclassical economists, according to which the market has an absolutely dominant role, is too narrow. The critical perspective of evolutionary economics, expressed so well by Delorme (1995), is more stimulating; it stresses the role of institutions and organizations as well as their dynamic character, marked by the diverse control mechanisms and by the context in which they operate.

31. Governance is a relatively new term that the World Bank is using. A comprehensive book on this issue was written by Frischtak and Atiyas (1996).

32. On the nature of the present crisis as essentially a fiscal crisis of the state see Bresser Pereira (1987, 1988, 1991, 1993b, 1996a).

33. In January 1995 I took office as Minister of Federal Administration and Reform of the State in Fernando Henrique Cardoso's administration. Besides preparing the *Plano Diretor da Reforma do Aparelho do Estado* (Ministério da Administração Federal e Reforma do Estado, 1995), I have published a few articles on the subject (Bresser Pereira, 1995, 1996b and 1996c).

34. In the reform under way, bureaucratic public administration is being replaced by managerial public administration. This, however, is not intended to diminish the role of state bureaucracy, which has a strategic role in the administration of the state.

35. There is a vast literature on managerial public administration. See, among others, Barzelay (1992), Osborne and Gaebler (1992), Fairbrother (1994), Ranson and Stewart (1994), Nunberg (1995), Gore (1995) , Abrucio (1997), Ferlie *et al.* (1996).

36. As observed by Melo and Costa (1995), governance is associated *inter alia* with the capacity for insulation of the professional bureaucratic élites *vis-à-vis* the political and party system, and the government élites *vis-à-vis* particularistic interest groups.

37. According to Evans (1995, p. 248): 'The autonomy (of the state bureaucracy) is essential in defining a developmental state, but it is not enough. The capacity of the state to undertake changes also depends on the relations between the state and society. Autonomous states, completely isolated from society, can easily be predator states. The states which aim at development must be embedded in a thick network of social relationships that links it with its allies in society based on transformation objectives. Embedded autonomy and not just autonomy, is what makes the developmental state effective.' This position is similar to the one I am presenting here, although the social-liberal state I assume is less interventionist in the economic field than Evans's developmental state.

38. See Diniz (1995, 1997) for a criticism of traditional governance analysis of the imbalance between the demand and supply of public services. On the governability crisis in Latin America see Ducatenzeiler and Oxhorn (1992).

39. This matter was extensively analysed by Bresser Pereira and Nakano (1997).

40. This wave started with democratic transition in Spain in the 1970s, going through the other southwestern countries of Europe; it transferred to Latin America in the 1980s, and continued with the democratization of the former Communist countries by the end of that decade. In the 1990s, they were democratic transitions in East and Southeast Asia and attempts at democracy in Africa. The literature on the subject is very large. On democratic transitions in general see Linz (1982), O'Donnell and Schmitter (1986), O'Donnell, Schmitter and Whitehead, eds (1986a), Palma (1990), Przeworski (1991) and Huntington (1991); on transition in Brazil, Bresser Pereira (1978, 1985), Martins (1983), Stepan (1989), Lamounier (1989), Cardoso (1986); on transitions in Eastern Europe, Przeworski (1993); and for an analysis of ongoing transition in Asia, Haggard and Kaufman (1995), whose work also presents their general view of the transition process based on a political economy prospect.

41. Przeworski identifies the 'Chicago model' as that in which politicians only aim at being re-elected, while in the 'Virginia model' politicians are rent seeking. In Chicago, the original contribution to that type of model was that of Stigler (1975), although Olson (1965) had already formalized the point of view by attempting to demonstrate the lack of feasibility of collective action by large groups.

42. Bobbio, however, pointed out that the democratic principle of rejecting the imperative mandate

has always been violated in contemporary democracies, in which the corporative principle that says that politicians would represent private interest, tends to predominate. In this model, intermediation would be in the hands of state bureaucracy and not in those of politicians.
43. Przeworski (1995a, p. 8) makes this fact clear when he rejects the imperative mandate and also when he observes that the citizens may ignore what is in the public interest. Institutions should reward those governors and citizens acting on behalf of the public interest and penalize those who do not: 'Private agents have to benefit for behaving in accordance with the public interest and they must suffer when they act in a different way, and the same should apply to governors'.
44. See John F. Kennedy's book *Profiles in Courage* (1956) for a fascinating set of short biographies of American politicians who had that courage.
45. See Przeworski and Limongi (1993, 1997) on this aspect. These authors question a 'theory of modernization', which linearly relates development to democracy, and state that the emergence of democracy is not simply the result of development, but is related to the political actors' action in pursuing their own objectives. Notwithstanding, based on broad empirical evidence, they admit, avoiding total indetermination, that 'once (democracy is) established, economic restriction plays a role: survival possibilities of democracies are greater the richer the country is' (1997, p. 177).

BIBLIOGRAPHY

Abrucio, Fernando Luiz (1997), *O Impacto do Modelo Gerencial na Administração Pública: um Breve Estudo Sobre a Experiência Internacional Recente*, Brasília: Escola Nacional de Administração Pública, Cadernos ENAP, **10**.

Alves dos Santos, Antônio Carlos (1996), *A Economia Política da Privatização*, São Paulo: Fundação Getúlio Vargas, PhD Thesis, September.

Armstrong, M., S. Cowan and J. Vickers (1994), *Regulatory Reform*, Cambridge, MA: MIT Press.

Audretsch, David B. (1989), *The Market and the State*, New York: Harvester Wheatsheaf.

Barzelay, Michael (1992), *Breaking Through Bureaucracy*, Berkeley: University of California Press.

Bobbio, Norberto (1984), *Il Futuro della Democracia*, Torino: Einaudi.

Bresser Pereira, Luiz Carlos (1972), 'A Emergência da Tecnoburocracia', in *Tecnoburocracia e Contestação*, Rio de Janeiro: Editora Vozes.

Bresser Pereira, Luiz Carlos (1977a), 'Notas Introdutórias ao Modo Tecnoburocrático ou Estatal de Produção', *Estudos CEBRAP*, **21**, April. Reproduced in Bresser Pereira, 1986, pp. 77–109.

Bresser Pereira, Luiz Carlos (1977b), *Estado e Subdesenvolvimento Industrializado*, São Paulo: Editora Brasiliense.

Bresser Pereira, Luiz Carlos (1978), *O Colapso de uma Aliança de Classses*, São Paulo: Editora Brasiliense.

Bresser Pereira, Luiz Carlos (1980), 'As Classes Sociais no Capitalismo Contemporâneo', unpublished.

Bresser Pereira, Luiz Carlos (1981), *A Sociedade Estatal e a Tecnoburocracia*, São Paulo: Brasiliense.

Bresser Pereira, Luiz Carlos (1985), *Pactos Políticos*, São Paulo: Editora Brasiliense.

Bresser Pereira, Luiz Carlos (1986), *Lucro, Acumulação e Crise*, São Paulo: Brasiliense.

Bresser Pereira, Luiz Carlos (1987), 'Changing Patterns of Financing Investment in Brazil', *Bulletin of Latin America Research*, 7 (2), October, pp. 233–248.

Bresser Pereira, Luiz Carlos (1989), 'O Caráter Cíclico da Intervenção Estatal', *Revista de Economia Política*, 9 (3), July. English version (1993): 'Economic Reforms and the Cycles of the State', *World Development*, 21 (8), August.

Bresser Pereira, Luiz Carlos (1991), *A Crise do Estado*. São Paulo: Nobel.

Bresser Pereira, Luiz Carlos (1992), *Privatization Through Institutionalization, when it is Necessary to Create the Market and the State*, Working Paper no. 23, São Paulo: Department of Economics, Fundação Getúlio Vargas, December.

Bresser Pereira, Luiz Carlos (1993a), 'Economic Reforms and the Cycles of the State', *World Development*, 21 (8), August.

Bresser Pereira, Luiz Carlos (1993b), 'Economic Reforms and Economic Growth: Efficiency and Politics in Latin America', in L.C. Bresser Pereira, J.M. Maravall and A. Przeworski (eds), *Economic Reforms in New Democracies*, Cambridge: Cambridge University Press. Published in Portuguese by Editora Nobel.

Bresser Pereira, Luiz Carlos (1995), 'A Reforma do Aparelho do Estado e a Constituição de 1988', in *Revista del Clad: Reforma y Democracia*, 4. (Working Paper ENAP, no. 1.) Brasília, 1995.

Bresser Pereira, Luiz Carlos (1996a), *Economic Crisis and State Reform in Brazil*, London: Lynne Rienner Publishers.

Bresser Pereira, Luiz Carlos (1996b), 'Da Administração Pública Burocrática à Gerencial', *Revista do Serviço Público*, 47 (1), January, pp. 7–39.

Bresser Pereira, Luiz Carlos (1996c), *Managerial Public Administration: Strategy and Structure for a New State*, Washington: Wilson Center, The Latin American Program, Working Paper Series no. 221, July.

Bresser Pereira, Luiz Carlos, José Maria Maravall and Adam Przeworski (eds) (1993), *Economic Reforms in New Democracies,* Cambridge: Cambridge University Press. Published in Portuguese by Editora Nobel, 1996.

Bresser Pereira, Luiz Carlos and Yoshiaki Nakano (1997), 'The Missing Social

Contract', in A. Ducatenzeiler and P. Oxhorn (eds), *What Kind of Democracy? What Kind of Market? Latin America in the Age of Neoliberalism.* Pensylvania: Penn State University Press, 1997.

Cardoso, Fernando Henrique (1986), 'Entrepreneurs in the Transition Process: The Brazilian Case', in A. O'Donnell, P. Schmitter and L. Whitehead (eds), *Transitions from Authoritarian Rule: Corporative Perspectives*, Baltimore: Johns Hopkins University Press.

Cardoso, Fernando Henrique (1996) 'Ideologias no Pós-Guerra Fria', in *Os Caminhos da Social-Democracia*, Brasília: Partido da Social-Democracia Brasileira, April (Cadernos do PSDB, nº 1).

Castells, Manuel (1994), 'Comentário no Seminário *O Brasil e as Tendências Econômicas e Políticas Contemporâneas'*, in F.H. Cardoso and L. Martins (1995), *O Brasil e as Tendências Econômicas e Políticas Contemporâneas*, Brasília: Fundação Alexandre Gusmão.

Coase, Ronald H. (1937), 'The Nature of the Firm', in A.J. Stigler and K.E. Boulding (eds) (1952), *Readings in Price Theory.* Originally published in *Economica*, 1937.

Cunill Grau, Nuria (1995), 'La Rearticulación de las Relaciones Estado-sociedad: en Busqueda de Nuevos Sentidos', *Revista del Clad – Reforma y Democracia*, **4**, July.

Delorme, Robert (1995), 'An Alternative Theoretical Framework for State-Economy Interaction in Transforming Economies', *Emergo: Journal of Transforming Economies and Societies*, **2** (4).

Diniz, Eli (1995), 'Governabilidade, Democracia e Reforma do Estado: os Desafios da Construção de uma Nova Ordem no Brasil dos Anos 90', in *Dados,* **38** (3), pp. 385–415.

Diniz, Eli (1997), *Crise, Reforma do Estado e Governabilidade*, Rio de Janeiro: Fundação Getúlio Vargas Press.

Ducatenzeiler, G. and P. Oxhorn (1992), *Democracy, Authoritarianism and the Problem of Governability in Latin America.* Paper presented to the Latin American Studies Association Conference, Los Angeles, 24–26 September.

Evans, Peter (1995), *Embedded Autonomy*, Princeton: Princeton University Press.

Fairbrother, Peter (1994), *Politics and the State as Employer,* London: Mansell.

Ferlie, Ewan, Andrew Pettigrew, Lynn Ashburner and Louise Fitzgerald (eds) (1996), *The New Public Management in Action*, Oxford: Oxford University Press.

Frischtak, Cláudio (ed.) (1995), *Regulatory Policies and Reform: A Comparative Perspective*, Washington: The World Bank, December.

Frischtak, Leila L. (1994), 'Governance Capacity and Economic Reform in Developing Countries'. (Technical Paper no. 254.) Washington: World Bank.

Frischtak, Leila L. and Izak Atiyas (eds) (1996), *Governance, Leadership, and Communication*, Washington: World Bank.

Genro, Tarso (1996), 'A Esquerda e um Novo Estado', *Folha de S. Paulo*, 7 January.

Gore, Al (1995), *Common Sense Government*, New York: Random House.

Haggard, S. and Kaufman, R. (1995), *The Political Economy of Democratic Transitions*, Princeton: Princeton University Press.

Hirschman, Albert O. (1991), *The Rhetoric of Reaction*, Cambridge: Harvard University Press.

Huntington, Samuel P. (1991), *The Third Wave*. Norman: University of Oklahoma Press.

Jessop, Bob (1994), 'Changing Forms and Functions of the State in an Era of Globalization and Regionalization', in J. Delorme and P. Dopfer (1994), *The Political Economy of Diversity*, Aldershot: Edward Elgar Publishing House and EAEPE.

Kennedy, John F. (1956), *Profiles in Courage*, New York: Harper and Row.

Krueger, Anne (1974), 'The Political Economy of the Rent-Seeking Society', *American Economic Review,* **64** (3), June.

Lamounier, Bolívar (1989), 'Authoritarian Brazil Revisited: The Impact of Elections on the Abertura', in Alfred Stepan (ed.), *Democratizing Brazil*, New York, Oxford: Oxford University Press.

Linz, Juan (1982), *The Transition from Authoritarian Regimes to Democratic Political Systems and the Problem of Consolidation of Political Democracy*. Paper presented at the International Political Science Association, Tokyo Roundtable, March.

Marshall, T.H. [1950] (1992), 'Citizenship and Social Class', in T.H. Marshall, *Citizenship and Social Class*, London: Pluto Press.

Martins, Luciano (1983), 'Le Regime Autoritaire Brésilien et la Liberalization Politique', *Problèmes d'Amérique Latine,* **65**. Also published in O'Donnell, Schmitter and Whitehead (eds), 1986b, pp. 164–187.

Melo, Marcus André (1996), 'Governance e a Reforma do Estado: o Paradigma Agente-principal', *Revista do Serviço Público*, **47** (1), January, pp. 67–82.

Melo, Marcus André and Nilson do Rosário Costa (1995), 'A Difusão das Reformas Neoliberais: Análise Estratégica, Atores e Agendas Internacionais', in E. Reis, M.H. Almeida and P. Fry (eds), *Pluralismo, Espaço Social e Pesquisa*, São Paulo: Editora Hucitec.

Ministério da Administração Federal e Reforma do Estado (1995), *Plano Diretor da Reforma do Aparelho do Estado*, Brasília: Nacional Press, November.

Nunberg, Barbara (1995), *Managing the Civil Service – Reform Lessons from*

Advanced Industrialized Countries, Washington, DC: World Bank. (Working Paper no. 204), April.

O'Donnell, Guillermo and Philippe Schmitter (1986), *Transitions from Authoritarian Rule: Tentative Conclusions about Uncertain Democracies*, Baltimore: The Johns Hopkins University Press. Published in Portuguese by Editora Vértice.

O'Donnell, Guillermo, Philippe Schmitter and Laurence Whitehead (eds) (1986a), *Transitions from Authoritarian Rule: Comparative Perspectives*, Baltimore: The Johns Hopkins University Press. Published in Portuguese by Editora Vértice.

O'Donnell, Guillermo, Philippe Schmitter and Laurence Whitehead (eds) (1986b), *Transitions from Authoritarian Rule: Latin America*, Baltimore: The Johns Hopkins University Press. Published in Portuguese by Editora Vértice.

Olson, Mancur (1965), *The Logic of Collective Action*, Cambridge, MA: Harvard University Press.

Osborne, David and Ted Gaebler (1992), *Reinventing Government*, Reading, MA: Addison-Wesley.

Palma, Giuseppe Di (1990), *To Craft Democracies*, Berkeley: University of California Press.

Przeworski, Adam (1986), 'Some Problems in the Study of Transitions to Democracy', in A. O'Donnell, P. Schmitter and L. Whitehead (eds), *Transitions from Authoritarian Rule: Comparative Perspectives*, Baltimore: Johns Hopkins University Press.

Przeworski, Adam (1990), *The State and the Economy under Capitalism,* Chur: Harwood Academic Publishers.

Przeworski, Adam (1991), *Democracy and the Market*, Cambridge: Cambridge University Press.

Przeworski, Adam (1993), 'Economic Reforms, Public Opinion, and Political Institutions: Poland in the Western Europe Perspective', in L.C. Bresser Pereira, J.M. Maravall and A. Przeworski (eds), *Economic Reforms in New Democracies*, Cambridge: Cambridge University Press.

Przeworski, Adam (1995a), 'O que os Países Civilizados Têm em Comum', *Folha de S. Paulo*, 2 April, pp. 1–3.

Przeworski, Adam (1995b), *Reforming the State: Political Accountability and Economic Intervention*. Paper presented at the conference 'Inequality, the Welfare State and Social Values', El Escorial, Espanha, July.

Przeworski, Adam (1996a), *On the Design of the State: a Principal-Agent Perspective*. Paper presented at the seminar 'Reforma do Estado na América Latina e no Caribe', Brasília, 16–17 May.

Przeworski, Adam (1996b), 'Nota sobre o Estado e o Mercado', *Revista de Economia Política*, **16** (3) July, pp. 115–120.

Przeworski, Adam and Fernando Limongi (1993), 'Political Regimes and Economic Growth', *Journal of Economic Perspectives*, **7** (3) Summer.

Przeworski, Adam and Fernando Limongi (1997), 'Modernization: Theories and Facts', *World Politics*, **49** (2), January.

Putnam, Robert D. (1993), *Making Democracy Work*, Princeton: Princeton University Press.

Ranson, Stewart and John Stewart (1994), *Managing for the Public Domain*. London: St Martin's Press.

Reis, Fábio Wanderley (1994), '"Governabilidade" e Instituições Políticas', in J.P.R. Velloso (ed.), *Governabilidade, Sistema Político e Violência Urbana*, Rio de Janeiro: José Olympio and Fórum Nacional.

Shepherd, Geoffrey and Sofia Valencia (1996), 'Modernizando a Administração Pública na América Latina: Problemas Comuns sem Soluções Fáceis', *Revista do Serviço Público*, **47** (3) September, pp. 103–128.

Stepan, Alfred (ed.) (1989), *Democratizing Brazil*, New York, Oxford: Oxford University Press.

Stigler, George J. [1971] (1975), The Theory of Economic Regulation', in George J. Stigler, *The Citizen and the State*, Chicago: Chicago University Press. Originally published in *Bell Journal of Economics and Management Science*, Spring.

Stigler, George J. (1975), *The Citizen and the State*, Chicago: Chicago University Press.

Stiglitz, Joseph E. (1989), 'The Economic Role of the State', in Arnold Heertje (ed.), *The Economic Role of the State*, Oxford: Basil Blackwell.

Stiglitz, Joseph E. (1992), 'Methodological Issues and the New Keynesian Economics', in A. Vercelli and N. Dimitri (eds), *Macroeconomics: a Survey of Research Strategies*, Oxford: Oxford University Press.

Stiglitz, Joseph (1993a), 'Post Walrasian and Post Marxian Economics', *The Journal of Economic Perspectives*, **7** (1), Winter.

Stiglitz, Joseph (1993b), 'The Role of the State in Financial Markets', *Proceedings of the World Bank Annual Conference on Development Economics*, supplement from *The World Bank Economic Review* and from the *World Bank Research Observer*.

Stiglitz, Joseph E. (1994), *Whither Socialism?*, Cambridge, MA: The MIT Press.

Stokes, Susan (1995), *Democratic Accountability and Policy Change: Economic Policy in Fujimori's Peru*, University of Chicago, Chicago Center on Democracy, Paper no. 6.

Velloso, João Paulo Reis (ed.) (1994), *Governabilidade, Sistema Político e Violência Urbana*, Rio de Janeiro: José Olympio and Fórum Nacional.

Washington Post (1997), 'Americans Oppose Cutting Entitlements to Fix Budget', *Washington Post*, 29 March, p. 9.

Williamson, Oliver E. (1985), *The Economic Institutions of Capitalism*, New York: The Free Press.

World Bank (1997), *World Development Report 1997: The State in a Changing World,* Washington: The World Bank, March (draft version).

9. Blockage *versus* continuance in Brazilian industrialization

Antonio Barros de Castro

INTRODUCTION

The blockage metaphor dominates studies on industrialization in Latin America. Since the second half of the 1950s, even the Economic Commission for Latin America (ECLA), an ardent champion of industrialization, has shifted its position to defend the argument that after a certain point industrial advancement becomes difficult and the economy tends to stagnate.

The intense surge of development initiated in 1968 and prolonged until 1980 made it clear that at least in the case of Brazil, industrial growth was far from exhaustion, as so many analysts had announced. In fact, during the thirteen years between 1968 and 1980 Brazilian industrial production tripled! (See Table 9.1.) Many, however, refused to give in: according to them, the resurgence of growth had simply put off the exhaustion of a 'model' that was doomed to crisis.

Based on other theoretical premises, a new version of industrial pessimism raised its head in the 1990s. According to this new view, an industry that had been created on a foundation of favours and subsidies and kept free of competition through huge (mostly tariff) barriers would not be able to free itself from its dependence on public resources (thus contributing to both fiscal crises and chronic inflation). It is important to stress that in this last version difficulties did not originate in the structural characteristics of underdevelopment, such as extreme inequality in income distribution. The problems supposedly arose from the vicious relationship between government and private interests and the behaviour of firms. It further pays to emphasize that according to this standpoint income concentration was viewed rather as a consequence than as the cause of problems in industry.

Through several formulations (which focused invariably on the rent-seeking behaviour of the industry) the foregoing view came to be irrefutably domi-

Year	Annual Index (previous year = 100)	1968/98 (1968 = 100)
1968	–	100.00
1969	111.20	111.20
1970	111.90	124.43
1971	111.81	139.13
1972	114.19	158.87
1973	117.04	185.94
1974	108.49	201.73
1975	104.90	211.61
1976	111.74	236.46
1977	103.14	243.88
1978	106.44	259.59
1979	106.80	277.24
1980	109.25	302.88
1981	91.16	276.11
1982	99.96	276.00
1983	94.08	259.66
1984	106.31	276.04
1985	108.27	298.87
1986	111.66	333.72
1987	100.99	337.03
1988	97.40	328.26
1989	102.86	337.65
1990	91.82	310.03
1991	100.26	310.84
1992	95.78	297.72
1993	107.01	318.59
1994	106.73	340.03
1995	101.91	346.53
1996	103.73	359.45
1997	105.52	379.29
1998	99.02	375.58

Source: Brazilian Institute of Geography and Statistics/DPE/Department of National Accounts

Table 9.1:   Evolution of Industrial GNP, 1968–98

nant. More importantly, its conclusions came to be taken as indisputable premises for subsequent work. Thus, for example, a recent study published by BNDES summarily refers to the manufacturing industry that existed in the country prior to the opening of the market as being characterized by 'low productivity, obsolete products and inefficient scales'. The explanation for this would seem to lie (according to the text) in the state-enterprise relationship prior to the current decade (Moreira, 1999).

That negative evaluation of industry has recently teamed up with another important thesis. I refer to the belief that industry has currently lost importance as a source of economic growth. To put it simply, growth during the so-called post-industrial era is said to be propelled by services. The combination of the aforementioned (local) pessimism with the general hypothesis that industry has become a thing of the past tends to have serious consequences. In the 1990s therefore, when owing to structural reforms the economy freed itself from the deleterious characteristics (supposedly) inherent in closed environments, public authorities paid no attention whatsoever (during the first half of the decade) to industry. This notorious omission of public powers in the face of economic difficulties in the real side of the economy was not only due to their belief that reforms and stability would create an environment favouring the appearance of competitive activities; worldwide manufacturing itself was (supposedly) no longer worthy of attention.

The ideas just evoked became the object of an international controversy in which the works of Robert Rowthorn (1999), representing one of the tendencies, appear to me to contain sound arguments in favour of the notion that the production of goods continues to carry great weight in advanced centres. As he points out, no less than two-thirds of employment in industrialized economies relate even today to 'goods-related' activities. Furthermore, the enormous changes and improvements introduced in the sphere of services proper, such as health and entertainment (free-standing services as opposed to the wide gamut of goods-related ones), have their basis in the new products incessantly created by the industry. It is likewise worth mentioning that the reduction in industry's relative weight in the GNP structure can largely be explained by the marked increase in its productivity (the so-called Baumol effect).

While basically agreeing with Rowthorn[1] and other authors where the importance of industry (in a broad sense) is concerned, I intend to discuss below only the first type of industrial pessimism, i.e. the deep-rooted notion that an industry generated by import substitution would not be capable of achieving sustained growth.

Let me state in advance that in my understanding, industrial growth ceased in the early 1960s not because the import substitution process had exhausted itself, but rather owing to the exacerbation of macroeconomic disturbances – as well as the growing political instability associated with it. As for the vigorous growth surge which started in 1968 and came to an end in 1980, it was aborted by an extraordinary conjunction of external shocks. Those worth mentioning are the second petroleum shock and above all the so-called interest shock, a precursor of the fatal blow struck by the collapse of external financing in 1981–2.

Once again we were faced with an abrupt interruption of growth, one that in no sense could have been explained by the alleged failure of industry to use (and create) new growth opportunities. I insist that no one has ever convincingly connected any of the two major growth interruptions either to the structural traits inherent in our economy (such as the aforementioned extreme inequality in income distribution) or to bad management or any other kind of deviation due to a (supposedly) vicious relationship with the state. More importantly – and as the facts seem to suggest – the industrial structure inherited from the import substitution process constitutes even today a wide and diversified basis from which growth will eventually resume in the now stabilized and open economy.

At the end of this work the hypothesis will be raised that perhaps today there are reasons to believe that industry – for the first time since its inception in the 1930s – may be abandoning its (rather bumpy) trajectory towards national replication of a modern industrial structure. However, understanding the present situation and discussing the country's industrial perspectives require us to look back in time. After all, the most peculiar characteristics of the economy are an obvious legacy of the past. But that flashback need not go beyond the period of accelerated growth and intense diversification that occurred between 1968 and 1980; during this phase decisions were made that shaped the Brazilian industrial structure (Castro, 1993).[2]

THE BUMPY TRAJECTORY OF BRAZILIAN INDUSTRIALIZATION: A STYLIZATION

We shall distinguish the periods 1968 through 1980, 1980 through 1993, and 1994 through 1998. Concerning the first two, which occurred prior to the opening of the market, I will attempt to emphasize the traits that remain as a strong and singular inheritance conditioning the present. I shall mostly attempt to show that interruptions rather than changes in trajectories have marked the Brazilian industrial experience. In other words, and contrary to what occurred in Chile and Argentina in their neo-liberal experiences (Foxley, 1988), and more recently in East Germany and Russia, structures did not disappear, whether or not they were replaced by new ones. Crises introduced changes and left scars that instead of calling into question or reversing industrialization, were incorporated into it as differences or idiosyncrasies. We can ultimately say that the decisions previously made, most of them induced by the state through policies that were scarcely coherent but rather effective, have shown an extraordinary resilience.

The Period 1968-1980

The decisions made during this phase largely defined the relative importance of sectors, production scales, technology and verticalization of factories (and firms), together with regional location. In other words, this phase shaped the country's modern industrial structure.

In terms of scales, the choices were decidedly ambitious. In the metalworking sector, for instance, Jorge Katz found an enormous discrepancy (in the order of four to one) between plants typically installed in Brazil and in Argentina (Katz, 1986). Opting for large-scale production found its justification in the high rate of economic growth, in incentives awarded through credit by public authorities (who were determined to catch up with advanced economies) and in the country's own culture. The latter, dominated by a 'growth convention' (Castro, 1993), was characterized by a firm belief on the part of Brazilian authorities, businessmen, and the general public that the country was destined for growth.

As far as technological choices are concerned, it may be said that in keeping with the ambitious scales then being adopted, they tended to favour state-of-the-art technologies.

A further trait that had been etched in the past and was strongly confirmed by the big step forward taken from 1968 to 1980 is to be found in the high degree of company and plant integration (or verticalization). The fact that part of the supply chain was absorbed by manufacturing companies themselves – a phenomenon that was taken to extremes in the capital goods sphere but which is also present, for example, in the large automobile plants of the ABC region (São Paulo) – can be understood as a response to environmental limitations. In other words, faced with the 'make or buy' alternative, companies opted for self-supply to a much larger degree than in industrialized countries.

Finally, a word on the industrial spatial configuration, undoubtedly a significant aspect in an economy of continental dimensions. Initially, the most advanced industries were highly concentrated in the city of São Paulo and its surrounding areas, but even during this period a few steps were taken toward regional decentralization. The petrochemical complexes of Camaçari and Triunfo (in Bahia and Rio Grande do Sul, respectively) and that of Fiat in

Betim (Minas Gerais) were the first attempts to build modern industrial centres away from São Paulo and Rio de Janeiro. The public subsidies and other inducement mechanisms used in those first attempts at decentralization were even stronger than in the overall industrial advancement.

As for inflation, this was the period that saw the beginning of the Brazilian experience of widespread (formal) indexation – which from 1968 onwards included the economy's exchange rate. During this stage, backward looking price determination (or correction) according to official inflation became a typical procedure – while the firms' attention remained focused on expanding and updating production capacity.

By the end of this period the country started being perceived in developed centres as an aggressive newly-industrialized country (NIC) whose manufactured exports were growing at extremely high rates.

The Period 1981-1993

The second period, which can be more precisely defined as extending from the second half of 1980 to the first half of 1993, was a phase of mere (and difficult) industrial survival. As is widely known, those were years of great macroeconomic turbulence comprising several failed attempts at stabilization.

During this phase, the industrial structure – drastically expanded during the previous period – suffered a virtual freezing. The same cannot be said of the typical behaviour of firms. In other words, the absence of new investments, the maintenance of the same techniques and the infrequent launching of new product lines did not mean that important changes were not taking place in company decision making.

In fact, the dominant patterns of behaviour on the real side of the economy were deeply changed. The new practices were unquestionably aimed at an adaptation to the new domestic environment, characterized as it was by chronically high inflation and a succession of radical (but failed) attempts at stabilization. In practice, this also meant a stop and go progression and overall stagnation (Ferraz, Kupffer and Serrano, 1999).

Among the characteristically reactive behaviour of the period one must emphasize first of all an inertial setting of prices according to the latest inflation figures. Nevertheless, as both the price race and anti-inflationary packages increased markedly with time, companies apparently tried to overtake inflation. This procedure, besides feeding the inflationary process, most certainly contributed to aggravating the country's income distribution. Firms however, could easily justify their more aggressive attitude as an effort to compensate for the higher risks they were facing (Frenkel, 1979).

Another form of behaviour developed in this particular context – and largely incorporated into the Brazilian firm's typical pattern of conduct – was a (marked) aversion to indebtedness. This attitude was in sharp contrast to what was taking place in East Asia: in Korea, for example, the debt/asset coefficient often ranged from 300 to 500 per cent. Debt of such magnitude would undoubtedly be too dangerous in an environment repeatedly submitted to radical institutional shifts. The resulting cautiousness (also) became notorious as regards the behaviour of banks, which found high and safe sources of profits in inflationary gains (float) and government borrowing.

A third characteristic is to be found in the overall swiftness achieved by firms in their reactions to environmental changes. It should be understood that the kaleidoscopic changes characterizing that period imposed permanent attention on new risks and opportunities – and obviously required quick answers. Equally associated with such a stressful environment was an ostensible and generalized practice of aggressively defending one's own interests. If on the one hand this meant a radicalization (or caricaturing) of the capitalist ethos, on the other it implied a marked predominance of short-term reactive behaviour rather than strategic positioning.

Still in the domestic sphere it is worth noting that this period marked the demise of the developmental state. Notwithstanding this, public authorities intervened intensively in the economy, not only through macroeconomic policies but also by trying to reform institutions and by redefining the rules of the game. From various standpoints therefore, there was an authentic reversal of some of the major characteristics of the preceding period.

For the central economy and the Asiatic NICs this was a period of great transformation. International competition was greatly intensified and new production techniques (and managerial methods) were rapidly diffused. Those techniques, more flexible and versatile than the former ones, favoured both product differentiation and a reduction of the average product's lifetime.

Whereas in the US and Europe the markets that had pushed the post-war growth were no longer dynamic, countries like Korea and Taiwan were not only boosting their exports explosively but also going through their own mass consumption revolution.

Brazilian industry was clearly unable to replicate the intense transformations that were taking place in advanced centres. Under these circumstances, Brazil ceased to be seen as a threatening NIC. Indeed, it rapidly acquired the reputation of an endemically unstable economy – and came to be referred to as a 'disposable' economy.

The basket of articles produced by Brazilian manufacturing industries (both nationally-owned and multinational) gradually came to be typical of the final stage of the 'product cycle'. This means that the corresponding production facilities in industrial centres were already being depreciated (and disappearing) – and new plants (in many cases) were being built in countries with low salaries and/or abundant natural resources.[3]

The supply structure being a prisoner of articles that were becoming 'inferior', Brazilian economy – whose industrial base in the early 1980s had approached that of developed countries – ran into obvious (relative) decline. However, the highly protected domestic market allowed its prices (in dollars) to remain well above the levels found on the external market. An important consequence of this was that, taking into account the articles that were being produced, domestic wages (in dollars) held a (paradoxically) privileged position. Yet this privilege was only an apparent one, as workers could not buy products (at their going prices) on the external market. For the same reason domestic firms were only in seeming disadvantage, given that external competition was rigidly contained. On the other hand, the fact that even multinationals (like Ford or GM) were now producing outdated articles made it clear that the problem was one of context – and not of individual firms.

The Period June 1994–December 1998

The opening up of the Brazilian economy decided upon in 1990 and intended for implementation in the four subsequent years, was inadvertently intensified by an exchange rate overvaluation during the second half of 1994. Moreover, for the great majority of firms (which had no access to external credit sources) the huge difference between domestic and international interest rates further accentuated the disparate conditions faced by domestic producers as compared to their external competitors.

Faced with such a scenario, no analyst would bet on the response capacity of the existing industry. Many, as has already been pointed out, predicted that it would be scrapped, following the example of other neo-liberal Latin American experiences and, more recently, of former socialist economies after the capitalist reforms. Enthusiasts of the new policies, on the other hand, were unaffected by the threat of disappearing producers (or even sectors). In their place new activities – industrial or otherwise – would supposedly spring up (Castro, 1999).

Against the background of drastically intensified competition in world markets and of the opening up of the Brazilian economy, the new period can be characterized by the following crucial facts: a strong drop in the relative prices of tradables – and a consequent broadening of their markets; a reluctant return of the state; an intense modernization and restructuring of firms; and the rediscovery of Brazil by direct foreign investment.

As far as the price reduction of tradables is concerned, the most important implications arose from the fact that wages belong in the non-tradable sphere. Authorities, however, tried to convince the public that the rise in real wages was a conscious and intentional consequence of the new economic policy. Some have even drawn a dangerous lesson from that episode: the living conditions of the population could be substantially improved without any change in the real side of the economy. And this could be almost instantly obtained!

Quite apart from central government rhetoric, four points are worth emphasizing as far as (industrial) policies are concerned. They are: the automobile industry regime; maintenance of the special status and advantages conferred upon the Manaus Pole (basically the electronics industry); some *ad hoc* tariff increases, usually combined with special credit programmes (sponsored by BNDES); and the aggressive decentralized (state) policy for attracting investments.

Let us have a look at the restructuring of firms.

Stimulated by the domestic market enlargement and using various resources (such as increasing their import coefficient), industrial firms at large reacted strongly to the import invasion of their markets. In order to do so, they were forced to review decisions made in the first of the aforementioned periods – especially with regard to the degree of vertical integration, managerial methods and markets to be challenged. In cases where survival proved difficult, they converted to being importers themselves or, as a last resort, sold their assets. Some had to retreat to mere assembling. No comprehensive study has yet been conducted on the mosaic of company reactions. But there are strong indications that only a few industrial sectors were seriously affected (Veiga, 1999).

As regards the rediscovery of Brazil by direct foreign investment, it should be remembered that (except for products derived from new technologies) most central markets have been showing signs of saturation in the last 20 years. Several of the so-called emerging markets display a noticeable contrast in this respect – and the perception of this fact has served as the basis for a strategic option made by the Clinton administration. Indeed, at the beginning of the President's first term of office, the Sub-Secretary of Commerce announced trade expansion with and investment penetration into the so-called BEMs (Big Emerging Markets) as an American priority. Those domestic markets (a total of ten, with some emphasis on the Brazilian case) would supposedly hold 'massive investment and commercial opportunities for US companies'. In the raw, straightforward language of the Sub-Secretary of Commerce those would be the places where it would be possible to find 'more jobs for us and for our children' (Garten, 1996). Indeed, several (large) North American (and European) companies had already started acting consistently in the belief that BEMs had become decisive to industries that had propelled growth in the 1960s and 1970s.

The broadening of domestic markets, the restructuring of companies (only rarely accompanied by a net discarding of productive capacity), and the arrival of new investments unfold a scene in which hope for resurrected and sustainable growth becomes quite plausible. However, the renewed growth potential has come into conflict with restrictions derived from current account deficits and, last but not least, the growing public sector deficit. The conflict between the microeconomic potential dynamism and strong short-term macroeconomic restrictions has translated itself into a remarkable stop-and-go trajectory (Castro, 1996). The result is the bumpy trajectory portrayed in Figure 9.1 below. Beyond the vigour revealed during expansion phases, the good news contained therein rests on the fact that since the launching of the Real Plan, increases in demand no longer brought with them inflation pressures. It is the quantities produced that grow rather than prices. The contrast with the previous periods is particularly noticeable here.

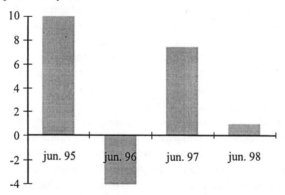

Source: Brazilian Institute of Geography and Statistics-Gross Internal Product Indicators,
            June–September 1998

*Figure 9.1:   Industry after the Real Plan, Growth Rate (%) of 12 Months
                Compared to the Previous 12 Months*

THE CURRENT SITUATION AND PERSPECTIVES: INITIAL REMARKS

There is no doubt that the opening up of the economy and other tests to which Brazilian industry has recently been submitted have generated enormous changes. Restructuring, outsourcing, mergers and changes in ownership and control have substantially altered the country's industrial scene. It would be incorrect, however, to say that the profusion of decisions recently made deny the basic options which originated in the past – as was the expectation of those who did not believe in an industrial structure grown out of import substitution and state aid.[4]

I will limit myself here to a couple of illustrations.

The (modest) pre-1973 Chilean automobile industry was literally wiped off the map by the country's neo-liberal experiment. Magnitogors, a steel complex sometimes referred to as the 'heart' of Soviet industry, appears to be in a terminal stage. The contrast between them and what occurred respectively with the Brazilian automobile and steel industries could not be any greater. The same (bumpy) continuity can be found in the shoe, chemical and even capital goods industries (whose losses have been quite considerable).

From a broader perspective however, the industrial revitalization now under way seems to be qualitatively different from the advances (or recoveries) of the past. This is due to the fact that until the early 1980s the Brazilian economy was effectively reducing the gap that separated it from advanced centres. We were in fact overcoming the international division of labour that had prevailed until 1930. By the mid-1980s this historical task had been completed – as strongly suggested by a jump in manufacturing exports from 13.4 per cent in 1970, to 43.7 per cent in 1985 (Bulmer-Thomas, 1996).

The recent and voluminous investments in the Brazilian automobile industry (to take a significant example) are undoubtedly designed to bring plants installed in Brazil closer to their North American and European counterparts. Additionally, numerous Brazilian companies operating in other sectors of the economy have been introducing equipment and managerial methods close to those used in developed centres. But stressing these facts may risk hampering the understanding of two serious questions.

Growth in the developed world – and most particularly in the US – has come to be led by firms (or networks) that are radically new in their nature. Their main characteristic is to operate directly through knowledge. Their primary asset is (also) knowledge, whose management raises new and important problems – besides introducing a high degree of unpredictability into medium and long-term strategies (Teece, 1999). Physical capital and a more or less trained work-force have little relevance here. The very notion of the (traditional) firm tends to be diluted, making way for new formations (networks and 'virtual companies'). The price of new products in this incipient world tends towards zero in a short time span. Evidently, mere manufacturing has relatively little importance. On the other hand, new services associated with the creation and development of ideas (to be incorporated into new products) multiply. Needless to say, Brazilian industry finds itself far away from all that.

A second change under way in developed centres must be pointed out. It can briefly be characterized as bringing to the fore a new international division of labour. Through that and as a reaction to the new environment, productive (in the traditional sense of the word) corporate functions are passed on to BEMs – whereas those which might be referred to as noble (Furtado, 1997) remain in the developed economies. The Brazilian economy at the moment would appear to be an outstanding candidate for this new sort of international arrangement.

I am optimistic about the growth possibilities of the restructured Brazilian industry, yet pessimistic about its entrance into the knowledge industry realm – as well as about the possibility of reversing the tendency to relegate Brazil (and other BEMs) to the condition of a mere material producer – unless a new and successful generation of industrial policies, both more subtle and more daring than those of the past, can be conceived, adopted and effectively implemented. These are open questions but they should be central to the debate on the perspectives of an economy that within two to three years may free itself from the macroeconomic restrictions that have curtailed its growth since 1980.

NOTES

1. See, however, the last item of this paper.
2. This proposition refers exclusively to the private sector.
3. This statement would not be entirely valid with regard to basic input industries. In this case, Brazilian scales and technologies have been kept up to date.
4. The statements made in this work have often derived from interviews undertaken by the author in several industrial branches in different regions of the country.

BIBLIOGRAPHY

Bulmer-Thomas, V. (1996), *The New Economic Model in Latin America and its Impact on Income Distribution and Poverty*, New York: St Martin's Press.

Castro, Antonio Barros de (1993), 'Renegade Development: Rise and Demise of State-Led Development in Brazil', in William Smith, Carlos Acuña and Eduardo Gamarra (eds), *Democracy, Markets and Structural Reforms in Latin America*, New Brunswick: Transaction Publishers.

Castro, Antonio Barros de (1996), 'A Capacidade de Crescer Como Problema', in João Paulo dos Reis Velloso (ed.), *O Real, o Crescimento e as Reformas*, Rio de Janeiro: José Olympio.

Castro, Antonio B. de (1999), 'O Lado Real do Real; o Debate e Algumas Surpresas', in *Vinte anos de política econômica*, Rio de Janeiro: Contraponto/Corecon.

Ferraz, João, David Kupffer and Franklin Serrano (1999), 'Macro/Micro Interactions: Economic and Institutional Uncertainty and Structural Change in Brazilian Industry', *Oxford Development Studies*, **3** (27).

Foxley, Alejandro (1988), *Experimentos Neoliberales en America Latina*, Mexico: Fondo de Cultura Econômica.

Frenkel, Roberto (1979), 'Decisiones de Precio en Alta Inflacion', *Estudios Cedes*, **2** (3)

Furtado, João (1997), 'La Transformation des Conditions d'Insertion des Économies à Industrialisation Tardive dans l'Économie Mondiale'. PhD thesis presented to the University of Paris XIII.

Garten, Jeffrey E. (1996), 'The Big Emerging Markets', *The Columbia Journal of World Business*, Summer.

Katz, Jorge (1986), *Desarollo y Crisis de la Capacidad Tecnologica Latinoamericana. El Caso de la Industria Metalmecanica*, Buenos Aires: CEPAL.

Moreira, Maurício Mesquita (1999), *Estrangeiros em uma Economia Aberta. Impactos Recentes sobre Produtividade, Concentração e Comércio Exterior*. Discussion Paper BNDES/DEPEC, no. 67, March.

Rowthorn, Robert (1999), *Manufacturing Industry: Growth, Trade and Decline*. Paper presented at the Brasília Seminar 'O Futuro da Indústria no Limiar do Século XXI', sponsored by Confederação Nacional da Indústria.

Teece, David (1999), 'Capturing Value from Knowledge Assets: The New Economy, Markets of Know-how and Intangible Assets'. Mimeo.

Veiga, Pedro da Motta (1999), 'A Indústria nos Anos 90: A Transição Inacabada'. Mimeo, February.

10. Central banking, democratic governance and political authority: the case of Brazil in a comparative perspective

Lourdes Sola

1. INTRODUCTION

With the recent transition to democracy in developing countries nearly complete, analysts have turned towards examining the conditions for effective democratic governance. Central to this research agenda has been a study of factors contributing to democratic accountability, transparency and public sector efficiency. Only by meeting those conditions will nascent democracies have a chance to consolidate fully their political institutions. This paper draws attention to a critical aspect of democratic governance which has so far been ignored in the literature – monetary authority. Despite the obvious and essential impact monetary authority has upon the political economy of developing countries, with notable exceptions the study of central banks has been largely left to economists.

We attempt to accomplish two tasks in this paper. First, we provide a justification for the study of monetary authority and central banks as an essential item on the research agenda of democratic governance for political scientists. In order to discuss effectively the relationship between democratic governance and monetary authority however, one must expand the conceptual framework used to study central bank institutions. Specifically, analysis should shift away from an exclusive focus on how central banks attain autonomy from the political arena towards a study of central banks as a special mode of political authority. Only by doing so can we discern the specific trade-offs within monetary authority regarding questions of transparency, democratic accountability and public sector efficiency.

Our second task is to suggest what an empirical study of monetary authority looks like if central banks are conceptualized as a mode of political authority.

Drawing upon the Brazilian case, we invert a common assumption within the study of central banks, i.e. that price stability follows from an autonomous central bank. In the case of Brazil we demonstrate that nearly the opposite has taken place. Only with price stabilization and the success of the recent Real Plan have the conditions for an autonomous central bank been created. The end of inflation weakened the very actors opposed to a centralization of monetary authority in the central bank, thus paving the way for its eventual autonomy from short-term political pressures. Price stability has led to a reform of central bank institutions, not the other way around. In order to demonstrate this however, our empirical study could not make a priori assumptions over who the relevant actors bargaining over monetary authority would be, nor that their relative bargaining positions would remain constant over time.

This paper consists of four sections. The first explains why the study of monetary authority is critical for democratic governance and proposes to expand the notion of monetary authority through treating it as a special mode of political authority. The second reviews the existing literature, and the third conducts an empirical case study of Brazil. Contrary to conventional arguments, we argue that the end of inflation has created the conditions for a centralization of monetary authority in the central bank, with its eventual autonomy from the political arena. The fourth section concludes.

2.   WHY THE INTEREST IN THE ESTABLISHMENT OF MONETARY AUTHORITY IS CRITICAL FOR EFFECTIVE DEMOCRATIC GOVERNANCE

We explore two sets of questions in this section. Why the interest of political scientists in central bank autonomy, and why is tackling this question necessary for an understanding of recent developments in Latin American neo-democracies? We argue that these questions should be placed on the comparative politics research agenda for two reasons: it is relevant to explain the diversity of current regional integration experiences and, in particular, it impinges upon the prospects of democratic consolidation and the quality of democracy. We claim that the current trend towards greater central bank statutory autonomy, and/or formal independence, should be approached in broader terms than those adopted by economists, who approach the topic in terms of a political economy of monetary authority. Specifically, monetary authority should be studied as a special mode of political authority. We hope to show that the development of such a perspective can yield insights into a specific family of Latin American neo-democracies – those which have been most exposed to protracted hyperinflationary pressures throughout their experiment in democratization, such as Argentina and Brazil. We believe the recent and convoluted Brazilian experience of central banking provides a wealth of insights regarding the linkages between economic stabilization and democratic consolidation. This is partly due to Brazil's status, in a regional perspective, as a late-late comer in achieving a modicum of economic stability within an unstable and shifting political context of democratization. At the same time, Brazil is an extreme case of the 'untidy praxis' of central banking mentioned by Whitehead as typical of many countries in the region, and more broadly, of neo-democracies.

One of the most striking developments of the 1990s has been the general trend towards greater central bank statutory autonomy, or even formal independence, in both the dominant capitalist democracies and neo-democracies (South and East). This is taking place quite independently of the political and ideological tradition and image of the parties whose leaders were able to push in that direction, as recent events in Great Britain show. Who would have expected that the formal independence of the Bank of England would be one of the first initiatives of a new Labour government? On the other hand, in most countries of Latin America and Southern Europe, the quest for greater autonomy from the Federal Executive and/or from the political arena is part of a broader process of economic stabilization and restructuring taking place in the shifting political context of democratization. In both cases politicians and governmental élites are confronted with an increasingly delicate dimension of state reform, for political and technical reasons.

Differences between the two groups of countries, however, should not be underestimated. In OECD countries a great many political resources have been spent in debating how much discretion should be delegated by individual central banks to a new institution responsible for monetary order at a regional level. The starting point of such a debate, however, is an established national monetary authority acknowledged not only by the associated members of the financial system, but also by the relevant populations. The question of how to obtain recognition of the specific powers central banks are expected to exercise has already been resolved within the territorial jurisdiction of each national state. As recent literature has shown, this is the long-run outcome of a number of different and convoluted institutional histories of European central banks (and of the Federal Reserve). Analogously, current research further indicates that the recent wave of greater central bank autonomy also contains a diversity of institutional designs – far more than are usually allowed for by the orthodox approach to central banking.

Evidence indicates, however, that instead of placing in jeopardy the effectiveness of monetary management, this outcome has challenged an essential assumption of traditional approaches to central bank reform: that there is just one effective model of central bank independence to be adopted by neo-democracies.[1] Undeniably though, strategic political actors and economic agents within dominant capitalist democracies have converged upon recognizing the authority of individual central banks within their national boundaries. However incremental the legitimization of central banks may have been in the past, and however diverse the political mechanisms and institutional devices by which they are accountable to other actors, critics of orthodoxy easily acknowledge central banks as an indispensable mode of authority. That is to say, they are seen as a necessary condition – and token – of an uncontested commitment to monetary order.

The economic and political motivations for such a legitimization of monetary authority in the central bank are diverse. One possible source may be a strong ideological commitment to price stability and/or concern with the uncontrolled passion of rulers, which in the case of England derived from the struggle of important sectors in civil society against mercantilism and/or the absolutist state. The other more recent example is given by the German Bundesbank. Its successful performance for 40 years as an institution independent from the political arena owes much to the devastating effect that hyperinflation had upon millions of Germans during the early 1920s, in addition to the political use of the Reichsbank as an instrument of the Nazi regime.[2] Jacques Delors, former President of the European Commission and one of the main architects of the European Monetary Union, makes a point and a caveat against the prescriptions of easy institutional transplants in the name of economic and political liberalism by way of an epithet: 'Not every German believes in God, but all Germans believe in the Bundesbank.'

Whichever way legitimization was achieved (either through an ideological and socially embedded commitment to price stability and the rule of law, or by way of an economic and political trauma), a second condition for the exercise of monetary authority in a democratic framework is the acknowledgement of price stability as a first priority public good. A number of other political requisites must be satisfied in order to reconcile the exercise of monetary authority with democratic governance. These are, to a great (although variable) extent, related to the premise of social legitimization discussed above.

A convenient starting point for discussing the impact that central bank autonomy may have upon democratic governance is to recall the special functions and powers attributed to central banks. By doing so, the reasons for placing the study of central bank autonomy as an important item on the research agenda should become clearer. A first question to answer is why, and on what grounds, economists have labelled central banks, or institutions performing similar functions, monetary authorities? The answer rests with their specific functions in shaping monetary and exchange rate policies, securing financial stability and ultimately acting as guardians of the currency. The effective performance of those tasks is closely related to the exercise of specific powers: the regulation of the financial system, monetary supervision and maintenance of external creditworthiness. In this capacity they are rule-givers as much as rule-enforcers, through their capacity to enforce penalties and generate acquiescence to existing regulations by all members of the financial system.

This function should be distinguished analytically, as Weber reminded us, from another, more indirect mode of power also enjoyed by those economic institutions. This consists of providing incentives for actors in the financial markets to respond to guidelines for credit and monetary policies in a co-opera-tive way, according to different criteria: their own variable individual calcula-tions of what is in their best interest. The latter mode of power derives from the fact that central banks enjoy a monopoly or quasi-monopoly over credit, whereas their capacity as rule-givers stems from their expected performance and legitimate intervention in the economy as guardians of an established mon-etary order. We can therefore infer that monetary authority is a special mode of political authority and of power, thus providing two reasons to approach central banks as an important chapter within the study of political economy.

Notwithstanding the key role the concept of authority has for political theory – democratic or otherwise – central banking still remains a topic ex-plored primarily by economists. This does not mean economists have neglected to explore the political dimensions of central banking. They tend, however, to leave aside a major problem, extremely relevant for political scientists, which encompasses normative issues and questions of institutional engineering – par-ticularly relevant for neo-democracies. Namely, how to reconcile the exercise of monetary authority with a modicum of democracy? That question is of no special concern for economic analysis because at best democracy has been treated as and remains a residual category.

This may help explain why much theorizing about the social and political role of those institutions has focused predominantly on two dimensions of poli-tics. The first relates to the impact central bank autonomy has upon growth and employment. The second dimension is both technical and normative, for it con-cerns the requisite political conditions for a central bank to perform its ex-pected economic functions.

The conventional approach takes for granted that central bank independence improves the quality of democracy, given the insulation of central bankers from undue particularistic pressures and a politicization of technically complex monetary issues. Due to the highly technical nature of monetary operations and the potential dangers from particularistic pressures, a delegation to monetary authorities may indeed have beneficial consequences. Analysts and policy makers alike, however, need to insert the issue of accountability within this act of delegation.

To the extent that, in the name of monetary order, insulation from the political arena is indispensable for protecting against self-serving particularistic interests, the analyst is confronted with one of the most fundamental (and oldest) challenges for democratic theory: who guards the guardians? And, by implication, which set of institutions are best equipped to counteract the risks of delegating the necessary autonomy to institutions regulating monetary authority? For more than just affecting the rate of growth and level of employment, decisions made by central banks impinge upon the country's strategy of development and indirectly upon the redistribution of resources between winners and losers.[3]

This question, as is well known, also applies to the judiciary, which as guardian of the law is often not democratically accountable. Tackling this question leads us to explore well-known dilemmas pertaining to democratic governance which are best explored by Dahl, namely, the permanent tension between autonomy and control in a pluralist democracy. Two questions follow: to whom should central bankers be accountable, and what are the limits to transparency? The latter is complicated by the fact that secrecy, or at least non-immediate disclosure, is often an important tool for effective monetary management, not only on the grounds of economic efficacy, but also as a means of protection against speculative attacks.

Economic liberalism takes for granted three assumptions. Firstly, price stability is a public good. The second, which follows from the first, is that because inflation is more detrimental to social sectors less able to protect their incomes from the 'inflationary tax', economic stabilization is instrumental in achieving a greater degree of equity in the long run. Thirdly, central bank independence is a principal condition for actors and the institutions in charge of price stability to act in the interests of society. In other words, the conventional approach presumes a conception of what constitutes good government and a good society. This has been, of course, a major criterion in the legitimization of central banks in dominant democracies, which the concept of monetary authority draws heavily upon.

To what extent do the same criteria for good government delineated above hold for neo-democracies? In our view, neo-democracies as an analytic category are too broad for our purposes. In order to explore the problems associated with the establishment of a legitimate and accountable monetary authority one must first make a distinction between two families of neo-democracies. On the one hand, there are countries that fall under the rubric of hyperinflationary regimes, having experienced a runaway inflation as a consequence of both the adjustments imposed by the 1982 external shock and past policy choices.[4] In such cases, economic stabilization became a priority, inseparable from economic restructuring and, in particular, the reform of the state. This is so because hyperinflation is in effect synonymous with the end of any monetary regime. This is a term which, translated into political science parlance, is nothing less than a disruption of the existing monetary order. Hyperinflation can therefore be interpreted as a process of accelerated loss of monetary – and political – authority. It may further be interpreted as the combined outcome of a fiscal and legitimization crisis of the state affecting both itself and its regulatory capacities, and therefore, the long-term relationship it established with the economy and the society. Most Latin American countries fit into this category, although one can draw additional distinctions among the most conspicuous hyperinflationary cases – Argentina, Bolivia and Brazil. Whereas in the first two countries hyperinflationary pressures developed into an effective hyperinflationary crisis, in Brazil such pressures were kept under permanent if precarious control, thanks to a generalized indexation lasting until 1993. This mode of control, as far as decision making was concerned, verged on a praxis of systematic brinkmanship.[5]

On the other hand, there are neo-democracies for which the task of reconciling economic restructuring with democratization could be achieved in the context of a comparatively manageable rate of inflation. This was due in great part to a more amenable fiscal crisis, related to a comparatively reduced exposure to the 1982 debt crisis and to an externally supportive environment created by the European Union, which provided incentives for a smooth change in the prevailing pattern of state financing. Portugal and Spain fit into this category.

In what follows we shall address problems typical of the first group of countries, resorting to evidence supplied primarily by Brazil, but eventually by Argentina and Bolivia. This family of neo-democracies have distinctive features. They represent extreme cases where economic restructuring and democratization are taking place in a context in which monetary order has been and still is a goal, not a reality. We are therefore assuming that although hyperinflationary pressures have been eliminated and inflation has been dramatically brought to unprecedented low levels, the achievement of self-sustained economic stabilization is a long-run process dependent upon the implementation of economic and institutional reforms, and the continuance of the external bonanza.

This context imposes a number of additional conditions upon an effective state reform compatible with democratic governance, which principally concerns the re-establishment of monetary authority in the context of a broader, and conflict-ridden, process of recreating democratic political authority. Two conditions are essential to this process. The first is the recognition of self-sustained economic stability as a public good, with the expectation that this goal is inseparable from greater equity. The second condition is an agreed process of institutional innovations geared to rendering the monetary authority accountable to society without becoming prey to the political arena. These conditions may be referred to as a quest for embedded authority, typical of a situation in which the state's capacity for regulation and supervision will be dependent *inter alia* upon a changing pattern of financing and composition of its expenditures. This implies, of course, a different state-society relationship, the implications of which have been covered elsewhere.

We therefore posit that the question of central bank autonomy[6] should be considered in a still broader perspective than the one proposed by critics of the conventional approach. We can begin with Laurence Whitehead's critique of a presumed convergence towards a single model of central banking in neo-democracies, an assumption resting at the heart of neo-liberal prescriptions. A distinction must be drawn, however, between two separate issues. The first is the observed and indispensable trend towards greater central bank autonomy from the contradictory pressures of competitive politics and its use as an instrument of party politics. This has become a standard condition for self-sustained economic stability and a critical chapter in state reform, a condition in the light of which the comparatively 'untidy praxis' of most central banks in Latin America should be measured. Such an exercise, however, does not imply an uncritical acceptance of the single-model version that bearers of the conventional approach tend to prescribe for neo-democracies. As Whitehead shows, the latter brush aside *inter alia* three important questions. Firstly, the convoluted history of central banks in dominant democracies and the variety of paths followed by them. Secondly, the present diversity of economically effective institutional designs, which vary according to governmental rules and praxis geared to strike a balance between monetary stability and other, possibly conflicting, goals. The third is the important analytical question of identifying the shifts in social interests underlying the dominant claim and the general trend towards central bank independence.

In countries like Brazil and Argentina we believe a second issue should be explored, concerning both the pace and the guidelines for this mode of state reform to be effective. The establishment of a new monetary order poses specific problems for democratic governance – such as the legitimization of monetary authority and the institutional innovations needed to make it more accountable to politicians and society. In our view, monetary authority has yet to be fully established in these neo-democracies. Furthermore, other dilemmas should be considered if democratic governance is to be counted as a legitimate competing goal (alongside other ones). One can consider a number of implications which follow from this proposal, which we will briefly review.

Firstly, the political dynamics of economic stabilization concentrates power, at least at its initial stage. A principal feature of neo-democracies consists in re-concentrating power within the institution responsible for monetary authority – a process which implies multiple acts of delegation. These acts of delegation range from politicians to experts and eventually to whole bureaucracies, from politicians situated in the executive and/or in Congress, from politicians holding executive positions at the state level in a federation, and from the judiciary as the authorized interpreter of the legal order. The other side of this multifaceted game is, of course, the multiplication of veto players.[7]

Secondly, the technical complexities of monetary management regarding its financial reorganization and regulation are further enhanced by another factor. When hyperinflation sets in, together with its inseparable companion, the fiscal crisis of the state, a tidy praxis of central banking requires a modicum of co-ordination between monetary and fiscal policies. This condition can be satisfied in many ways, one of which is to provide the President of the Central Bank with veto power over (expansionist) fiscal policies – thus preventing the risks derived from indirect challenges to the established monetary guidelines, that is to say, to its own authority.

Exploring the links between fiscal and monetary policy for stabilization in a hyperinflationary context is out of the scope of this paper. We do, however, wish to make a point pertaining to this relationship. A major constraint facing the delegation of power to monetary authority is the usually low level of understanding of its technical issues and systemic policy consequences. Stated in a more positive light, technical expertise among politicians within a democratic framework is a precondition for establishing a new monetary and regulatory financial system.[8] This is an ideal long-run condition, which is far from being satisfied even in dominant democracies, yet still more difficult to achieve in countries where uneven development – social, economic and political – is the rule. The problem, however, is more critical in neo-democracies under hyperinflationary stress. The question for us is: which modes of political and institutional intermediation are required in order to bridge the gap between technical knowledge and expertise concentrated in the hands of a given economic team, on the one hand, and on the other, the actual level of understanding of politicians with a mandate, and whose fiat is indispensable?

Incentives to bridge the gap more or less quickly may come from various sources. We posit that in cases in which institutions are not flexible and effective enough to secure the legitimacy derived from the representative system, the incentive to bridge that gap and to help check hyperinflationary disruption may come directly from a definite change in the preferences of the population. Such was the case in Brazil and most Latin American countries. This is why beyond all differences related to diversity of the relevant party systems, and in particular beyond the technical differences in their stabilization programmes, Bolivia (1986), Argentina (1991–92) and the latest comer Brazil (1993–94) show a political denominator in common.

In all three cases, the building up of an agreed economic strategy was dependent upon three conditions. Firstly, a shift in the ordinal preferences of society towards making stabilization a first order priority goal. This process of conversion may be translated as the emergence of a new criterion of legitimacy owing much to the role of hyperinflation in the wake of a number of stabilization programmes within new democracies. Under such circumstances there is a shift in what should be expected from democracy. Above all, there is a gradual de-linking between immediate economic welfare and treating democracy as a goal and value on its own. The second condition is related to the quality of the leadership. An executive must have the political capacity to propose a technically adequate stabilization programme in addition to creating a political coalition necessary to respond to a newly emerging anti-inflationary coalition.[9] From this follows a third condition, still related to the quality of the leadership. In order to bridge the gap between technocrats and politicians within the framework of a disrupted monetary order, one must delegate a high degree of autonomy to the economic team, and therefore to the monetary authority, while at the same time securing the support of Congress, and eventually of local executives. This was a condition satisfied in the case of Brazil under Cardoso, Menem in Argentina, and in particular, of Bolivia under Victor Paz Estensoro.[10] In the case of Brazil, we can speak of a paradox by which, in the absence of an institutionalized fully autonomous power of the monetary authority, the Central Bank was granted the right to proceed as if it were 'independent' in the wake of the Mexican crisis of 1994–95. The de-politicization of the Central Bank was dependent upon a political decision – an indicator of the precarious statutory autonomy of the Brazilian monetary authority.

Finally, decentralization poses a crucial problem for countries (like Brazil and Argentina) that face the need to establish a credible monetary authority while improving the conditions for democratic governance. Economic and political decentralization is often claimed to be essential for viable democratic governance owing to its beneficial effects upon accountability, transparency and public sector efficiency. The literature on decentralization, however, has to date not explicitly incorporated the question of monetary authority within its analysis. That analysis tends to conduct studies either on inter-governmental fiscal relations or on specific sectors like education, health or infrastructure. The distinctive features of monetary management, the conditions for its effectiveness and the special dilemmas it poses for democratic control are left aside. Furthermore, it fails to make a satisfactory analytical distinction between the political logic of decentralization and that of federalism in a democratic framework. Only by doing so can one fully understand the active role played by states and municipalities in the passage from high inflation to hyperinflation within the context of democratization and their claims for greater autonomy. The ability of local banks to create quasi-money through their administration of state government fiscal deficits – either through carrying state bonds or providing direct loans – has had important consequences in Brazil, and to a lesser extent in Argentina. Specifically, state banks became a favourite mechanism of state governors to evade meeting the elementary requirements of transparency and accountability established by monetary and fiscal authorities at the federal level. As we shall see in the case of Brazil, this implied a deliberate challenge to the constitutionally established monopoly over money creation at the federal level.

In other words, the disruption of the monetary order in democratic Brazil since the early 1980s was closely related to the operation of centrifugal intergovernmental forces which effectively created rival centres of monetary power between levels of government. This was part and parcel of the dramatic loss of both monetary and fiscal authority, which is inseparable from hyperinflation and constitutes the absence of any monetary and fiscal regime. In effect, Brazil's source of monetary disorder (and to a lesser extent Argentina's) can be characterized as a monetary tragedy of the commons. While state governments effectively used their state banks as printers of money in order to finance their budget deficits, one could argue that the collective good of price stability was jeopardized – which is a federal, not a state responsibility.

That is why, when examining the more extreme case of Brazil, it is possible to speak of a monetary and fiscal rebellion inseparable from hyperinflation.[11] The complex bargaining act required for self-sustained economic stabilization in such a neo-democracy places additional strains on political leadership, for it constitutes a permanent trade-off between two goals: on the one hand, the need to check and to bring under permanent control the centrifugal forces which deny central monetary authority – a need which must first be turned into a political goal by the rulers; on the other hand, the executive is faced with the need to build an agreed economic and political strategy to reshape the political order consonant with federalist principles.

In what follows we demonstrate that the study of decentralization, at least in the Brazilian case, must incorporate the question of inter-governmental monetary authority. A coherent monetary authority is essential for the viability of a new federalist pact, in addition to reconciling decentralization with the objectives of democratic governance: accountability, transparency, predictability in the rule of law and public sector efficiency.

3. ALLEGATIONS IN THE LITERATURE

Despite the evident impact monetary authority has upon the establishment of effective democratic governance, few analysts have studied monetary authority as a political authority in the Latin American context. This section will first review the prevailing wisdom concerning monetary authority, and subsequently two lines of research which attempt to explain the conditions under which politicians delegate monetary authority to an independent central bank. While the prevailing wisdom approximates a normative vision resting on tenuous grounds, the latter provides promising lines of research but suffers from two deficiencies which we attempt to address in the country case study of Brazil: one should not presume who the relevant actors surrounding monetary policy will be, and analysts should be sensitive to the dynamic element surrounding political negotiations over monetary authority.

Conventional wisdom over monetary policy in the 1990s stipulates the independence of central banks from the political arena as a precondition for achieving durable price stability. If monetary authority is governed directly by elected officials, their electoral incentives will inevitably lead them to pursue an expansionist monetary policy in order to bolster economic growth. Such a strategy, however, increases employment only in the short term. As consumers cease to be myopic, an expansionist monetary policy is most likely to result in stagflation (the combination of persistent inflation and unemployment). In order to uphold the economy's long-term interest in price stability, monetary authority should be delegated to a central bank independent from short-term electoral interests. According to this line of reasoning, economic growth and price stability therefore rest on 'getting the institutions right'. The moment central bank governors have fixed mandates which do not coincide with an electoral calendar, price stability and economic growth should follow.

Adherents to the above argument often cite the well-known study by Alesina which finds a positive correlation between independent central banks and price stability.[12] One must be careful, however, in viewing such studies as evidence of the hypothesis that independent central banks cause price stability. Firstly, such quantitative studies are robust only in OECD countries, hence one cannot assume that such a relationship will also hold in developing countries. More importantly, however, such studies demonstrate a correlation between price stability and independent central banks, not causation. As we demonstrate in the Brazilian case study, the conditions for creating an independent central bank have only recently been generated because of price stability, not the other way around. While not dismissing the potentially large impact political institutions have on policy outcomes, the Brazilian case qualifies the generalizability of arguments that focus on 'getting the institutions right'.

Before entering into our specific argument, however, we will review two positive (instead of normative) lines of research which attempt to explain the conditions under which politicians delegate monetary authority to an independent central bank, respectively from an international and a national level of analysis. Drawing attention to the unparalleled recent trend in developing countries to establish independent central banks, Sylvia Maxfield argues that politicians delegate monetary authority to an independent central bank as a mechanism to signal international creditors.[13] In order to attract investment when international credit is tight, governments need a credible commitment to a policy of price stability. 'Tying one's hands' through delegating monetary authority to an independent central bank is one mechanism to do so. Maxfield's argument is specifically relevant in a context of a growing internationalization of securities markets in the 1990s.

While an international approach provides a good first cut, there still exists a considerable amount of 'slack' at the domestic level which an approach like Maxfield's cannot account for. In her country case study of Brazil, she herself recognizes that in certain moments 'domestic political pressures, specifically the incentives stemming from constant uncertainty, swamped the need for international creditworthiness.' (Maxfield, 1995, p. 169). Except for a short interim period during Brazil's first military government of Castello Branco (1964–67), monetary authority has either been dependent upon the federal executive[14] or effectively divided between levels of government. Such a dispersal of monetary authority persisted throughout sustained periods of tight international credit and economic stagnation in the 1980s and 1990s. Brazil therefore constitutes a case which warrants the analyst's development of domestic level hypotheses.[15]

Domestic approaches to central bank independence have primarily been developed in the OECD context and can be divided into two categories: institutional and social preference explanations. Institutional explanations generally presume that delegating authority to a central bank is costly. Countries with strong corporatist institutions capable of coordinated wage bargaining are therefore more likely to have independent central banks,[16] and once established, central banks are more likely to endure in polities with high political competition and a large number of veto gates.[17] Social preference explanations, however, treat institutions as intervening variables and focus instead on the preferences of dominant groups which influence economic policy making. Central bank autonomy is therefore most likely in countries where the financial sector is relatively stronger than labour-intensive industries – which have an interest in promoting monetary policy as a means of increasing employment.[18]

The argument we develop for the Brazilian case study adopts a domestic level of analysis which contains elements of both a social preference and an institutional explanation. Our explanation, however, differs from the above orientations in a few significant ways. On the institutional side we agree that policy change in polities with a large number of veto gates is difficult,[19] but the Brazilian case indicates how the relative bargaining position of actors occupying those veto gates can change over time. A strictly institutional orientation would not have the tools necessary to examine when such change is possible, hence in Brazil it would be unable to explain the recent centralization of monetary authority in the central bank.

In order to account for the dynamic element inherent in the politics of monetary authority, the analyst must turn to the relevant actors involved. Unlike the social-preference explanations previously cited, however, we do not assume that the relevant actors impinging upon monetary policy will be the same across countries, nor, as we stated above, that their relative bargaining positions will remain constant. In Brazil the relevant actors disputing control over monetary authority include the federal executive, state governments and the private financial sector, whereas other countries may have very different actors bargaining over monetary authority. Furthermore, we demonstrate in the case of Brazil how the stalemate over monetary authority and its eventual independence is beginning to dissolve, because the end of inflation reduced the relative bargaining strength of the actors opposed to a centralization of monetary authority in the central bank.

An approach which does not make a priori assumptions over who will be the relevant actors, nor what their relative bargaining strengths will be over time can further shed light on accounting for the wide empirical variation in the central banking models adopted. As Whitehead has recently pointed out, there is no single central bank autonomy model.[20] There are a variety of ways to structure monetary authority in order to sustain the goals of price stability, thus analysts should turn their attention away from how to arrive at central bank autonomy and try instead to answer the question 'autonomy from whom?' Our country case study takes a step in this direction.

4.   BRAZIL'S QUEST FOR EMBEDDED AUTHORITY

4.1 The Political Game Prior to the Real Plan

Brazil has achieved a dramatic reversal of its hyperinflationary pressures in 1994–95 under the aegis of the Real Plan, initiated by then Minister of Finance Fernando Henrique Cardoso. In a regional perspective Brazil can be considered a late-late comer regarding price stabilization, because of its numerous and unsuccessful heterodox shocks in 1986, 1987, 1989 and 1990. By 1992 the government resorted to orthodox monetary and fiscal short-run policies with only partial success. The repeated stabilization failures, in addition to political constraints preventing the implementation of fiscal and administrative reforms, are the principal reasons why the Brazilian case has been approached in economic literature as a typical case of muddling through.

As in other parent countries, the recent Brazilian economic stabilization brought about a dramatic change in perspectives. Price stability came to be reckoned as a first order public good, reflecting a clear change in social preferences and criteria for political legitimization – something unprecedented in contemporary Latin American history. The experience of hyperinflation and/or hyperinflationary crisis instigated a lowering of expectations concerning economic welfare and democracy. Given that social preferences often translate into electoral outcomes and political rhetoric, the election of Fernando Henrique Cardoso confirmed this recent trend. All over the region such changes inflicted a dramatic blow to economic populism. It became clear that the populist policies and style of problem solving would not yield electoral dividends as they had in the past. This change in the political and economic climate holds true for economic structures, political regimes and systems of representation across countries as diverse as Peru, Bolivia, Argentina, Mexico and Brazil.

Why has Brazil been one of the slowest reformers? Although answering this question thoroughly is beyond the scope of this paper, its importance must be highlighted, for two reasons. Firstly, economic stabilization is a process still under way. As a goal it is far from consolidated, for its continued success depends upon fiscal, social security and administrative constitutional reforms that require Congressional approval. Secondly, some of the political constraints on managing hyperinflation are still at work and impinge heavily upon the difficulty in establishing an embedded monetary and fiscal authority as a specific mode of political authority.

In what follows we will be concerned with two kinds of constraints. The first is long-run and refers to how monetary authority was handled under a national and federal perspective prior to the democratization of the 1980s. This discussion will provide the background necessary to address the main question of this section: how has the exercise of monetary authority changed subsequent to economic stabilization?

From a regional perspective, one of the distinctive traditions of Brazilian policy making, in addition to an explicit vocation towards continuous growth at all costs, has been a difficulty in establishing a single monetary authority. From the 1930s until the breakdown of the populist democracy in 1964, the establishment of a single monetary authority was not politically viable. Except for a brief interlude in 1964–67, the Central Bank has experienced, since its creation in 1964, a convoluted history of very little autonomy. Thus Brazil is also a late-late comer in terms of establishing a statutory monetary authority. Most Latin American countries had established their own central banks long before 1964, with a wave being created as a response to the economic crisis of the 1930s.

Moreover, one could describe the history of the eight failed attempts at stabilization throughout the populist democracy (1945–64) in terms of the political constraint posed by the protracted dispute between two rival centres of monetary authority – each subjected to different political and economic pressures. Politicization of monetary management in that period therefore prevailed under the guise of the contradictory policies made possible by the existence of a dual monetary authority: Banco do Brasil and Sumoc (Superintendência da Moeda e do Crédito).

Subsequently, the convoluted history of Brazilian central banking since 1964 provides a wealth of insights for political analysts concerned with explaining the contrast between economic programmes and ideas, on the one hand, and the effective results of economic policy making, on the other. For, although the intentions and the rules laid down by the architects of the Central Bank's reform in 1964 were clearly stated in terms that established a central bank which would be autonomous from the political arena, such a proposal was easily defeated, three years later, under the subsequent military government committed to expansionist policies.[21] It was only in 1986 and later in 1988, under the first civilian government, that two reforms were implemented to establish basic mechanisms for effective monetary management and a minimum degree of transparency in national accounting.[22]

The convoluted history of monetary authority in post-war Brazil has therefore less to do with the nature of the political regime than with a commitment to economic performance cast in terms of accelerated growth at all costs.[23] International liquidity, of course, played an important role during 1974–78, as Sylvia Maxfield argues. The decision taken by General Geisel in 1974, however, to prolong the period of accelerated growth and deepen import substitution despite the first oil shock (which required adjustments) was a domestic political option. Two reasons explain this. Firstly, continuous growth may have appeared necessary to the military in order to cement a political coalition they wished to create in support of a strategy of gradual and controlled political liberalization. Secondly, the choice in favour of growth at the expense of infla-tion and an exchange rate crisis had always been made by previous Brazilian governmental élites.

Brazil has become one of the slowest reformers for a second reason, one that is directly related to the kind of dual monetary authority which emerged in tandem with democratization. This dual monetary authority is intimately linked to the federal question and to decentralization, for the governors acted as centrifugal forces which pressured for fiscal decentralization and used their state banks to produce money, thus fiercely challenging the constitutional au-thority of the Central Bank. An important explanation for the ability of gover-nors to use their state banks in such a manner, and thus undermine all stabiliza-tion plans undertaken by the new civilian regime (1986, 1987, 1989, 1990 and 1991), relates to the sequence by which democracy was restored. The contrast between the Brazilian and Spanish strategies may help clarify this point.

By the time Brazilian civilian rule was re-established in 1985–86, the strategy of political devolution adopted by the military had been under way for almost 10 years. For our purposes it is sufficient to stress two major aspects. Firstly, devo-lution at the state level occurred prior to that at the federal level. Open guberna-torial elections were re-introduced first in 1982, with the opposition party (PMDB) electing a significant number of governors committed to democratiza-tion in the most economically and politically powerful states (São Paulo, Minas Gerais, Rio de Janeiro and Rio Grande do Sul). Secondly, the economic strategy adopted by the military government of Ernesto Geisel (1974–78) resulted in a process of accelerated economic decentralization at an early stage of political liberalization. Geisel radically changed the previous pattern of industrialization which focused on the already industrialized southeast.

This sequence is critical in order to understand the manner in which the political drive for autonomy at the state level translated into a centrifugal pull. Economic, and eventually democratic, devolution at state level, prior to liberal-ization at the federal level,[24] helps explain the difficulties later faced by the federal executive in exercising a coordinated authority and implementing an agreed strategy and support among governors. A political economy of federal-ism should take into account such a political and economic sequencing.[25]

From the standpoint of federalist devolution Brazil and Spain are polar cases. A large part of the success of the devolution strategy adopted in Spain was due to the opposite sequence – that is to say, general elections and conditions of legitimacy were established before devolution took place. This is all the more striking inasmuch as the Spanish case represents a far more extreme case, i.e. a multinational federalism which requires multiple balancing acts from central authorities.

In our view the protracted challenges to central political authority on behalf of states owes much to this sequence. Any explanation of the difficulty of any subsequent civilian government in building a governing coalition should take into account this kind of political constraint. For this sequence set the stage for a second type of political constraint to economic policy making and stabilization – the new Constitution promulgated in 1988. This transferred a fixed percentage of federal taxes to states and municipalities without a concurrent transfer of spending responsibilities, and represented the culmination of a process of fiscal decentralization initiated in 1974. Such a constitutionally-determined fiscal allocation imposes an important constraint upon economic management and the crafting of social policies.

In what follows we are principally concerned with examining monetary authority despite the fact that such a study is intimately linked to the fiscal arena. Within monetary authority we further focus on the relationship between the Brazilian Central Bank and state banks. Although fiscal and monetary rebellion is also practised by the private sector, our focus on state banks is justified for three major reasons. Democratic governance is first predicated upon coherent control by the incumbent government over the proper state apparatus.[26] Secondly, the creation of quasi-money by the latter has an obvious impact on the expansion of the monetary base. Finally, private banks such as the Banco Econômico in Bahia or Bamerindus in Paraná enjoyed an enormous bargaining power, given their effective role as regional banks.[27]

4.2 The Political Game After the Real

The transition to democracy and political decentralization in Brazil created an effective division of monetary authority between state and federal governments. The previous section argued that this outcome derived from a political game in which governors were able effectively to transform their state banks into producers of money. This section argues that monetary authority has been increasingly centralized in the Central Bank because the federal executive has increased its bargaining power over governors since the implementation of the 1994 Real stabilization plan.

The federal executive has been able to centralize monetary authority in the Central Bank for both purely political and economic reasons. On the political end, both the interests and bargaining power of the federal executive have changed. Not only does the current administration have an unprecedented interest in sustaining the present stabilization plan, but the executive has gained leverage over the legislature, and therefore governors, due to the concurrent presidential, legislative and state-wide elections in 1994. On the economic end, the federal government increased its bargaining power over governors because the end of inflation substantially weakened state government finances, thus making governors dependent upon a federal bailout. We argue that Fernando Henrique Cardoso took advantage of both of these political and economic factors to make a federal bailout conditional upon a centralization of monetary authority in the Central Bank – an essential element to sustain the current stabilization programme.[28]

The federal executive is usually the branch of government held electorally accountable for maintaining macroeconomic stability, therefore any federal executive would have an interest in maintaining a stabilization programme. The government of Fernando Henrique Cardoso, however, differs from previous administrations in the extent of its interest in upholding a stabilization programme. Fernando Henrique Cardoso launched and won his bid for the presidency almost entirely on the basis of his role in crafting the Real stabilization programme as Minister of Finance under the outgoing Itamar Franco administration (1993–94). Whereas previous presidents could craft a stabilization programme after being elected, see it fail and still have time for a second 'go', Fernando Henrique Cardoso did not have that option because he had won the presidency on a specific stabilization programme – the Real Plan. Fernando Henrique Cardoso's political career and his chances for re-election in 1998 were dependent upon the continued success of the Real Plan.[29]

In addition to an unparalleled interest in sustaining the current stabilization programme, the executive branch gained added leverage over the legislature and governors through the concurrent presidential, legislative and state elections of November 1994. The Brazilian transition to democracy was marked not only by the re-introduction of direct elections for governor prior to the presidential elections, but also by concurrent gubernatorial and national legislative elections in 1982, 1986 and 1990. Direct presidential elections were only re-introduced in 1989 – an 'off' election year. Brazilian legislative candidates during the 1980s and early 1990s therefore benefited from riding 'gubernatorial coat tails' rather than presidential ones.[30] Fearing the possible victory of the presidential candidate for the Worker's Party (PT), the legislature passed a constitutional amendment shortening the presidential term to four years, thus making presidential, legislative and state-wide elections coincide in 1994. For the first time in Brazil's recent democracy, legislative and gubernatorial candidates had the potential of riding presidential coat tails. The successful presidential bid of Fernando Henrique Cardoso (PSDB) indeed appears to have influenced both the legislative and gubernatorial elections. PSDB increased its representation in the Chamber of Deputies from 38 to 62 seats (out of 513), in the Senate from one to nine (out of 54), and maybe more importantly, its gubernatorial posts from one to six (out of 27), including the most prominent states of São Paulo, Rio de Janeiro and Minas Gerais.[31]

However, the unparalleled interest in sustaining a stabilization plan and a concurrent election in 1994 do not constitute sufficient causes for a successful centralization of monetary authority in the Central Bank. Essential to this process has been the economic impact of the end of inflation upon state government finances. State governments had been running fiscal deficits for quite some time before 1994. The end of inflation, however, made those deficits unsustainable. The Real stabilization plan squeezed state finances through both a monetary and a fiscal mechanism. On the monetary end, state governments could no longer use the large 'floating' revenue of state banks, and on the fiscal end, states could no longer use inflation to corrode real spending on items like public wages and were compelled to disburse significantly higher debt payments because of the higher interest rates.

High inflation generates winners and losers. A clear winner under high inflation in Brazil was the financial sector, thanks to its ability to appropriate a significant portion of the famous 'inflation tax'. The banking sector (public and private) is estimated to have derived at least 20 per cent of its revenue from inflation.[32] In fact, floating revenue became a principal reason for preventing many state banks from entering complete bankruptcy during much of the 1980s and early 1990s. While most of their credit operations (assets) were directed to the public sector in the form of long-term financing, their liabilities derived primarily from short-term deposits, or bank bonds (CDBs etc). Without the floating revenue, state banks had increasing difficulties in meeting their cash requirements. When a bank does not balance its account by the end of the business day, it has two options: either borrow the money over the 'inter-bank market' (mercado inter-bancário) at a hefty interest rate, or resort to the Central Bank's discount line (linha de redesconto). By the end of 1994 the private market was no longer accepting state bank CDBs or RDBs (bank bonds), and thus prominent state banks like Banespa and Banerj (which make up 60 per cent of the financial sector) repeatedly turned to the Central Bank – thus providing the impetus for the latter's subsequent intervention. In sum, without inflation revenues many state banks became insolvent, thus inducing a Central Bank intervention. This placed a pinch upon state finances because state banks were essentially the managers of state government debt, and through that role they subsidized state finances.

With the end of inflation state government finances further deteriorated through two fiscal mechanisms. Firstly, states could no longer keep budgetary costs down by using inflation as a means to corrode real spending on items like public payroll. Spending on payroll often followed an electoral calendar. Governors and mayors would swell the public sector with political appointments prior to elections in order to help elect their successors, and once in office the newly-elected governments would reduce spending on payroll by allowing inflation to corrode the real wage bill. This was done either through poorly indexing wages, or through tardy payroll disbursements. With the end of inflation this mechanism to reduce spending also came to an end, and as a result the public payroll consumed an increasing percentage of state budgets.

Secondly, the end of inflation had the effect of dramatically increasing debt obligations. Much like the stabilization programme in Argentina, the Real Plan was based upon a stabilization of the currency through the exchange rate. Such a stabilization plan forced the government to keep a high interest rate in order to attract foreign capital, which consequently had the effect of higher debt payments on behalf of state and municipal governments. Figure 10.1 demonstrates how state level debt mushroomed at an astonishing rate after the stabilization programme was implemented. Note, however, that the dramatic increase derived from the two categories of debt whose interest rates are not fixed: bonds and debt owed to state banks.

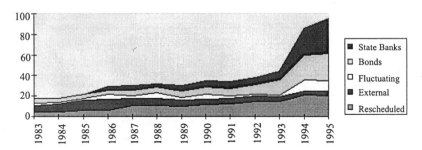

Source: World Bank. 1995. Brazil, State Debt: Crisis and Reform.

Figure 10.1: Bonds and Debt Owed to State Banks.

Before proceeding with the argument, however, two qualifications are in order. Firstly, we do not argue that the end of inflation caused the fiscal crisis many state governments are currently experiencing. The first major state-borrowing boom began in the 1970s under the military government's developmental project, and during the 1980s state governments were able to roll over that debt and to contract new debt by using their state banks. Rather than create the fiscal crisis, the end of inflation eliminated the mechanisms which sustained chronic state government fiscal imbalances.

Secondly, it is important to note that the weakening bargaining position of state governments began prior to the imposition of the Real Plan. State and municipal governments began a process of debt rescheduling during the early 1990s, and both the Senate and the Central Bank imposed more stringent limits on the ability of subnational governments to contract new debt. With each new round of state debt crisis during the 1980s and 1990s, the federal government and the Central Bank gained incremental leverage over state government finances. Following the state bank crisis of 1987, for example, the Central Bank, through Decree Law 2321, gained the ability to assume temporary control over insolvent state banks. The same decree law further established more stringent rules regarding the judicial accountability of state administrators for improper banking practices. While the state banks placed under federal intervention in 1987 were eventually returned to their respective state governments with no significant judicial action taken against their bank managers, the Central Bank gained a new tool to discipline state banks.[33]

The next round of the state government financial crisis during the early 1990s further placed new limits on state banks and state government finances. In 1990 the National Monetary Council imposed more stringent limits on the ability of state banks to loan to the public sector,[34] and in 1992 the judicial accountability of public administrators for their actions in state enterprises was further tightened.[35] In addition to imposing more restrictions on state banks, the Senate, as the branch of government responsible for setting legal debt limits for states and municipalities, further limited the ability of subnational governments to contract new debt.[36]

Thus we do not argue that the end of inflation in 1994 initiated the process through which the federal government is exerting greater control over state finances – either through Central Bank discipline over state banks or through legislative restrictions over the permissible level of debt states are able to contract. The ability of the Central Bank to exert discipline over state banks must be viewed as an incremental process beginning in the early 1980s, which was imposed with each successive state banking crisis. These periodic crises were induced both by the political use of such banks at the time of elections and by the various, and inevitably failed, stabilization programmes which temporarily ended inflation. Not coincidentally, each state banking crisis has coincided with the electoral calendar (1982, 1986 and 1990) and with stabilization plans (1986, 1989–90).

We do argue, however, that the recent crisis of state banks induced by the end of inflation in 1994 differs from the previous state banking crisis on two and potentially three fronts. Firstly, as we demonstrated, the executive branch has an unparalleled interest in disciplining state banks in order to sustain the stabilization programme, and secondly, the Real Plan has so far proven a much more sustainable stabilization plan than its predecessors, thus inducing a more drastic pinch on state bank and state government finances.[37] Thirdly, the central bank had more tools at its disposal to discipline state banks in 1994 partly because of the periodic state banking crisis described above. The federal government therefore took advantage of both political and economic factors that weakened the bargaining position of state governors in order to, in addition to other measures, make a federal bailout conditional on a centralization of monetary authority in the Central Bank.[38]

The evaluation by the federal government that disciplining state-level financial institutions was a necessary component to making the Real Plan work was made evident by declarations of members of Fernando Henrique Cardoso's economic team soon after his electoral victory in November 1994.[39] The government did not waste any time. On 31 December 1994, the last day of the presiding state government administrations, the Central Bank intervened in the two largest state banks belonging respectively to the states of São Paulo and Rio de Janeiro: Banespa and Banerj. In addition to infusing 'national' elements into a predominantly local and regional congressional election, Fernando Henrique Cardoso further took advantage of a concurrent turnover of state and federal governments.[40] With an intervention on the exact date of turnover, the outgoing governor does not have a chance to mobilize his political allies against the intervention, and the incoming governor does not have as large an incentive. On the one hand, the incoming governor is not directly accountable for the intervention and, more importantly, the governor may have a financially healthy bank returned to the state halfway through his term.[41] While legislators from São Paulo and Rio fought against the stated aims of the Central Bank to privatize both banks eventually, initial opposition to the intervention might have been greater if it had taken place during the middle of a gubernatorial term.

The intervention in both Banespa and Banerj in itself constituted an important advance over the Central Bank's ability to impose discipline over the financial system. The economic team created by Fernando Henrique Cardoso were well aware that the Real Plan could not survive without providing a resolution to the question of state banks, and taking care of Banespa and Banerj went a long way towards a solution for the entire sector.

Once the Central Bank had conducted the intervention in both banks, the government used whatever tools it had at its disposal to increase the effective threat of privatization – and this was accomplished by slowly opening the financial market to foreign competition, a policy more recently made evident by the purchase of Bamerindus by HSB. With new foreign competitors looking to establish themselves in the Brazilian market, the privatization threat became much more credible due to potential buyers.

In short, the political game between the executive, legislators and governors has substantially changed during the 1990s. The end of inflation made the fiscally precarious state finances unsustainable, and thus dependent upon federal financial rescue. Subnational dependence on federal rescue, however, was combined with an unprecedented interest on the part of the president in preserving the Real Plan and with a stronger executive, owing to the concurrent elections. Fernando Henrique Cardoso was elected because of the Real, hence his political fate is intimately tied to its continued success. Since discipline over the monetary system is a precondition for holding inflation down, Fernando Henrique Cardoso has made federal rescue of state finances conditional upon a centralization of monetary authority in the Central Bank.

4.3 Evidence of Increased Central Bank Discipline over the Monetary System

The federal government has been able to make a bailout of state finances conditional upon a centralization of monetary authority in the Central Bank through two mechanisms: the rescheduling of state debt, and Central Bank bailouts of state banks. While the former is also a prerogative of the Senate, the latter is exclusively a Central Bank one.[42] Unlike previous federal bailouts of state finances, the recent round of Central Bank interventions and state debt rescheduling has demanded greater counter-measures on behalf of state governments. Through monetary authority, states have been induced to adhere strictly to existing Central Bank resolutions and, more importantly, to privatize or transform their state banks into development agencies. Central Bank discipline over the financial sector, however, has not been limited to state governments – the recent rescue of private banks has been conditional on similar measures.

As the previous sections demonstrated, Central Bank intervention in state banks is not a novelty of the 1990s. State bank crises and subsequent Central Bank rescue have coincided with Brazil's electoral calendar and its stabilization programmes.[43] The Central Bank attempted to impose restrictions on the likelihood of such crises re-occurring, but those measures either lacked scope or were simply ignored. At the extreme, state non-compliance with Central Bank resolutions took the form of a blatant public defiance. In 1993, for example, a state bank from Brazil's northeast region opened six new agencies without the requisite prior approval of the Central Bank. The state bank's president was summoned to Brasília and verbally censured for his actions. Following the meeting, the bank opened another six agencies, upon which the governor stated to a Central Bank director, 'The bank is mine and I do as I please'.[44] Such defiance clearly demonstrates that the political weight of the governor trumped the legal and statutory authority of the Central Bank.

As is indicated by the foregoing example of the opening of new agencies, much of the history of Central Bank-state bank relations has been one of successive non-compliance with Central Bank regulations. In addition to ignoring the Bank's stipulations for opening new agencies,[45] state banks further ignored various measures which tried to restrict state bank credit operations with their respective state governments. Despite the 1964 banking reform legislation which stipulated that no banking institution could compromise more than 10 per cent of its credit operations with its controllers, by the mid-1980s state banks allocated more than half their assets to their respective state governments. While some exceptions to the above regulation were permitted by Central Bank resolutions,[46] states clearly passed the legal limits permissible for credit operations with their states.[47]

The current interventions of state banks differ from those of the 1980s and early 1990s on two important counts. The first pertains to the adherence to Central Bank regulations. While the Central Bank began to tighten the ability of state banks to loan to their controllers during the early 1990s, the Real Plan further tightened the controls over state banking practices which were adhered to. The National Monetary Council re-established limits on the concessions of new loans to the public sector, including the carrying of state bonds (Resolution 1990 of 30 June 1994), prohibited the rescue by the Central Bank or the Treasury in order solely to recapitalize state banks (Resolution 1995 of 30 June 1994) and further increased the judicial accountability of state bank administrators.

Secondly, and probably more importantly, full federal rescue has since been conditional on either an eventual privatization or a transformation of the bank into a development agency. According to Provisional Measure 1.514, edited by the executive, states are provided with two options for federal rescue of their state banks. In order for the federal government to refinance the entire portion of state debt owed to the respective state bank, the state government must agree to either privatize, liquidate or transform the institution into a development agency. State governments, however, can retain control over their banks if they are willing to accept a federal restructuring of only half their debt to the state banks. Given the acute stage of the crisis, however, the latter alternative is often not an option.[48]

In sum, the bargaining game between the federal executive, governors and the legislature has shifted. While the federal government had initiated the slow process of controlling state finances and state banks during the early 1990s, the Real Plan added great impetus to it. The end of inflation imposed by the Plan has pinched state finances and made many state banks insolvent. In order to guarantee the continued success of the current stabilization programme the federal government has made the restructuring of state debt and the bailout of state banks conditional upon a centralization of monetary authority in the Central Bank.

CONCLUSION

An important dimension of state reform and of economic restructuring in neo- and Western-dominant democracies pertains to the function and changing jurisdiction of central banks in the context of globalization and regional integration. International factors such as the liquidity crisis of the 1980s and the acute need to attract investments in peripheral economies in Latin America, Africa, East Europe and more recently South Asia, have provided important incentives to improve international creditworthiness. This indeed is the international background against which the world-wide trend towards the greater central banks' statutory autonomy observed in the 1990s becomes intelligible.

The problems we addressed in this paper, however, led us to propose an analytical shift of focus which we reckon is also policy-relevant. We started by exploring three related questions. The first and more general one is why, despite the critical impact the exercise of monetary authority has upon democratic governance, has this topic been nearly absent from the relevant political literature? A second set of questions has to do with an uncritical acceptance of the way monetary authority is currently used by economists – for whom democracy is (at best) a residual category. If, as we believe, the exercise of monetary authority is relevant for political scientists because it impinges directly on the question of democratic governance, the distinctive attributes of this specific mode of authority should be incorporated into our analytical framework. Finally, a third question was raised in connection with the comparatively 'untidy praxis' of central banking in most Latin American countries, notwithstanding the legal changes geared towards granting them an ever greater autonomy in the 1990s. We followed the criticisms of the conventional approach raised by Laurence Whitehead, who challenged the notion of a single effective central banking model by which to measure countries. At the same time, we tried to advance a step further by introducing another question: to what extent are categories such as peripheral economic systems and neo-democracies too broad to explore the dilemmas posed by the need to reconcile the tasks (ideally) performed by central banks as rule-givers, on the one hand, and democratic governance, on the other?

A first conclusion is that monetary authority is a mode of political authority which, like the judiciary, poses an important question for the democratic framework: who guards the guardians of both the currency and the law? The process of legitimization of such authority depends in great measure on the value attached to economic stability as a first order public good.

With support from empirical evidence supplied by a sub-family of Latin American countries like Argentina and Brazil, we conclude that the process of legitimization by which economic stability is reckoned a first order public good is especially convoluted in Latin American neo-democracies. In order to demonstrate this we thought it crucial to draw an important distinction between two kinds of neo-democracies: those where monetary disorder reached the stage of hyperinflation (accompanied or not by a hyperinflationary crisis), and those where political stresses inseparable from economic restructuring were less threatening to the maintenance of a modicum of monetary order. Argentina and Brazil belong in the former category. We thus chose as examples these extreme cases, in which, together with Bolivia in 1986, the issue at stake was the construction of a new monetary order. Hyperinflation is inseparable from the absence of a monetary and fiscal regime of any sort – the state is rendered powerless to impose the rule of law (if there is one). Brazil found itself in this predicament for reasons linked to the federal structure, and in particular to the influence governors had exerted in the Congress owing to Brazil's logic of democratization. Brazilian governors illustrated how challenges to fiscal and monetary authority tend to take the form of fiscal and monetary rebellion, in the name of democracy. We tried to show that the mode of economic and political federalism adopted during political liberalization and subsequent democratization impinged directly upon the monetary order because it created a multiplication of rival centres of power prepared to create money – which in principle is an exclusive prerogative of the centralized monetary authority.

We conclude, where the case of Brazil is concerned, that at least one of the conditions for legitimization of central bank authority has been achieved, to the extent that economic stabilization became a first order public good for both the population at large and the existing government. The Real Plan's redistributive impact in favour of lower economic segments, however, should not be dismissed as a factor in the endorsement to and popularity enjoyed by the Real Plan, and subsequently by its major architect, Fernando Henrique Cardoso.

The recent centralization of monetary authority in the Central Bank yields a final and valuable analytical lesson. The Central Bank in Brazil has been able to gain increasing discipline over the monetary system partly because of the

economic stabilization plan – not the other way around, as predicted by conventional wisdom. Economic stabilization has less to do with 'getting the institutions right', and is rather a consequence of a dynamic bargaining game between the federal executive, legislators and subnational governments. When
studying monetary authority and central bank institutions, the analyst should
identify the relevant actors, their interests, and how economic and political
conjunctures can shift the relevant bargaining position of those very actors.
Only then can the analyst study monetary authority as political authority.

NOTES

1. Laurence Whitehead makes this point in a forthcoming work.
2. This was not the only motivation. As is well known, the Allied powers played an important
    role in the restructuring of the monetary order and finances of the German state, in order to
    prevent the German economy from being subordinated to a new war effort. The independence
    of the Central Bank *vis-à-vis* the domestic political arena was crucial for this purpose. The
    question is, however: can this model be transplanted to Latin America?
3. Moreover, to the extent that effective autonomy has in practice been accompanied by the
    exercise of a veto power by central banks over fiscal policy, there is no question of the specific
    problems raised for effective democratic governance.
4. The author has developed this point in other works (Sola, 1994).
5. (Sola and Kugelmas, 1997). For our purposes, generalized indexation can be interpreted as
    the device by which the distributive conflicts underlying accelerating inflation were accom-
    modated and prevented from turning into uncontrolled hyperinflation for a long time. It may
    be interpreted as part and parcel of the Brazilian style of policy making and was first adopted
    under the military regime.
6. We note, however, that many make a distinction between autonomy and independence. While
    the latter refers to a severance from the political arena, the former indicates the ability to resist
    short-term political pressures. Independence never really exists in practice.
7. This is more so in cases like Brazil, where a very new and minutely detailed constitution
    opens multiple fronts for divergent interpretations, not to speak of the infra-constitutional
    legislation to be derived from the Constitution of 1988, which is still (in 2000) pending Con-
    gressional decision. For the legal constraints posed by the Constitution, see Sola, 1996.
8. We are assuming that deregulation of the financial system does not preclude regulation at
    another level on behalf not only of monetary order but also of transparency, accountability
    and predictability (the rule of law depends on much legislative work related to infra-constitu-
    tional legislation).
9. We are following Albert Hirschman in his assumption that at a certain point inflation gener-
    ates a new social coalition in favour of stabilization. Our point, however, is that political
    intermediation and the quality of leadership are additional conditions which may or may not
    be met but are relevant for the choice of effective policies also in the sense that they are
    adequate to the social profile of that coalition. This implies, of course, the choice of the eco-
    nomic team.
10. For the Bolivian experiment, see especially Malloy and Conaghan, 1996. For the Brazilian
    case, see Sola and Kugelmas, 1997.
11. See Sola, 1994. While it is out of the scope of this paper, monetary and fiscal rebellion oc-
    curred in the private and public sector alike. Public and private actors often financed their

investments by evading tax payments and delaying social security payments. Under high inflation, such practices became a source of revenue.

12. See Alesina, 1988; see also Grilli, Masciandaro and Tabellini; for the use of such arguments in Brazil see Campos, 1995.
13. See Maxfield, 1995.
14. Not only dependent upon the federal executive, but also divided between two federal organs: SUMOC and Bank of Brazil prior to 1964, and the Central Bank and Bank of Brazil after the military coup. For details see Sola (forthcoming).
15. Maxfield's country case studies do not focus exclusively on the need to obtain credit. In most of her cases she blends international with national level variables, whereas we contend that her general theoretical orientation is ill-suited to explain the Brazilian case.
16. See Hall, 1994.
17. For examples of the latter type of arguments see Lohmann, 1994; also Banaian, Laney and Willett, 1986. Notice, however, that the relationship posited by these two authors between federalism and central bank autonomy would be the opposite in a context where the central bank is not autonomous. A large number of veto gates hinders institutional change, hence federal countries without an independent central bank would be the slowest to implement those institutions.
18. Goodman, 1992; Woolley, 1985.
19. Stepan makes this type of argument for federal countries.
20. Whitehead, 1996.
21. See Campos, 1995.
22. The separation between monetary and fiscal budgets introduced by the economic team under the first civilian government, in 1986, made it viable to eliminate one of the black boxes created by Antonio Delfim Neto, namely the non-discrimination between those two budgets – a mechanism by which the executive evaded accountability.
23. Except for the short interlude of 1964–67. For stabilization plans under the populist regime, see Sola (forthcoming).
24. We refer here to the federal executive. Congressional elections were held during most of the military period.
25. Stepan makes this argument in connection with the electoral sequencing.
26. Malloy and Connaghan (1996) make this point succinctly.
27. This would partially explain the Central Bank's belated action in disciplining those banks – in both cases, after the Real Plan was under way.
28. In addition to centralizing monetary authority in the Central Bank, the federal government has made state bailouts conditional upon a series of other measures beyond monetary authority (future revenues, administrative reform and privatization of state-owned enterprises).
29. The Brazilian Congress approved a constitutional amendment to permit executives in all three levels of government to run for re-election. Again, this institutional change further increased the power of Fernando Henrique Cardoso, as noted by an increased flocking of congressmen to the president's party after the amendment was approved.
30. For the effect that this electoral calendar had upon subnational influences on the national legislature, see Linz and Stepan e Fernando Abrucio, 1994; Garman, Haggard, and Willis, 1996.
31. Nicolau, 1996.
32. FGV, Balanços de bancos, and *Gazeta Mercantil*.
33. It might be argued that the federal interventions of 1987 indicated the strength of state governments in relation to the federal executive. Most governors in fact desired a federal intervention in their insolvent state banks upon taking office in 1987 (the only opposition came from Leonel Brizola, governor of Rio de Janeiro), for they correctly assumed that their banks would be returned to them in good financial health at the end of their administration, in time for the next elections. The way the Central Bank decided to use its ability to intervene in state banks, however, was analytically distinct from the incremental process we are trying to de-

pict, whereby the Central Bank acquired more tools to discipline state financial agents. For the willing participation of governors in the 1987 interventions, see *Folha de São Paulo*, 31 January 1988; *Isto É*, 4 March 1987; *Correio Brasiliense*, 10 August 1987.

34. CMN (Conselho Monetário Nacional) Resolution 1718 of 29 May 1990; CMN Resolution 1775 of 26 December 1990.
35. Lei da Improbidade – Código Penal – Law 8429 of 2 June 1992.
36. Senate Resolution n. 94, 15 December 1989; Senate Resolution n. 58, December 1990; and Senate Resolution n. 36, June 1992. In 1993 a Constitutional Amendment (n. 3, 17 March 1993) was further passed which prohibited the production of any new state bonds except for the payment of principal.
37. The Real Plan has recently celebrated three years of price stability. For details on what differentiates the Real Plan from other stabilization plans, and on the mechanisms which brought about its success, see Lourdes, 1997.
38. Since this paper focuses on monetary authority, we limit our discussion primarily to how federal bailout of state finances has affected Central Bank credibility in the financial sector. The current rescheduling of state finances, however, involves many elements which go beyond the monetary sector. In order to receive federal financing, state governments are further being forced to yield guarantees on future revenue (from their own taxes and constitutionally allocated shares of federal taxes), as well as assets of their state-owned enterprises.
39. In the Senate confirmation hearing for the President of the Central Bank, Persio Arida, for one, declared that he was in favour of privatizing state banks in order to sustain price stability. *Jornal do Brasil*, 14 December 1994.
40. Since prior to 1997 governors and presidents were not permitted to run for re-election, an election, by definition, constituted a turnover in government.
41. The Central Bank's intervention in both banks was also helped by the fact that incoming governors Mario Covas of São Paulo, and Marcelo Allencar of Rio de Janeiro belonged to the same political party as the president (PSDB). Their belonging to the same party, however, could influence the outcome either way. One might equally expect each governor to reduce state 'rebellion' against the federal government, and expect the federal government to give those governors favourable treatment.
42. As will become clear, the two cannot in practice be separated. Because state banks have been the administrators of state government debts, negotiation over state banks by the Central Bank must often be made in tandem with a restructuring of the state government debt – a senate prerogative.
43. Brazil's gubernatorial elections were first held in 1982, with subsequent elections for the governor's office held every four years: 1986, 1990 and 1994. The first Central Bank bailout of state banks occurred in 1983, followed by a series of interventions in 1987 and 1991. These crises, however, also coincided with the various stabilization programmes adopted over the last 10 years: the Plano Cruzado of 1986, and the Plano Collor of 1990.
44. *Estado de São Paulo*, 17 January 1993.
45. Not only did state banks open new agencies without approval, but they also failed to close deficit agencies which they had agreed to close upon receiving Central Bank relief during the early and mid-1980s. In fact, the state banks that received Central Bank assistance on the condition of closing deficit agencies had their total number of agencies increased. See Andrade, 1992.
46. There were, however, various exceptions thanks to this banking law. In 1972, for example, the Central Bank passed BC Resolution 346, allowing state banks to make loans to their respective states, which participated in their 'social capital' – if authorized by the Central Bank (Andrade, 1992). Other resolutions would chiefly make exceptions to the National Housing Bank (BNH) and, subsequent to its dissolution, the CEF.
47. By the late 1980s state banks in some cases invested more than 80 per cent of their credit operation with their respective state governments. See Andrade, 1992.
48. Medida Provisória n. 1514, 7 August 1996.

BIBLIOGRAPHY

Alesina, Alberto (1988), 'Macroeconomics and Politics', in Stanley Fischer (ed.), *NBER Macroeconomics Annual*, Cambridge: Cambridge University Press.

Andrade, Eduardo de Carvalho (1992), *Os Bancos Comerciais Estaduais no Brasil: do Final dos Anos Sessenta à Crise dos Anos Oitenta*, MSc thesis, Rio de Janeiro: PUC.

Banaian, King, Leroy O. Laney and Thomas D. Willett (1986), 'Central Bank Independence: An International Comparison', in E.F. Toma and M. Toma (eds), *Central Bankers, Bureacratic Incentives, and Monetary Policy*, Boston: Academic Publishers, pp. 199–219.

Campos, Roberto (1995), *A Lanterna na Popa*. Rio de Janeiro: Topbooks.

Garman, C., S. Haggard and E. Willis (1996), 'Decentralisation in Latin America', paper presented at APSA.

Goodman, John B. (1992), *Monetary Sovereignty: The Politics of Central Banking in Western Europe*, Ithaca: Cornell University Press.

Grilli, Vittorio, Donato Masciandaro and Guido Tabellini, 'Political Monetary Institutions and Public Financial Policies in the Industrial Countries', in *Economic Policy: A European Economic Forum*, 13 October, pp. 342–392.

Guardia, E.R. (1993), *O Processo Orçamentário do Governo Federal: Considerações Sobre o Novo Arcabouço Intitucional e a Experiência Recente*, IESP – Intituto de Economia do Setor Público/Fundap.

Hall, Peter A. (1994), 'Central Bank Independence and Coordinated Wage Bargaining: Their Interaction in Germany and Europe', *German Politics and Society*, **31**, Spring, pp. 1–23.

Linz and Stepan e Fernando Abrucio (1994), *Os Barões da Federação: o Poder dos Governadores no Brasil Pós-autoritário*, MSc thesis, University of São Paulo.

Lohmann, Susanne (1994), 'Federalism and Central Bank Autonomy: The Politics of German Monetary Policy, 1957–92', Department of Political Science, UCLA, October.

Loyola, Gustavo (1992), *Bancos Estaduais: Experiências e Perspectivas*. Banco Central do Brasil. Seminário Internacional, Brasília.

Malloy, James M. and Catherine Conaghan (1996), *Unsettling Statecraft, Democracy and Liberalism in the Central Andes*, Pittsburgh: Pittsburgh University Press.

Maxfield, Sylvia (1995), 'Gatekeepers of Growth: The International Political Economy of Central Banking in Developing Countries' (draft), July.

Nicolau, Jairo Marconi (1996), *Multipartidarismo e Democracia*, Rio de Janeiro: Fundação Getúlio Vargas.

Santos, Gilton Carneiro dos (1993), *Contingenciamento de Créditos e Finanças Estaduais*.

Sola, Lourdes (1994), 'State, Structural Reform and Democratisation', in William C. Smith, Carlos Acuña and Eduardo Gamarra (eds), *Democracy, Markets and Structural Reforms*, New Brunswick: Transaction Books.

Sola, Lourdes (1995), *Reforma Econômica, Democratização e Ordem Legal no Brasil*, Santiago do Chile, CEPAL.

Sola, Lourdes (1996), 'Reforma do Estado, Ordem Legal e Democratização', in *Projeto de Reforma do Estado e Políticas Públicas*, no. 38, Comissão Econômica para a América Latina, Santiago do Chile.

Sola, Lourdes (forthcoming), *Idéias econômicas, decisões políticas: Desenvolvimento, estabilidade e populismo*, Editora da Universidade de São Paulo.

Sola, Lourdes and Eduardo Kugelmas (1997), 'Statecraft, Economic Liberalisation and Democracy: the Case of Brazil in Comparative Perspective', paper presented at the Congress of the Latin American Studies Association, Guadalajara, 17 April.

Whitehead, Laurence (1996), 'Models of Central Banking: How Much Convergence in Neo-Democracies?' (draft).

Woolley, John T. (1985), *Monetary Politics*, Cambridge: Cambridge University Press.

11. Public administration in Central and Eastern Europe: considerations from the 'state science' approach

Wolfgang Drechsler

1. INTRODUCTION

In Central and Eastern Europe, the reform impetus of 1989–1991 has subsided by now, and not only as regards state matters. Nonetheless, 'keeping on going, keeping on going' is still no viable policy, because – regardless of the fact that in the West not everything is that great either – things are hardly going as well as they should be and, more importantly, as they could. The fundamental challenge to Central and Eastern Europe is still a restoration or (re)creation of the positive concept of the state, indeed of the *polis*, i.e. of structured human social life. Democracy, the generally chosen form of government in the region, needs to be filled out and given meaning, and the chosen form of the allocation of scarce resources – the (more or less free) market economy – does not function without a well-functioning state either. Many, if not most, of the problems facing Central and Eastern Europe right now are therefore related to questions of what the state is or should be.

In this brief essay, I want to focus on the crucial role of public administration for such a state, or indeed any state. The legitimacy of the state as such often springs from a working public administration, this being the state in action. Bad public administration, inversely, can and probably will cause citizens to turn away from the state in its current form. Yet, in Central and Eastern Europe, any state matter, and particularly public administration, usually suffers from the legacy of a justifiably bad reputation after Soviet rule.

2.   THE CASE OF ESTONIA

As an illustration, let us look at the case of Estonia. This is the westernmost country of Central and Eastern Europe (CEE), bordering to the east on Russia, to the south on Latvia, and bathed to the north and west by the Baltic Sea. It covers 45 000 square kilometres and has a population of 1.5 million inhabitants. From 1227 to this day, there has been no Estonian self-government except for a period of 27 years. Until 1991–92, the country was a Soviet Republic.

On the whole, Estonia's transition – we can use the term in this context because its origin and goal will be stated shortly – from a colony within a totalitarian empire to a pluralistic free-market democracy, which took place during the last decade or so, has been swift and extremely successful. The country is already called the 'Tiger of the Baltic' (Schießl, 1997, p. 129), although at present this is a rather back-handed compliment, and the economic bubble did in fact collapse to a certain extent (even if this is an unfortunate metaphor) during 1998. Estonia is a parliamentary democracy headed by a president, a prime minister and cabinet, and a one-chamber diet. There are no extremist parties of any significance; by 'Atlantic' standards, its political outlook might be called liberal in the classical sense. The currency is pegged to the German mark, which has led to a low outer inflation.

In a way, Estonians have had the best of both worlds, because its people have surely experienced an increase both in voting and freedom of speech *and* in personal safety, decent food, education, housing, health services, and the like (cf. Chang and Nolan, 1995, pp. 4–5) . And as far as national pride is concerned, the majority of the population enjoys all this to an amazing degree that is entirely incomparable with previous times. There are some serious problems, however, such as a society in which the lower 20 per cent of the population do not enjoy an acceptable standard of living, and a Russian-speaking minority of 30 per cent; this is far too big a problem to be even briefly addressed here. However, the Council of Europe's decision to admit Estonia in its first round has been the grand reward for this policy. Whatever one may say about the EU, membership would be an amazing advantage for the general welfare of the Estonian people. I might even venture to say that Estonia is more or less 'home and dry'.

Yet, Estonia is a fine illustration of the claims made in the introduction, in spite or perhaps because of its peculiarities. Its most serious problem is still the lack of a prevailing state identification on the part of its citizens. There is not even a concept of 'state' as such, which leads to serious problems that Estonia cannot afford. These include the citizens' lack of automatic loyalty to and co-operation with the government, or of true respect for legal or administrative decisions. Estonians very generally identify with the Estonian nation in the sense of the Estonian people, i.e. they identify with their fellow Estonians (usually excepting the national minorities), but hardly anyone – including judges, politicians, and intellectuals – identifies with the Republic of Estonia.

This somewhat extreme libertarianism is an unsurprising reaction against the Soviet past, and it finds resonance in Estonians' predisposition to individualism and to a historical distrust of the state. During the days of Soviet rule, the state was excluded from their everyday life. The independence movements of the late 1980s concentrated on the Estonian nation, not on an Estonian state. But, indeed, how could it have been otherwise?

This lack of trust in the state prevails towards judges as well – few really respect them or their judgements, and they are appointed in a way that is not transparent to most – and certainly to lawmakers, who are often not credited with representing anyone, not even their constituents. Added to this there is the dominance of a rather primitive marketeerism on the one hand, and a lack of market infrastructure on the other. I think it goes without saying, in the present context, that low taxes and individualism do not make for a market economy. When even the World Bank has realized as much (see World Bank, 1997), there seems to be hardly any more reason to labour this point. Social stability, a savings banks system, a contract culture, and the *Rechtsstaatlichkeit* are the key elements of a free market culture, and to the extent that they are still lacking, even though many aspects have undergone improvements for other reasons, they are lacking because of a lack of state-orientedness.

Even that issue, however, is being dealt with as of late. In 1997, a group of Estonian politicians led by the current Foreign Minister released a rather indicative manifesto on state reform, *Millist riiki me tahame?* [What kind of state do we want?] (Aaviksoo *et al.*, 1997). They claimed that the 'Estonian State and society have reached a point where once again we need to decide on how to proceed; gone are the days when we could base our attempts at reform on anti-Sovietness and consider only economic reforms'. 'Estonia deserves more than it has nowadays, i.e. we must pay closer attention to social problems and to the problems of those who have not "succeeded", so that our society may not be made up of only winners and losers' (Aaviksoo *et al.*, 1997). At the current time, in late 1998, we may safely say that this kind of thinking has certainly not been implemented as yet, but it has significantly reshaped the overall discourse.

3. THE IMPORTANCE OF PUBLIC ADMINISTRATION

What, then, is the importance of public administration in this context? The reason why public administration and the state are so important has been well phrased by Christian Wolff (1679–1754), who is arguably the founder of public administration as a scholarly discipline in Europe. He put the matter thus:

> We can very easily realise that single households can neither provide themselves with the means to satisfy their needs, their comfort and pleasure, indeed their happiness, nor can they enjoy their rights or be definitely granted what they are entitled to receive from others, nor can they be protected against violence from the outside. It is thus necessary to guarantee to common, communal powers what individual households cannot achieve by themselves. (1740, § 972)

To put the matter still more precisely: the need for the state arises from the fact and the insight, as Hannah Arendt put it, that 'Man is not God and lives in this world together with his like' (Safranski, 1994). In a *polis*, things do not just 'happen'. Some structure is necessary, and if there is no planning, regulation, supply of public goods, etc., we cannot live together, or at least not in close contact; nevertheless, that is the situation almost all of us are 'thrown into'. If this living together is not organized and well-administered, not only will the *polis* die, but so shall we.

But what does the reality of public administration in Central and Eastern Europe look like? The main problem here is usually not to be found in administrative structures, despite the fact that external advice and scholarly attention tend to focus on them, but rather in the lack of well-qualified, highly motivated civil servants. According to Aristotle,

> Those who wish to hold decision-making offices must have three characteristics: first, an adherence to the existing constitution of the state; second, a supreme talent to exercise the office in question; and third, a kind of virtue and justice that within each respective constitution concern precisely that constitution. (*Politika* 1309a)

Public administration therefore requires a special virtue on the part of its main protagonist, the civil servant, in order for the system to work properly or even function at all. This virtue cannot be created artificially and is highly dependent on tradition. How, then, is a good civil service to be obtained, if there is neither a good tradition nor ethos, as is generally the regional situation observed? Servants could perhaps be highly paid, but in Central and Eastern Europe the consensus seems to be that the state cannot afford that. Hence the state must offer what it can best provide: security, honour, stability, civility, and fulfilment. If the state does so, it becomes more prestigious to work for the government. This in turn will lead to a greater general faith in the state, which again will lead to higher civil service prestige – and so on, and so forth.

In other words, good public administration, a good civil service, and a good state are interdependent. But this is as much a problem as it is an answer: if one of the elements is bad, the other two will suffer as well. It is in any case necessary to begin the improvement somewhere, carefully raising the level as much as possible and covering all areas at the same time.

In a popular textbook, Jan-Erik Lane of the University of Oslo has stated that 'Public administration as an academic discipline has more or less crumbled during the recent decades of research into the public sector. It has become outdated, losing its status as the main approach to the interpretation of the state or government' (1993, p. vii). But the opposite is true. Public administration, in my opinion, has to, and is going to, focus on the areas neglected by other, neighbouring disciplines that equally deal with the public sphere: where they do not deliver, public administration must do so. The classic canon of Western public administration must surely be followed – if in a critically adapted form – but this is not enough in the East nor in the West.

What dimension is it that must be added, or better still, regained? It is taking up the old and venerable tradition of public administration as a 'state science', *Staatswissenschaft*. Within the social sciences, public administration is characterized by being academic and professional at the same time. Because of its implemental, action-based focus, public administration can concentrate on the state in a way that the field supposedly in charge of doing it, *viz*. political science, so often appears to be incapable of, at least at the moment, as it often gets stuck in an empirical-positivist matrix that condemns it to self-referentiality.

What is so bad about empirical-positivist social science is, as Ted McAllister paraphrased Eric Voegelin, that 'positivists allow their method to define the subject and ... the most important political and social questions get tossed aside because a crucial component of human experience is effectively devalued as "subjective" (1996, p. 74). And this actually means (this time, in McAllister's words narrating Leo Strauss's view) that the

> social scientists most relevant to the political arena – political scientists – are utterly incapable of understanding their subject. The rich, valuative political and social world is a terra incognita for the political scientist who transforms the world as experienced into discrete facts. These 'facts' have the advantage of being easily grasped and manipulated; they have the disadvantage of possessing little relationship to the subject. (p. 164)

That may perhaps be all right in political science, although I do not believe it. At the end of the millennium, mainstream political theory, at least on the higher level of discourse, fortunately seems to be reverting slowly to the Aristotelian ethical foundations of that which is common or usual in a good community of citizens, plus the wise application of the implicit norms of local traditions. But political science is a field that does not necessarily have to do with reality: it can be self-referential, an intellectual game that is perhaps even beautiful and aesthetically pleasing, such as pure mathematics, neoclassical economics, ana-lytical philosophy, and other self-referential constructs. In those fields one can say, 'If we assume x, y, and z, then a, b, and c', and once that is written down it can make an acceptable article. But in public administration one must ask: Can we assume x? Is y the case? Is z real? If not, who cares?

Professionalism, as Richard Rose correctly states, means 'diagnosing spe-cific problems in light of general principles' and recommending action rather than explaining them (1993, p. 11; cf. also Berlin, 1996, p. 47). But public administration, in its professional orientation, must focus on truth, on how things actually are – on truth defined as congruence with reality (see Drechsler, 1999). And by doing so, one can actually cut through the problem of self-refer-ential systems and end up with productive normative state thinking.

Admittedly, the description of reality which includes normative and ethical points is an immense problem, but what else can we do? According to Nicolai Hartmann, the difficulty of a problem is not a good reason to put it aside. Con-cepts such as tyranny, betrayal and loyalty are not quantifiable, yet if one leaves them out of consideration when talking about the state, one is screening out determining variables just because they do not fit in with the chosen methods. If one asks scientific questions in a field concerning human beings, one will get wrong, meaningless answers. As the late Sir Isaiah Berlin put it, 'To demand or preach mechanical precision, even in principle, in a field incapable of it is to be blind and to mislead others' (Berlin, 1996, p. 53). In public administration, one cannot, and thus usually does not, ask the wrong questions. This allows for talking meaningfully about the state, about humans living together. In other words, the key task in thinking about the state, about 'What is the state', is now often simply left to public administration, which by taking it up is re-trans-formed into state science.

All the more must public administration in Central and Eastern Europe be watchful not to fall prey to an already receding fashion of its Western variant, i.e. the use of economic analysis and management techniques that is associated with the term 'new public management'. It must rather be remembered that the state is precisely the area in which those approaches cannot work. Their use misinterprets the most basic requirements of public administration, particularly in a democracy, such as greater attention to openness, regularity, and due process, rather than to (business) efficiency and speed as a liability. However, attention to the latter has been caused by an awareness of the awesome compulsoriness and power which the state inevitably has – something that is perhaps less easily forgotten in our region than in the West, at least for a while. The Schumpeterian entrepreneur outside the market context has a strong tendency to become a tyrant. In addition, the use of both certain economic models and 'scientific management', the old, Taylorite concept behind the 'new' public management, will lead immediately to the problems previously ascribed to political science, depriving public administration precisely of the vital potential it has at present.

4.   EDUCATION

All this must then be reflected in public administration instruction. As Christian Wolff already put it 250 years ago, 'One does not teach "state art" [public administration] for any other reason than to learn what is beneficial for the state, so that one can then be a prudent leader of the state. But the kind of "state art" which is usually taught in universities is not very useful for this...' (Wolff, 1740, p. 409). And how can it become useful? By teaching practical skills? Undoubtedly, but not only that.

These days, so many 'practical' things are changing so rapidly that to teach them responsibly would be a waste of time, if not downright impossible. Information and communications technology is a case in point. Public administration teaching therefore needs to focus also on the basics, as I have briefly outlined them. One cannot concentrate only on basic questions, of course. But in our complex, rapidly changing times all one can do, yet what one must do, is to strive for a learned, creative, adaptable yet intellectually secure public administration professional who is aware of the basic questions and therefore able to address the day-to-day ones once they pose themselves, often in unforeseen forms.

That kind of education, of course, is the role of the university as opposed to polytechnics, teachers' colleges, professional schools, or state training institutes, all of which also have their place in public administration as well as elsewhere. But public administration is and must be a university field and a true academic discipline. Besides its unique capability of genuinely educating, rather than just training civil servants, is it only in the university that independent, fundamental thinking on public administration and constructive criticism of the present state are possible, and that is what is required.

5. REFORM OF ADMINISTRATIVE UNITS

On the other hand, academic competence and its application are very much needed, because 'common-sense' solutions are often plainly wrong, especially as regards public administration. For instance, at first sight a layman might think that if there are two administrative units in one area, combining them into one unit (especially if they are small) would lead to a saving in costs and bureaucratic jobs. Therefore, administrative unit reforms often call for the combination of units – ministries, counties, departments, etc. However, even a quick look at similar reforms made in Europe during this century will show that this is simply not the case. More often than not, there are no savings at all; on the contrary, all job positions continue to exist and some others are created to *coordinate* their work.

There is, after all, no abstract 'ideal' size for an administrative unit – the ideal size depends on the actual tasks to be performed as well as on the environment (traditions, laws, personnel, etc.). But even if we ignore for a moment the special demands of the public sphere and apply simple business standards of efficiency, units that are excessively large, be they administrative or commercial, are difficult to manage on the personnel level, and difficult to coordinate and to communicate in. They actually create the need for a more hierarchical and less horizontal structure (which even in small units, incidentally, is only possible if one has an exceptionally highly-motivated, responsible, well-paid, and well-educated staff).

But when it comes to combining regional administrative units, units that people actually live in, considerations other than business efficiency are even more important. The minimizing of municipalities and counties, for instance, has a tendency to create less responsive governments; the offices are physically more difficult to reach; and bureaucrats are less informed about and less interested in local matters. Such was the German experience of the *Gebietsreform* of the 1970s, in which such combinations were made in some states, against the will of most citizens.

Perhaps even more importantly, creating artificial larger units is a typical feature of centralist, non-representative and even non-democratic governments. Regional and community identity and responsibility, based on traditional smaller units, is one of the best safeguards against an over-involved central government, even against totalitarianism. This is why the terror regime during the French Revolution imposed new regional departments as administrative units upon the French, in order to destroy their county loyalty, and it is also why traditional states were abolished by Communists in East Germany, while anonymous, non-traditional districts were created.

All this is especially important to remember in Estonia, which we will again use as an example, as a knee-jerk unification of several small local units was taken into consideration there on the basis of the naïve assumption that it would be (business) efficient, without any regard to the fact that those municipalities were and are the cradle of democracy, having been historically (1) the place where Estonians organized themselves, (2) where centuries ago there appeared some sort of *polis*, and (3) the most important units during the times of oppression. Furthermore, centralism goes against all that is at the core not only of Estonian but of European political ethos at large nowadays; it removes identity and responsibility at all levels and among all concerned parties – and it is inefficient even by business standards.

None of this is to say that some form of administrative unit reform in Estonia might not be beneficial, appropriate, and even called for. However, that reform, just like any other, should be based on a careful, professional analysis of the tasks and environment involved, which takes some time. Hasty and ill-considered administrative reform, after all, is not only very expensive in every respect but also counterproductive.

6. BUREAUCRACY

But now to the fundamental problem of public administration: bureaucracy. Here, Hans-Georg Gadamer must be quoted at some length:

> Feelings mutual to all are coming into words in language, in new words that come into use. There are primarily two words which by their very formation betray the loss of freedom and the lack of identification possibilities we all feel with what is general – a new word and an older one, both encompassing however almost unlimited areas of use: Technocracy and Bureaucracy. Both word formations apparently rely on the word 'autocracy', or at least share with it (and not with similar words, such as aristocracy and democracy) the stigma of powerlessness in face of the over-powerful, and that not only in the sense that all rational force of the facts limits and disempowers the individual will. For it is precisely the need of reason, the need to understand and to identify through understanding, that is claimed in these words. ...
>
> ... bureaucracy, this acknowledged basic evil of the rational administration of the world, regretted and opposed in every state form, [is] nevertheless perkily progressing everywhere, due to apparently unbreakable factual forces. This oldest of epithets used by the farmer and the citizen against rulers and public offices unleashes its attack, in the name of a common reason, a reason that seeks to be general, against not only the incomprehensibility but also the ineptness of administrative action. What is defended by these opprobrious epithets are the last bastions of common reason, which Heraclitus demanded to be followed and

for which – as something commonly held to be valid, as the *nomoi* – Heraclitus admonished to fight even more bravely than for the walls of the city. (Gadamer 1991, pp. 63, 64)

Properly understood, public administration, good public administration, is precisely not bureaucratic in this sense – it is rather the implementation, the exercise, and the guarding of the *nomoi*.

But bureaucracy in the sense in which it is commonly used nowadays is indeed the opposite. And since it has been emphasized how important good public administration is, the truly catastrophic consequences of the action of those who are not civil servants but bureaucrats in Gadamer's sense cannot be overstressed. That is not only bad public administration but actively making people turn away from the state. Unfortunately, it would be ignoring the facts not to admit that this is still happening frequently in the region. There are perhaps two main reasons for this: first, in Central and Eastern Europe there is still far too much of a traditional, Soviet-style bureaucracy that persists in ignoring who exists for whose sake. If the *homo sovieticus* lives on anywhere, it is in the branches of public administration that come into contact with citizens and other people.

A second but related reason is that one often observes that a strange rigidity in bureaucratic processes is mixed up with the concept of the *Rechtsstaat*, due process of law; it is sometimes precisely well-meaning civil servants who in their narrow-minded pursuit of the letter of the law forget that the strictest pursuit of the law may cause the greatest injustice. That is the danger of 'state playing', if we may put it that way. In Central and Eastern Europe, however, there is no room and no excuse for state playing or for Soviet-style bureaucracy, and it is up to public administration scholars and experts to point out the problems, just as it is up to the government to improve the situation.

7. SOME ANSWERS

So, what can one do? After all the theoretical points concerning the need to be practical, I would like to offer a catalogue of types of public administration reform or improvement which I believe to be a valid checklist for virtually any public administration structure. In classical public administration tradition, I have couched it in an acronym, as in the case of POSDCORB and SLOCUS (see Thomas, 1989, pp. 77, 86–87), and called it FINMOUSE.

Finance: are budgeting, accounting, and controlling done transparently and efficiently, and are they cost-effect-related?

Incentives: does the unit get, promote, and keep the best members available through specific incentives offered by the state (job security, promotion, prestige)?

Niceness: can anything be done to improve citizen satisfaction and control without causing financial or other problems?

Minimal State: would the task be better or equally well performed by a non-state entity?

Output-Orientation: is task performance measured by output, while keeping in mind that excessive control costs more than it saves, yet easily prevents the development of the civil service ethos?

Unit Size: are the units in the hierarchy small enough to allow for humaneness and supervision but big enough to avoid too much red tape?

Subsidiarity: is the lowest functioning unit in the hierarchy performing the task?

Efficiency: given the requirements of democracy and the *Rechtsstaat*, are the task performed and the office structured with (business) efficiency?

Public administration is a field that looks *prima facie* unattractive to many if not most people in Central and Eastern Europe, because of what bureaucracy does even to those who value the state: inefficiency, corruption, and boredom seem to be associated with it. Rightly understood, however, public administration is the key academic discipline of our administratively-structured times, hence one that we neglect both academically and professionally at our own peril. A high-quality, sound, competent, and responsible administration is perhaps the one factor, apart from the aforementioned *nomoi*, that singly contributes most to the happiness and well-being of the *polis* everywhere, not only in CEE – and therefore of all of us.

BIBLIOGRAPHY

Aaviksoo, Jaak *et al.* (1997), *Millist riiki me tahame?* [What kind of state do we want?], Manifesto on the State of Estonia. First published in *Paevaleht*, 27 September.

Appel, Karl-Otto (1993), 'Das Problem einer universalistischen Makroethik der Mitverantwortung', *Deutsche Zeitschrift für Philosophie*, **41** (2), pp. 201–215.

Backhaus, Jürgen G. (1997), 'Christian Wolff on Subsidiarity, the Division of Labor, and Social Welfare', *European Journal of Law and Economics*, **4** (2–3), pp. 129–146.

Berlin, Isaiah (1996), *The Sense of Reality: Studies in Ideas and their History*, London: Chatto & Windus.

Chang, Ha-Joon and Peter Nolan (1995), 'Europe versus Asia: Contrasting Paths to the Reform of Centrally Planned Systems of Political Economy', in H.-J. Chang and P. Nolan (eds), *The Transformation of the Communist Economies: Against the Mainstream*, New York: St Martin's; Basingstoke: Macmillan, pp. 3–45.

Drechsler, Wolfgang (1995), 'Estonia in Transition', *World Affairs*, **15** (3), pp. 111–117.

Drechsler, Wolfgang (1997), 'Avalik haldus kui riigiteadus' [Public Administration as 'State Science'], in W. Drechsler (ed.), *Avaliku halduse alused: valimik Euroopa esseid* [Foundations of Public Administration: A European Collection], Tartu: Tartu University Press, pp. 11–21.

Drechsler, Wolfgang (1999), 'Natural vs. Social Sciences: On Understanding in Economics', in E.S. Reinert (ed.), *Evolutionary Economics and Income Inequality*, Aldershot: Edward Elgar.

Ebbinghaus, Julius (1969), *Traditionsfeindschaft und Traditionsgebundenheit*, Frankfurt/Main: Klostermann.

Gadamer, Hans-Georg (1991), 'Über die Macht der Vernunft', in *Lob der Theorie. Reden und Aufsätze*, 3rd edn., Frankfurt/Main: Suhrkamp, pp. 51–66.

König, Klaus (1996), *On the Critique of the New Public Management*, Speyer: Forschungsinstitut für öffentliche Verwaltung.

Lagerspetz, Mikko (1996), *Constructing Post-Communism. A Study in the Estonian Social Problems Discourse*, Annales Universitatis Turkuensis, ser. B, **214**, Turku: Turun Yliopisto.

Lane, Jan-Erik (1993), *The Public Sector: Concepts, Models and Approaches*, London: Sage.

McAllister, Ted V. (1996), *Revolt Against Modernity: Leo Strauss, Eric Voegelin, & the Search for a Postliberal Order*, Lawrence: University Press of Kansas.

Rose, Richard (1993), *Lesson-Drawing in Public Policy: A Guide to Learning Across Time and Space*, Chatham: Chatham House.

Safranski, Rüdiger (1994), *Ein Meister aus Deutschland: Heidegger und seine Zeit*, Munich and Vienna.

Schießl, Michaela (1997), 'Estland sollte lächeln', *Der Spiegel*, 13 October, pp. 129–136.

Strauss, Leo (1998), 'What Is Political Philosophy?', in *What Is Political Philosophy? And Other Studies*, Chicago and London: University of Chicago Press, pp. 9–55.

Thomas, Rosamund (1989), *The British Philosophy of Administration*, 2nd edn, Cambridge: CBPSE.

Wilson, James Q. (1994), 'Reinventing Public Administration', *PS: Political Science & Politics*, **27** (4), pp. 667–673.

Wolff, Christian (1740), 'Von einer Erwegung der Staatsgeschäffte', in *Gesammelte kleine philosophische Schrifften, Sechster und letzter Theil, darinnen besonders die zur Staatsklugheit und der damit verbundenen Rechtsgelehrsamkeit gehörige Stücke enthalten*, G[ottlieb] F[riedrich] H[agen] (tr. and ed.), pp. 323–528. Repr. as *Gesammelte Werke*, Ist Ser., **21**, pt. 6, Hildesheim – Zürich – New York: Olms.

Wolff, Christian (1754), *Grundsätze des Natur- und Völckerrechts, worin alle Verbindlichkeiten und alle Rechte aus der Natur des Menschen in einem beständigen Zusammenhange hergeleitet werden*. Repr. as *Gesammelte Werke*, Ist Ser., **1**, Hildesheim – Zürich – New York: Olms.

World Bank (1997), *World Development Report 1997: The State in a Changing World: Selected World Development Indicators*, Washington, DC: The World Bank.

Index